Security as Politics

Security as Politics

Beyond the State of Exception

Andrew W. Neal

EDINBURGH
University Press

Edinburgh University Press is one of the leading university presses in the UK. We publish academic books and journals in our selected subject areas across the humanities and social sciences, combining cutting-edge scholarship with high editorial and production values to produce academic works of lasting importance. For more information visit our website: edinburghuniversitypress.com

© Andrew W. Neal, 2019

Edinburgh University Press Ltd
The Tun – Holyrood Road
12(2f) Jackson's Entry
Edinburgh EH8 8PJ

Typeset in 11/13 Adobe Sabon by
IDSUK (Dataconnection) Ltd

A CIP record for this book is available from the British Library

ISBN 978 1 4744 5092 8 (hardback)
ISBN 978 1 4744 5094 2 (webready PDF)
ISBN 978 1 4744 5095 9 (epub)

The right of Andrew W. Neal to be identified as the author of this work has been asserted in accordance with the Copyright, Designs and Patents Act 1988, and the Copyright and Related Rights Regulations 2003 (SI No. 2498).

Contents

Acknowledgements	viii
1. In Defence of Politics against Security?	1
Security as a threat to politics	2
The growth of security and the Hobbesian trap	4
In defence of politics	7
Normative politics against security: From extraordinary politics to normal politics	12
From Hobbes to Machiavelli: From state survival to political survival	19
From Schmitt to Weber: From sovereign exception to the profession and vocation of politics	23
The UK example	28
Notes	34
2. How Do We Know Security When We See It? Problematisation as Method	42
The 'everything becomes security' trap	45
The problem with 'strictly defined criteria' of security	47
Contextual security	50
Foucault's historical empiricism: Dispensing with definitions	56
Problematising security	62
History as war?	67
Foucault contra Foucaultians	71
From governmentality to politics	73
Notes	76

3. Securitisation and Politicisation 84
   Critique of the norm/exception binary 87
   Spheres and activities of politics 90
   The politicisation/depoliticisation debate 95
   Politicisation and arena migrations 100
   The UK example 106
   Conclusion 110
   Notes 110

4. Politicians, Security Politics and the Political Game 115
   Understanding the political game 117
   Political sociology: Discourses, norms, structures 120
   Unequal parliamentary power relationships 125
   The power relationships and norms of security politics 127
   The dilemma of bad faith 139
   Habitus and the House of Lords 145
   The breakdown of trust and deference 147
   Notes 154

5. Can One Person Make a Difference? Fearless Speech vs. Security Politics 161
   Parresia and its problematisations 167
   The problematisation of truth in security politics 175
   Parresia as a rejection of the rules of the game 178
   Conclusion: 'Nevertheless, in spite of everything' 185
   Notes 188

6. Security as Normal Politics: The Rise of Security in Parliamentary Committees 194
   The stakes of committee politics: Democratic legitimacy and executive oversight 198
   The 1980s as 'traditional' security politics and the beginnings of change 204
   The 1990s: Intelligence oversight and post-Cold War security issues 209
   The 2000s: Post-9/11 politicisation 216
   2010 onwards 223
   Conclusion: The migration of security into the political arena 227
   Notes 231

7. Security as a Whole-of-Government Project: Risk, Economy, Politics	236
Osborne goes to China: The NSC, risk assessment and balance	237
Threat and risk in the National Security Strategy	241
Risk as depoliticisation?	245
Security as not Blair: Security from the joined-up centre	250
Security, risk and political economy	257
Conclusion: Security as economy, security as politics	260
Notes	264
Conclusion: More Security, More Politics	269
Notes	282
Bibliography	285
Index	316

Acknowledgements

Writing a book is inevitably autobiographical. Authors are not the same person at the beginning of the process as they are at the end. I have been writing this book longer than I have known many dear and important people in my life. In many ways they have been part of the story. My wonderful wife Rebecca and our growing children have brought so much love to these years, for which thanks is not enough. I am becoming increasingly forgetful in my middle age, so I begin with an apology to everyone I forgot to thank here by name. I have presented ideas and drafts for the book at many conferences, workshops and seminars over the last few years, where I have received many wise questions, suggestions and words of encouragement, as well as a few quizzical looks as to why I would want to research anything so unfashionable as parliamentary security politics (hopefully the answer is clear in the book). I am grateful to everyone who has taken an interest and helped me in the process. I would like to extend personal thanks to Angharad Closs, whose friendly invitation to a workshop on austerity helped forge Chapter 7; Christian Bueger, whose enthusiasm for my project has been a tremendous spur; Didier Bigo, who has always taken it seriously; Mike Slaven, ever thoughtful with his comments; Jonas Hagmann and Hendrik Hegemann, who have become partners in crime on the politicisation of security (watch this space); Hugh Bochel, Andrew Defty and Marc Geddes for helpful comments on the committees chapter; and Karen Lund Petersen, whose invitation to spend a short time as a visiting fellow at the 'Copenhagen School' helped the project's conception. I am ever grateful to the International Relations Research Group at the University of Edinburgh, where I presented drafts of every

Acknowledgements

chapter (I think some accidentally more than once) and received more excellent suggestions than I can remember from colleagues and our fantastic PhD students, and also to the broader Politics and International Relations subject area at Edinburgh, which is chock full of colleagues whose wisdom I could not do without, and where I am still grateful to work after eleven years. Thanks to the Carnegie Trust for the Universities of Scotland for a small research grant that enabled me to conduct my research interviews in London, and to Polity for permission to recreate Figure 3.2 from Colin Hay's *Why We Hate Politics*. Finally, thank you to Alison Howell, who called me out on the parts where I was insufficiently political; Rita Floyd, who told me she'd never thought of it like that before; and Jonna Nyman, who said 'meh' and 'more oomph' in all the right places.

1. In Defence of Politics against Security?

This book investigates security from the perspective of professional politics. This arena of political activity is not the totality of politics. It is narrow compared to the huge scope of all that could be considered 'political'. But the professional politics practised by politicians in democratic institutions is a distinct and significant type of political activity with a historically changing relationship to 'security'. It has been neglected by scholarship.

The reason for this neglect is the assumption that 'security' is a kind of 'anti-politics'. The practice of 'security' is considered to be something illiberal and undemocratic at the heart of politics. Security studies remains preoccupied with manifestations of Thomas Hobbes's security state – the *Leviathan* – in the forms of sovereign power, executive action, high politics, military force and these days increasingly diverse forms of security governance.[1] The 'Copenhagen School' authors of securitisation theory – one of the most influential security theories to emerge since the Cold War – go as far as defining security as an exception to 'normal politics'. They argue: '"Security" is a move that takes politics beyond the established rules of the game and frames the issue either as a special kind of politics or as above politics.'[2]

This book challenges the idea that security is a form of 'anti-politics'. In recent years the character and location of 'security' has changed. Its relationship to professional politics has altered. The majority of professional politicians who were once marginalised by 'security' are now actively engaged with multiple aspects of security governance. The book argues that whereas 'security' was once institutionalised as the anti-political 'exception' in liberal democracies – a 'black box' of secret intelligence and military decision making at the dark heart of the state – it has now permeated 'normal' professional political life. In the arena of professional politics specifically, security is now subject to any number of debates, votes, hearings, inquiries, reports, questions and struggles. Security has become part of the activity of politics. The relationship of security to politics can no longer be understood as pathological and exceptional. Security is no longer an anti-politics. It is politics.

Security as a threat to politics

The fear that the pursuit of security threatens politics is as old as modern Western political thought itself. Hobbes's *Leviathan* has become a synonym for the security state.[3] Hobbes argued that without the security guaranteed by the state, civilised life would be impossible.[4] Security was the minimum necessary condition for civil, economic and political life.[5] Yet for Hobbes and others such as John Locke and J. S. Mill this posed a dilemma. The 'security' provided by the *Leviathan* could become tyranny, itself a form of insecurity for the people.[6] Even so, Hobbes thought this was better than the terror of a stateless anarchy in which life would be 'nasty, brutish and short'.[7] Others thought this too great a price to pay.

They were prescient. History is littered with examples of the activity of politics being curtailed in the name of security. Populist and fascist regimes have risen to power by stoking fears of real or imagined enemies. Neither have liberal democracies been immune. In the wake of 9/11, US politics suffered a stifling of dissent: a 'rally round the flag' effect that diminished pluralism.[8] 'Security' has all too often trumped diversity, deliberation, parliamentary procedure, rule of law and civil liberties. The very meanings associated with 'security' – survival, threat, necessity, decision, secrecy, emergency, crisis – all challenge the openness, pluralism and tolerance that are central to liberal democratic political life.

The debate loosely known as 'critical security studies' has made this a starting point for critiques of security. To mention a few important examples, Claudia Aradau has argued that 'democratic politics is incompatible with the politics of security'.[9] For her, security has an inherently 'exclusionary and non-democratic logic'; it is a 'non-democratic politics'.[10] For Jef Huysmans, 'security practice is a danger for democratic politics in the sense that it limits the possibility to act democratically upon security'.[11] From a neo-Marxist perspective, Mark Neocleous sees politics as the chief victim of security, where 'politics' is the possibility to think and act differently. For him, not only does security pervert the normal procedures and principles of democratic politics, it reorders society and colonises the political imagination, causing a 'paralysis experienced in the face of security'.[12] From a more social democratic perspective, Ian Loader and Neil Walker argue that we should 'civilise security' by re-imposing democratic political control. For them, security must be 'made safe by and for democracy'.[13] And for the political sociologist Didier Bigo, the growing field of security professionals has simply 'discarded some actors, like parliaments'.[14]

These academic assumptions are a product of historical experience. Historically, states, governments and political systems have indeed been structured to keep the business of security at arm's length from the business of organised democratic politics. In the UK, the very existence of the security and intelligence services was taboo until the late 1980s. Parliamentary rules prevented politicians from even asking questions about them.[15] In the US, it took Watergate and the subsequent Church Committee hearings to bring the US intelligence agencies under democratic oversight.[16] At times in the history of these two countries, there have been suspicions that not even democratically elected leaders have had full control over their state's security apparatuses. Prime Minister Harold Wilson was convinced he was under electronic surveillance by MI5 (a fear now discredited by historians, although MI5 did hold files on many prominent Labour politicians).[17] Senator Frank Church described the US intelligence agencies as 'rogue elephants' – a term which has stuck.[18] In many other countries, particularly new democracies, there have been intense struggles to bring 'security' into the light of democratic politics.[19]

The growth of security and the Hobbesian trap

Until the early 1990s the study of security was essentially the study of international relations (IR) and war. In 1991, the realist scholar Stephen Walt argued that 'security studies may be defined as the study of the threat, use and control of military force' and the 'specific policies that states adopt in order to prepare for, prevent, or engage in war'.[20] Security was the problem of international insecurity, a product of relations between states under the formal 'anarchy' of the international system. Security was thus a matter of 'high politics' and statecraft, not the 'low politics' of the domestic realm. This dissociation of security and 'low politics' remains integral to the structure of academic disciplines. Political science, the domestic cousin of IR, still sees 'security' as an exotic specialism that is marginal to its field of analysis. In security studies the study of domestic politics remains a novelty. Foreign policy analysis is an exception in the sense that it examines domestic political factors, but only as a variable affecting executive foreign policy making, rather than a focus in its own right.[21]

The scope and machinery of 'security' have expanded since the end of the Cold War, particularly since 9/11. Insecurities have proliferated, accompanied by the extension of 'security' as a concern and activity of government. In the process, 'security' has become more than Hobbes's foundational guarantee of order or Walt's 'threat, use and control of military force'.[22] Many scholars (although not all) recognise that the meaning and scope of 'security' has become 'wider' and 'deeper' than traditional military and intelligence matters.[23]

Until the late twentieth century, the sections of government concerned with security such as defence and intelligence were not small, but they were insulated from the wider apparatus of government. Today, behemoths such as the US Department of Homeland Security and 'whole-of-government' projects such as the UK National Security Strategy sprawl across the state and beyond. Policy areas such as cyber security, energy security, health security (for example pandemics), financial security (for example anti-terrorist finance) and counter-radicalisation did not exist in those terms thirty or even fifteen years ago. Elements of the traditional security 'black box' at the dark heart of the state still exist, such as secret intelligence, but 'security' could now be a concern of any part of government, from ministries of industry and health to energy and transport.

'Security' has also become the business of a whole army of technicians, private companies, quasi-autonomous agencies and what Didier Bigo calls 'security professionals'.[24] In the UK, the practice of security even encroaches into the duties of what Francesco Ragazzi calls the 'unprofessionals of security', with teachers, doctors, university lecturers and other public servants required by law to report their suspicions about individuals who may be, in the words of Charlotte Heath-Kelly, 'at risk of becoming risky'.[25] Some commentators have noted an irony in all this, given that by any objective measure citizens in affluent liberal democracies are safer than they have ever been.[26]

In parallel to these transformations the study of security has become sprawling and diverse, spilling out of IR into sociology, geography and science and technology studies, to name but a few avenues. Innovative scholars offer incisive critiques of surveillance, algorithms, border technologies, resilience, risk management and countless other 'technologies of government' designed to manage proliferating insecurities.[27] Nevertheless, the study of security still falls into a Hobbesian trap. Traditional IR approaches do this in their state centrism and focus on the executive, but 'critical' studies of security do something similar.[28] Even when scholars look beyond the *Leviathan* to examine alternative security governance techniques they assume that the field of professional politics is irrelevant to, or distorted by, the practice of security. As Huysmans argues, whether the aim of the critical security scholar is to undermine the traditional Hobbesian logic of security, deconstruct it, account for its operation sociologically or offer emancipatory alternatives, the starting assumption is that 'security' is Hobbesian at root.[29] The *Leviathan* – wielding the sovereign instruments of power and towering above the land – remains a key expression of the logic through which security imperatives are assumed to trump politics.

In the aftermath of 9/11, it was understandable that security scholarship was drawn towards the 'exceptional' responses of the state and the expansion of security practices, although many question how 'exceptional' these responses, such as torture, really were.[30] In the so-called 'War on Terror', the executive branch of several governments did indeed curtail politics by reasserting sovereign security prerogatives and repressing democratic deliberation and choice.[31] Yet despite dramatic political moments in the aftermath of violent events when politicians have marched to the beat of war and exceptionalism, the post-9/11 expansion of 'security' has not damaged or hindered the activity of politics in democratic institutions. And with 9/11 receding into history the logic of emergency has faded. Diverse forms of political activity around security have taken its place. Continuing with the traditional analytical lens of anti-politics, sovereign decision, executive action, increased governmental powers and the proliferation of innovative techniques of security governance makes an analytical blind spot of the changing nature of security politics.

The Hobbesian trap and the analytical lens of anti-politics divert attention from the diverse ways in which professional politicians are increasingly mobilising and organising around security issues. In the US and the UK, security has become the subject of multiple congressional and parliamentary committee hearings, fractious legislative bargaining, governmental restructuring, negotiation over the allocation of resources, interactions with lobbyists and interest groups and electoral struggle. Far from being marginalised by 'security', politicians continue to contest policies, set up inquiries, scrutinise budgets and play the political game. Yet the Hobbesian trap means that parliaments, for example, are assumed to be at worst irrelevant, at best a variable affecting the decisions of states, governments and leaders. As Kaarbo and Kenealy put it, 'there is little systematic research on parliaments' role in security policy because it is assumed that parliaments are unimportant'.[32] The Hobbesian trap distracts from the sheer range of professional political discourse and activity on security that no longer defers to Hobbesian executive prerogatives. This political activity involves backbench politicians, opposition parties and committee members. It includes political leaders and ministers in their capacity as politicians rather than as executive office holders. Scholars have failed to notice the migration of security into the arena of professional politics.

Securitisation theory is the archetypal expression of security as an anti-politics. It assumes that when issues get socially constructed as *security* issues they are lifted out of the arena of 'normal politics' – with its debates, procedures and negotiations – and shifted into a rarefied arena of executive decision and narrowed choice. However, in response to criticisms about the inflexibility of the theory, founding securitisation author Ole Wæver recently asked: 'Did securitization theory maybe appropriately capture only the politics of security of 1995 or 1985? Was it more accurate for 1955 than for 2015?'[33] This book answers yes. The theory is the product and expression of a world that once existed. Since then, 'security' as an issue and policy area has become less secretive, less confined to a metaphorical and institutional 'black box' at the dark heart of the state and less politically rarefied. This does not mean that the traditional facets of security such as executive dominance have disappeared altogether. Rather, they have come to exist – often uneasily – alongside other kinds of security politics that are more like 'normal politics'. To paraphrase Foucault, the new security politics does not 'erase' the old but does 'penetrate it, permeate it'.[34]

With all this in mind, the book asks: what happens if we refuse to understand security as an 'anti-politics'? What happens if we refuse the pathological opposition of security to 'normal politics'? What happens if we examine security from the perspective of professional politics? What would it mean to rethink security as politics?

In defence of politics

This book is concerned with the activity of politics and its changing relationship to 'security'. Fifty years ago, in an influential book called *In Defence of Politics*, Bernard Crick argued that politics is an activity not reducible to government. Nor is it to be confused with rule, ideology, democracy, ethics, the common good or any set of fixed ideals or principles.[35] For Crick, politics is not everything, nor it is another term for power struggle.[36] Elements of politics may exist under coercive, illiberal, non-democratic systems.[37] Government can be undertaken in a variety of more or less coercive ways, with differing degrees of political consent and legitimacy.[38] But ultimately for Crick (unfortunately in the gendered words of his time): 'Politics are the public actions of free men.'[39] Politics is an activity – a specific type of free human activity.

This book investigates a type of political activity relating to 'security' that has been missing, presumed dead, in security scholarship: professional politics. Professional politics is something more specific than Crick's understanding of politics as an activity. It is a complex area of social activity in its own right. It is characterised by institutionalised hierarchies, relationships, boundaries and routines. It is not the totality of politics and it is not the same as government. Professional politics certainly relates to government – indeed Max Weber defined 'politically oriented' action as that which 'aims at exerting influence on the government' – but it has its own specific problems, logics, games, rationalities and practices.[40]

Defining what is and is not politics is no simple matter and is itself political. The very act of defining 'politics' can have the effect of dismissing certain issues as non-political. For example, one of the most important achievements of feminist politics has been to redefine what is political and therefore what should be treated as a matter of public and governmental concern. Behind the phrase 'the personal is political' lies decades of work to take issues such as domestic violence and reproductive freedom out of the private sphere and on to political agendas. Cynthia Enloe argues:

> One of the simplest and most disturbing feminist insights is that 'the personal is political'. Disturbing, because it means that relationships we once imagined were private or merely social are in fact infused with power, usually unequal power backed up by public authority.[41]

The question of what is or could become 'political' is thus an expansive one, expressed succinctly by Colin Hay: 'All events, processes and practices which occur within the social sphere have the potential to be political.'[42] It matters if issues are considered political or not and it matters if issues get politicised or depoliticised.

For the same reasons, the presence or absence of issues in specific institutional arenas of politics is significant. By extension, it matters if professional politicians are prevented from engaging with security or choose not to engage with it through a lack of information or deference to the executive. And it matters if politicians then choose to become active on security, bringing issues into debate, contention and parliamentary process where once they did or could not.

The choice of this book to focus on professional political activity is thus unavoidably political. Its choice to call this activity 'normal politics' is not a value judgement but a direct reference to the distinction made by securitisation theory between 'normal politics' and 'exceptional' security politics. For the Copenhagen School authors Buzan, Wæver and de Wilde, 'normal politics' means simply: 'the issue is part of public policy' or 'merely politicized'.[43] This stands in contrast to the ostensibly 'exceptional politics' of security.[44] The negated, relational place of 'normal politics' in securitisation theory is the starkest expression of a near ubiquitous assumption in security studies: the implicit or explicit view that 'normal politics' of the kind described by the Copenhagen School is by definition uninteresting to the study of security. 'Normal politics' is the state of affairs from which 'security' deviates in its qualities, practices, institutions and effects.

For many commentators, the Copenhagen School view of 'normal politics' is not innocent or unproblematic. In his call for 'Less security, more politics!' founding securitisation author Wæver has been criticised for valorising a privileged Western European experience of politics that overlooks the many exclusions and injustices it has produced.[45] The institutionalised structures of 'normal politics' in liberal democracies are all too often still 'male, pale, and stale', and struggle to reflect the diversity of the societies they ostensibly represent.[46] To many members of the public, institutionalised forms of 'normal politics' appear archaic, alien, irrelevant, distasteful and a discouragement to political engagement generally.[47] To others in the history of liberal democratic states, the lived experience of 'normal politics' has been far worse; for indigenous communities, racial, ethnic, religious and sexual minorities, irregular migrants, the mentally ill and the poor, 'normal politics' has all too often meant repression, exclusion, incarceration and violence.[48] Alison Howell adds that 'to speak of "securitisation" is to mistakenly assume that there is something pure, merely, or normally political prior to security that is not permeated with relations of force'.[49]

Andreas Kalyvas captures some of this disillusionment with political 'normality' when he argues that 'normal politics' is itself a form of depoliticisation:

> Normal politics seems to boil down to relations of bargaining and negotiation among organized interests and state officials. In ordinary times, in short, politics as usual fits a utilitarian and statist model that is characterized by civic privatism, depoliticization, and passivity and carried out by political elites, professional bureaucrats, and social technicians.[50]

Kalyvas intends his description to be disparaging: it describes a politics that lacks transformative potential, is alienating and uninspiring and certainly not the kind of politics that most critical theorists would like. As we will see, Kalyvas's notion of 'normal politics' captures the attitude of many critical security scholars towards existing liberal democratic political systems.

In normative terms, this book disputes none of these critiques of 'normal politics', which is all too often alienating and depoliticising for the public and is responsible for a multitude of sins. However, normative distaste of 'normal politics' among critical security scholars has led to the analytical neglect of the security-related transformations that have been happening in that arena. If the implication of their critique of 'normal politics' is that we should ignore it altogether, then this book rejects that position. This book does not take an explicit normative stance towards 'normal politics' but rather examines it with empirical curiosity and treats it as an analytical category. It argues that the migration of 'security' into the 'normal' political arena – an institutional site of professional political practice – is not unambiguously good or bad. It is an empirical development that is complicated, multifaceted and has implications for our assumptions about security.

To examine professional politics as an activity in its own right – and not simply as a cog in the policy-making machine, an interest-based power struggle, a 'variable' affecting government decision making or a symptom of wider social and political injustices – is to follow a scholarly tradition with its own lineage. German sociologist Max Weber is a key author here; his 1919 valedictory lecture 'The Profession and Vocation of Politics' is a landmark expression of the pressures and dilemmas of professional political life.[51] Another, perhaps surprisingly, is Michel Foucault, who late in his career turned his attentions to the practice of politics, in contrast to the 'rationalities of government' that had occupied him previously and for which he is best known. In his work on classical Greece he focused on the practice of politics itself; his concern was to understand 'the political game, its rules and instruments, and . . . the individual who engages in it'.[52]

This book follows the efforts of Weber, Foucault and others such as Pierre Bourdieu to understand professional politics, and specifically as it relates to the changing pursuit and practice of security. The book does this in order to challenge the assumption that security is a form of anti-politics. It demonstrates empirically that security is becoming part of the activity of professional politics where it was once excluded. More specifically, it argues that the orthodox assumption that security is an anti-politics should be dated to a particular time and place. Using an extended case study of the UK, the empirical chapters show that while this account was a persuasive description of institutionalised forms of security politics until around the mid-1990s, it is no longer. Following a genealogical methodology derived from Foucault, one aim of the book is therefore not to refute the orthodox view of security as an anti-politics, but to date it as the product of a particular time and place that has now passed. The overriding aim is to examine the evolution of the new security politics, 'its rules and instruments, and . . . the individual who engages in it'.[53]

Normative politics against security: From extraordinary politics to normal politics

For some critics, the Copenhagen School distinction between 'normal politics' and 'exceptional security politics' overlooks too many normative issues. These critics make much stronger normative claims about what democratic politics should be in relation to the anti-politics of security. They call for politics to be defended from security but go further by articulating positive visions of politics distinct from the status quo of 'normal politics'. The CASE Collective calls this a difference between 'politics as normality' (the status quo) and 'politics as normativity' (its transformation).[54] These interventions still reproduce the underlying assumption that security is a form of anti-politics.

Claudia Aradau made one of the most important interventions on this issue, which has influenced the direction of the debate since. She argued that the Copenhagen School 'preference' for 'normal politics' over security is not enough, for it may simply mean a return to an elite politics that suffers from injustice, inequality and exclusions.[55] This is close to Kalyvas's negative reading of 'normal politics'. Aradau criticises the Copenhagen School for being overly analytical and taking a weak normative stance against the politics of security. Their mere 'preference' for 'desecuritisation' – that is, taking issues back into open political deliberation by reversing the securitising move that closes down politics – does nothing to challenge the logic of security itself. For her, the question of what security does to politics cannot simply be analytical. Rather, it must be a normative question about 'the type of politics we want'.[56] For Aradau, the normative aim of a critical approach to security must be to 'un-make' security in favour of a radically equal, fair and open form of democratic politics, and not simply a return to politics as usual.[57]

Aradau's work rests on the assumption that security is an anti-politics. On this she is quite categorical: 'democratic politics is incompatible with the politics of security.'[58] In this sense, she agrees with the Copenhagen School that the core logic of security is a closing down of politics. Hence for Aradau, a properly critical security theory needs to commit to a different kind of politics that challenges the 'exclusionary logic of security'.[59] Like Kalyvas, what Aradau wants is not 'normal politics' but 'extraordinary politics'. She opts for an emancipatory tradition found in two strands of French philosophy: the poststructuralism of Jacques Rancière and the cosmopolitanism of Étienne Balibar. In these she identifies 'democratic politics . . . extensively defined in terms of equality and fairness, voice and slow procedures open to public scrutiny'.[60]

Aradau's normative vision of politics is laudable but comes with an analytical cost. She assumes that any politics of security is by definition 'exclusionary and non-democratic'.[61] This excludes, a priori, the analytical possibility of finding forms of security politics that are not exclusionary and non-democratic. It also dismisses traditional political forms such as parliamentary politics and the significance they may have for transformations in the security/politics relationship.

Mark Neocleous goes further in his *Critique of Security*, taking a more neo-Marxist perspective. Like Aradau, he affirms the basic logic of securitisation theory when he writes: 'casting an issue as one of security tends to situate that issue within the logic of threat and decision.'[62] He amplifies this by arguing that security 'magnifies the dangers and ratchets up the strategic fears and insecurities that encourage the construction of a certain kind of political reason centred on the violent clampdown of the moment of decision'.[63] Neocleous does not simply see security as a deviation from the normal liberal democratic state of affairs, but as a pervasive tendency within liberal-capitalist societies. For him, security is not the foundation and guarantor of politics (as in the Hobbesian tradition), but a 'master narrative' at the centre of a liberal-capitalist reordering of society.[64] For Neocleous, security is a catalyst for a tendency already present within the 'normal politics' of liberal democracy; it is 'a political technology through which individuals, groups, classes, and, ultimately, modern capital is reshaped and reordered'.[65] To support this he offers a compelling genealogy of security, ranging from early modern political theory through to Roosevelt's New Deal and anti-communism, in which security has always been a means to expand the alliance between the liberal state and capitalism. Hence, like Aradau, the normative aim of his critique is not a return to 'politics as normality' but 'to play a part in freeing the political imagination from the paralysis experienced in the face of security'.[66] Again, this comes with the analytical cost of closure towards the possibility of transformations in the security/politics relationship arising from within the status quo.

In *Civilizing Security*, Ian Loader and Neil Walker argue that 'security' is a fundamental public good. Following the social democratic themes of Crick, they see security as the foundation that makes politics among humans possible in place of violent alternatives. Yet for Loader and Walker, all too often this public good is undermined by the egregious way the state pursues security, damaging liberties and amplifying social exclusions. This is their version of security as anti-politics.

They go on to argue that security presents four 'pathologies' (which in turn reflect other parts of the critical security debate). The first is 'paternalism', where security professionals and experts such as police and intelligence officers gain undue authority in shaping security policy at the expense of 'the will of elected political actors'. This is akin to Bigo's arguments about security professionals.[67] The second is 'consumerism': a form of populism in which politicians 'sell' tough measures on crime and security to a lowest-common-denominator consuming public at the expense of democratic scrutiny, deliberation and social solidarity. This is somewhat akin to securitisation and its focus on the 'speakers' and 'audience' of securitising speech acts.[68] The third is 'authoritarianism', which links back to the constitutional dilemmas faced by Hobbes, Locke and others. Here, security creates 'a sense of impatience and urgency; with calls for the unhindered, speedy hand, and visible display, of executive authority'.[69] The fourth is a depoliticising 'fragmentation' in which the provision of security as a public good is replaced by fragmented services in the marketplace and a multiplication of arm's-length governmental agencies, much like the governmentality literature.[70] Like Neocleous, Loader and Walker are concerned that security is pervasively reordering society, replacing public democracy with a market-driven authoritarianism.

Loader and Walker have a wide notion of social democratic politics that is not simply institutional 'normal politics' in the Kalyvasian sense, but rather expresses normative ideals of solidarity and egalitarianism. Again, there is a danger that their 'pathologies' and normative concerns become a priori assumptions about the security/politics relationship. In theory, their concerns could be addressed through traditional parliamentary politics, but analytically their normative approach does not prompt them to look here for potential transformations.

Jef Huysmans is more innovative. He argues that security does not simply repress or damage politics but creates forms of politics that limit democracy. He defines security as 'the technique of enacting democratic limits'.[71] He reinterprets the meaning of 'securitisation' to go beyond the 'speech act' framework of the Copenhagen School by revising 'act' to mean the 'enactment' of new political situations. He identifies three forms of this. In the first, 'security is about enacting situations in which democracies threaten themselves, where democracy encounters its own limits'.[72] This is akin to the foundational problem in modern politics discussed above, where the practice of 'security' guarantees the possibility of politics but also threatens it. In his second form, security 'limits the possibility to act democratically upon security'.[73] This is recognisable as the narrowed form of political action and decision making found in securitisation theory and the normative concerns of Aradau, Neocleous, and Loader and Walker. Huysmans' third form concerns the ways in which security technologies and technologies of government exceed democratic controls, akin to the concerns of Bigo and the wider critical governmentality literature (which is explored further in Chapter 2).[74]

Huysmans' work is interesting because it does not offer an a priori conceptualisation of security politics as an 'anti-politics'. Rather, it maintains empirical openness by asking what kind of politics is enacted through security practices. For example, Huysmans argues that when computer or weapon-systems failure gets framed as a security threat, this enacts a form of 'technocratic politics' in which technical experts carry significant authority.[75] Alternatively, when mass migration is framed as a security threat, this calls human rights into question and thus enacts a legalistic politics that often plays out between the executive and judiciary.[76] Huysmans thus leaves open the empirical and constitutive possibilities of the security/politics relationship. Yet his approach is still built on the core assumption that security limits politics, or, more accurately, that security enacts forms of politics that limit democratic politics. So again, security is political, but also an anti-politics.

These normative interventions on the politics of security, particularly that of Aradau in 2004, have been influential, prompting some authors to rearticulate securitisation theory with renewed visions of politics. Instead of a mere preference for 'politics as normality' as articulated in the 1990s version of securitisation theory, they have called for more open and authentic modes of politics against the political dangers of security.[77] This follows Aradau's point that security is important precisely because it throws into sharp relief the normative valuation of different forms of politics. For example, Wæver has developed a positive vision of politics based on the work of Hannah Arendt in which he posits politics as a broad, productive and creative activity that takes place between people.[78] He argues that the political question attached to security must therefore be to consider the negative effect security has on the Arendtian potential of politics to be a 'truly open, political, constitutive space of human inter-/co-action'.[79] Wæver claims this was always implicit in securitisation theory because of its concern with intersubjective discourse in the public sphere.[80] Yet even from this renewed perspective, the underlying problematisation of security remains unchanged, namely its negative effect on politics. For Wæver it remains the case that 'the inevitable negative effects of any securitization [are] the logic of necessity, the narrowing of choice, [and] the empowerment of a small elite'.[81]

In 2003 Michael C. Williams argued that because securitisations are speech acts they remain within the realm of discourse, and speech always 'entails the possibility of argument, of dialogue'.[82] This does not mean that such dialogue is free from power, exclusion or coercion, but nevertheless, according to Williams, transformative possibilities remain.[83] He has since developed this into a more radical normative response to the politics of security in which he sets aside the negative conceptualisation of security found in securitisation theory, which is 'defined by a politics of emergency and exception' and influenced by the work of Carl Schmitt.[84] Citing Kalyvas, he raises the possibility of a 'positive securitization' that would bring about an 'extraordinary democratic politics' based on the 'constituent power' of radical moments of self-determination.[85] These extraordinary moments could refigure political structures and value systems; they present illimitable creative potentialities.[86] This is similar to Sergei Prozorov's reading of 'the exception' as a moment of radical freedom and transgression, following the work of Jacques Derrida.[87] But whereas Prozorov does this through a seemingly ironic flirtation with Schmitt (arguing that the only alternative to Schmitt's enmity is love), Williams grounds his move in republican democratic theory. Wæver's recent position is similar, insisting that meaning is always co-produced in the relationship between the speaker and the audience, and not just through the one-sided act of speech.[88] Like Williams, Wæver's intention is to reduce the executive, decisionistic, Schmittian aspect of securitising speech acts, and to refocus on wider socio-political arrangements.[89] Both wish to emphasise the transformative and constitutive possibilities of dialogue even under invoked conditions of security.

What unites these authors, in contrast to the original 1990s articulation of securitisation theory, is their ambivalence towards status quo 'normal politics' as something to be defended from security. Like Aradau and Kalyvas, they see 'normal politics' as stale, exclusionary and ultimately depoliticising. Ironically, they have this in common with Schmitt and his desire to 'break through the crust of a mechanism that has become torpid by repetition'.[90] Of course, the ways in which they want to do this are different, such as Williams' rethinking of security as 'extraordinary' rather than 'exceptional'. And none reject 'normal' liberal democratic politics entirely (in favour of sweeping revolution, for example). All use the challenge of security to affirm more authentic and vital forms of democratic politics. This critical-normative debate opens up important questions about 'the type of politics we want', but it still rests on the assumption that security is an anti-politics.

There is another strand of critical security studies that also calls for more equality, emancipation and authentic democracy. This is what is often known as the Welsh or Aberystwyth School of security studies, although the debate has since become broader than that.[91] Based on Frankfurt School critical theory more than the poststructuralist-inspired authors discussed above, scholars such as Ken Booth and Karen Fierke began the debate by challenging the restrictive 'national security' focus of traditional security policy and scholarship.[92] They argued that in the everyday lives of most humans, real security threats come not from enemy states but from 'other challenges, such as economic collapse, political oppression, scarcity, overpopulation, ethnic rivalry, the destruction of nature, terrorism, crime and disease'.[93] Jonna Nyman argues that many authors in this debate present a positive rather than negative view of security, which calls for a security conceived not only as 'an absence of threat' but also as 'the presence of conditions furthering human "flourishing" of some form'.[94]

For the most part, the positive security debate does not explicitly frame security negatively as damaging to politics. It says little about security as an anti-politics. Its concern is more that state security policies target the wrong threats and insecurities instead of those experienced by most people. Yet it does start from the same Hobbesian problem: the *Leviathan* and the ambiguous 'security' it provides. As Booth said, 'people are more threatened by the policies and inadequacies of their own government . . . To countless millions of people in the world it is their own state, and not "The Enemy" that is the primary security threat.'[95] Since Booth's intervention the debate has flourished, with sensitive discussions of the possibilities (and inevitable ambiguities) of alternative forms of security based on ethics of care, feminism, cosmopolitanism, decolonisation and posthumanism, to name a few.[96] Directly or indirectly, they take Aradau seriously in her call for the problematisation of 'security' to be posed as a normative question about 'the type of politics we want'.[97]

However, these authors are united in their neglect of 'normal politics' – the traditional arena of organised professional political practice discussed in this book. While we can only speculate in absence of direct comment, presumably the assumption is that change in security policy would not arise from this political arena. From this perspective, parliamentary politics is inherently uninteresting, perhaps seen merely as an extension of the state. As argued above, this creates an analytical blind spot. It misses important empirical developments in the domain of 'normal politics' that have implications for how we understand the security/politics relationship. Even if we do not like 'normal politics', what happens there may be significant for the practice and concept of security. 'Normal politics' is still politics, however staid.

From Hobbes to Machiavelli: From state survival to political survival

To rethink security as part of the activity of politics requires different starting assumptions drawing on different traditions of thought. The Hobbesian trap expresses a particular ontology – a particular understanding of the nature of political being – in which the sovereign state is the primary category. To understand security as politics an alternative ontology is needed. One such alternative ontology comes from Nicolo Machiavelli, author of *The Prince*. At first glance this is counter-intuitive, because Machiavelli has often been claimed as part of the 'realist' tradition of international relations that also claims Hobbes. But as R. B. J. Walker argues, to consider Machiavelli in a realist vein is to misunderstand the quite different world of ontological contingency he occupies.[98] If Hobbes represents an ontology of state security, then Machiavelli represents an ontology of politics.

For Hobbes and Machiavelli, the stakes are different. In Hobbes, the existential survival of the state – and thus the existential survival of individuals and all aspects of civil life under the state – is at stake. In Machiavelli's *The Prince*, the existence of the state and civic life is not in doubt. Rather, it is the reign of the prince that is at stake. Princes come and go. They acquire states and lose states. They may win at being a prince for a while, but the rules of *fortuna* dictate that they will lose in the end. Yet in Machiavelli this is not an existential problem. The eventual failure of the prince's reign is part of the rules of the game. This is exactly what the controversial British politician Enoch Powell meant when he wrote: 'All political lives, unless they are cut off in midstream at a happy juncture, end in failure, because that is the nature of politics and of human affairs.'[99] This is very different from the existential logic of security in which – to quote innumerable Hollywood films – failure is not an option. To understand security as politics, we need to start not from Hobbes but from Machiavelli. We need to escape the Hobbesian security trap that reaffirms the existential security logic. Instead we need Machiavelli's political logic.

Under a Hobbesian ontology, the state is sovereign. The ideal state for Hobbes is a secure state in full command of its fate. In this sense the sovereign state is a mortal God.[100] It identifies what is a threat, decides what needs to be done about it, and does it. In Hobbes, the threat does not usually come from other states, but from civil war and a reversion to the terrifying insecurity of anarchy. (The discipline of international relations extends the Hobbesian existential logic to the insecurities that stem from competing states, although this is a problematic intellectual stretch for many reasons, as Hedley Bull and many others have discussed.[101]) The core logic of Hobbesian insecurity is that in face of existential threat, 'there is no alternative'. In these circumstances, the absolute rule of the *Leviathan* is an existential necessity. Indeed, Hobbes put *necessity* at the centre of his argument from the outset; his was a logic that could 'admitteth no other Demonstration'.[102] Security studies reproduces this logic. For example, the Copenhagen School argues that securitisation 'construct[s] a plot that includes existential threat, point of no return, and a possible way out'.[103] This is the core claim of Hobbes: without security there is a 'danger of violent death'.[104]

In contrast, Machiavelli's prince is not a mortal God. The prince remains subordinate to the superior forces of what Machiavelli calls *fortuna*, or contingency, chance or fate.[105] He should build defences against the vicissitudes of *fortuna*. He may learn some historical lessons of how to perpetuate his reign, as supplied by Machiavelli's writings. Yet *fortuna* always wins in the end. The prince cannot master contingency indefinitely. He is ultimately at the mercy of events.

For Machiavelli there are no necessities and no unchanging truths. There are only historical examples, and there are always alternatives. Machiavelli does not offer an irrefutable logic, but only a series of loose pointers, merely 'something that will prove of practical use to the inquirer'.[106] Jonathan Powell, former chief of staff to Tony Blair, calls Machiavelli's guidance 'useful maxims, precepts, practical hints, historical parallels and general laws for a ruler'.[107] Yet one is not to follow the rules as if there were no alternative. When trying to hold on to a state, office or seat, it is just as important to judge when not to follow maxims or rules. Even this offers no security against *fortuna*. As Walker puts it: 'Machiavelli offers maxims, mere tennis play as Hobbes would insist, advice about how to prepare for the coming of *fortuna* . . . [But] once *fortuna* arrives, even such maxims are of little use.'[108]

The political life of Machiavelli's *Prince* is akin to political life generally. The reign of the prince is akin to the reign of a government or the life of a political career, not the existence or sovereignty of a state. Governments fall as a matter of course; all political lives end in failure unless they are cut off at a happy juncture. The key point is that this is not an existential catastrophe. As David Runciman puts it: 'The great thing about democracy is that no politician is too big to fail.'[109] In contrast, Hobbes's *Leviathan* is too big to fail. But politicians and governments are not, at least in liberal democracies. Political failure does not mean existential destruction. Governments and politicians accept this as part of the rules of the game, as must the prince. Pierre Bourdieu argues that politicians know the rules, must play by them if they want to be successful, and consider the game worth playing.[110] They must build their political defences and hold on.

From the perspective of professional politicians, whatever other concerns and principles they may have, the primary 'threat' is not to the state or some other valued 'referent object', but to the life of a government or their own political careers. Threats to political life, at least in stable liberal democratic states, are not existential but political; the survival at stake is merely political survival. The argument here, and of this book generally, is that politics has its own logic, its own ontology, which is different from that of security. Or to put it differently, security from the perspective of politics looks different to politics from the perspective of security.[111] (As an aside, the Copenhagen School argues that 'politics' itself can be existentially threatened according to the existential logic of security. This is when the political system is threatened with overthrow or a fatal blow to its legitimacy.[112] This is Hobbes again, and merely applies the security logic to the political system. It does not capture the contingent, non-existential ontology of political life as expressed by Machiavelli.)

A prince and a politician are not the same thing of course. A prince acquires and rules a state; a lowly politician acquires a parliamentary seat or other elected office, at least at first. Yet in the first instance both have to hold on and survive being a prince or a politician in order to continue being one. This does not mean existential survival but surviving the vicissitudes of their position. A prince may lose his state; a politician may lose her seat. They may keep their corporeal life but lose their political life. This is the distinction between existential survival and political survival. In *The Prince* it is never in question that the state will survive; the only question is how long the prince can keep hold of it. Similarly, to be a politician in the first place, and to continue being one, a politician must above all else save their seat. Thus, for the prince and the politician the primary concern is how to survive politically, not existentially.

The MP Paul Flynn recently published a book called *How to Be an MP* that is unconsciously rather like *The Prince*. Parliament scholar Philip Cowley described it as 'The single best thing ever written about being an MP'.[113] It was the book most borrowed by MPs from the parliamentary library in 2012.[114] Its stated aim is to help MPs 'survive life in Parliament'.[115] It is a deceptively light-hearted 'how-to' guide for almost every conceivable parliamentary situation. *How to Be an MP* is not an academic book. It offers no theories or concepts. Nevertheless, the non-theoretical nature of the book, its attitude towards its subjects, and its implicit notion of contingent history make it rather like *The Prince*. Not because of some caricatured Machiavellianism, but because Flynn and Machiavelli have the same approach towards their eponymous subjects. Neither of them offers a general theory of politics. Like Machiavelli, Flynn has merely 'diligently analysed and pondered [these matters] for a long time', and 'summarized them in a little book'.[116]

The Prince deals with the situations a prince is likely to encounter from the beginning to the end of his reign. *How to Be an*

MP does the same. For example, it starts with 'How to Arrive' in parliament as a newly elected MP, which is akin to Machiavelli's opening concern with 'newly acquired states'.[117] The two books combine personal wisdom with tales of historical figures who have got it wrong, ruining their reputations, careers or worse. The books are addressed directly to their subjects. The question is not whether to be a prince or a politician but what to do if you are one. They concern not the best constitution of politics in the Aristotelian sense but, as Foucault puts it, 'the practice of the political game'.[118] Again, the point in Machiavelli, Flynn and also Foucault is that the practice of politics has its own specific concerns, which are separate from the logic of security, the state, government or any particular political doctrine, ideal or end.

From Schmitt to Weber: From sovereign exception to the profession and vocation of politics

The specific concerns of the 'political game' do not mean that politicians are uncaring about 'security' or approach it cynically – far from it. The empirical research presented in this book shows that politicians take security seriously and would rarely, if ever, belittle its importance. They express genuine concern and a sense of responsibility for the safety of the public and the national security of their country. Indeed, this responsibility towards security is one of the unspoken 'rules of the game' of professional politics. It does not mean that security is a form of anti-politics. On the contrary, professional politics goes on.

This sense of responsibility in political life has a genealogy in understandings of professional politics. While this introductory chapter cannot unpack this exhaustively, a crucial treatment remains Max Weber's lecture 'The Profession and Vocation of Politics'. The responsibility Weber ascribes to professional politics is distinct but related to other meanings of responsibility in IR and security studies. For example, the godfather of realism Hans J. Morgenthau makes a Weberian argument that a good 'statesman' takes responsibility for the foreseeable consequences of their actions.[119] However, his focus on statecraft in international relations is exactly the kind of preoccupation this book rejects. Weberian responsibility is also related to an underlying concern of the securitisation debate: the attribution of political responsibility for security threat constructions. Wæver argues:

> The securitization approach points to the inherently political nature of any designation of security issues and thus it puts an ethical question at the feet of analysts, decision-makers and activists alike: why do you call this a security issue? What are the implications of doing this – or of not doing it?[120]

Securitisation theory wants political actors to confront the potentially violent or political deleterious consequences of their actions and indeed their inactions.

For Weber, the profession of politics is riven with tensions and contradictions that largely stem from his view that 'The decisive means for politics is violence'.[121] This does not mean that all policies are implemented through violence in the first instance, but rather that the state reserves the right to use violence as the ultimate means of policy enforcement. The state for Weber is 'a human community that (successfully) claims the *monopoly of the legitimate use of physical force* within a given territory'.[122] This may be expressed, for example, as the use of 'reasonable force' in the maintenance of order, the sanction of imprisonment in law enforcement, the Clausewitzian use of war as an instrument of policy, or indeed the violence sometimes involved in security practice.[123] For Weber, politicians must reconcile themselves with this fact, because 'he who lets himself in for politics, that is, for power and force as means, contracts with diabolical powers'.[124] This applies as much to those who do not themselves govern but who aim to exert 'influence on the government' or attain government office at a future date.[125]

In contrast to Weber's 'ethic of responsibility', he posits an 'ethic of conviction' that implies absolutism. This might be expressed as an unshakable commitment to pure means, with no sense of responsibility for the inevitably impure consequences of action or inaction, as in the case of unconditional pacifism.[126] Alternatively, conviction could be expressed as a commitment to ultimate ends that justify any means, as in certain revolutionary doctrines, which entail only a sense of responsibility to the revolutionary cause itself.[127] Weber argued: 'The person who subscribes to the ethic of conviction feels "responsible" only for ensuring that the flame of pure convention . . . is never extinguished.'[128]

Weber's 'ethic of responsibility' is an ethic of moderation. Yet it is not opposed to conviction. Indeed, a commitment to the largely thankless and morally perilous calling of politics requires conviction in the first place. An 'ethic of responsibility' implies being able to temper conviction with prudence, moderation and being able to answer for the '(foreseeable) *consequences* of one's actions'.[129] Thus Weber was concerned with what it meant for an individual to surmount these inevitable and intractable tensions residing at the heart of politics. For Weber, a serious politician with a genuine 'vocation for politics' combines 'passion, a feeling of responsibility, and a sense of proportion'.[130]

Weber believed that politics was under threat, not from 'security' but from the rise of bureaucracy and the more general process of rationalisation entailed by modernity. Weber's concern was that in modern life, rationalisation was everywhere increasing its reach. Nowhere was off limits to its relentless march.[131] Even political parties increasingly resembled bureaucratic election machines, and most politicians were no more than 'yes men' in thrall to their party managers or, worse, to officialdom.[132] For Weber, responsibility in politics was fundamental to winning the struggle against the forces of rationalisation and in particular the ever-growing bureaucratic machinery of the state. Indeed, finding a way to resist the 'iron cage' of rationalisation and the rise of bureaucratic authority was the defining problem of modernity.

In particular, Weber was concerned by the growth of the bureaucratic state and its eclipse of democratic control:

> In view of the growing indispensability and hence increasing power of state officialdom, how can there be any guarantee that forces exist which can impose limits on the enormous, crushing power of this constantly growing stratum of society and control it effectively? How is democracy even in this restricted sense to be at all possible?[133]

Again, he related this to the problem of responsibility, or lack of. For Weber, the task of officials is to 'master organisational problems . . . and official tasks of a *specialised* nature', but they have a 'vested interest in holding office *without responsibility*'.[134] They can always say they were only following instructions.[135] To shift registers from German to English, the constitutional essayist Walter Bagehot would say that government by officials is not *'come-at-able'*; it is not an 'available authority' to serve as a locus for the public's ire.[136] Weber argued that 'It is *politicians* who must provide a counter-balance to the rule of officialdom'.[137] The duty of the politician is to *'answer for his actions'*.[138]

On this point, it is worth spending a moment to consider an influential alternative to the Copenhagen School approach to security: the so-called 'Paris School' of security studies, founded by Didier Bigo. For Bigo, a field of security professionals has displaced the political arena altogether: it has 'discarded some actors, like parliaments'.[139] This is a fear about the displacement of politics from the public realm, akin to Max Weber's fear of the rise of bureaucracy.[140] For Bigo, the significant struggles over security do not take place in traditional political institutions. The public security discourses articulated by politicians are only a shop front for a competitive and bureaucratic industry of security experts and professionals, which supplies the discursive framework through which security can be discussed at all. In this view, this is where the politics that really matters is to be found: in a behind-the-scenes struggle between professionals in the bureaucratic 'field' for position, power and the authority to frame security priorities.[141] Analytically and politically, Bigo thus abandons the field of professional politics as already 'discarded'.

In contrast, against the extension of bureaucratic rule, the only limited hope Weber saw was in politics. For Weber, the profession of politics contained at least a few genuine individuals capable of expressing value convictions through the responsibilities of political rule. In the face of all this, the individual with a genuine calling for politics needed to overcome 'Embitterment or philistinism, sheer, dull acceptance of the world and of your job' and to 'withstand even the defeat of all hopes'.[142] For Weber, it was a special kind of individual who could continue to practise politics under these modern conditions by saying '"Nevertheless" in spite of everything'.[143]

A common criticism of Weber's ethic of politics is that it is elitist in its extolling of heroic and charismatic leaders.[144] Indeed, Weber often made a disparaging distinction between 'leading politicians' and mere 'lobby fodder'.[145] Furthermore, he advocated only a limited form of democracy rather than its extension.[146] Perhaps this makes Weber an inappropriate thinker to invoke in debates about security politics. Weber's political elitism may bring him too close to Carl Schmitt, a kind of fascistic Hobbes on steroids with his statement that 'Sovereign is he who decides the exception'.[147] Indeed, Weber was involved in drafting Articles 41 and 48 of the Weimar Constitution, which gave provision for exceptional presidential powers and ultimately facilitated the rise of Hitler.[148]

However, there are important distinctions between Weber and Schmitt. McCormick argues that Schmitt's emphasis on exception and decision was a direct response to Weber's paralysing account of the 'iron cage of modernity' with its 'irresistible, objectively rational structures'.[149] When Schmitt writes 'In the exception the power of real life breaks through the crust of a mechanism that has become torpid by repetition', this is a direct antithetical reference to Weber's 'iron cage'.[150] McCormick describes Schmitt's concept of the exception as 'a miracle-like monkey wrench to be thrown into the works of the liberal-positivist machine'.[151]

Schmitt offers a way out of the Weberian impasse of rationalisation, but it is through the inhuman figure of the sovereign, which in the form of Hobbes's *Leviathan* he saw as a 'powerful monster that combined god, man, animal, and machine'.[152] Although it is difficult to ascribe a single set of political implications to Schmitt's protean works, McCormick puts it sharply when he explains that Schmitt 'takes far too literally Weber's claim that politics involves the subjectively personal choice between God and the devil, as well as the likelihood that one will "contract with diabolical powers"'.[153] We do not need to dwell here on the permanent tainting of Schmitt by his involvement with the Nazi party, but suffice it to say that Schmitt's existential concept of 'the political' – in which 'the enemy is, in concrete clarity, recognized as the enemy' at 'the high points of politics' – squarely aims to destroy the ethic of politics that is the final destination of Weber's oeuvre.[154] There is thus a contrast between Schmitt's exceptional sovereign and Weber's concern with 'what kind of human being one must be'.[155] Weber's politician is human in a way that the *Leviathan* and the grey march of technocracy are not. Despite Weber's political elitism, as Tamsin Shaw puts it, 'Instead of surrendering political power altogether to impersonal processes, submission to charismatic authority permits politics to be brought under human control'.[156]

There are limits in applying Weber's analysis to the relationship between professional politics and security. For example, it does not appear that Weber would have approved of the migration of 'security' from the executive into the wider political arena. Although the current broad concept and practice of 'security' did not exist in Weber's time, his comments on foreign policy suggest that he favoured elite decision making on such matters. As he argued, 'the most responsible decisions on *foreign* policy are made by a *small* group of people'.[157] This is akin to 'the empowerment of a smaller elite' in securitisation theory.[158] In fact, Weber's position reflects the executive-skewed understanding of security politics expressed by the Hobbesian trap, although of course he pre-dates the 'broadening' and 'deepening' of 'security' by a century.

That said, the value of Weber to this project is not his view on security or foreign policy but his concern with professional politics as an activity with a specific set of responsibilities and concerns. Weber provides a window on to this neglected dimension of security politics that has fallen between the gaps of critical security studies. Much like the later Foucault, Weber is concerned with 'the specific problem and set of problems of politics . . . [T]he practice of the political game.'[159]

The UK example

Bagehot once wrote 'we may easily miss the permanent course of the political curve if we engross our minds with its cusps and conjugate points'.[160] His advice applies here. Security scholarship tends to be drawn towards controversies and dramatic moments, but this reaffirms the prevailing understanding of security as an exception to 'normal politics'. Scholars direct their critiques at the most contentious security policies and practices, the 'cusps and conjugate points' of security, but they miss the 'permanent course of the political curve'.[161]

This book explores trends and changes in security politics using an extended UK case study, and with good reason. The UK is emblematic of the normalisation of security politics. It has long been a cockpit of security innovation, exporting its models and methods globally. When states rushed to develop new counter-terrorism laws after 9/11, spurred by UNSC Resolution 1373, the UK offered an extensive body of law and parliamentary review from its painful experience in Northern Ireland. This 'mother of all parliaments' has given birth to many 'Westminster model' constitutions across the former British Empire, such as Australia, Canada and many others in the Commonwealth. To this day these draw heavily on UK jurisprudence and parliamentary procedure on security policy.[162] The UK is an intelligence superpower, second only to the US in the unique Anglosphere 'Five Eyes' intelligence-sharing relationship, the largest defence spender in Western Europe, a key player in Europol and an engine of the neoliberal reforms driving new models of security governance such as 'risk' and 'resilience'. Once a secretive Cold War player with intelligence agencies that did not officially exist, no democratic oversight and a parliament mostly excluded from security policy, its political actors have become increasingly politicised and active as security policy has spilled out of the deep security state, across government departments and into further areas of social, political and economic life.

The choice of an extended UK case study represents depth over breadth. It allows examination from multiple angles across an extended historical period. This in itself is a reaction against the reductionism towards domestic politics usually displayed by security studies approaches. It would of course be interesting to build on this study of historically changing security politics with case studies on other countries. Evidence suggests findings would be similar. Many countries, for example Finland, Canada and the

Netherlands, now produce comprehensive national security strategies that go far beyond the traditional security issues of defence and intelligence.[163] As these strategies reach into areas of social, political and economic life not traditionally associated with security, it would not be surprising if they also created new professional political activity, as they do in the UK.

Let us now quickly survey the UK case. Put simply, it shows two things. First, that there was a period in history, lasting roughly until the mid-1990s, when security did resemble a kind of anti-politics along the lines assumed by security studies, securitisation theory in particular. Second, the relationship between security and politics has changed, with a demonstrable growth in professional political activity relating to security. As security has spread out of its historical 'black box' and into almost every policy area of government, parliamentary activity has shadowed this with more legislative scrutiny, topical debates, select committee inquiries and other parliamentary instruments.

At the start of the 1980s, security was truly a 'black box' at the heart of the British state. MI5 and MI6 had no legal status and did not officially exist. There was no democratic intelligence oversight other than through government ministers. Opportunities for parliament to openly debate intelligence and security barely existed. The four decades since have seen significant changes in this core area of security governance. First, the domestic security service MI5 was put on a statutory footing in 1989, followed in 1994 by the foreign intelligence service MI6 and the signals intelligence service GCHQ. That year also saw the creation of an intelligence and security oversight committee (the ISC). This consisted of trusted parliamentarians hand-picked by the prime minister. It had limited resources and powers and met off the parliamentary estate in government offices. The 2013 Justice and Security Act reformed the ISC, giving it new powers and more independence from the executive.[164] Over the same period, the intelligence services have become more open (from the lowest possible base), with their chief officers making occasional public appearances and giving regular informal private briefings to other parliamentary committees.[165]

However, intelligence alone represents a narrow understanding of 'security', the institutional scope and meaning of which has broadened considerably over time. For example, since 2008, the UK government has published a National Security Strategy that lists an extensive range of risks and threats. This list is so broad that one commentator has argued that its 'full range of existing and potential risks to our national security' in effect encompasses 'everything'.[166] The incoming government in 2010 then created a National Security Council, designed as a forum for resource bargaining and policy coordination between ministers and civil servants across government. This supplanted some of the traditional security prerogatives of the prime minister with more institutionalised procedures, increasing security policy coordination across government departments. The effect is that 'security' is no longer confined to Downing Street and the traditional lead security ministries of Defence, Foreign and Home (interior). Security has ostensibly become a 'whole-of-government' problem with institutional structures to match.[167]

These changes relate in the first instance to government but have been mirrored by transformations in parliamentary politics at Westminster. The historical norm in the politics of security was parliamentary marginalisation and deference to the executive on security matters, accompanied by a pattern of consensus on national security between the frontbenches (if not always from the more rancorous backbenches). For example, in the 1980s only a handful of parliamentary committees had any kind of engagement with security matters, and even then very minimally. Parliamentary interest and engagement with security has since grown steadily. This trend began with increased intelligence oversight in the early 1990s. At the same time the committees of Home Affairs, Foreign Affairs, and Trade and Industry (relating to arms exports) started taking a greater interest in intelligence and security matters (see Chapter 6 for full details). Tony Blair's foreign military interventions from 1998 onwards played a role in raising parliamentary interest in security issues, as did 9/11 and the accompanying expansion of security governance. In the same period, security became a more politicised issue in the sense that it became more controversial. A relentless legislative agenda on counter-terrorism prompted multiple parliamentary rebellions and intense inter- and intra-party struggles on civil liberties and human rights.[168] To the present day, approximately twenty-five parliamentary committees have now conducted substantive inquiries into security-related matters, roughly a quarter of all committees, representing a significant upswing from an almost non-existent base.[169] This trend cannot be taken in isolation, however; it not only reflects increased parliamentary engagement and politicisation on security, but also mirrors the broadened meaning and application of 'security' to include areas of governance that simply did not exist thirty or even fifteen years ago, such as energy and health security.

Some professional political activity is automatically tied to government activity, such as legislative scrutiny when the government tries to enact new security laws through parliament. Other activity is more loosely tied, as with departmental select committees that have the freedom to inquire into any topics they choose, but generally oversee the policies and policy areas of the departments they shadow. There are also many instruments that parliamentarians can use to independently initiate activity on issues of concern (including those relating to security), such as written and oral questions to ministers, early day motions, committee inquiries and the formation and mobilisation of all-party parliamentary groups. A few parliamentarians have taken a strong interest in security and have become active campaigners and questioners. Others have remained more muted through choice or lack of opportunity. However, when examining the overall trend, it is difficult to argue that it has been driven by particular actors. Although individual decisions and acts may lie behind specific activities, when examining the increasing range of security topics and activities in parliament over the course of decades, it becomes clear that parliamentary activity mirrors governmental, expert and social problematisations of security, and rarely, if ever, initiates them.

It is not a stretch to argue that security politics in the UK increasingly resembles what Kalyvas and the Copenhagen School call 'normal politics'.[170] It is an elite politics conducted within and between the ministries of Whitehall and the debating chambers and committee rooms of Westminster. It is peopled by ministers, MPs, peers, civil servants, clerks, expert witnesses and interest groups. The most dramatic of their activities, hearings, inquiries, reports and debates may 'engross our minds' at their 'cusps and conjugate points', of which there have been many.¹⁷¹ But the rise in more prosaic parliamentary activity – the 'permanent course of the political curve' – has been little noticed by security scholars.

Security politics in the UK is for the most part no longer 'exceptional' in the institutional sense.¹⁷² Instead it increasingly resembles what the Copenhagen School calls the 'merely politicized' rather than the 'securitized', meaning that 'the issue is part of public policy, requiring government decision and resource allocations'.¹⁷³ Legacies of the old anti-politics of security still exist, such as limited parliamentary access to intelligence, but even this is under challenge.

However, more professional political activity on security does not necessarily mean all is well. At first it might be assumed that more democratic political engagement is a good thing given the history of parliamentary exclusion on security. But more activity can mean that security more often gets played for cynical political ends, with politicians succumbing to the temptations of scaremongering and scapegoating. It can also mean that it becomes harder for the government to formulate coherent security policy as it tries to reconcile the increasing number of concerns and interests in the political arena.

What is clear is that security can no longer be defined as an anti-politics, as an exception to 'normal politics', as a pathology of politics. Security is no longer confined to war rooms or executive decision making. The historical conventions and taboos that worked to keep security out of the political arena are losing their grip and have been for some time. Yet whatever process is under way, it is incomplete. Security is migrating out of its traditional black box and into the arena of professional politics, but it is an incomplete migration often characterised by struggle and controversy. The politics of security does not yet fully resemble the politics of other 'normal' policy areas, such as health, education or taxation, as we shall see. The legacy of the old security politics still exerts an influence.

The rise of security as normal politics raises a number of questions that this book explores. What do we mean by 'security'? Is the 'security' of two or three decades ago the same as the 'security' of today? If not, how can we identify 'security' and analyse it? What does it mean for security to 'enter' the arena of professional politics? Is this a form of politicisation or desecuritisation? Chapters 2 and 3 comprehensively address these conceptual and methodological questions and provide a framework for the rest of the book. The subsequent chapters then take a more empirical focus, exploring questions such as: what does 'security' mean in professional political practice? Are there 'rules of the game' of security politics? If so, is it possible to change or subvert them? If security is becoming more akin to 'normal politics', is there anything still distinctive about it? Chapter 4 explores security from the perspective of politicians, drawing on interview data. Chapter 5 examines what it might mean for politicians to break free of the norms and rules of security politics. Chapter 6 analyses the four-decades-long trend of security entering the 'normal' political arena via the work of parliamentary committees. And Chapter 7 investigates the changing meaning of 'security' – from narrow to comprehensive – in the politics of government policy making.

Notes

1. Buzan, Wæver and de Wilde, *Security*; Buzan and Hansen, *The Evolution of International Security Studies*; Peoples and Vaughan-Williams, *Critical Security Studies*; Walt, 'The Renaissance of Security Studies'.
2. Buzan, Wæver and de Wilde, *Security*, p. 23.
3. Huysmans, 'Defining Social Constructivism in Security Studies', p. 60.
4. Hobbes, *Leviathan*, p. 89.
5. Ibid.
6. Locke, *Political Writings*, p. 269; Mill, *'On Liberty' and Other Writings*, pp. 5–6.
7. Hobbes, *Leviathan*, p. 89.
8. Chowanietz, 'Rallying around the Flag or Railing against the Government?'; Chang, *The Silencing of Political Dissent*.
9. Aradau, 'Security and the Democratic Scene', p. 399.
10. Ibid. pp. 406, 401.

11. Huysmans, *Security Unbound*, p. 30.
12. Neocleous, *Critique of Security*, pp. 9–10.
13. Loader and Walker, *Civilizing Security*, p. 7.
14. Bigo, 'Security and Immigration', p. 83.
15. May, *A Treatise on the Law, Privileges, Proceedings and Usage of Parliament*, 21st edn, p. 292.
16. Miller, *US National Security, Intelligence and Democracy*.
17. MI5, 'The "Wilson Plot"'.
18. Born and Caparini (eds), *Democratic Control of Intelligence Services*, p. 18.
19. Gill and Andregg, *Democratization of Intelligence*.
20. Walt, 'The Renaissance of Security Studies', p. 212.
21. Hudson, *Foreign Policy Analysis*, pp. 125–42; Kaarbo, *Coalition Politics and Cabinet Decision Making*.
22. Walt, 'The Renaissance of Security Studies', p. 212.
23. Buzan and Hansen, *The Evolution of International Security Studies*, p. 188.
24. Bigo, 'Security and Immigration', p. 72.
25. Heath-Kelly, 'Counter-Terrorism and the Counterfactual', p. 397; Ragazzi, 'Countering Terrorism and Radicalisation' and 'Preventing Radicalisation in the EU'.
26. Furedi, *Invitation to Terror*, p. 133; Pinker, *The Better Angels of Our Nature*, pp. 344–7.
27. Amoore and de Goede, *Risk and the War on Terror*; Amoore, 'Algorithmic War'; Aradau, 'The Promise of Security'; Heath-Kelly, 'Securing through the Failure to Secure?'; Salter, 'Passports, Mobility, and Security'; Squire, *The Contested Politics of Mobility*; Vaughan-Williams, *Border Politics*; Bigo, 'Security and Immigration'; Kindervater, 'The Emergence of Lethal Surveillance'; Schouten, 'Security as Controversy'; Lundborg and Vaughan-Williams, 'Resilience, Critical Infrastructure, and Molecular Security'; Adey and Anderson, 'Anticipating Emergencies'; Corry, 'Securitisation and "Riskification"'; Vaughan-Williams, '"We Are Not Animals!"'; Squire, 'Desert "Trash"'; Joseph, 'Resilience as Embedded Neoliberalism'; Zebrowski, *The Value of Resilience* and 'The Nature of Resilience'; Leese, 'The New Profiling'; Bellanova, 'Digital, Politics, and Algorithms'; Amoore and Raley, 'Securing with Algorithms'; Aradau and Blanke, 'The (Big) Data-Security Assemblage'; Dunn Cavelty, Kaufmann and Kristensen, 'Resilience and (in)Security'.
28. Waltz, *Theory of International Politics*, p. 105; Vasquez, *The War Puzzle*.

29. Huysmans, 'Defining Social Constructivism in Security Studies', p. 60.
30. Richter-Montpetit, 'Empire, Desire and Violence' and 'Beyond the Erotics of Orientalism'; Roberts, 'Torture and the Biopolitics of Race'; Dayan, *The Story of Cruel and Unusual*; Feldman, *Formations of Violence*.
31. Scheuerman, 'Survey Article: Emergency Powers and the Rule of Law after 9/11'; Bigo and Tsoukala, *Terror, Insecurity and Liberty*; Gearty, '11 September 2001'.
32. Kaarbo and Kenealy, 'No, Prime Minister', p. 30.
33. Wæver, 'Politics, Security, Theory', p. 473.
34. Foucault, *'Society Must Be Defended'*, p. 241.
35. Crick, *In Defence of Politics*, p. 19.
36. Ibid. p. 6.
37. Ibid.
38. Ibid. p. 15.
39. Ibid. p. 4.
40. Hindess, 'Politics and Governmentality', p. 261, citing Weber, *Economy and Society*, p. 55.
41. Enloe, *Bananas, Beaches and Bases*, p. 195.
42. Hay, *Political Analysis*, p. 3.
43. Buzan, Wæver and de Wilde, *Security*, p. 23.
44. Huysmans, *The Politics of Insecurity*, p. 135.
45. Wæver, 'Securitization and Desecuritization', p. 56; Howell, 'The Global Politics of Medicine', p. 969.
46. Kenny, *Gender and Political Recruitment*; Childs, *Women and British Party Politics*.
47. Hansard Society, 'Audit of Political Engagement 14'.
48. Richter-Montpetit, 'Beyond the Erotics of Orientalism'; Howell, 'The Global Politics of Medicine'.
49. Howell, 'The Global Politics of Medicine', p. 969.
50. Kalyvas, *Democracy and the Politics of the Extraordinary*, p. 6.
51. Weber, 'The Profession and Vocation of Politics'.
52. Foucault, *The Government of Self and Others*, pp. 159–60.
53. Ibid.
54. CASE Collective, 'Critical Approaches to Security in Europe', p. 455.
55. Aradau, 'Security and the Democratic Scene', pp. 395–7; CASE Collective, 'Critical Approaches to Security in Europe', p. 456; Elbe, 'Aids, Security, Biopolitics'.

56. Aradau, 'Security and the Democratic Scene', p. 390.
57. Ibid. p. 401.
58. Ibid. p. 399.
59. Ibid. p. 401.
60. Ibid.
61. Ibid. p. 406.
62. Neocleous, *Critique of Security*, p. 4.
63. Ibid. p. 9.
64. Ibid. p. 4.
65. Ibid. p. 5.
66. CASE Collective, 'Critical Approaches to Security in Europe', p. 455; Neocleous, *Critique of Security*, pp. 9–10.
67. Loader and Walker, *Civilizing Security*, p. 197.
68. Ibid. p. 202.
69. Ibid. p. 206.
70. Ibid. p. 209.
71. Huysmans, *Security Unbound*, p. 30.
72. Ibid.
73. Ibid.
74. Ibid.
75. Ibid. p. 12.
76. Ibid. p. 13.
77. CASE Collective, 'Critical Approaches to Security in Europe', p. 455.
78. Wæver, 'Politics, Security, Theory', pp. 468, 478.
79. Wæver, 'The Theory Act', p. 29; see also his 'Politics, Security, Theory', p. 468.
80. Wæver, 'Politics, Security, Theory', p. 468.
81. Ibid. p. 469.
82. Williams, 'Words, Images, Enemies', p. 523.
83. Ibid.
84. Williams, 'Securitization as Political Theory', p. 19.
85. Ibid. pp. 20–1.
86. Ibid.
87. Prozorov, 'X/Xs: Toward a General Theory of the Exception'.
88. Wæver, 'The Theory Act', pp. 27–8.
89. Ibid.; see also Balzacq, 'The "Essence" of Securitization'; Vuori, 'Illocutionary Logic and Strands of Securitization'.
90. Schmitt, *Political Theology*, p. 15.
91. For example see the wide-ranging contributions in Nyman and Burke, *Ethical Security Studies*.

92. See Booth, 'Security and Emancipation'; Fierke, *Changing Games, Changing Strategies*.
93. Booth, 'Security and Emancipation', p. 318.
94. Nyman, 'What Is the Value of Security?', p. 826. See also Roe, 'Is Securitization a "Negative" Concept?'; Browning and McDonald, 'The Future of Critical Security Studies'; McDonald, 'Securitization and the Construction of Security'; Floyd, 'Towards a Consequentialist Evaluation of Security'; Burke, 'Security Cosmopolitanism'.
95. Booth, 'Security and Emancipation', p. 318.
96. Nyman and Burke, *Ethical Security Studies*.
97. Aradau, 'Security and the Democratic Scene', p. 390.
98. Walker, *Inside/Outside*, pp. 44–6.
99. Powell, *Joseph Chamberlain*, p. 151.
100. Hobbes, *Leviathan*, p. 120; Schmitt, *The Leviathan in the State Theory of Thomas Hobbes*, p. 19.
101. Bull, *The Anarchical Society*, pp. 41–3; Suganami, 'Reflections on the Domestic Analogy'.
102. Hobbes, *Leviathan*, p. 11.
103. Buzan, Wæver and de Wilde, *Security*, p. 33.
104. Hobbes, *Leviathan*, p. 89.
105. Machiavelli, *The Prince*, p. 84; Pitkin, *Fortune Is a Woman*, pp. 138–72.
106. Machiavelli, *The Prince*, p. 49.
107. Powell, *Joseph Chamberlain*, p. 5.
108. Walker, *Inside/Outside*, p. 40.
109. Runciman, *Politics*, p. 92.
110. Bourdieu, 'Political Representation', p. 180.
111. For an earlier version of this argument, see Neal, '"Events Dear Boy, Events"'.
112. Buzan, Wæver and de Wilde, *Security*, pp. 141–2.
113. Flynn, *How to Be an MP*, back cover.
114. Holehouse, 'How to Be an MP Is the Most Borrowed Book in Parliament'.
115. Flynn, *How to Be an MP*, back cover.
116. Machiavelli, *The Prince*, p. 1.
117. Ibid. p. 5.
118. Foucault, *The Government of Self and Others*, p. 159.
119. Morgenthau, *Politics Among Nations*, pp. 4–15.
120. Wæver, 'Securitizing Sectors?', p. 334.
121. Weber, 'The Profession and Vocation of Politics', p. 365.

122. Weber, 'Politics as a Vocation', p. 78.
123. See Frazer and Hutchings, 'Virtuous Violence and the Politics of Statecraft in Machiavelli, Clausewitz and Weber'; Ryan, 'Reasonable Force'.
124. Weber, 'Politics as a Vocation', p. 123.
125. Hindess, 'Politics and Governmentality', p. 261, citing Weber, *Economy and Society*, p. 55.
126. Weber, 'The Profession and Vocation of Politics', p. 364.
127. Ibid. p. 360.
128. Ibid.
129. Ibid.
130. Weber, 'Politics as a Vocation', p. 115. The genealogy of the term 'vocation' and its translation from the German context is rather complex, but it is connected to Protestantism (hence 'calling') and Weber's work on society and capitalism; see *The Protestant Ethic and the Spirit of Capitalism*.
131. Weber, 'Parliament and Government in Germany under a New Political Order', p. 159.
132. Weber, 'Politics as a Vocation', p. 106.
133. Weber, 'Parliament and Government in Germany', p. 159.
134. Ibid. pp. 177, 205.
135. Ibid. p. 160.
136. Bagehot, *The English Constitution, and Other Political Essays*, p. 82.
137. Weber, 'Parliament and Government in Germany', p. 178.
138. Ibid. p. 208.
139. Bigo, 'Security and Immigration', p. 83.
140. Weber, 'Parliament and Government in Germany', p. 159.
141. Bigo, 'Security and Immigration', p. 73.
142. Weber, 'The Profession and Vocation of Politics', pp. 368–9.
143. Ibid. p. 369.
144. Kalyvas, *Democracy and the Politics of the Extraordinary*, pp. 46–64.
145. Weber, 'Parliament and Government in Germany', pp. 206–7, and 'The Profession and Vocation of Politics', p. 343.
146. Weber, 'Parliament and Government in Germany', p. 159.
147. Schmitt, *Political Theology*, p. 5; Neal, *Exceptionalism and the Politics of Counter-Terrorism*.
148. Kalyvas, *Democracy and the Politics of the Extraordinary*, p. 19; Mommsen, *Max Weber and German Politics*, pp. 332–45.

149. McCormick, *Carl Schmitt's Critique of Liberalism*, pp. 34–5.
150. Schmitt, *Political Theology*, p. 15; McCormick, *Carl Schmitt's Critique of Liberalism*, p. 75.
151. McCormick, *Carl Schmitt's Critique of Liberalism*, p. 75.
152. Schmitt, *The Leviathan in the State Theory of Thomas Hobbes*, p. 81.
153. McCormick, *Carl Schmitt's Critique of Liberalism*, pp. 76–7.
154. Schmitt, *The Concept of the Political*, p. 67.
155. Weber, 'The Profession and Vocation of Politics', p. 352.
156. Shaw, 'Max Weber on Democracy', p. 38.
157. Weber, 'Parliament and Government in Germany', pp. 206–7.
158. Wæver, 'Politics, Security, Theory', p. 469.
159. Foucault, *The Government of Self and Others*, p. 159.
160. Bagehot, *The English Constitution, and Other Political Essays*, p. 17.
161. Ibid.
162. Rhodes, Wanna and Weller, *Comparing Westminster*.
163. Ministry of Defence (Finland), 'Security Strategy for Society (Government Resolution 16.12.2010)'; Canada, 'Securing an Open Society'; Ministerie van Justitie en Veiligheid, 'National Security – Counterterrorism and National Security'.
164. Bochel and Defty, 'Parliamentary Oversight of Intelligence Agencies', pp. 109–10.
165. Bochel, Defty and Kirkpatrick, *Watching the Watchers*, pp. 16–17.
166. HM Government, 'A Strong Britain in an Age of Uncertainty', p. 25; Crowcroft, 'A War on "Risk"?', p. 173.
167. HM Government, 'A Strong Britain in an Age of Uncertainty', p. 9.
168. Cowley, *The Rebels*.
169. Counting numbers of committees is not straightforward over such a long time period, because often new ones are created and old ones are refashioned to mirror government reorganisations. Interpretation of which activity relates to security is not straightforward either. As will be explained in Chapters 2 and 6, the interpretive criterion 'substantive' means committees have dedicated inquiries or substantial sections of inquiries to issues found in the declared security policies of government, or else to other issues that the committees feel should be on the security agenda of government. These are cases where the actors themselves discuss the issues as security issues and are not simply cases that meet abstract criteria of 'security' supplied by theory. See Ciută, 'Security and the Problem of Context'.

170. Kalyvas, *Democracy and the Politics of the Extraordinary*, p. 6; Buzan, Wæver and de Wilde, *Security*, pp. 4–5.
171. Bagehot, *The English Constitution, and Other Political Essays*, p. 17.
172. See Ackerman, 'The Emergency Constitution'; Agamben, *State of Exception*.
173. Buzan, Wæver and de Wilde, *Security*, p. 23.

2. How Do We Know Security When We See It? Problematisation as Method

Flinders and Kelso have argued that 'Scholars have a public duty to correct rather than propagate the myths that surround their chosen subject matter'.[1] To this end, this book challenges the assumption that security is a form of anti-politics. This challenge is based on the empirical research set out in later chapters. In short, the argument is that 'security' is increasingly present in the arena of professional political practice. It is no longer confined to a 'black box' at the dark heart of the state in the way it once was, at least in the structures and practices of institutionalised democratic government and politics. The way security is handled in the political arena increasingly resembles what the Copenhagen School calls normal politics: 'the normal bargaining processes of the political sphere'.[2] This is opposed to the exceptional politics that securitisation theory and the Hobbesian lineage of security studies more generally have assumed security to be. From a Copenhagen School perspective, 'security as normal politics' is a contradiction in terms. The very idea challenges its concept of security and its assumed relationship between security and politics.

This challenge poses a fundamental methodological problem, which must be addressed before this study can proceed. If it is no longer tenable to define 'security' as the exception to 'normal politics' – as that which suspends, limits, threatens, damages, distorts or destroys politics – then how is it possible to identify and analyse 'security' at all? If 'security' is not something that can be recognised by its 'anti-political' logic, then how do we know 'security' when we see it? This is a methodological question that Ole Wæver has continued to press. For example, in response to Jef Huysmans' recent work on banal, everyday, routine and unspectacular security practices – 'little security nothings' as he calls them – Wæver poses the 'how do we know security when we see it?' question: 'If the securitization form is the definition that allows us to "observe" security, how does [Huysmans] then see these new forms of security and know they are security?'[3] In order to rethink the relationship between politics and security (as this book intends), we must first answer this question.

To this end, this chapter sets out a method for analysing 'security' without assuming or imposing a singular definition. This method is problematisation, based on the work of Michel Foucault. The method is four things. First it is empiricist. It analyses what people said and did when they articulated problems and responded to them. In the case of this study, the problematisation is 'security', its relationship with 'politics' and various associated sub-problems, such as how to identify emergent threats, provide the government with appropriate security powers, hold the government to account for the use of those powers, gain appropriate parliamentary access to secret intelligence and ensure democratic legitimacy. Second, the method is historical. It assumes that problematisations are specific to certain times and places and that they change over time. This means that problematisations are distinct from logics, criteria or definitions that are assumed to be stable across time and space. Thus there can be no core or objective definition of 'security', only historically specific problematisations of security. Third, the method is reflexive. It reflects on the role and position of the analyst. The analyst does not have a God's eye view or a view from nowhere from which to construct objective and ahistorical definitions and concepts. Rather, the analyst's view is from a particular position within history, politics and theoretical debates. The collection, curation and analysis of empirical material is motivated by a critical intent to challenge prevailing theoretical and political assumptions in the present. In the case of this study, the aim is to challenge the assumption that security is a kind of anti-politics. Fourth, the method of problematisation is always a double move: it aims first to identify and describe problematisations in context, and second to amplify and problematise them further for critical purposes. This latter move makes the analyst into an active player in the problematisation, not a dispassionate and disinterested observer.

It is also worth stating what problematisation as method is not. First, it is not necessarily an analysis of government or wider forms of what Foucault called governmentality.[4] Indeed, this chapter aims to recover Foucault from the overriding scholarly focus on his idea of governmentality. A Foucaultian analysis should not be synonymous with an analysis of techniques or rationalities of government. Second, problematisation as method is not primarily textual, linguistic or discursive (and this sets it apart from the focus of securitisation theory on 'speech acts' and their 'felicity conditions'[5]). Although the method does consider what people said and wrote, its idea of discourse is not reducible to those things, but may also include other practices and artefacts, such as architectures or organisational forms, as they cohere around specific problematisations. Third, problematisation as method is not explicitly normative: it does not subscribe to the promotion of particular social or political ideals through its work. However, it is critical and pursues a critical ethos: its criticality resides in its aim to marshal the raw material of history to challenge our present assumptions and to think differently. Problematisation as method is thus directed at ourselves and our thought. There is of course an implicit normativity in this aim, but not a political programme.

This chapter performs several steps of work. It begins by discussing the methodological stakes of current debates in security studies. This starts with Ole Wæver's defence of the methodological choices built into securitisation theory and the methodological challenges he poses to its critics. It then discusses in detail the 'contextualist' challenge from Felix Ciută, who rejects the 'strictly defined criteria' of the Copenhagen School in favour of an approach that privileges contextual actors' changing usages and meanings of 'security'.[6] From here, the chapter introduces the methodology of Foucault and works through a number of issues. First, his ontological stance towards historical empirical material and what this says about the possibility of 'strict criteria' or 'core logics'. Second, his method of problematising and how this may be put into practice. Third, the risk that such a method may be partisan and empirically dubious, particularly in its 'genealogical' form. Fourth, the need to recover Foucault from 'governmentality', which has come to dominate interpretations and applications of Foucault at the expense of other dimensions. And finally, a move towards Foucault's work on politics rather than government.

The 'everything becomes security' trap

In periods of historical change, security scholars have found existing concepts of 'security' to be inadequate for understanding new and novel security-related practices. For example, it is common to argue that the end of the Cold War prompted analytical innovation because the focus on the state and military in what was then known as 'strategic studies' had become limiting.[7] Even before the fall of the Berlin Wall, many argued that the meaning of 'security' had to be 'widened' to include non-state threats, the environment, human security, gendered security issues and so on, and 'deepened' to ask more profound questions about what it means to experience security or insecurity.[8] If security is defined too narrowly it potentially excludes empirical developments that do not fit the definition. This is the same as the problem of defining politics too narrowly, as discussed in Chapter 1.

Some traditional security scholars resisted the conceptual expansion of 'security' vehemently.[9] One reason was that to endlessly expand the meaning of security would risk analytical incoherence.[10] The Copenhagen School authors of securitisation theory accepted this warning. They argued that if everything is security, then the ability to distinguish between security and 'non-security' would be lost.[11] Ole Wæver calls this the '"everything becomes security" trap'.[12] Huysmans explains the problem as follows:

> If everything can in principle become an item on a security agenda, defining what determines the difference between a security question and a non-security question becomes controversial. If this difference cannot be established, security will be a trivial concept; it will be everywhere.[13]

They thus founded securitisation theory as a solution to this problem. It aimed to offer a middle ground. It kept the core focus of traditional security studies on existential threat but added a dose of social constructivism to open up a broader conceptual and empirical universe of different possible threats, different threatened objects and different security actors. It also posed the ethico-political question of what it means to choose security policies over more 'normal' political policies.

The Copenhagen School proposed that security analysis could maintain conceptual coherence in the face of the endless widening of security agendas by defining 'the logic of security itself'.[14] By fixing 'the essential meaning of security', they could then investigate the specific character that security took in different 'sectors' of social and political life.[15] The Copenhagen School held that 'security' could be recognised through its 'grammar', by which they meant the basic logical structure of security arguments. In this grammar, actors use 'speech acts' to invoke threats to 'referent objects' and legitimise security responses, a process which involved 'exception, emergency and a decision'.[16]

Through this conceptual move, the Copenhagen School broke the traditional link between security and military affairs because this 'grammar' or 'logic' of security could be found in other 'sectors' of social and political life too. For example, 'societal securitisation' could involve social and political actors decrying immigration as an existential threat to a particular identity or way of life.[17] Huysmans explains how the conceptual shift proposed by the Copenhagen School constituted a new research programme of securitisation studies, which 'consists of "discovering" social practices structured according to the security logic – i.e. practices of securitization'.[18]

Thus Wæver and the associated authors of securitisation theory did embrace the need to widen the concept of security, but at the same time insisted that methodological credibility depended upon preventing this from going too far. As 'wideners' they argued that '[t]hreats ... can arise in many different areas'.[19] But to defend against traditionalist criticisms they found a way to address the problem that if widened excessively, 'security' could mean anything, losing its analytical value and becoming 'intellectually incoherent'.[20] In retrospection on the theory, Wæver says that the Copenhagen School answer to the 'everything becomes security' dilemma was that

> Security is tied to a particular figure, that of securitization. This was how securitization theory 'solved' the widening impasse. Until the invention of the concept of securitization, 'widening security' ... risk[ed] the 'everything becomes security' trap.[21]

Their solution was to use 'strictly defined criteria' to set analytical limits on the meaning of security.[22] At its core this aimed to 'distinguish [security] from the normal run of the merely political'.[23] As they explained: 'We seek to find coherence ... by exploring the logic of security itself to find out what differentiates security and the process of securitization from that which is merely political.'[24]

The problem with 'strictly defined criteria' of security

The Copenhagen School criteria have proved too strict for many scholars. The problem is primarily one of empirical fit. Apparent instances of securitisation do not always follow the 'grammar' or 'strict criteria' set out by the Copenhagen School. For example, Rita Floyd argues that 'securitizing actors do not always revert to exceptional security policies when they address a threat'.[25] Similarly, Rita Abrahamsen writes: 'Rather than emergency action, most security politics is concerned with the much more mundane management of risk.'[26] Paul Roe takes issue with a different element of the theory, arguing that 'the extent to which securitization necessitates a lack of openness and deliberation has been overexaggerated'.[27] Indeed, most aspects of the Copenhagen School 'grammar' of security have been problematised in the literature.[28]

Wæver addressed these critiques by arguing that theories are not meant to be mirrors of reality but rather tools of comparison to highlight how far reality strays from the model.[29] However, the excessive 'strictness' of the theory is not just a problem of empirical fit but also a problem of the conceptual, definitional and methodological basis of the theory itself. Its requirement for conceptual coherence aims at meeting a disciplinary demand: to appease the concerns of traditionalist security scholars. Yet analysts do not have a monopoly on concept definition. This is to assume a kind of sovereignty over the subject matter that does not exist. As Jens Bartelson puts it (in reference to the concept of sovereignty rather than security), if we insist that 'this concept has some immutable core meaning . . . then [it] will keep running away from us, performing new tricks behind our backs'.[30] It is not just that empirical instances of securitisation do not always fit the theoretical criteria, but that 'security' more generally – its meaning and practice – has a life of its own that is not under theorists' command.

Several scholars have made points to this effect. Huysmans writes that the Copenhagen School model creates 'difficulties in including social challenges to their understanding of the logic of security itself'.[31] Felix Ciută argues that securitisation theory 'locks-in the meaning of security and insulates it from conceptual variation or practical reformulation'.[32] Philippe Bourbeau considers that '[the Copenhagen School] model is ill equipped to deal with the idea that mechanisms of security are proliferating'.[33] It is not only new and transformed meanings of security that challenge the 'strict criteria' of securitisation theory, but also historically prior meanings: Alison Howell argues that the theory is limited to 'national or international security speech acts, which only emerged after World War II', thus excluding what she sees as the 'biopolitical social warfare' of 'social security' dating from the 1930s.[34]

In recent years, Wæver has broadly accepted these criticisms, calling the original formulation of securitisation 'too restrictive'.[35] He says, 'the fixation of security in definite form became inflexible . . . [A] contemporary security theory should be able to explore changes to the security form itself.'[36] He has even suggested that securitisation theory, in its search for the 'essential meaning of security', was of its time, and that that time may have passed.[37] He asks: 'Did securitization theory maybe appropriately capture only the politics of security of 1995 or 1985? Was it more accurate for 1955 than for 2015?'[38] As discussed in the previous chapter, this book answers 'yes'. Securitisation theory – specifically its anti-political assumption that is also expressed in related literatures and in modern Western political thought more generally – should be dated as the product of a particular time and place.

To argue that securitisation theory is dated is not a question of 'falsifying' it. Rather, the problem is that the theory and the more widely held assumption that security is an anti-politics enables a certain view of security and disables others.[39] Existing theorisations of the security/politics relationship come with an analytical cost. They condition our expectations of what we will see when we go looking for the politics of security. Wæver is right to say that theories are not meant to be mirrors of reality. However, as Pierre Bourdieu argues, theories are nevertheless 'programmes of perception' that shape how we see reality.[40] They prompt us to see things one way and not another. This has political implications.[41] As Wæver himself argues: 'A theory is political primarily through the way it conditions analyses, because a theory is a construct that enables particular observations about cases.'[42] If this is so, then the inverse is also true: a theory can disable particular observations. Again this is a criticism that Wæver has acknowledged; referring to R. B. J. Walker, Wæver writes: 'a theory of the exceptionalist dimension of politics ... can fortify a conceptual universe where exceptionalism is central to the political field, and thereby limit our political imagination.'[43] This is indeed the case.

Felix Ciută puts a historical slant on this criticism. He argues that securitisation theory was built on a historically situated understanding of security, but it has 'fixed' this in conceptual form. He writes: 'Securitisation theorists are ... right to note the sedimentation of a certain meaning of security, but they transform this observation into a conceptual axiom.'[44] This book argues that the empirical universe on which securitisation theory was built did exist: the experience of security politics in the UK until the mid-1990s is a close expression of it. Yet this empirical universe has changed; so too, therefore, must the Copenhagen School's 'conceptual universe where exceptionalism is central to the political field'.[45]

To put it differently, to study 'security' over time is to study a moving target. Apparent instances of 'security' should not be identified by the same criteria regardless of their historical position. In the period under investigation – the early 1980s to the present day – the meaning and scope of 'security' expanded. Many of the issues that political actors discuss in security terms today, they did not discuss in those terms thirty years ago. For example, many of the issues detailed in the UK National Security Strategies of 2010 and 2015 are not new, such as flooding, pandemics and disruptions to energy supply and trade, but policy-makers did not frame them in national security terms until recently. It is not that new issues have been constructed as security problems according to an underlying 'logic' of security, but rather that new qualities, meanings and institutional locations of 'security' have come to supplement the old ones. The next section will explore Ciută's critique in greater detail. The methodology of this book adopts much of it, but with important departures inspired by Michel Foucault.

Contextual security

In response to the restrictiveness of securitisation theory, several scholars have called for a more 'contextualist' approach to security, loosened from any insistence on a core meaning or 'logic' of security. Ciută has called for a 'contextual-hermeneutical perspective' that would 'privilege ... the actors' definition of security' as opposed to that of the analyst.[46] Nils Bubandt has proposed the study of 'vernacular security'.[47] Holger Stritzel has explored 'translations' of security in which new meanings of security emerge in the travel, iteration and usage of the concept.[48] This section will explore the challenge from Ciută in detail because it is the best expression of the underlying methodological dilemmas. However, the argument is ultimately that Ciută's proposed actor-centric hermeneutic approach needs to be supplemented with more reflexive and critical considerations from Foucault.

Ciută's critique relates to what Stritzel calls 'a principal (and, in my view, irreconcilable) tension between traditionalism and reflectivism in Wæver's thinking'.[49] 'Traditionalism' here refers to the Copenhagen School desire to meet the disciplinary demand that the concept of security should not be diluted to the point of incoherence. 'Reflectivism' refers to the more discursive and constructivist aspects of the theory which consider 'security' to be the constructed product of securitising speech acts.

Ciută argues that the theory tries to have it both ways and in effect contains two definitions of security. On the one hand it opts for a 'reflectivist', constructed, actor-led approach in which security is 'what actors make of it'.[50] The theory expresses this in its openness towards the possibility of (constructed) security threats emerging in non-military 'sectors'. Securitisation theory thus resists an objectivist position about 'what *real security threats are*'.[51] As a constructivist approach, the Copenhagen School authors are clear that there are no convincing analytical grounds for objectivism about security issues. They argue: 'some measure of whether [an] issue is "really" a threat ... would demand an objective measure of security that no security theory has yet provided.'[52] On the other hand, securitisation theory fixes 'strictly defined criteria' for the meaning of security.[53] Ciută argues that this results in 'a much stronger claim about what *real security means*: security always means survival in the face of existential threats'.[54] Herein lies the contradiction: the fact that threats are constructed and may vary empirically is ultimately irrelevant to the immutable core logic of security.[55] Security is thus not what securitising actors make of it after all.

Ciută detects a further problem. What if actors *do* use or construct meanings of security that do not conform to the 'core logic' of security?[56] For example, Ciută points out that the eastward expansion and integration of NATO, the EU and the OSCE was 'defined by policy-makers as a security policy' but not as a set of 'exceptional measures'.[57] According to Wæver, because this does not fit the core meaning of security, it is not security.[58] But Ciută argues that this example can still be considered a security practice, just one with a different meaning that confounds the Copenhagen School definition. This poses a hermeneutic dilemma that pits the security analyst against the contextual security actor. Which is to take priority? Ciută cites philosopher Charles Taylor to describe this as the problem of 'confronting one's language of explanation with that of one's subjects' self-understanding'.[59]

The Copenhagen School is conflicted on this hermeneutic question. At one point they suggest that analysts' definitions should take priority over contextual uses and meanings:

> The analyst can . . . intervene to countersay actors in relation to the use of the *word* security. Sloppy talk of "economic security" or "environmental security" can be questioned by arguing that the security act has not really been performed and that the securitizing actor has not managed to establish a case for treating the threat as existential.[60]

This is at odds with their constructivist claim that the 'meaning of a concept lies in its usage and is not something we can define analytically or philosophically according to what would be "best"'.[61] In other words, the Copenhagen School is not clear how much definitional leeway to give to contextual actors.

Ciută's solution is a contextual approach to security. This would prioritise the meanings of security employed by actors.[62] By this view, actors' contextual use of security language and construction of security meanings should be considered an endlessly empirical variable, and not constrained by analytical criteria. Ciută argues: 'students of security *must* take the self-understandings of the actors for real, because there is nothing outside these self-understandings to validate the exercise.'[63]

Ciută cites several influences from the hermeneutic tradition for his proposed approach, including Hans Gadamer, Paul Ricoer and Quentin Skinner. Skinner offers one of the clearest accounts of a contextual-hermeneutic approach. The aim of his 'Cambridge School' form of historical analysis is 'to use the ordinary techniques of historical enquiry to grasp [actors'] concepts, to follow their distinctions, to appreciate their beliefs and, so far as possible, to see things their way'.[64]

Ciută argues that such an approach would mean breaking the traditionalist taboo in security studies, or what Wæver calls the '"everything becomes security" trap'. From Ciută's perspective, 'security' really could mean anything.[65] Yet this would not mean anything goes; that is not how context works. It would still be necessary to pay heed to the institutionalised and sedimented discursive structures that shape the production of meaning. Usages and meanings are thus not completely fluid but often sticky. Indeed, the Copenhagen School attaches much importance to these sedimented aspects of security meaning, which they translate into their 'grammar' of security.[66] But Ciută argues that they reify them, 'rather than maintaining the theoretical principle and practical possibility that sedimented categories of meaning can change'.[67]

Ciută claims his radical contextualism entails a commitment to a broader form of constructivism than that of the Copenhagen School.[68] He argues that such a constructivist approach should consider not only how actors construct security threats and threatened things ('referent objects'), but also how security measures get constructed as security measures, how securitising actors get constructed as securitising actors, and, most importantly, how the meaning of security itself gets constructed.[69]

The central pillar of his approach is that despite the historical and institutional sedimentation of many aspects of security, the meaning of security can change. Specifically, actors can change it through language. This follows Skinner's approach to history, which focuses on precisely such phenomena: it studies historical actors 'who legitimate novelties through referring to their use in the everyday vocabulary, which they then extend or revise for their own specific purposes'.[70] In fact, Skinner's focus on the performative use of language, or 'speech acts', has the same theoretical roots as securitisation theory. However, Ciută and Skinner give their actors more freedom to change contextual meanings, unlike the Copenhagen School, which distils historically specific, sedimented meanings into timeless concepts.[71]

Ciută proposes that instead of going looking for the recognisable logic of security as it appears in different contexts (which poses a risk of what Thierry Balzacq calls 'confirmation bias'), the aim is to interpret meanings of security as they appear in different contexts, with the assumption that these meanings may depart from sedimented meanings.[72] Ciută argues that the primary aim of contextual hermeneutics is 'To offer an interpretation in the name of a better *description* . . . to point out meaning already inherent in context'.[73]

Ciută's intervention in the debate is important for making the case against 'strict criteria' of security. He argues that 'contexts of security can be studied confidently even in the absence of a perennial category of security'.[74] However, his proposal is not a complete answer to the 'how do we know security when we see it?' question. It suffers from certain problems and blind spots. For example, he stresses that there is 'nothing outside' the 'self-understandings' of actors.[75] Yet, accessing those self-understandings is not straightforward. The legible and recoverable traces of what actors say or write in public may not necessarily signify their subjective 'self-understanding' but may rather be their outward 'self-presentation', which may be quite different. This problem can be seen as the age-old problem of rhetoric, in which actors may say things for strategic purposes rather than as a statement of their true beliefs (Chapter 5 explores this problem in depth through Foucault's work on ancient Greek politics). It could also be seen through Erving Goffman's dramaturgical analysis as the problem of 'front stage' and 'back stage'.[76]

There is also an important difference between language as the intentional utterances of actors and discourse which is a wider system of meaning.[77] Stefano Guzzini points out that discourses or intersubjective systems of meaning may be beyond the comprehension and manipulation of individual contextual actors.[78] It is possible that actors may not correctly discern the contextual system of meaning in which they are enmeshed. Guzzini gives the example of red traffic lights, which possess a socially embedded, constructed meaning, calling on traffic to stop. However, 'An actor coming from another society where such a convention does not exist would at first be at a loss to understand the meaning of the red traffic light. Hence, correct behaviour presupposes a type of background knowledge.'[79] In this case, analytically 'seeing things their way' would not help, because the alien under analysis does not understand the system of meaning in which it has become entangled. As Guzzini points out, this means that 'meaning is not limited to the actor itself, but must comprise the significance given to it by other actors, and also observers'.[80]

This draws the analyst back into the equation, because analysts are observers who impart significance. In other words, there is a role for the analyst beyond interpreting and describing the meanings and intentions of actors, and this role is to interpret systems of meaning and their significance in ways that may not be apparent to contextual actors themselves. Contextual actors may not always be able to tell us about things that are absent from their immediate context. And as Hay points out, such absences and exclusions may be politically significant, such as whether or not an issue is accessible to political actors or on their agendas.[81] This is a central concern of this book, as the next chapter will elaborate. There may also be other areas of analytical significance that are not reducible to the level of contextual actors' 'self-understandings', such as the growth of a 'field' of security professionals or the rise of techniques and technologies of security governance that do not speak for themselves.[82]

There are also historical examples in which contextual actors did not realise the security implications of what they were discussing at the time, but which in hindsight can be identified as significant. For example, in November 2015 it transpired that MI5 had been conducting a secret telephone metadata surveillance programme under a clause in the Telecommunications Act 1984, which was not foreseen by parliamentary legislators at the time.[83] Analysts thus have a different critical vantage point from which to interpret the historical, contextual and conceptual significance of empirical material, and they may have access to different material than the contextual actors had themselves.[84]

Ciută's contextualist move remains important for pointing out the analytical costs of rigid conceptual assumptions. More conceptual flexibility and contextual nuance is certainly needed in order to maintain analytical openness to historical and empirical change. But an actor-centric analysis does not fully answer the methodological question 'how do we know security when we see it?'. Analysts with a different institutional or historical vantage point may see much that contextual actors cannot. Questions also remain about where to look and what sort of materials or data to gather, especially those that may not be encompassed by the 'self-understandings' of actors. The next section turns to Foucault to address some of these issues. As we will see, Foucault's approach has much in common with Ciută and Skinner (who cites Foucault as one of his inspirations).[85] However, a Foucaultian approach based on problematisations offers a way to avoid the conceptual restrictiveness of securitisation theory and the potential actor-centric myopia of contextual hermeneutics.

Foucault's historical empiricism: Dispensing with definitions

> I wouldn't want what I may have said or written to be seen as laying any claims to totality. I don't try to universalize what I say.[86]

The Foucaultian methodology is a form of historical empiricism. It is historical because it concerns historically situated practices and systems of thought that can be dated to a particular time and place, rather than immutable concepts or core logics. And it is empirical because it works with source material drawn from the 'archive' of things that have been said, done, written, built, organised and instituted. This 'archive' is literal, in the sense of libraries and documents, and metaphorical, in the sense that discourses and practices have a history and can be situated in time. Sometimes discourses and practices carry a great weight of history, such as long traditions of thought or institutionalised ways of doing things (as with 'sedimented' meanings and edifices of 'security'). Sometimes they have a forgotten history, which it may be politically or conceptually significant to recover. Sometimes they represent new and significant departures from the old.

A Foucaultian methodology is critical in at least two ways. First, it is critically *directed* at theory. By historical and empirical demonstration, it aims to make the assumptions of existing theories problematic. Second, it is critically directed at present-day practices, with the aim of contributing to change. It does not say how things should be (it is not explicitly normative). Rather, it points out that things are not necessarily as we assume. Graham Burchell writes that the 'starting point is the non-necessity of what passes for necessary in our present'.[87] Foucault thus says that his aim is

> To give some assistance in wearing away certain self-evidences and commonplaces about madness, normality, illness, crime and punishment; to bring it about, together with many others, that certain phrases can no longer be spoken so lightly, certain acts no longer, or at least no longer so unhesitatingly performed; to contribute to changing certain things in people's ways of perceiving and doing things.[88]

This book adds 'security' to this list of 'self-evidences', specifically the assumption that it is a kind of anti-politics.

Readers of Foucault will know that his work is often described as a 'history of the present'.[89] Foucault reads the past in order to put our present concerns in a new light. He makes the past strange in order to make the present strange, so that we may see our present concerns in their particularity and distance ourselves from our assumptions. Foucault offers an empiricist reading of the past that is directed at the present. Of course, all historical work is directed at its own present in terms of its audience. But Foucault does not offer a straightforward historical account, nor a contextual-hermeneutic approach in the Skinnerian sense of 'seeing things their way', nor a 'follow the actor' approach in Bruno Latour's sense of describing 'actor networks'.[90] His methodological criticality is to be found in a historical empiricist methodology aimed at unsettling existing theoretical and political assumptions. In other words, it is an empiricism shaped and directed by a critical purpose. Burchell writes:

> It is by modifying their own and others' relation to the present through a modification of their relation to truth that historians of the present 'play their part', reshaping the space of public debate, for example.[91]

Foucault argues that we should not apply generalised definitions, assumptions or theories when we study particular historical episodes or events. He writes: 'The world . . . does not work hand in glove with what we already know.'[92] Kendall and Wickham call this 'suspending second order judgements'.[93] If we arrive at our analysis with prior assumptions, then we are merely looking to confirm what we already think we know. This includes using generalised theories or a priori criteria to explain particular cases, such as the 'core logic' of security in securitisation theory, or more generally the idea that security is an anti-politics. Foucault's aim is not to offer a more truthful account, a better-theorised account or a more accurate account, but to make the past appear strange in order to make the present appear strange and in turn to prompt scholars and practitioners (or 'analysts' and 'actors' in the earlier parlance) to rethink their assumptions.

Much like any historian, Foucault could see that people's thoughts about things change over time, to the extent that there could be no universal or transhistorical definitions of those things. His method is thus always to begin his inquiries by suspending existing definitions. The typical example in Foucault's work is 'madness', to which he frequently refers to explain and develop his methodology. His *History of Madness* shows that for one age, madness was a form of demonic possession or divine message; for another it was a form of unreason and a lack of liberty; and for another, closer to our own time, it was a pathology that could be diagnosed by psychology or psychiatry.[94]

Paul Veyne argues that Foucault's point is not that 'we were doing better than our ancestors and had discovered the truth around which they had stumbled'.[95] Rather, it is that our recent ideas are no less strange and historically specific. They are yet another variation piled upon all the rest.[96] Rather than correcting the errors of the past by coming up with a new and better definition of madness, for example, Foucault's point is that the phenomenon of madness should be understood in its historical contingency, through the 'customs, words, bodies of knowledge, norms, laws and institutions' that accompanied it and therefore defined its reality at particular historical moments.[97] Thus his method was 'to start off with detailed practices, details of what was done and what was said'.[98] Foucault's notion of practice includes what people do and their reasoned reasons for doing it; in other words, thought informs practice, is part of practice and is practice in its own right.[99]

For Foucault, the 'reality' of a thing is to be found in the practices that surround it and not in any underlying essence of the thing itself. Foucault was in this way an empiricist: not in the sense of using measurements or data to get closer to an object, but by adding contemporaneous detail to an object – including what people thought about it – until it can no longer be contained by a universal definition. As Veyne explains, Foucault did not aim to reduce phenomena to some underlying 'nugget . . . of the truth', such as reducing homosexuality to 'anatomy or physiology'.[100] Foucault instead asks us to begin our inquiries by suspending the assumption that objects of inquiry have a core truth at all.[101]

This has epistemological, ontological and methodological significance, which Bruno Latour illustrates in his own additive and empiricist approach which is in many ways similar. Latour complains that realist philosophers all too often use simple solid objects like rocks as examples to demonstrate the factual materiality and core truth of things.[102] However, he argues that something like a parliament – which in Nordic languages often has a name deriving from the word 'thing', such as the Icelandic *Althing* – is not a solid lump but a gathering.[103] It is a gathering of people, ideas, hopes, practices, architectures, movements and so on. For Latour, like Foucault, critical inquiry should add to reality, not subtract from it.[104] The aim should not be to reduce a thing to a general category or even to critique the conditions that made people erroneously believe it was a solid fact, but to build a richer empirical understanding of what goes into making it a 'thing' at all. Latour thus calls for 'a multifarious inquiry launched with the tools of anthropology, philosophy, metaphysics, history, sociology to detect how many participants are gathered in a thing to make it exist and to maintain its existence'.[105] This is similar to Foucault, although as we will see, Foucault has a stronger notion of the politics of such an approach.

In one of his later works, Foucault said that his method was to approach history through problematisations. A problematisation is when people begin using their freedom of thought to question something, identify difficulties in it and start treating it as a problem.[106] It is when a problem is identified as such and enters thought as a result. External events might prompt this questioning – for example in security studies the Cold War or 9/11 – but a problematisation is not reducible to those events. A problematisation is when, for whatever reason, developments 'provoke . . . a certain number of difficulties' with something and make it 'lose its familiarity'.[107] It is when something that was unquestioned, accepted or not actively thought about becomes problematic to contemporaneous actors.

Explaining this idea of problematisations, Foucault describes his method as a 'critical analysis in which one tries to see how the different solutions to a problem have been constructed'.[108] A problematisation is when, for whatever reason, the self-evidence of an established set of assumptions or practices breaks down or an issue becomes problematic. This leads actors to rethink their practices, assumptions, knowledges or rationalisations. When people identify something as a problem, they begin to offer responses and solutions, which may be diverse and even incompatible.[109]

The empirical focus of the method is thus on how people articulated a problematisation and the interventions, discourses and practices that the problematisation animated. This constitutes a terrain for analysis, but a problematisation is more than the sum total of what people said and did about a problem they identified. Problematisations create a space or 'discourse' in which people express the problem, propose solutions to it and put those solutions into practice.[110]

The Foucaultian term 'discourse' is somewhat misleading because it is not meant to be purely linguistic, unlike the Copenhagen School focus on 'speech acts'.[111] At different times, in different translations and in different commentaries, Foucault is said to have talked of 'discursive formations', 'discursive practices', 'grids of intelligibility', assemblages and *'dispositifs'*.[112] The last is notoriously difficult to translate from the French, having an everyday meaning akin to apparatus (as in the general apparatus of the police) but also a more critical connotation as used by Foucault to bring into question the assumed boundaries of that apparatus (for example, to understand 'policing' as a social practice that is not confined to the concrete apparatus of the police itself).[113] The translation of *dispositif* used by Janet Lloyd, Paul Veyne's translator, is 'set up'.[114] This works almost colloquially in English to convey a loose but inclusive notion of the things that surround a particular issue, problem or practice, as in 'the whole set up'. This is somewhat akin to Latour's 'gathering'.

The choice of what to include in this 'set up' lies with the analyst and their critical intent and is part of the methodology.[115] In Foucaultian methodological terms, it is the role of the analyst to identify and interpret problematisations via their specific 'set up' or *dispositif*. This *dispositif* may include all manner of things and is not limited. Foucault talks of

> a thoroughly heterogeneous ensemble consisting of discourses, institutions, architectural forms, regulatory decisions, laws, administrative measures, scientific statements, philosophical, moral and philanthropic propositions – in short, the said as much as the unsaid.[116]

Mitchell Dean argues that while this is an empirical methodology, it is not a naïve empiricism aimed at a 'reconstruction of the past ... [using] historical sources to discover the reality of which these sources are traces'.[117] Nor is it akin to a pure hermeneutics that sees interpretations all the way down, nor a contextual hermeneutics that tries to 'see things their way'.[118] Foucault's methodology rests upon a particular understanding of discourse as ontologically and empirically concrete. The method is not about uncovering the hidden meaning, subtext or historical forces behind a discourse that are only accessible to the analyst; it is not about discerning and accessing the intentions of actors, which remain subjectively internal and therefore inscrutable. Nor is it about the recovery of reality through discourse. Discourse is a reality in itself. Foucault's methodology is to remain 'within the dimension of discourse':[119] 'There is no subtext.'[120] As Dean explains: 'It is this affirmation of the reality of discourse as something to be analysed, described, and organised that prevents archaeology from retracing the interpretative spiral of hermeneutics.'[121] This does not mean that working with discourse is epistemologically straightforward, despite its ontological concreteness. As Foucault famously claimed in his related writings on genealogy (which we will discuss shortly): 'Genealogy is gray, meticulous, and patiently documentary. It operates on a field of entangled and confused parchments, on documents that have been scratched over and recopied many times.'[122]

Problematising security

To say that security and its relationship to politics has become something strange and unfamiliar – that it has breached its conceptual packaging – means in Foucaultian terms that it has been problematised. Parliamentarians have problematised 'security' explicitly, implicitly and sometimes inadvertently in their speech and practice. For example, when they question the extent to which the executive should keep intelligence secret, from them in particular, they problematise the traditional executive monopoly on secret intelligence. When they inquire into the legitimacy and propriety of the government's use of secret intelligence, they problematise the executive prerogative to make security decisions on that basis. When they question the scope and content of a national security strategy, they problematise the traditional right and capacity of the executive to identify threats. When parliamentary committees with no traditional security remit launch their own inquiries on aspects of security policy, they problematise the constitutional settlement that restricts intelligence oversight to special committees that meet behind closed doors. All these activities problematise the 'logic' of security as an 'anti-politics'.

Events may have prompted this problematisation of the security/politics relationship, but it is not reducible to them. Nevertheless, there are historical points at which the questioning intensified. Later chapters will examine these in more detail, but an obvious example is the 2003 Iraq War, specifically the contentious way that the UK and US governments used intelligence to make their case for war. The effects of this are still being felt. The UK parliamentary vote on intervention in Syria in the summer of 2013 revealed a widespread distrust of government use of intelligence.[123] The parliamentary debate leading up to the vote featured implicit and explicit questioning of the intelligence prerogatives of the government and state. Some MPs offered their own assessments of the situation on the ground in Syria, calling into question the exclusive remit of the intelligence agencies to do this for the government.[124]

Taking a longer view of the UK, a problematisation of the traditional constitutional settlement around security emerged after the end of the Cold War. Around this time, for example, UK policy-makers first put the country's intelligence agencies on a statutory footing. They also created democratic intelligence and security oversight mechanisms for the first time.[125] All this represents a problematisation of the historically sedimented conventions through which security was practised, conventions that kept most politicians out of any meaningful engagement with security and kept security out of 'normal politics'.

This all begs the methodological question of what to include in a problematisation, which is another way of asking the question 'how do we know security when we see it?'. What criteria should be used, who should decide what they are and should this be led by the practices of contextual actors or the choices of the analyst? From a Foucaultian perspective, this actor/analyst distinction is problematic and blurred. As discussed by Guzzini above, analysts are actors who can affect others through their analysis; their observations have the ability to feed into social situations and affect them.[126] This implicates analysts in the things they research and makes them another actor in the *dispositif*. From a Foucaultian perspective there is no external, neutral vantage point from which the 'analyst' can describe and delimit discourses or problematisations. As Bartelson explains: 'historians of ideas or sociologists of knowledge are in want of a suprahistorical vantage point from which history can be written, validated, judged and criticized with a claim to truth or verisimilitude.'[127] Because there is no such vantage point, we cannot expect to find one, or indeed any 'truth' outside of historical 'regimes of truth'.[128] To put it differently, the 'analyst' is always already contextual.[129]

A Foucaultian historical-empiricist methodology thus places considerable judgement with the analyst over what artefacts to include in their identification of problematisations and their attendant *dispositif* or 'set up'. In so doing it loses securitisation theory's rump 'traditionalist' objectivism of identifying the 'core criteria' of security in empirical cases. Indeed, the analytical task is the opposite of abstracting 'conceptual axioms' or generalisable 'truths' from history.[130] Such an approach should highlight the change and contingency of the meaning and practice of 'security'. From a historical-empiricist point of view, one cannot ask 'what is security?', only 'what is security here?'. As argued above, *dispositif* is a loose notion of a 'set up' drawn widely by the analyst that can include, for example, the knowledges, rationalities, languages, practices, artefacts and technologies that surround a particular problematisation.[131] This method does not therefore establish the parameters of a *dispositif* as positive criteria of identification (of 'security' in this case), but rather the choice of where and how to describe a *dispositif* is part of the critical intentionality of the analyst.

Thus, this book aims to draw the *dispositif* of security politics differently to other approaches in security studies. It includes a growing range of parliamentary activities on security that have hitherto gone unnoticed or been considered unimportant. Unlike a contextual-hermeneutic approach, such as that of Ciută and Skinner, the aim is not primarily to 'see things their way' by giving interpretive expression to contextual actors' discourses and meanings. Rather the aim is to identify and interpret contextual problematisations in the first instance, but simultaneously to intervene in them, amplify them and draw out their significance for rethinking categories in the present.[132] In other words, the aim is to question how this problematisation should make us think about security politics differently.

A historical angle is not in itself novel. Most historical methodologies would emphasise that meanings change over time. Robert Castel argues that the historical materials used by Foucault are much the same as any historian would use. But he adds, 'One who studies a problematisation' is not a historian like others; 'A problematisation is a historical account that differs from an account written by a historian even though it is often based on the same materials.'[133] Castel then asks: what right does the analyst of problematisations claim in writing histories different to those of other historians, if not that of offering a 'better' interpretation?[134] Castel argues that a problematisation-based approach 'must contribute something to what has already been achieved by a classical historical approach'.[135] And since it is directed at the present, it must also offer something different to other non-historical approaches such as sociology or ethnography.[136] According to Castel, therefore, a Foucaultian 'history of the present' adds something to historical interpretation in order to say something pertinent about the present. It is not a story of 'how we got here', but an analysis of historical materials to prompt a rethinking of current theories and narratives.

To put it another way, what matters in this method is the specific kind of critical emphasis. Again, the aim is not simply to identify and describe problematisations in their historical context from an external vantage point, but to make an explicit choice to intervene in those problematisations and amplify them for critical purposes.[137] Thus a history of problematisations always rests on a double move: first to identify and describe, and second to amplify and problematise further. It is not only the contextual actors who problematise, but also analysts. This again blurs the actor/analyst distinction.

In the case of this study of security politics, historians and parliamentary scholars have often already worked on many of the same materials. For example, there are numerous histories of intelligence agencies and their relationship with politicians; there are accounts of various scandals concerning executive overreach (particularly in the US); and there is some specialist parliamentary literature on the UK Intelligence and Security Committee and its contentious position in the political field. To a large extent, the Foucaultian approach of this book works with the same or similar materials and faces the same challenges with sources and archives, as Castel suggests. But the purpose of the work is not the same as that of archetypal historians who aim to reinterpret or add to our knowledge of the past. Rather, it is to add something different to our knowledge that other approaches do not. As Castel puts it, 'a problematisation constructs another account from historical data'.[138]

This takes us back to the starting point of this chapter, Wæver's question 'how do we know security when we see it?'. A problematisation-based approach does give an answer to this question, but also rejects its objectivist or 'traditionalist' premise. This is because there is no 'neutral' or transhistorical 'standpoint' from which to make an objective judgement about what is 'security'.[139] The analyst must instead make a judgement about what is significant, not on the basis of ideology or a normative programme to which the analyst subscribes, but in order to point out the consequences of otherwise continuing with an orthodoxy of unquestioned assumptions. Graham Burchell puts it as follows:

> By plotting the historically contingent limits of present thought and action, attention is drawn to what might be called the costs of these limits: what does it cost . . . for its truth to be produced and affirmed in this way?[140]

In this study, for example, the consequences of continuing to ignore developments in professional politics as they relate to security include not only the intellectual risk of being uninformed or out of touch, but also the political risk of failing to notice the emergence and influence of new players, arguments and practices in the game of security politics.

The Foucaultian critical approach developed here treads some old ground in security studies debates. For example, as long ago as 1999 Johan Eriksson published an insightful article entitled 'Observers or Advocates? On the Political Role of Security Analysts' in which he argued that any security analysis had to take political responsibility for how it drew the boundaries of 'security', and that this could not simply be seen as a form of scientific observation.[141] And while other scholars have argued for security analysis to have explicitly normative or even emancipatory motivation (as discussed in Chapter 1), the problematisation approach outlined here is more critically reflexive in being motivated to work against the limits and blind spots of prevailing theoretical assumptions.[142] It is motivated by a concern identified by Annick Wibben: 'As scholars – even as conscious, accountable, and engaged scholars – we can easily be complicit in maintaining dominant Security Studies frameworks.'[143] Wibben sees the role of critical security scholarship as 'an opening of security . . . to generate new security imaginaries', which she suggests should include gendered and postcolonial concerns.[144] The point of this book is that dominant security studies frameworks (including 'critical' ones) make a blind spot of many practices of professional politics that relate to security.

History as war?

So far, this chapter has discussed problematisation as method, or, to put it differently, the methodology of Foucaultian historical empiricism as a 'history of problematisations'. This approach cannot avoid certain traditional methodological concerns. For example, Castel demands 'validity' from such an approach.[145] Problematisations must not be fictions. They must be empirically justified. Castel writes: 'The right to choose one's materials and refocus them in light of a current issue . . . is not permission to rewrite history.'[146] For Castel, the normative ends of such work do not justify any interpretive means necessary. He demands a criterion of validity under which problematisations must remain open to refutation by historians: 'a problematisation can be refuted if it contradicts historical knowledge.'[147] Foucault himself struggled with more extreme forms of this question: is his methodology partial or partisan? Can history serve as a weapon in political struggles? Moreover, Foucault struggled with these methodological questions in the context of questions about the relationship between politics and war, making them even more relevant for this study. It is worth examining Foucault's intellectual progression through these questions because it captures some of the political stakes involved in the question 'how do we know security when we see it?'.

Thomas Biebricher argues that in Foucault's 'genealogical' phase around the publication of 'Nietzsche, Genealogy, History' (1971) and *Discipline and Punish* (1975), Foucault was writing provocative histories using 'highly rhetorical textual strategies' with the aim of provoking political transformations, or at least critical questioning, in his present.[148] One of the core assumptions of genealogy was that truth existed only in a servile relationship to power. For this reason, Foucault could not himself claim to be making power-free truth claims in his historical works.[149] Because one of the core claims of genealogy is that partisan struggles and even war are the very substance of history, any historical work must be seen as an intervention into those struggles.[150] At this time, therefore, Foucault embraced the notion that his works were provocative fictions, flippantly saying: 'Of course, there's no question of it being anything else but fiction.'[151] Biebricher tries to explain the reasoning behind the apparent methodological licence of genealogy as follows:

> Foucault's historical depictions in *Discipline and Punish* are provocations and challenges aimed at the reader: if this narrative of punishing, its link to pedagogy, medicine, the legal system and religious confessional practices were really 'true', what would you do? To be sure, a more measured account would have to introduce qualifiers, caveats and nuance, but the point of genealogy cannot be historical accuracy if it does not want to risk relapsing into a framework in which truth can be disentangled from power.[152]

This raises methodological challenges. For example, it breeches Castel's demand for validity. However, Foucault was soon to leave this provocative stance. As a scholar he was unusually honest in expressing dissatisfaction with his earlier work (although this impression might be because of the accessibility of his lectures, which are more reflexive than his monographs). For example, at the beginning of the 'Society Must Be Defended' lectures he says:

> I've just about had enough; in other words, I'd like to bring to a close, to put an end to . . . the series of research projects . . . that we've been working on for four or five years . . . I realize that there were more and more drawbacks, for both you and me.[153]

This lecture series marks a key moment in Foucault's methodological development. Their purpose is to ask whether history really can be thought of as a form of 'war'.[154] Foucault asked, 'If we have to think of power in terms of relations of force, do we therefore have to interpret it in terms of the general form of war?'[155] Foucault does so by historicising the question, investigating where and when in history was history itself understood as partisan. In this way, using his empiricist historical methods, and with no irony, Foucault answers his own question about history as war in the negative. Biebricher calls this a 'genealogy of genealogical thought'.[156] The end result is that Foucault puts to bed the idea that history is 'war'. He makes that idea into just another historically contingent discourse.[157] In other words, the idea that 'history is war' cannot be transhistorically true once it has been historicised. Or, to look at it differently, following Nietzsche's point that 'Only that which has no history can be defined', once something has been given a history, it can no longer be fixed with a definition.[158] This encapsulates the method described in this chapter: by giving the idea that 'security is an anti-politics' a history by dating it to a certain time and place, it can no longer be taken as a definition of security.

Going back to Foucault's methodological development, in the opening of the 'Security, Territory, Population' lectures of the following year, we can see a remnant of the battlefield metaphor. He says the role of the lectures is 'that of showing the knowledge effects produced by the struggles, confrontations, and battles that take place within our society, and by the tactics of power that are the elements of this struggle'.[159] But he immediately qualifies this by stating that there is no normative imperative, no call to arms, implied in his work: '[S]aying "strike against this and do so in this way" seems to me to be very flimsy when delivered from a teaching institution or even just on a piece of paper.'[160] In this way he disavows the notion that his work is an incitement to some sort of struggle or resistance against a particular institution or power structure. Foucault then offers a further methodological imperative before beginning the lectures proper: 'Never engage in polemics.'[161] He explains this more fully in a 1984 interview:

> The polemicist . . . proceeds encased in privileges that he possesses in advance and will never agree to question. On principle, he possesses rights authorizing him to wage war and making that struggle a just undertaking; the person he confronts is not a partner in the search for the truth, but an adversary, an enemy who is wrong, who is harmful and whose very existence constitutes a threat.[162]

By dissociating himself from polemics he moves a long way from his 1971 declaration of genealogical war in 'Nietzsche, Genealogy, History', in which he claimed 'knowledge is not made for understanding; it is made for cutting'.[163] After 'Security, Territory, Population', battlefield metaphors disappear from Foucault's substantive historical research and from his methodological comments. Indeed, Biebricher argues that in Foucault's later works there is no assumption that struggle is the substance of history, either methodologically or as empirical content. For example, the 1978–79 'Birth of Biopolitics' is an apparently quite un-genealogical evolution of neoliberalism that leads directly to the present; it is not a discontinuous history of struggles and reversals as would be expected in a genealogy.[164]

In the 'Birth of Biopolitics' lectures, Foucault rearticulates his methodology with no trace of battlefield metaphors. Here we find an account of the historical empiricism described above, which refuses universal or transhistorical concepts.[165] From then onwards, his historical works are squarely about the emergence of rationalities and their accompanying practices: the reasoned way that people do things and the reasoned way they think things should be done – 'The reasoned way of governing best', as Foucault puts it.[166] The 'Biopolitics' lectures are about the problematisations animating the forms of knowledge and truth that make up those rationalities (in this case: neoliberal economics) and the forms of subjectivity constituted by them (in this case: populations as economic actors).

This discussion of partisanship in the study and writing of history is an important consideration for a Foucaultian methodology. It addresses the positionality of the 'analyst', which has proved controversial in the critical security studies debates discussed above. A Foucaultian methodologist does not stand outside history and does not occupy a position that enables the distillation of timeless concepts from contingent historical events. Such a scholar is motivated by the intellectual and political stakes of the contemporary debates in which they are enmeshed and uses their empirical study to bring into question the assumptions permeating those debates. However, if such a scholar does not claim the epistemological rights and privileges of a quasi-scientific 'analyst' who stands outside history, then what right do they claim? Are they just another partisan antagonist in political and historical struggles, undermining any claim to analytical authority they may have had? This was a question that troubled Foucault, and which he answered with his own methods. The conclusion reached here is that such a methodology should claim epistemological authority on the basis of empirical validity, and critical authority on the basis of the assumptions it challenges.

Foucault contra Foucaultians

To proceed with this chapter's methodological reading of Foucault, further moves are needed. It is necessary to extricate Foucault's methodology from the predominant reading of Foucault in critical security studies. This predominant reading overly focuses on one particular problematisation in Foucault's work: liberal or neoliberal practices of government, under the label 'governmentality'. This chapter now needs to clarify the distinction between 'Foucaultian governmentality' research on the one hand – which has a particular substantive and normative content – and a more general methodological reading of Foucault on the other. To put it another way, the aim is to develop a Foucaultian methodology for researching security politics that is not all about governmentality.

Karen Lund Petersen identifies the influence of what she calls a 'Foucaultian governmentality approach' in this critical security studies. She argues that its critical aim is to identify the 'disciplining power of . . . neoliberal logic', as found in the 'daily practices of governments and companies'.[167] With reference to scholarship on risk, she gives the examples of '[Mark] Salter's work on airport security, [Claudia] Aradau and [Rens] van Munster's article on terrorism insurance and [Louise] Amoore's work on private security companies'.[168] From another angle, we could say this work is united by what Mitchell Dean calls an 'analytic of government': the 'study of the organized practices through which we are governed and through which we govern ourselves'.[169] This encapsulates the general scholarly concern with 'governmentality', which in Dean's words is an expansive notion of government that includes not only the traditional 'conduct of conduct' but also 'practices for the production of truth and knowledge ... [and] multiple forms of practical, technical and calculative rationality'.[170] This book acknowledges the importance of this research, but aims to disassociate a Foucaultian methodology from it. This is because if Foucault becomes synonymous with the 'Foucaultian governmentality approach', it may hinder analytical openness.

To explain this in more detail, there are two reasons why this methodological disassociation is necessary. First, the predominance of the 'Foucaultian governmentality approach' in critical security studies may create an expectation about the content of Foucault-inspired research. O'Malley et al. once posed this problem as 'abstract restrictions on what governmentality is to study, that is, what its theoretical object is taken to be'.[171] This is not to identify a flaw in such research, but to express concern that the name 'Foucault' has become a shorthand for critiques of the ways in which 'we' are governed in liberal polities. Mitchell Dean's now standard work on governmentality is an example of this problem. In the following quotation we can see how Dean ties Foucault's historical method to a substantive problematisation: 'genealogy strives to make intelligible forms of liberalism in relation to the practices of government to which they are linked.'[172] However, contra Dean, there is no necessary connection between genealogy as a method and the critique of liberalism or neoliberal governmentality. In security studies, governmentality-focused research has been invaluable for understanding how security works as a practice, particularly by moving attention away from the international interactions studied by more traditional forms of security research. Yet that is not the concern of this book.

Breaking the connection between Foucaultian method and governmentality is important if this book is to address the analytical neglect of practices of professional politics in security studies. As discussed in Chapter 1, government and politics are not synonymous. Foucault was at times guilty of blurring this distinction, as we will discuss shortly. Yet the diversity of Foucault's empirical work, such as his later lectures on the Greeks, demonstrates its applicability to more varied political concerns than the 'Foucaultian governmentality approach' implies. It is only in this later work that he introduces a specific problematisation of politics as distinct from government.

The second reason for disassociating Foucaultian methods from the 'Foucaultian governmentality approach' follows Petersen's concern that governmentality scholars 'tend to define *a priori* the main political stakes in today's world'.[173] In other words, that approach assumes to know what the political problem is in advance – the problem of liberal or neoliberal government – and thus assumes a particular normative stance. Latour poses this concern in a more general and provocative way when he bemoans 'explanations resorting automatically to power, society, discourse'.[174] He attacks a heroic mode of scholarship in which 'the courageous critic, who alone remains aware and attentive, [says] "You ... believe you are free but, in reality, you are acted on by forces you are not conscious of"'.[175] To be fair, research in critical security studies offers an empirical richness quite unlike the old-fashioned critical theory that Latour criticises here, but nevertheless there is a grain of truth in the concern that critical inquiry too often comes with an a priori normative slant. Petersen argues that this risks closing down 'analytical sensitivity' to the emergence of conceptual change and new political stakes.[176] Given the earlier focus of this chapter on the need for analytical openness, this last point is especially important.

From governmentality to politics

Foucault himself partly caused the problem. Barry Hindess points out that when Foucault talked about 'political rationality' he most often meant the 'governmental rationality' of the modern state: 'In his writings on government Foucault commonly uses the term "political" as if it were equivalent to a certain understanding of "governmental".'[177]

Hindess argues that the novelty of Foucault's work on governmentality is found in the way it described the emergence of an 'art of government' separate from the problematisation of the right and legitimacy of the prince.[178] This understanding of governmentality is an autonomous rationality of government . . . clearly predicated on an understanding of the state, first, as distinctive institutional structure, not reducible to the court and other appurtenances of the ruler, and, second, as containing its own principle of rationality.[179]

Foucault explained that the aim of this work was to 'account for real governmental practice . . . as it is given, but at the same time as it reflects on itself and is rationalized'.[180] However, O'Malley et al. argue that

> The concept of governmentality was designed to form a mid-range explanatory level between the history of political philosophy and an empirical study of social relations. The consequence of this kind of explanatory strategy has been the reduction of politics to a 'mentality of rule'.[181]

Hindess argues that having developed so much important work on rationalities of government, Foucault nevertheless failed to consider forms of political action which are not 'identified with the action of government itself'.[182] One example would be Max Weber's understanding of 'politically oriented' action as that which 'aims at exerting influence on the government'.[183] Another is implied by the Foucaultian idea of liberal government through freedom, as popularised by Dean, Nikolas Rose and others; Hindess argues that free individuals, groups, parties and factions – although 'governed' through their freedom – may nevertheless still be free to influence or even dominate the state.[184] The possibility of freely influencing the state also challenges the idea that there is an autonomous rationality of governing that is independent from competing political influences.[185]

Meera Sabaratnam makes a similar criticism of scholars who adopt Foucaultian governmentality frameworks to explain and critique liberal interventions and what Mark Duffield calls the 'development-security nexus' in the global south.[186] Like Dean, Rose and the 'powers of freedom' literature, such frameworks argue that forms of liberal governmentality produce liberal subjects who are governed through their very freedom.[187] However, Sabaratnam argues that such accounts tend to 'ignore the exteriority of power through the discounting of Southern subjecthood'.[188] In other words, a totalising understanding of governmentality leaves no room for the agency of the subjects 'targeted by intervention'.[189] Vivienne Jabri points out that this is partly a product of Foucault's own blind spot regarding empire and his positionality in a time and space of French imperialism.[190] However, the more general point is that governmentality frameworks all too often leave little room for agency outside the umbrella of governmental powers. In the context of Sabaratnam's critique of Eurocentrism it may seem perverse to argue here that the professional political elite in liberal democracies suffer the same erasure of agency in the governmentality framework, but in fact the point about maintaining analytical space for political agency is the same.

A different way of looking at this problem of subsuming 'politics' under 'government' is that Anglo-American social science has had many decades to engage with Foucault's problematisations of government, but only a few years to engage with his problematisation of politics. Foucault's final lectures have only recently been published in English and it is only now possible to see that Foucault did not always mean 'governmental' when he said 'political'. In the 1982–83 and 1983–84 lectures on 'The Government of Self and Others' (numbered I and II), the problematisation under analysis is not what people thought government should do and for what reasons ('the reasoned way of governing best'), nor the liberal problem of how to maintain individual freedom in relation to the state, but rather the problem of how to live a political or philosophical life.

In his earlier 'genealogical' work discussed above, Foucault gave an account of politics as partisan struggle, which formed the substance of history. In his final lectures, he offers a different understanding of politics. Foucault goes back to the Greeks to explore 'the problem of the political game, of its rules and instruments, and of the individual who engages in it'.[191] His methodology has not changed; it is the identification and amplification of historically situated problematisations. The problematisation in this case is that of practising politics. For example, when an individual becomes a politician or enters the political arena, they claim a certain right to speak for others, to exhort others to follow or to govern others.[192] This creates the problem of 'an ascendancy exercised by some citizens over others'.[193] Furthermore, by entering the 'political game' the players enter a dangerous game of rivalries, factions and performance. The rules of the game require them to govern themselves in a certain way to maintain their credibility and position, hence the title 'The Government of Self and Others'.

Note that a problematisation is not a concept and this is of fundamental importance to the methodology developed in this chapter. A problematisation is not the expression of a general problem that can then be refined, distilled and applied elsewhere as an explanatory tool. Unlike securitisation theory which takes a 'sedimented meaning' of security and turns it into a 'conceptual axiom', problematisations are always specific to times and places and are as likely to be historically discontinuous as continuous.[194] Although it may be possible to identify the contextual problematisation of political practice in varied times and places, this problem and contemporaneously proposed solutions may be quite different in different political situations, such as the democratic assembly or the court of a tyrant. Moreover, the problematisation of professional politics is specific to the Western democracies of the past two centuries at most and did not enter Foucault's analysis. It is Weber's 'Profession and Vocation of Politics' that remains one of the earliest and most important expressions of this particular problematisation.

Nevertheless, Foucault's work on politics offers an opening to an analysis of political practices and their problematisation, distinct from the familiar 'Foucaultian governmentality approach' in critical security studies. The empirical chapters will ask, therefore, what is 'the problem of the political game, of its rules and instruments, and of the individual who engages in it'?[195] And how does this relate to 'security'?

Notes

1. Flinders and Kelso, 'Mind the Gap', p. 265.
2. Buzan, Wæver and de Wilde, *Security*, pp. 4–5.

3. Huysmans, 'What Is in an Act?'; Wæver, 'Politics, Security, Theory', p. 473.
4. Foucault, 'Governmentality'.
5. Wæver, 'The EU as a Security Actor', pp. 252–3; Buzan, Wæver and de Wilde, *Security*.
6. Ciută, 'Security and the Problem of Context'.
7. See Buzan and Hansen, *The Evolution of International Security Studies*, pp. 1–3; Krause and Williams, *Critical Security Studies*.
8. Buzan, *People, States and Fear*; Brundtland, 'Our Common Future'; Ullman, 'Redefining Security'; Mayall, 'Reflections on the "New" Economic Nationalism'; Cohn, 'Sex and Death in the Rational World of Defense Intellectuals'; Buzan, Wæver and de Wilde, *Security*, p. 5.
9. See Eriksson, 'Observers or Advocates?', pp. 312–13; Walt, 'The Renaissance of Security Studies', p. 213; Goldman, 'Miljöhot, Migration Och Terrorister I Tokyo-Om Begreppet Säkerhet'.
10. Buzan, Wæver and de Wilde, *Security*, p. 4.
11. Ibid. p. 19.
12. Wæver, 'Politics, Security, Theory', p. 469.
13. Huysmans, 'Revisiting Copenhagen', p. 491.
14. Buzan, Wæver and de Wilde, *Security*, p. 4; Huysmans, 'Revisiting Copenhagen', p. 500.
15. Buzan, Wæver and de Wilde, *Security*, p. 19.
16. Wæver, 'Politics, Security, Theory', p. 478.
17. Ilgit and Klotz, 'How Far Does "Societal Security" Travel?'; Buzan, Wæver and de Wilde, *Security*, pp. 119–40.
18. Huysmans, 'Revisiting Copenhagen', p. 500.
19. Buzan, Wæver and de Wilde, *Security*, p. 5.
20. Ibid. p. 4.
21. Wæver, 'Politics, Security, Theory', p. 469.
22. Buzan, Wæver and de Wilde, *Security*, p. 5.
23. Ibid.
24. Ibid. pp. 4–5.
25. Floyd, 'Extraordinary or Ordinary Emergency Measures', p. 678.
26. Abrahamsen, 'Blair's Africa', p. 59.
27. Roe, 'Is Securitization a "Negative" Concept?', p. 250.
28. See, inter alia, Salter, 'When Securitization Fails'; Stritzel, 'Towards a Theory of Securitization'; McDonald, 'Securitization and the Construction of Security'; Boswell, 'Migration Control in Europe after 9/11'; Balzacq, 'The Three Faces of Securitization'.
29. Wæver, 'Politics, Security, Theory', p. 467.

30. Bartelson, *A Genealogy of Sovereignty*.
31. Huysmans, 'Revisiting Copenhagen', p. 500.
32. Ciută, 'Security and the Problem of Context', p. 307.
33. Bourbeau, 'Moving Forward Together: Logics of the Securitisation Process', p. 191.
34. Howell, 'The Global Politics of Medicine', pp. 965, 966, 970.
35. Wæver, 'Politics, Security, Theory'.
36. Ibid. p. 469.
37. Buzan, Wæver and de Wilde, *Security*, p. 19.
38. Wæver, 'Politics, Security, Theory', p. 473.
39. Ibid. p. 466.
40. Bourdieu, *Language and Symbolic Power*, p. 128.
41. Ibid.
42. Wæver, 'Politics, Security, Theory', p. 466.
43. Ibid. p. 470. Wæver is citing Walker's critique of international relations theory *Inside/Outside*.
44. Ciută, 'Security and the Problem of Context', p. 321.
45. Wæver, 'Politics, Security, Theory', p. 470.
46. Ciută, 'Security and the Problem of Context', p. 314.
47. Bubandt, 'Vernacular Security'.
48. Stritzel, 'Security, the Translation', p. 343.
49. Ibid. p. 344. His brackets.
50. Ciută, 'Security and the Problem of Context', p. 302; Buzan and Waever, *Regions and Powers*, p. 48.
51. Ciută, 'Security and the Problem of Context'.
52. Buzan, Wæver and de Wilde, *Security*, pp. 30, 40.
53. Ibid. p. 5; Ciută, 'Security and the Problem of Context', p. 306.
54. Ciută, 'Security and the Problem of Context', p. 307.
55. See Buzan, Wæver and de Wilde, *Security*, pp. 21–3.
56. Ciută, 'Security and the Problem of Context', p. 309.
57. Ibid. p. 312.
58. Ibid., citing Wæver, 'European Security Identities', p. 120.
59. Ciută, 'Security and the Problem of Context', p. 302.
60. Buzan, Wæver and de Wilde, *Security*, p. 47, fn. 9.
61. Ibid. p. 24.
62. Ciută, 'Security and the Problem of Context', p. 318.
63. Ibid. p. 315.
64. Skinner, *Visions of Politics*, p. 3.
65. Ciută, 'Security and the Problem of Context', p. 320.
66. See Buzan, Wæver and de Wilde, *Security*, pp. 27–9.
67. Ciută, 'Security and the Problem of Context', p. 321.

68. Ibid. p. 317.
69. Ibid.
70. Palonen, *The Struggle with Time*, p. 16.
71. See also Howell, 'The Global Politics of Medicine', p. 966.
72. Balzacq, *Securitization Theory*, p. 34; Huysmans, 'Revisiting Copenhagen', p. 500.
73. Ciută, 'Security and the Problem of Context'.
74. Ibid.
75. Ibid. p. 315.
76. Goffman, *The Presentation of Self in Everyday Life*; Salter, 'Securitization and Desecuritization', p. 327.
77. Howarth, *Discourse*, p. 9.
78. Guzzini, 'A Reconstruction of Constructivism in International Relations', p. 164.
79. Ibid. p. 161.
80. Ibid.
81. Hay, *Why We Hate Politics*, p. 64.
82. Bigo, 'Security and Immigration'; Huysmans, *The Politics of Insecurity*.
83. BBC News, 'MI5 "Secretly Collected Phone Data" for Decade'.
84. Castel, '"Problematization" as a Mode of Reading History'.
85. Vucina, Drejer and Triantafillou, 'Histories and Freedom of the Present'; Making History, 'Interview with Professor Quentin Skinner'.
86. Foucault, 'Questions of Method', p. 73.
87. Burchell, 'Liberal Government and Techniques of the Self', p. 279.
88. Foucault, 'Questions of Method', p. 83.
89. Burchell, 'Liberal Government and Techniques of the Self'; Dean, *Critical and Effective Histories*.
90. Skinner, *Visions of Politics*, pp. 1–8; Latour, *Reassembling the Social*.
91. Burchell, 'Liberal Government and Techniques of the Self', p. 279.
92. Foucault, 'The Discourse on Language', p. 328.
93. Kendall and Wickham, *Using Foucault's Methods*, p. 13.
94. Foucault, *History of Madness*, pp. 153, 56, 538. Foucault's *History of Madness* was of course neither comprehensive nor the last word on the historical critique of 'madness', least of all the international dimension of the governance of mental health, which Alison Howell examines in *Madness in International Relations*.
95. Veyne, *Foucault*, p. 5.
96. Ibid. p. 7.

97. Ibid. p. 10.
98. Ibid.
99. Foucault, 'Questions of Method', p. 75.
100. Veyne, *Foucault*, p. 8.
101. See for example Foucault, *The Birth of Biopolitics*, p. 3.
102. Latour, 'Why Has Critique Run out of Steam?', p. 234.
103. Ibid. p. 233.
104. Ibid. p. 232.
105. Ibid. p. 246.
106. Foucault and Rabinow, 'Polemics, Politics and Problematizations', p. 388.
107. Ibid.
108. Ibid. p. 389.
109. Ibid.
110. Ibid.
111. Particularly if we consider how Foucault distanced himself from his earlier preoccupation with linguistic 'statements' in *The Archaeology of Knowledge*. Dreyfus and Rabinow, *Michel Foucault*; Bonditti et al., 'Genealogy'.
112. Dreyfus and Rabinow, *Michel Foucault*, pp. 120–1.
113. For a further discussion of *dispositif*, see Howell and Neal, 'Human Interest and Humane Governance in Iraq', pp. 215–18.
114. Veyne, *Foucault*, pp. 10, 149.
115. See also Howell and Neal, 'Human Interest and Humane Governance in Iraq', and the chapters in Aradau et al. (eds), *Critical Security Methods*.
116. Foucault, 'The Confession of the Flesh', p. 194.
117. Dean, *Critical and Effective Histories*, p. 14.
118. Ibid. p. 15; Skinner, *Visions of Politics*, p. 1.
119. Foucault, *The Archaeology of Knowledge*, p. 85.
120. Ibid. p. 135.
121. Dean, *Critical and Effective Histories*, p. 16.
122. Foucault, 'Nietzsche, Genealogy, History', p. 76.
123. House of Commons, 'Syria and the Use of Chemical Weapons, House of Commons Hansard Debates for 29 Aug 2013'; Strong, 'Interpreting the Syria Vote'.
124. House of Commons, 'Syria and the Use of Chemical Weapons, House of Commons Hansard Debates for 29 Aug 2013'.
125. Bochel, Defty and Kirkpatrick, '"New Mechanisms of Independent Accountability"'.

126. Guzzini, 'A Reconstruction of Constructivism in International Relations', p. 162.
127. Bartelson, *A Genealogy of Sovereignty*, p. 55.
128. Foucault, 'Truth and Power', p. 131.
129. This is the key distinction between Foucault's early 'archaeological' approach and his later 'genealogical' approach.
130. See Ciută, 'Security and the Problem of Context', p. 321.
131. Veyne, *Foucault*, pp. 10, 149.
132. See also Aradau et al. (eds), *Critical Security Methods*, pp. 1–22.
133. Castel, '"Problematization" as a Mode of Reading History', p. 240.
134. Ibid. pp. 239–40.
135. Ibid. p. 251.
136. Ibid.
137. Bonditti et al., 'Genealogy'.
138. Castel, '"Problematization" as a Mode of Reading History', p. 251.
139. Bartelson, *A Genealogy of Sovereignty*, p. 55.
140. Burchell, 'Liberal Government and Techniques of the Self', p. 279.
141. Eriksson, 'Observers or Advocates?'.
142. Nunes, *Security, Emancipation and the Politics of Health*; Nyman and Burke, *Ethical Security Studies*; Booth, 'Security and Emancipation'.
143. Wibben, 'Opening Security', p. 137.
144. Ibid. pp. 137, 148.
145. Castel, '"Problematization" as a Mode of Reading History', p. 252.
146. Ibid.
147. Ibid.
148. Biebricher, 'Genealogy and Governmentality', pp. 366–8.
149. Ibid. p. 370.
150. Foucault, 'Nietzsche, Genealogy, History'. For a longer discussion see Neal, 'Cutting Off the King's Head'.
151. Foucault, 'Interview with Michel Foucault', p. 242. Cited in Biebricher, 'Genealogy and Governmentality', p. 370.
152. Biebricher, 'Genealogy and Governmentality', p. 370.
153. Foucault, *'Society Must Be Defended'*, p. 3.
154. Neal, 'Cutting Off the King's Head'.
155. Foucault, *'Society Must Be Defended'*, p. 266.

156. Biebricher, 'Genealogy and Governmentality', p. 384.
157. Neal, 'Cutting Off the King's Head'.
158. Nietzsche, *The Genealogy of Morals*.
159. Foucault, *Security, Territory, Population*, p. 3.
160. Ibid.
161. Ibid. p. 4.
162. Foucault and Rabinow, 'Polemics, Politics and Problematizations', p. 382.
163. Foucault, 'Nietzsche, Genealogy, History', p. 88.
164. Biebricher, 'Genealogy and Governmentality', p. 382.
165. Foucault, *The Birth of Biopolitics*, p. 2.
166. Ibid.
167. Petersen, 'Risk Analysis', p. 701.
168. Ibid.
169. Dean, *Governmentality*, p. 28.
170. Ibid. pp. 17, 28.
171. O'Malley, Weir and Shearing, 'Governmentality, Criticism, Politics', p. 509.
172. Dean, *Governmentality*, p. 61.
173. Petersen, 'Risk Analysis', p. 702.
174. Latour, 'Why Has Critique Run out of Steam?', p. 229.
175. Ibid. p. 238.
176. Petersen, 'Risk Analysis', pp. 708–9.
177. Hindess, 'Politics and Governmentality', pp. 257–8, 261.
178. Ibid. p. 258.
179. Ibid.
180. Foucault, *The Birth of Biopolitics*, pp. 2–3.
181. O'Malley, Weir and Shearing, 'Governmentality, Criticism, Politics', p. 504.
182. Hindess, 'Politics and Governmentality', p. 261.
183. Ibid., citing Weber, *Economy and Society*, p. 55.
184. Rose, *Powers of Freedom*; Hindess, 'Politics and Governmentality', p. 262.
185. Hindess, 'Politics and Governmentality', p. 262.
186. Sabaratnam, 'Avatars of Eurocentrism in the Critique of the Liberal Peace'; Duffield, 'The Liberal Way of Development and the Development–Security Impasse', p. 54.
187. Rose, *Powers of Freedom*; Miller and Rose, 'Governing Economic Life'. See also Dillon and Reid, *The Liberal Way of War*.
188. Sabaratnam, 'Avatars of Eurocentrism in the Critique of the Liberal Peace', p. 265.

189. Ibid.
190. Jabri, 'Michel Foucault's Analytics of War', p. 75.
191. Foucault, *The Government of Self and Others*, p. 158.
192. Ibid.
193. Ibid.
194. Ciută, 'Security and the Problem of Context', p. 321.
195. Foucault, *The Government of Self and Others*, p. 158.

3. Securitisation and Politicisation

Modern Western political thought, and more specifically the discipline of security studies as a sub-discipline of international relations, has understood 'security' through a negative relationship to politics. Key security literatures consider 'security' to be that which is removed from 'normal politics' or the 'merely political'.[1] By this view, 'security' is that which threatens to restrict political activity in the name of existential necessity. Security is seen as a high politics or an exception to 'normal politics': an anti-politics. More specifically, in securitisation theory and many 'critical' security literatures, the anti-politics of security is considered to work through executive secrecy and prerogative, the narrowing of choice and dialogue, the favouring of elite circles of expertise and decision making, and the shift of security governance away from democratic control.[2]

These assumptions have led to the analytical neglect of certain kinds of political activity by assuming their marginalisation or irrelevance to 'security'; in particular, politics as practised by professional politicians. As the previous chapters have made clear, this book's focus on this kind of politics is not intended to represent the totality of politics, nor all that is political. Rather, the practices of professional politicians in democratic institutions such as parliaments represent a distinct and significant type of political activity that has been neglected in security studies.

So, the book poses the question: what would it mean for security to be understood as part of 'normal politics', when 'normal politics' is understood as the activity of professional politicians within a specific institutional political arena? The question itself challenges the very concept of 'security', which as discussed has widely been understood as something institutionally and qualitatively distinct from 'normal politics'. This book deliberately departs from this assumption by looking for 'security' in the activity and arena of 'normal politics'. To this end, the empirical chapters, through an extended case study of the UK, tell the story of how the once 'exceptional' policy area of security has entered 'normal politics' over the past three decades. Professional political activity on security has increased to such an extent that it must prompt a rethink of the assumed pathological relationship between 'politics' and 'security'. Before that can be done, however, more conceptual work is needed.

While there is value in understanding a neglected area for its own sake, the critical implications of this study go further. As discussed in Chapter 1, the way politics is defined, and what it includes and excludes, is politically significant. This is demonstrated by feminist struggles to politicise issues such as domestic violence and have them recognised as political rather than merely private concerns.[3] By politicising domestic violence and putting it on to political agendas, feminists brought the issue into the 'arena' of politics. By the same token, it is politically significant if 'security' was once excluded from the activity and arena of 'normal politics' – as defined by Kalyvas and the Copenhagen School – and is now present there. This chapter is concerned with understanding this movement of issues into and out of the 'arena' of politics, and the inclusion and exclusion of actors in that 'arena'.

The subsequent empirical chapters of this book argue that professional political actors once marginalised by 'security' are now actively engaged with it and that security is increasingly present in the arena of their political activity. Again, following Hay, this book does not define politics as an activity that takes place in a specific institutional arena, but rather considers the presence or absence of an issue in that activity and arena to be politically significant.[4] Given that before the 1990s the UK parliament was almost entirely prevented from engaging with 'security', but is now substantively engaged across a whole spectrum of security-related topics, there is a significant development to understand and explain here. This is more than just a matter of the expansion of democratic intelligence oversight, which has been addressed in detail elsewhere.⁵ The meaning and scope of security policy and practice have expanded in this time beyond the traditional and narrow understanding of security as related to defence and intelligence, which is why Chapter 2 spent so much time on developing a way to identify changing iterations of 'security' in context.

What is now needed is a way of conceptualising this apparent 'shift' or 'migration' of 'security' into 'politics'. Securitisation is in fact already conceptualised as a form of 'arena shifting': a special type of 'arena shifting' that works through speech acts. Securitisation theory holds that when securitising actors discursively construct issues as security issues, they are lent the qualities of urgency, exceptionality and necessity, which facilitates their removal from 'normal politics' to more exclusive circles of decision making. This chapter will discuss the point that while the theory does not contain an explicit theorisation of 'arena', it contains implicit understandings of 'spaces' that are both metaphorical – in terms of exceptionally moving 'beyond' normal rules or procedures through the intensified qualities of security politics – and institutional – in the sense of transferring issues out of 'normal bargaining process' and into 'more elite circles of decisionmaking', such as specialist government committees.⁶

The previous chapters have shown that the securitisation framework makes the idea of 'security' being present in the activity and arena of 'normal politics' a conceptual impossibility. In this framework, security issues are by definition those that are elevated above the 'merely politicized'. By the same token, when issues are moved out of 'security' they get 'desecuritised', so by definition they are not security issues any more.⁷ In this framework, an issue cannot be 'security' and 'merely politicized' at the same time.

The aim of this chapter is therefore to conceptualise a form of arena shifting that does not result in this conceptual impossibility. To this end, as well as further interrogating the securitisation framework, it investigates the literature on politicisation and depoliticisation (which includes Hay). Like the securitisation framework, the literature on politicisation considers that when issues are successfully made more politically important or salient, they get elevated up political hierarchies to more politically important arenas and institutions, such as the issue of domestic violence being shifted from the private realm to the realm of politics and government. The chapter finds similar conceptual difficulties at work in this body of literature.

This chapter argues that the literatures on securitisation and politicisation conflate the political quality of issues with their institutional arena in hierarchies of government and politics. Qualitative changes in politics – such as issues or interactions becoming more important or intense – should not necessarily be tied to shifts in their institutional location, such as when issues get moved into or out of a particular political arena. Although qualitative changes and institutional shifts are often linked, there is no necessary conceptual link between the two. Therefore, this chapter argues that in order to analyse such a thing as 'security as normal politics', which would otherwise be a contradiction in terms, it is necessary to decouple political quality from political arena. Only with this conceptual move is it possible to analyse the shift of 'security' into the arena of normal, non-exceptional 'politics', without reproducing the assumption that security is by definition a form of anti-politics.

Critique of the norm/exception binary

As discussed, securitisation is a move that takes issues 'beyond' normal politics. The ostensible 'exceptionalism' of security is the 'breaking free of rules' and a move into a 'narrowed down and constrained' form of politics.[8] In practice, however, the meaning of the 'exceptionalism' of security is not always clear. For example, does the security 'exception' mean a formal constitutional state of emergency, as declared in France following the Paris attacks in November 2015? Does it mean the creation of 'exceptional' governmental powers beyond the established 'norm', such as those handed to the US President by Congress with the 14 September 2001 Military Authorization Act? Does it mean invoking existing national security clauses within legal regimes such as the European Convention on Human Rights, as with the indefinite detention of foreign 'terrorist suspects' by the

UK in 2001?[9] Or is 'exceptionalism' merely a more general pressure or feeling: an affective 'atmosphere'?[10]

The literature tends to treat several qualitatively and ontologically different signifiers of 'security' as overlapping. These range from the concrete and institutional, such as the institutional shift to smaller circles of elite decision; to the formal or processual, such as the enactment of legal exceptions or restriction of democratic scrutiny; to the discursive and affective, such as the invocation of emergency in speech.

It is therefore difficult to maintain 'exceptionalism' as a defining criterion of security. Several scholars have challenged the norm/exception binary in securitisation theory. In the counter-examples they invoke, security policies and practices do not enact formal exceptions to the law or to other 'normal' institutionalised political procedures. A few examples include the following. Elsewhere, I have argued that in the UK, security policy has historically been pursued through constitutionally 'normal' practices of lawmaking, even though deliberation and scrutiny have often been lacking.[11] Reflecting on the same UK example, Rita Floyd has argued that 'securitizing actors do not always revert to exceptional security policies when they address a threat'.[12] Paul Roe – commenting on Ole Wæver's point that in securitisation theory, 'The concept of security is Schmittian, because it defines security in terms of exception, emergency and a decision' – has argued that, 'in the context of liberal democracies, securitization rarely resembles Schmittian decisionism'.[13] Jonathan Bright, again on the UK case, examines whether security legislation is rushed and lacking in scrutiny. He concludes that, 'Far from being overwhelmed by the politics of security, it appears legislators are more likely to respond in kind, raising their efforts to conduct more scrutiny on legislation of increased importance.'[14]

Examining changes in Western security policies towards Africa, Rita Abrahamsen argues that these

> are not to be understood exclusively in terms of existential threats or external enemies but also relate to more mundane, everyday practices of managing and containing risks . . . an issue can move along a continuum of risk/fear without ever reaching the stage of 'existential threat' where it merits 'emergency action'.[15]

Mark Salter has reconceptualised 'successful' securitisations as policy changes rather than as formally or intersubjectively accepted 'exceptions'.[16] And Alison Howell, Melanie Richter-Monpetit, and Shampa Biswas and Sheila Nair argue in different ways that the violence of 'security' has always been a 'normal' part of social and political life for specific repressed groups, and so reject the norm/exception distinction.[17] From this varied research we can conclude that in practice the 'exceptionalism' of security can take many forms, if indeed it exists at all. Moreover, whether or not a security policy or practice is 'exceptional' may be more a matter of situated perception and discursive construction than formal distinction. (As discussed in Chapter 2, the Copenhagen School seems confused on this point, maintaining that security is on the one hand formally characterised by 'exception, emergency and a decision', and on the other hand by intersubjective 'audience acceptance' of discursive constructions of threat. This is what Holger Stritzel calls an 'irreconcilable tension'.[18])

However, although the critique of these binary distinctions can have powerful implications – such as exposing the historical 'norm' rather than 'exception' of racial oppression or torture – it may also limit analytical possibilities. Problematising binary categories such as norm/exception or politics/security is an important critical move that can unsettle scholarly orthodoxies – for example, R. B. J. Walker's 1993 *Inside/Outside* did this for the domestic/international binary that is central to the discipline of international relations – but blurring such binaries may have the effect of diminishing the possibility to make significant analytical distinctions.[19] Again, Hay's point about being able to distinguish whether political issues or actors are included or excluded from particular political arenas or agendas is key.[20]

It is for this reason that rather than simply dispense with the security/politics terminology and its associated conceptual schema, this chapter argues that there is analytical and political significance to be found in unpacking the ambiguities in the debate and treating them more concretely. For example, what would it mean to treat 'shifts' in politics to different arenas or locations as signifiers of change? Similarly, what would it mean to treat changes in the character, intensity or quality of politics as signifiers of politically significant developments? In other words, if the general assumption about security politics is that it closes down debate or shifts issues to more elite and exclusive circles of decision making, let us investigate empirically if that is, or was ever, the case. While scholars such as Bright have done this for some of the processes involved in security politics, such as legislating, the literature has yet to consider the significance of arena for identifying political change.

Spheres and activities of politics

Let us now return to securitisation theory to unpack its meanings of politics. For securitisation theory, the concept of 'security' presupposes a concept of 'politics'. It frames the 'exception' of security in relation to 'normal politics'. In their now canonical 1998 book *Security: A New Framework for Analysis*, Buzan, Wæver and de Wilde define security in contrast to 'the normal bargaining processes of the political sphere' and 'the normal run of the merely political'.[21] And also: '"Security" is a move that takes politics beyond the established rules of the game and frames the issue either as a special kind of politics or as above politics.'[22]

What 'politics' and 'political' mean in this context is not straightforward. There are ambiguities. For example, Huysmans points out that 'politics' has a double status in the Copenhagen School formulation. First, it is a 'sector' distinct from others such as the military, economy and society.[23] This is closest to what this book refers to as 'arena'. In the securitisation theory framework, different 'sectors' imply different kinds of 'securitising actor', different kinds of threat and different threatened things (the 'referent object').[24] 'Political security', for example, would involve threats to the existence of a political system or political actors.[25] But, second, 'politics' is also the general process through which issues are subject to extreme politicisation to become securitised.[26] Buzan et al. acknowledged this when they wrote:

> The problem with the political sector is that, paradoxically, it is the widest sector and is therefore also a residual category. In some sense,

all security is political ... All threats and defences are constituted and defined politically. Politicization is political by definition, and, by extension, to securitize is also a political act.[27]

Building on this tension, Buzan et al. situate their meaning of 'politics' between two existing theorisations. The first is Max Weber's understanding of politics as relating to institutionalised political structures and forms of authority, mainly the state; in securitisation theory, therefore, Weber represents the 'political sector' and 'the relatively stable institutionalization of authority'.[28] This is a slightly different emphasis from the focus on Weber's political professionals in Chapter 1, although this can still be understood as 'politically oriented' action which 'aims at exerting influence on the government'.[29] The second is Ernesto Laclau's understanding of politics as the destabilisation and hence politicisation of those same structures and forms; Laclau thus represents the process involved in politicisation and securitisation.[30]

Furthermore, in the Copenhagen School formulation, security is an anti-politics but still a kind of politics. It is 'a special kind of politics or ... above politics'.[31] Maria Mälksoo captures this ambiguity when she questions whether securitisation should be regarded as '*hyperpoliticization* or rather *depoliticization*'.[32] On the one hand securitisation is a hyperpoliticisation through which issues are increased in their 'intensity of importance', as Michael Williams puts it.[33] On the other hand this increased importance justifies a 'logic of necessity, the narrowing of choice, [and] the empowerment of a smaller elite'.[34] This is a form of depoliticisation.

So, in this original formulation of securitisation theory, there are several meanings of 'politics' at work. 'Politics' is a 'sector' consisting of institutionalised actors and structures. 'Politics' can become a 'referent object' of security if its structures and forms of legitimacy get constructed as existentially threatened. 'Politics' is also the general process through which securitisation takes place. 'Normal politics' or the 'merely political' is the state of affairs from which 'security' deviates, which is akin to Kalyvas's understanding of 'normal politics' discussed in the previous chapters. And 'security' is always a kind of politics, albeit a 'special kind'.[35] For the Copenhagen School to argue that security is 'an anti-politics or the politically constituted limit to politics' is to say that security replaces one kind of politics with another.

Ulrik Pram Gad and Karen Lund Petersen argue that the idea of a shift between different 'spheres' – such as between 'normal' and 'exceptional' politics, from wider to smaller 'circles' of decision, or from political professionals to security professionals – represents a distinct 'conversation' in the securitisation literature.[36] They point out that this speaks to a wider theme in modern social and political thought that concerns 'the societal organization of space – a sector, the public sphere – in a certain historical setting'.[37] Examples include the functional differentiation of societies found in the classical sociology of Durkheim and Weber, the functionalist political science of David Easton and the systems theory of Niklas Luhmann.[38]

As discussed, the security literature has an ambiguous understanding of 'sectors', 'spheres', 'spaces' or 'arenas'. The shift from 'politics' to 'security' can, for example, be conceived as a shift from one set of rules to a 'space' beyond those rules, or from 'open' dialogue to more 'closed circles' of discussion and decision making. These are in some ways metaphorical shifts, but they often also imply shifts between institutional locations, such as from parliament to the executive.[39] At times in their analysis, Gad and Petersen tend to reproduce these ambiguities. For example, they write that 'politics in [this] conversation is understood in terms of institutions', but then go on to discuss 'spatially demarcated spheres' that are 'marked as qualitatively different and functionally differentiated'.[40] It is this distinction between institutional arena and political quality that this chapter will clarify and develop.

To begin to unpack this ambiguity, we can look to the work of political theorist Kari Palonen, on whom Gad and Petersen draw. Palonen argues that spatial metaphors appear frequently in the history of political thought: 'Politics has been seen ... as a "domain," a "realm," a "field," a "sector," a "sphere," an "arena," a "stage," a "scene," etc.'[41] For Palonen these remain metaphors, and he adds: 'Nobody seems to claim that politics "exists" in such a space.' Rather, 'The conceptualization of politics through spatial metaphors is an attempt to approach politics indirectly by indicating the character of the space to which it is metonymically connected.'[42]

Palonen argues that spatial metaphors are limited in their ability to offer more precise and detailed understandings of politics. The alternative, he argues, is to conceptualise politics as an activity: a temporal rather than spatial concept that denotes what actors do rather than the realm in which they do it.[43] Thus Palonen sets up his work on politics as an activity in specific opposition to the understanding of politics as a sphere. As he states, 'my aim here is to understand politics as an activity that is independent of spheres and inherently in opposition to the necessitarian jargon.'[44] Such an approach would foreground contingent and contextual phenomena, because actors' understandings of what a particular activity means is contingent upon time and place. As Palonen explains, 'My first criterion is to construct modes of conceptualizing that do not *a priori* reduce the contingency in order to render the activity of politics intelligible.'[45] Márton Szabó puts it as follows in a review of Palonen:

> If we know that politics is an open and ambiguous practice, then we also know that political characters are theoretically free to consider anything to be the business of politics, not only those things which the sphere concept considers relevant. In other words, it is highly problematic if somebody claims to know what, in principle, *cannot* be part of politics.[46]

We can link this back to the discussion of contextual security in Chapter 2 and the importance of not excluding practices that may not fit overly rigid analytical categories of security. Yet, as Palonen notes, this alternative temporal concept of politics poses its own analytical difficulties, because 'activity as a contingent phenomenon remains fleeting and unforeseeable'.[47] Palonen's concern is similar to the analytical dilemma posed by Hay.[48] It is problematic if modes of analysis are so 'spatially' rigid as to define things 'out' of 'politics' or 'security'.

However, although analysis that focuses on contingent 'activities' may bring more detail, it may be unable to make important distinctions about what or who is included or excluded in different 'spaces'. Palonen creates a binary choice between 'sphere' and 'activity', opting for the latter. Yet what is needed is an analysis that captures both. This might mean identifying activities within spheres, or activities that move issues between spheres, such as forms of arena shifting. This is not to restrictively define politics as that which occurs in a particular institutional 'space', but to note that the spheres, arenas and locations of politics, however conceived, can be analytically and politically significant.[49] So to reiterate the discussion in previous chapters, defining what is 'political' and what is part of 'politics' has political stakes. Too narrow a definition may be analytically restrictive; too broad a definition risks losing analytical precision. And these analytical choices have political consequences.

To return to our original example in Chapter 1, Hay argues that too narrow a definition of 'politics' risks obscuring non-traditional political struggles, again such as feminist campaigns to politicise domestic violence.[50] Defining these activities out of politics would be to dismiss and delegitimise them. But too broad a definition of politics may diminish the ability to make important distinctions, such as 'whether or not a particular issue or set of concerns has been incorporated into the formal political process'.[51] For example, when did domestic violence become part of legislative agendas? And by what process? It matters politically if an issue was once not part of formal 'politics' and now is. This is something that can be studied and dated empirically, for example by examining the first parliamentary debate, the first committee inquiry, the first legislation and so on. The same is true of 'security': it matters if what was once institutionalised as an 'exception' to normal politics is now part of it.

Detecting these inclusions and exclusions may be a task for analysts with a different perspective to that of the contextual actors involved. However, as discussed in Chapter 2, it is problematic to make a strict separation between actors and analysts. That chapter made the point that analysts are also contextually situated and do not have a God's eye view. This is the basis for a

Foucaultian 'history of the present' that aims to unsettle taken-for-granted assumptions in the present. A different way to look at this is that sphere-based analyses are not exclusive to detached analysts. The interview material presented in the next chapter will show that contextual actors are perfectly capable of reflecting on the fact and meaning of their own exclusion from particular 'spheres'. Indeed, Anthony Giddens has long since stressed 'the need to avoid impoverished descriptions of the agents' knowledgeability'.[52] With these analytical and political considerations in mind, we will now turn to Hay's approach and the related literature on politicisation.

The politicisation/depoliticisation debate

Hay sets out a conceptual schema that aims to capture the movement and contingency of processes (or in Palonen's terms 'activities') of politics, but also aims to maintain the analytical purchase and political significance of different political arenas. Hay's schema avoids setting analytical limits on what can and cannot be politics, or on where politics can and cannot be found. Indeed, in an earlier work Hay maintains that 'the political' should be defined as expansively as possible:

> The political should be defined in such a way as to encompass the entire sphere of the social . . . All events, processes and practices which occur within the social sphere have the potential to be political.[53]

In later work, his aim is to understand the ways in which 'events, processes and practices' get politicised and to note the significance of this occurring within and between different political arenas.[54] Hay explains:

> We need: (i) to differentiate between the contexts within which political processes might be seen to occur; (ii) to see such contexts or arenas for potential political deliberation as politicized publicly to differing degrees; (iii) to order, and identify a hierarchy amongst, such arenas

of potential public politicization; and (iv) to consider the processes of politicization and depoliticization by which issues of contention are 'promoted' or 'relegated' from one arena to another.[55]

The idea of 'promoting' or 'relegating' issues between different arenas maps on to the Copenhagen School's shift between the 'merely political' and the 'securitised' through processes of securitisation and desecuritisation.[56] Buzan et al. actually discuss three spheres rather than two: the 'non-politicised', the 'politicised/normal politics' and the 'securitised/security politics', which we can see here:

> Securitization can . . . be seen as a more extreme version of politicization. In theory, any public issue can be located on the spectrum ranging from nonpoliticized (meaning the state does not deal with it and it is not in any other way made an issue of public debate and decision) through politicized (meaning the issue is part of public policy, requiring government decision and resource allocations or, more rarely, some other form of communal governance) to securitized (meaning the issue is presented as an existential threat, requiring emergency measures and justifying actions outside the normal bounds of political procedure).[57]

The following diagram of concentric circles illustrates the Copenhagen School's 'spatial' framework, with a larger circle representing the 'politicised' or 'normal politics' and a smaller circle within representing the 'securitised' or 'security politics'. Security here is still a form of politics, but a special one with anti-political qualities. The realm of the 'non-political' exists outside the circles and is unbounded. Securitisation is the move that takes issues to the inner circle. Desecuritisation is the move through which issues are moved back into the wider sphere of politics.[58]

In comparison to the three 'levels' posited by securitisation theory (the non-politicised, the politicised and the securitised), Hay adds further stages into the politicisation process. He conceptualises a hierarchy of differentiated 'arenas', each representing an increased level of politicisation.[59] In Hay's schema, politicisation is the transfer of issues up the hierarchy of arenas.

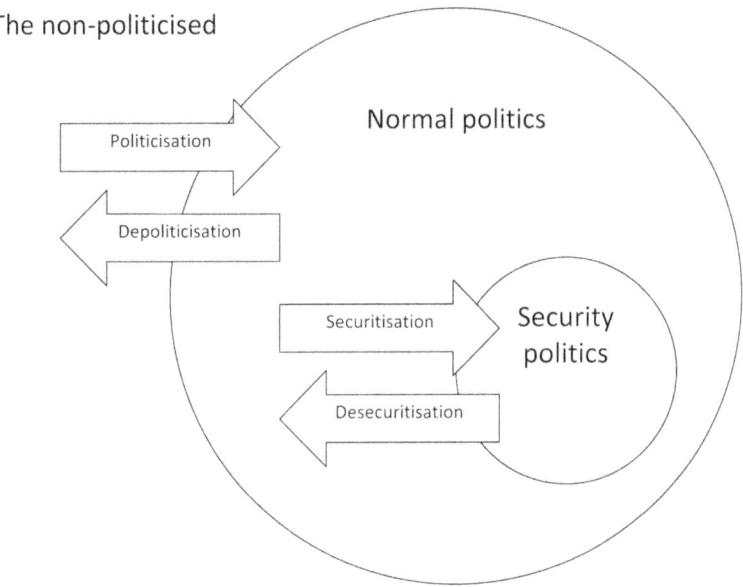

Figure 3.1 Movement between 'spheres' of politics in securitisation theory

Interestingly, Hay links politicisation to the capacity for agency. This is because 'Politics occurs, and can only occur, in situations in which actors can make a difference', or at least when actors recognise that they could acquire the 'capacity to make a difference' if they do not yet have it.[60] This is a way to understand political inclusion and exclusion and the degree to which actors have agency on any given issue. Hay's first or 'lowest' arena is the 'non-political': the arena of necessity or fate. This, he argues, is because 'Fatalism and resignation are the antithesis of politics. The extent to which our destiny is determined by processes beyond our control is the extent to which it is non-political' (note that 'necessity' is also one of the anti-political qualities posited by securitisation theory).[61] Hay's second arena is the 'non-governmental', which he subdivides into private and public arenas.[62] In the private arena, issues may be considered a matter of personal choice or questioning. Thus a first level of politicisation – 'Politicization 1' – is the move from 'fate' to the 'private arena', where humans may begin

Security as Politics

to consider that they have agency and choice where previously they did not, such as choosing one's religion instead of unquestioningly following one's religious upbringing.[63] 'Politicization 2' is the shift from the 'private' to the 'public' arena, which may be the result of 'consciousness-raising' efforts to bring issues into public attention and debate, but not yet on to governmental agendas. 'Politicization 3' is the shift of issues from public debate on to governmental agendas and into the 'governmental sphere' in which legislators and policy-makers subject issues to formal deliberation.[64] Depoliticisation is simply the reverse process.

In the Copenhagen School schema, securitisation is an extreme form of politicisation, so the 'securitised' sits beyond 'normal politics' or the merely 'politicised'. This suggests that security could be added to Hay's schema as a further stage of politicisation, which would create an extra 'exceptional' sphere of

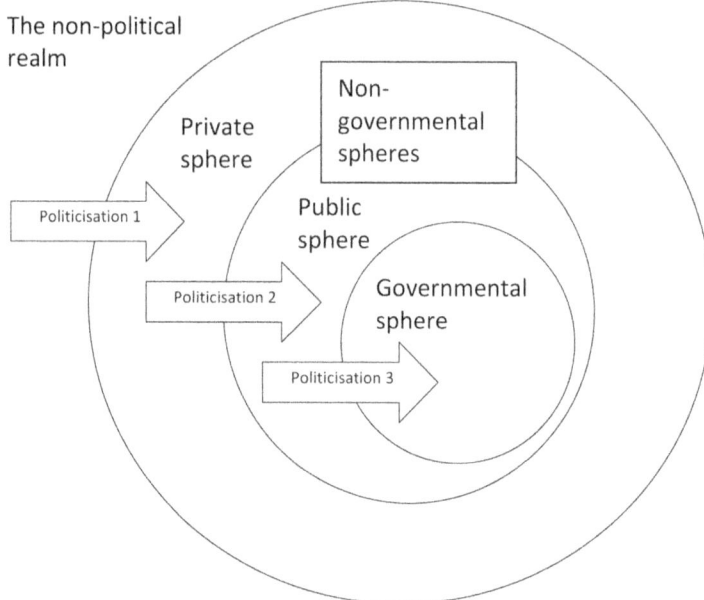

Figure 3.2 Movement between 'spheres' of politics in Colin Hay's schema
Source: Adapted from figure 2.2 of Colin Hay's *Why We Hate Politics*, reproduced with the permission of Polity.

'security politics' beyond his uppermost 'governmental sphere'. However, this is where the ambiguities of the security/politics distinction become apparent. The concept of securitisation cannot be conceived as an extension to Hay's schema because each shift up Hay's hierarchy of arenas – from private, to public, to the governmental – is meant to be characterised by an increase in agency, political importance and governmental/political attention. But although 'securitisation' represents an increase in the importance of an issue, it is simultaneously considered to be a reduction in public choice, agency and deliberation. So, while it could be argued that securitisation increases the agency of the government by legitimising extra executive powers with fewer checks and balances, securitisation is also a claim about conditions of necessity in which 'there is no alternative' and therefore a lack of choice about what needs to be done. These ambiguities are why Mälksoo questions whether securitisation should be regarded as '*hyperpoliticization* or rather *depoliticization*'.[65] Politicisation scholars Matthew Flinders and Matt Wood similarly express this when they describe securitisation as a tool of 'hyper-politicisation . . . through which to then impose a definitive position that closes down political debate (thereby depoliticising the issue)'.[66]

These frameworks result in conceptual and analytical contradictions when applied to the changing relationship between politics and security, and the apparent migration of security issues into the arena of 'normal politics'. For example, if a security issue moves 'down' from the realm of executive security prerogative into the wider arena of parliamentary activity, should it be understood as depoliticised because it has been shifted to a 'lower' arena? Or should it be understood as politicised, because it has been moved into open democratic contention in the arena of 'normal' politics? Should it be understood as securitisation, because there are more actors being more active on a greater number of security issues? Or is it desecuritisation because this activity is qualitatively and institutionally part of 'normal' political processes rather than forms of 'exceptionalism'? Furthermore, are these issues still security issues if they no longer have the special qualities of intensified importance associated with 'security' in the securitisation framework, such as 'urgency' and 'necessity'? What if contextual actors still discuss these as security issues and they fall within the practical scope of specified government security policies? In other words, is it conceptually and empirically possible for 'security' to be qualitatively 'normal' and institutionally located in a 'normal' political arena, or is 'security as normal politics' a contradiction in terms?

Politicisation and arena migrations

Some of these ambiguities – such as those around exceptionalism and hyperpoliticisation/depoliticisation – are already understood in the literature. However, what has yet to be considered is the analytical problem created by the conceptual linkage of arena and political quality in the politicisation and securitisation frameworks. For example, Hay understands politicisation as the simultaneous movement of issues up hierarchies of qualitative importance and political-governmental arena, such as from private sphere to public sphere to governmental sphere. He assumes that when an issue shifts 'up' from one arena to another it becomes politicised, and depoliticised when it shifts 'down'. Similarly, securitisation theory holds that when issues are constructed with qualities of 'security' – such as being existentially threatening – they are at the same time removed from 'normal' political processes and wider circles of democratic deliberation to more elite circles of decision making. This framework is thus built on the assumption that the process of securitisation involves a qualitative and institutional shift 'up' to a more rarefied 'sphere' and 'out' of 'normal politics'.

This conflation of the political quality of issues with their institutional location is a hindrance to understanding the phenomenon of security as 'normal politics'. Instead, in order to be able to capture the migration of 'security' into the arena of 'normal politics' without conceptual contradiction, the political quality of issues – for example their controversy, urgency or importance – must be decoupled from their institutional location or arena. In other words, security issues are not by definition those that are elevated above the 'normal' political arena because of their special qualities. If they were, it would be conceptually impossible to locate 'security' in the arena of 'normal politics'. 'Security' should instead be identified via the discourses and practices of historically contextual actors rather than its qualities. Its institutional location should be analysed separately without normative or conceptual assumptions.

The recent debate in British political science on politicisation and depoliticisation (of which Hay is part) illustrates why this disaggregation is necessary. This debate began as a problematisation of a specific kind of depoliticisation that appeared to be occurring in the UK, whereby governments would attempt to remove issues from political contestation by delegating them to technical agencies or to impersonal processes such as globalisation or market forces. Matthew Flinders and Jim Buller, for example, conceptualise this as a depoliticisation that divests the government of responsibility, with the effect of making ministers less accountable for certain issues and policies.[67] Flinders and Buller see this as a deliberate political strategy for ministers to dissociate themselves from controversial or risky issues, thereby 'insulating them from the adverse consequences of policy failure'.[68] Similarly, Flinders and Wood write: 'The concept of depoliticisation, while contested, essentially refers to the denial of political contingency and the transfer of functions away from elected politicians.'[69]

One example is the Labour government's decision in 1997 to hand the power to set interest rates to the Bank of England, thus distancing itself from the contentious perception that previous Conservative governments adjusted interest rates to manipulate political sentiment rather than for sound economic reasons. The Labour government thus 'depoliticised' interest rate setting.

The depoliticisation literature holds that the process is reversible and contestable.[70] Fawcett and Marsh call this 're-politicization'.[71] For example, a concerted political campaign or a failure of judgement by delegated experts could prompt a re-politicisation and bring issues back into public debate and political contestation. And attempted depoliticisations could themselves become politicised if they prompt complaints about democratic deficit or unaccountable and distant technocrats, as with many examples of anti-EU politics.

Flinders and Buller argue that this kind of depoliticisation does not 'in reality' remove the political nature of such issues, but rather transfers the politics to other arenas that are less accessible and contestable for the public and politicians.[72] As they argue:

> In reality the politics remains but the arena or process through which decisions are taken is altered (i.e. the form of politics changes or the issue is subject to an altered governance structure).[73]

In this understanding of 'depoliticisation', politics gets 'hidden' under claims that experts are apolitical. This resembles Didier Bigo's notion of a shift in authority away from public politics towards security professionals: there is still a politics, but it is not where it is supposed to be.[74] The 'politics' is shifted to a different arena and made less contentious and accessible in the process, but remains latent. Indeed, Flinders and Buller argue that such 'depoliticisations' may not be 'depoliticisations' at all, and thus 'the processes or procedures that are commonly referred to under the rubric of depoliticisation might therefore more accurately be described as 'arena-shifting'.[75]

Empirically speaking, these scenarios are entirely plausible. However, these two analyses – those of the depoliticisation literature and of Bigo – are not based solely on analytical observations but also on normative judgements about the motivations of the actors and the proper place and form of politics. Buller, Flinders and Wood assume that depoliticising actors want to divest themselves of risk and responsibility, and that their acts of arena shifting are a deliberate strategy to this end. For Bigo, security professionals have an interest in competing for resources and symbolic authority over security, which they attempt to wrest away from public politics. Furthermore, these analyses must themselves be seen as discursive and critical strategies to challenge such depoliticisations and to re-politicise them. The critical aim of these scholars is to reassert the politics and contestability of these situations against such attempted depoliticisations.

However, these processes could take different forms and have other drivers. For this reason Hay points out a danger in the depoliticisation literature, which is to 'associate too closely the mode of depoliticisation with the arenas or sites from which/to which responsibility is passed when issues become depoliticised'; in other words, we should not always assume that depoliticisation is a strategy by government ministers to offload risk and responsibility to technocrats.[76] In the same vein, building on Hay, the term 'arena shifting' implies a deliberate strategic act, which may not always be the case. More general 'arena migrations' of issues could occur without such acts.

This chapter proposes that greater analytical purchase can be achieved by distinguishing between changes in the political quality of an issue and changes in its institutional location or arena. These are two different issues that are not always connected. Both are significant, but they should be disaggregated. We should reserve the terms 'politicisation' and 'depoliticisation' for qualitative changes, which can be understood, for example, through Williams' idea of an increasing or decreasing 'intensity of importance'.[77] We should then reserve the term 'arena migration' (rather than deliberate 'shifting') for the movement of issues, policies or activities between different institutional locations. There is no necessary connection between the two. An issue may gain a greater 'intensity of importance' without a corresponding shift to a 'higher' political arena such as central government. And an issue may move from one arena to another, such as from central government to an arm's-length agency, without necessarily becoming more or less 'political'.

Analysing quality and arena separately implies different epistemological considerations. Identifying the qualitative politicisation or depoliticisation of an issue could in theory be done through empirical observation, but in practice such analysis is likely to contain some normative and political judgement. See, for example, the implicit normative aims of the depoliticisation literature. Hence Hay points out that 'there is a discursive component to all depoliticisations'.[78] This calls to mind the constructivist basis of securitisation theory and the Copenhagen School's point that 'some measure of whether [an] issue is "really" a threat . . . would demand an objective measure of security that no security theory has yet provided'.[79] In contrast, analytically locating issues or activities in particular arenas has more of a material empirical basis, since it is possible to locate contextual problematisations of 'security' (on the basis described in Chapter 2) in specific institutional settings such as parliament.

The depoliticisation literature does not offer this level of institutional precision. The problem is that Hay, Flinders, Buller, Wood and others do not distinguish between the institutional arenas of government and politics. For example, Hay's highest level/arena of politicisation is where issues enter the governmental sphere. However, he makes no distinction between government and the wider arena of professional politics. As discussed in Chapter 1, government and professional politics are not the same thing (and this is also overlooked by security studies debates). In parliamentary systems such as the UK, the institutional arenas of 'politics' (taken here as parliament) and 'government' (the executive) do overlap, but they are not identical. In the simplest terms, the UK government usually draws its 100 or so ministers from a parliamentary pool of 650 members of the House of Commons (sometimes with a few extras drawn from the 800+ peers in the House of Lords). Thus (quite obviously) all government ministers are politicians but not all politicians are in government. (The arena of 'government' may also include the civil service and the extended agencies of the state, and this of course would entail further distinctions within this arena between ministers and state officials. Chapter 6 will address issue migration within government in more detail.)

It is entirely possible for an issue to be in the institutional arena of 'professional politics' but not in the institutional arena of 'government' and vice versa. For example, an MP or parliamentary committee may decide to pursue a campaign or inquiry on an area they feel deserves government attention where there is currently none. Alternatively, an issue could be in the institutional arena of 'government' – specifically central government – but barely present in the institutional arena of 'politics'. Ministers and the civil service make daily governmental decisions on small policy matters that get little parliamentary or public attention, such as signing procurement contracts, responding to interest groups, appointing staff to agency posts or updating regulations in technical areas. These are only likely to get attention if they go wrong.

This distinction between the institutional arenas of government and professional politics matters not only analytically but also politically. For example, because of the historical exclusions of security politics, it matters if 'security' is no longer confined to the exclusive arena of executive prerogative and sovereign decision as it once was. This 'arena migration' does not necessarily correspond to an increase or decrease in how political, important, controversial or intense security issues are, nor to deliberate strategies of arena shifting by the most powerful actors. The reason for these 'migrations' is a matter for empirical analysis. For example, an issue may appear in the arena of parliament because it has been deliberately politicised by MPs; alternatively it may appear there because the government has attempted to depoliticise it by 'kicking it into the long grass' of a special parliamentary committee; or it may simply appear because it is the job of a departmental select committee to shadow the activities of particular government departments.

In fact, there is an overlooked and underdeveloped element of securitisation theory that expresses the distinction between institutional arenas on the hand and qualitative 'intensity of importance' on the other. This is the idea of 'institutionalised securitisation'. This is a situation in which the existence of a threat has become so widely accepted, implicit and normalised that it no longer needs to be explicitly constructed or reproduced through securitising discourse. There is a qualitative and an institutional aspect to this. Buzan et al. explain the qualitative aspect with the following example:

> It is implicitly assumed that when we talk of *this* (typically, but not necessarily, defense issues), we are by definition in the area of urgency: By saying 'defense' (or, in Holland, 'dikes'), one has also implicitly said security and priority ... If a given type of threat is persistent or recurrent, it is no surprise to find that the response and sense of urgency become institutionalized.[80]

Thus, the qualitative aspect refers to how, for example, a 'sense of urgency' becomes 'institutionalised' or, more accurately, 'normalised' in a discursive sense. The institutional aspect refers to how securitisations may become incorporated into institutionalised responses and implicit rationales for special security agencies, structures and powers. Once institutionalised it is no longer necessary to repeatedly legitimise the existence and special status of the security apparatus because this rests upon, as Buzan et al. put it, the 'repetition of a security argument so well established that it is taken for granted'.[81]

Buzan et al. go on to use the concept of 'institutionalised securitisation' to describe a historical situation that is quite familiar: 'In well-developed states, armed forces and intelligence services are carefully separated from normal political life.'[82] Indeed, historically, intelligence services in particular have been closed and secretive. Their workings have been kept from the eyes of the public, most of the political arena and even most ministers. This is not simply a metaphorical separation but a concrete institutional arrangement. As the next section will discuss, this captures the way that in the UK until the mid-1990s, 'security' was confined to a 'black box' at the heart of government from which the wider arena of politics and politicians was excluded. At times this was a politicised issue, particularly for politicians on the left who had suspicions (often correctly) that they and their activist and trade union allies were being spied on by the state.[83] But for the most part, the 'black box' of security was accepted as legitimate by most professional political actors and therefore not extensively politicised, as Chapters 4 and 5 discuss in detail.

The UK example

In the past, the UK secret services were the blackest of black boxes, their very existence not officially acknowledged until the late 1980s. Interestingly, these agencies were not created through any kind of public legitimation, but rather through the wartime decisions of prime ministers behind closed doors.[84] Their public legitimation only came many decades later with the 1989 Security Service Act and 1994 Intelligence Services Act. This shows one assumption of the Copenhagen School to be a little shaky: the idea that such institutional arrangements 'must' be legitimated publicly at some point. As they argue:

> In a democracy, at some point it must be argued in the public sphere why a situation constitutes security and therefore can legitimately be handled differently . . . When this procedure has been legitimized through security rhetoric, it becomes institutionalized as a package legitimization, and it is thus possible to have black boxes in the political process . . . In all cases, the establishment of secret services has some element of this logical sequence.[85]

This 'logical sequence' might be true of the way President Truman created the CIA through a public act of law in 1947. However, the origins of MI5, MI6 and GCHQ stem from non-public decisions that preceded public legitimation by almost a century. In the UK, then, the 'logical sequence' is backwards. It also renders the idea of 'audience acceptance' redundant.[86] This peculiarity could be explained by the fact the UK was not founded as a democracy but has evolved into one, and that the Crown claimed spying powers many centuries before the advent of universal suffrage in 1928.[87]

The history of the UK intelligence agencies shows the need to capture the way in which an issue can exist in a black-boxed part of government, but not be present in the institutional arena of politics. It also demonstrates the importance of treating questions of institutional arena and political quality as separate. Furthermore, we should not presume it always takes controversy and politicisation, or alternatively acts of depoliticisation, to bring about arena migrations.

There are examples where the arena migration of 'security' occurred through qualitative politicisation, such as Watergate and the subsequent Church Commission hearings in the US, which opened the security black box of the CIA to stronger democratic oversight.[88] However, Christopher Andrew, official historian of MI5, argues that in the UK it was not primarily public, parliamentary or even internal government politicisation that led to the opening up of the British intelligence apparatus to statutory regulation and limited parliamentary oversight in the late 1980s and early 1990s.[89] Rather, the impetus came from the services themselves after a series of court cases made ongoing disavowal increasingly impractical.[90] It could be argued that these court cases represented a kind of politicisation, but this was a by-product of litigation rather than an intentional political campaign. It is also important to dissociate the empirical analysis of such arena shifts from the question of who may be doing the shifting and why; it may not be a case of deliberate acts of politicisation or depoliticisation as with the Flinders and Buller approach, but more of an undirected 'arena migration' that is the product of slow trends or the unintended consequences of other developments.[91]

There are several mechanisms and processes by which this 'arena migration' could happen, not a single type of act or pathway. Qualitative changes in the complexion of an issue may cause or accompany arena migrations or they may not. In some instances, a parliament may wrest forms of access from the government, as with struggles to increase democratic oversight of the intelligence services. In other instances, committees with no historical security remit may independently decide to launch inquiries on what they problematise as security issues, thus bringing 'security' into the political arena. Committees may have varying motivations for doing this, such as raising constitutional concerns, understanding the security implications of events or developments, trying to put their own perception of threats and risks on to government agendas (which would be a form of securitisation), or simply shadowing what government departments are doing.

Such processes may also work from the top down rather than the bottom up. Governments may willingly place security issues into the political arena by convening special committees, which would be an attempt at depoliticisation in a qualitative sense, enacted via a deliberate arena shift. There may also be a more general trend of arena migration related to the general 'widening and deepening' of the concept and practice of security itself.[92] The point is that security may migrate or get shifted between different institutional arenas of politics for a variety of reasons that do not necessarily involve the qualitative transformations implied by the concepts of securitisation, desecuritisation, politicisation and depoliticisation. Seen in light of the history of security politics, 'arena migrations' such as these are politically and

Securitisation and Politicisation

analytically significant for they challenge constitutional and conceptual assumptions about the relationship between 'politics' and 'security'.

Again, the UK case is instructive here. In 1963, Prime Minister Harold Macmillan responded to a parliamentary question about an intelligence issue by saying: 'It is dangerous and bad for our general national interest to discuss these matters.'[93] At the time most of government, let alone parliament, was isolated from security matters. Security was kept to an innermost circle or often only the prime minister.

Two decades later in the early 1980s, parliament was still almost irrelevant to security. Parliament was actively prevented from engaging with it by a combination of parliamentary rules, constitutional convention, self-exclusion by MPs and executive prerogative, as Chapter 4 will discuss. At most, parliament provided a prime minister to whom the security services answered, and enacted the government's anti-terrorism laws. It was not until the 1989 Security Service Act that the British government and law acknowledged the existence of the security services. It was only in 1994 that a system of parliamentary intelligence oversight was created. Even then, it was arguably an extension of the security black box, given the prime minister's powers of appointment and redaction.

More than two decades on in the present, security has 'migrated' across government, parliament and into the arena of 'normal politics'. There is now extensive activity across parliament on security. For example, Chapter 6 shows that twenty-five or so parliamentary committees have now substantively engaged with 'security', compared to a mere handful in the 1980s. It is the location of issues within this arena that offers the primary analytical purchase, rather than the qualitative politicisation or depoliticisation of the issues.

Chapter 7 discusses how arena migration has also taken place within government, with 'security' spreading out from its traditional black box to ostensibly become a 'whole-of-government' problem, to use the terminology of the UK National Security Strategy.[94] Issues and competences that were once only in the remit of the prime minister and two or three senior ministers have come to involve potentially any and every ministry. In the same vein, the UK counter-terrorism strategy CONTEST invokes twenty-nine ministries and agencies as playing some role in security policy.[95]

Conclusion

Chapter 1 discussed the idea of security as an 'anti-politics' and the resultant neglect of professional politics in the security literature. Chapter 2 discussed how to identify instances of 'security' in context – not by an 'essential core' of qualitative and institutional criteria as found in securitisation theory, but according to the problematisations of contextual actors as seen from a critical eye in the present. This chapter has addressed how to analyse migrations of 'security' between institutional arenas – such as from the 'black box' of executive decision and the intelligence agencies to the activities of parliament – without becoming mired in conceptual contradictions and normative judgements. With this conceptual work now done, the following chapters will turn to an extended case study of the UK. They will examine changes in security politics empirically, using the methodology and conceptual framework the initial chapters have established.

Notes

1. Buzan, Wæver and de Wilde, *Security*, p. 23; Aradau, 'Security and the Democratic Scene', p. 399; Huysmans, *Security Unbound*, p. 30; Neocleous, *Critique of Security*, pp. 9–10; Loader and Walker, *Civilizing Security*, p. 7; Bigo, 'Security and Immigration', p. 83.
2. Wæver, 'Politics, Security, Theory', p. 478; Williams, 'The Continuing Evolution of Securitization Theory', p. 217.
3. Hay, *Why We Hate Politics*, p. 64.
4. Ibid. p. 78.
5. For example Bochel and Defty, 'Parliamentary Oversight of Intelligence Agencies'; Bochel, Defty and Kirkpatrick, *Watching the Watchers* and '"New Mechanisms of Independent Accountability"'; Caparini, 'Controlling and Overseeing Intelligence Services in Democratic States'; Gill, 'Evaluating Intelligence Oversight

Committees'; Gill and Phythian, *Intelligence in an Insecure World*; Leigh, 'The UK's Intelligence and Security Committee'; Phythian, 'The British Experience with Intelligence Accountability' and '"A Very British Institution"'; Rifkind, 'Intelligence Oversight in the UK'.
6. Buzan, Wæver and de Wilde, *Security*, pp. 4–5; Wæver, 'Politics, Security, Theory', p. 478; Williams, 'The Continuing Evolution of Securitization Theory', p. 217.
7. Hansen, 'Reconstructing Desecuritisation'; Wæver, 'Securitization and Desecuritization'; Aradau, 'Security and the Democratic Scene'; Salter, 'Securitization and Desecuritization'; Behnke, 'No Way Out'.
8. Wæver, 'Politics, Security, Theory', p. 478.
9. A policy the House of Lords – acting in its former judicial capacity – found to be incompatible with the ECHR in 2004. See Law Lords, *Opinions of the Lords of Appeal for Judgment in the Cause, a (Fc) and Others (Fc) (Appellants) V. Secretary of State for the Home Department (Respondent)* (2004). The 'Law Lords' were replaced by the Supreme Court in 2009.
10. Adey, 'Security Atmospheres or the Crystallisation of Worlds'.
11. Neal, 'Normalization and Legislative Exceptionalism' and 'Terrorism, Lawmaking and Democratic Politics'.
12. Floyd, 'Extraordinary or Ordinary Emergency Measures', p. 678.
13. Wæver, 'Politics, Security, Theory', p. 478; Roe, 'Is Securitization a "Negative" Concept?', p. 252. See also CASE Collective, 'Critical Approaches to Security in Europe', p. 455; Alker, 'Emancipation in the Critical Security Studies Project', p. 197.
14. Bright, 'In Search of the Politics of Security', p. 601.
15. Abrahamsen, 'Blair's Africa', pp. 61, 71.
16. Salter, 'When Securitization Fails', p. 121.
17. Howell, 'The Global Politics of Medicine'; Richter-Montpetit, 'Beyond the Erotics of Orientalism'; Biswas and Nair (eds), *International Relations and States of Exception*.
18. Stritzel, 'Security, the Translation', p. 344.
19. Walker, *Inside/Outside*.
20. Hay, *Why We Hate Politics*, p. 65.
21. Buzan, Wæver and de Wilde, *Security*, pp. 4–5.
22. Ibid. p. 23.
23. Huysmans, 'Revisiting Copenhagen', p. 488.
24. Buzan, Wæver and de Wilde, *Security*, p. 7.
25. Ibid. p. 142.
26. Huysmans, 'Revisiting Copenhagen', p. 488.

27. Buzan, Wæver and de Wilde, *Security*, p. 141.
28. Ibid. p. 143.
29. Hindess, 'Politics and Governmentality', p. 261, citing Weber, *Economy and Society*, p. 55.
30. Buzan, Wæver and de Wilde, *Security*, p. 143.
31. Ibid. p. 23.
32. Mälksoo, '"Memory Must Be Defended"', p. 8.
33. Williams, 'The Continuing Evolution of Securitization Theory', p. 217.
34. Wæver, 'Politics, Security, Theory', p. 469.
35. Buzan, Wæver and de Wilde, *Security*, p. 23.
36. Gad and Petersen, 'Concepts of Politics in Securitization Studies', p. 319.
37. Ibid.
38. Ibid.
39. Ibid. p. 320.
40. Ibid. pp. 318, 319.
41. Palonen, *The Struggle with Time*, p. 56.
42. Ibid. p. 61.
43. Ibid.
44. Ibid. p. 15.
45. Ibid.
46. Szabó, 'Review Article: The Conceptual History of Politics as the History of Political Conceptualizations', p. 281.
47. Palonen, *The Struggle with Time*, p. 61.
48. Hay, *Why We Hate Politics*, pp. 64–6.
49. Ibid. p. 65.
50. Ibid. p. 64.
51. Ibid. p. 65.
52. Giddens, *The Constitution of Society*, p. 289.
53. Hay, *Political Analysis*, p. 3.
54. Ibid.
55. Hay, *Why We Hate Politics*, p. 78.
56. Buzan, Wæver and de Wilde, *Security*, pp. 4–5.
57. Ibid. pp. 23–4.
58. Whereas once it could be argued that 'desecuritization' was 'largely under-theorised' (Aradau, 'Security and the Democratic Scene', pp. 389–90), the concept has now been subject to discussion and development. For example, Lene Hansen argues that desecuritisation can take a number of forms or 'ideal types' ('Reconstructing Desecuritisation', p. 5). These include 'stabilisation', when a conflict is

becalmed as in *détente*; 'replacement', when one constituted threat is replaced by another; 'rearticulation', when a security issue is recast as a political issue; and 'silencing', when an issue is removed from public debate and political agendas altogether (ibid. p. 15). Note that none of Hansen's 'ideal types' permit the idea of security as 'normal politics', nor do they question the concept of security as anything other than the anti-politics originally offered by the Copenhagen School.

59. Hay, *Why We Hate Politics*, p. 68.
60. Ibid. pp. 66–7.
61. Ibid. p. 67.
62. Ibid. p. 79.
63. Ibid. p. 81.
64. Ibid. p. 82.
65. Mälksoo, '"Memory Must Be Defended"', p. 8.
66. Wood and Flinders, 'Rethinking Depoliticisation', p. 164.
67. Flinders and Buller, 'Depoliticisation'.
68. Ibid. p. 296.
69. Flinders and Wood, 'Depoliticisation, Governance and the State', p. 135.
70. Wood and Flinders, 'Rethinking Depoliticisation'; Hay, *Why We Hate Politics*, pp. 79–80.
71. Fawcett and Marsh, 'Depoliticisation, Governance and Political Participation', p. 184.
72. Flinders and Buller, 'Depoliticisation', p. 296.
73. Ibid.
74. Bigo, 'Security and Immigration'.
75. Flinders and Buller, 'Depoliticisation', p. 296.
76. Hay, 'Depoliticisation as Process, Governance as Practice', p. 299.
77. Williams, 'The Continuing Evolution of Securitization Theory', p. 217.
78. Hay, 'Depoliticisation as Process, Governance as Practice', p. 299.
79. Buzan, Wæver and de Wilde, *Security*, pp. 40, 30.
80. Ibid. p. 27.
81. Ibid. p. 28. See also Vuori, 'A Timely Prophet?'.
82. Buzan, Wæver and de Wilde, *Security*, p. 28.
83. Bochel, Defty and Kirkpatrick, *Watching the Watchers*, p. 51.
84. Secret Intelligence Service, 'Our History'.
85. Buzan, Wæver and de Wilde, *Security*, p. 28.
86. See Balzacq, 'The Three Faces of Securitization'.
87. Hutchinson, *Elizabeth's Spymaster*.

88. Smist, *Congress Oversees the United States Intelligence Community*, pp. 9–15.
89. Andrew, *The Defence of the Realm*, pp. 1911–31.
90. Ibid.
91. Flinders and Buller, 'Depoliticisation: Principles, Tactics and Tools'.
92. Holland and Jarvis, *Security*, pp. 26–32.
93. HC Deb 16 July 1963 vol. 681 cc. 334–6, cited in Farson, Stafford and Wark, *Security and Intelligence in a Changing World*, p. 12.
94. HM Government, 'A Strong Britain in an Age of Uncertainty', p. 34.
95. Secretary of State for the Home Department, 'CONTEST: The United Kingdom's Strategy for Countering Terrorism', pp. 121–3.

4. Politicians, Security Politics and the Political Game

This book argues that security has been entering the arena of 'normal politics' and that therefore 'security' can no longer be defined as an 'anti-politics'. Over the last thirty years, while the concept and practice of 'security' has 'widened' and 'deepened', 'security' has migrated out from a historically institutionalised 'black box' at the core of government to become a problematisation potentially found in any part of government and politics. In this book's extended case study of the UK, security was once the preserve of an innermost core of government, the Ministry of Defence and a small number of secretive intelligence agencies such as MI5, MI6 and GCHQ. Today, 'security' is a problematisation that could involve almost any ministry or executive agency. For example, the list of risks published in the UK National Security Strategy implies that almost any aspect of social, political and economic life could become a threat.[1]

The growth of 'security' has been well discussed in the literature in terms of new forms of security governance, but not in terms of its implications for the practice of professional politics. Thus this chapter – following Foucault's problematisation of 'the problem of the political game, . . . its rules and instruments, and . . . the individual who engages in it' – analyses changes in professional politics related to security.[2] If 'traditional security studies' has tended to analyse security through the rationality of state (*raison d'état*), and critical security studies has tended to analyse security through rationalities of government (governmentality), then this chapter analyses security through the rationalities and problematisations of the 'political game' and the 'individual who engages in it'.³

As explained, the aim of this book is not to refute assumptions about the relationship between security and politics but to date them. Thus, in large part this chapter discusses the historical norms, conventions and power structures that have shaped the security/politics relationship. These resemble the Copenhagen School understanding of security to an extent, but – to agree with Ole Wæver's recent comments – they 'appropriately captur[e] only the politics of security of 1995 or 1985'.⁴

In 1995 or 1985, issues such as energy security, health security and cyber security did not exist in those terms and were not problematised as such. Therefore, it is not simply that political activity on security has increased, but that the meaning and practice of security have broadened to encroach on a greater number of policy areas, a greater number of government departments and, as a result, a greater part of professional political life. Similarly, as successive governments have pursued security agendas through legislation, politicians have found greater opportunity to engage with security topics.⁵ This is not to say that they have set the agenda or worked as 'securitising actors'. Sometimes they have, but generally they have followed the growth of security as a policy area and broader social and political trends. For example, professional politicians have mirrored the government and public interest in security spurred by 9/11, the Iraq War and the Snowden leaks.

This chapter describes how the historical 'rules of the game' of security politics marginalised most actors in the political arena. It also describes the traditional institutional and symbolic dominance of the state on security. These 'rules', conventions, norms and power structures represent a historical legacy. This has not disappeared. It continues to shape the politics of security but is being diluted. The latter part of the chapter describes how parliamentarians are increasingly questioning, resisting and even rejecting the constitutional conventions of security, such as deference to the executive on intelligence assessments, which had in the past helped to perpetuate executive dominance and their own marginalisation. However, there have always been tensions and struggles.

Understanding the political game

Chapter 3 argued that the presence or absence of an issue or activity within a particular institutional 'arena' is important because it can signify the inclusion or exclusion of political actors. The chapter thus constructed an analytical framework for identifying the 'migration' of issues into the 'arena' of 'normal politics' over time. Andreas Kalyvas describes 'normal politics' as 'monopolized by political elites, entrenched interest groups, bureaucratic parties, rigid institutionalized procedures, the principle of representation and parliamentary-electoral processes'.[6] This extends the description of 'normal politics' offered by the Copenhagen School: 'the normal bargaining processes of the political sphere' and 'the normal run of the merely political'.[7] If 'security' is found in 'normal politics' where it was once excluded, then this represents a challenge to historical norms of political practice on security and to conceptual assumptions about the relationship between security and politics.

Although the previous chapter made a case for the political and analytical importance of 'arena', this is nevertheless a reductive category designed primarily to identify change. 'Arena' is not a comprehensive empirical description of a complex institution such as a parliament. Parliamentary politics is polymorphous, structured and hierarchical; it cannot be understood in the singular, at least not without serious reductionism. As the former MP and parliamentary reformer Tony Wright argues, there is no such thing as 'parliament as a whole'.[8] Parliamentary discourse and practice exist only in the plural. Parliamentary activity on security or any other matter is not unified, collective, coordinated or even coherent. This chapter therefore builds on the analytical category of 'arena' to examine professional politics from the more detailed perspective of parliamentary problematisations, rationalities, practices and structures. In other words, the aim is to examine what happens within the 'arena' of 'normal politics' as it relates to security and why, and how this has changed over time.

Parliament is a number of different things: although it can be understood as an 'arena' in analytical terms, it is also a tool of government, a place of work and social life, a stepping stone into government for parties and individual MPs, a legislating body, and the institution that holds the government to account. To analyse parliamentary politics is not simply to analyse the legislative branch of government, but to analyse a complex social and political world. This world features multiple and overlapping relationships including (to name but a few) the relationships between political parties, within parties, between upper and lower chambers, and between those who are members of the government and those who are not. This is before we even mention the relationship of parliament to the outside world of the media, public, interest groups, lobbyists, constituents and so on (the chapter cannot comprehensively cover all of these).

It would be wrong to try to understand parliamentary security politics simply in terms of the legislature acting as a check and balance to an overmighty executive. This framing is common in the debate about liberty versus security but is a product of the American constitutional system which was built from the beginning on a separation of powers and a fear of strong government. The British constitution does not feature a strict separation of the legislative and executive branches: the executive overlaps with the legislature, is constituted from it and acts through it.[9]

The character of the historical security/politics relationship in parliament endured until the late 1990s. Its features transcended the specific actors and threats implicated in any given historical problematisation of security (for example communism or Irish nationalism) and were reproduced and institutionalised over political generations. The main part of this chapter examines why this was and, in many ways, continues to be the case. It examines how the power structures of parliamentary politics and the traditional edifices of security such as secrecy combined to reproduce a relationship of executive dominance and parliamentary marginalisation. This has been manifested in institutional arrangements, such as the historical separation between parliament and the intelligence agencies, and in constitutional conventions, such as parliamentary deference to the executive on intelligence and security. These conventions and institutionalisations represent a historical norm or legacy.

The latter part of the chapter discusses departures from this legacy. One important development is that parliament has become more assertive and active on security matters (Chapter 6 on committee activity will discuss in more detail how the expansion of the meaning, scope and governmental practice of 'security' has created many more opportunities for them to do so). Many parliamentarians no longer see security as a matter for the executive alone, even though they continue to recognise executive prerogatives to an extent. These changes challenge aspects of the 'unwritten' constitution of the United Kingdom itself. For example, when parliament voted against military intervention in Syria in August 2013, it in effect rejected the government's historic right to take the country to war, which is exercised as a 'Royal prerogative' derived from ancient monarchical powers.[10] This represented a milestone in a process begun by Robin Cook in the weeks before the 2003 Iraq War. His epitaph in Edinburgh reads: 'I may not have succeeded in halting the war, but I did secure the right of parliament to decide on war.' The final part of the chapter will return to this example.

This chapter approaches the subject of parliamentary security politics from two angles: the problematisations expressed by politicians and a broader analysis of the structured power relationships in which they are enmeshed. As such the chapter is partly theoretical and partly empirical, much like the rest of this book. The aim here is to reconstruct the 'rules of the game' of British parliamentary security politics and consider how these are changing. The chapter is built upon interviews conducted by the author with twelve UK parliamentarians, including three former cabinet ministers who held security-related briefs. The interviews date from late 2012 to early 2013, and their content reflects decades of parliamentary experience on the part of the interviewees. All had been in parliament at least fifteen years, some much longer. The interviewees themselves are not the direct subjects of this chapter, in the sense that the aim is not, for example, to map and explain differences in their views or behaviour according to party, government or parliamentary position, or to gossip about who said what about whom. This is why the interviewees have been anonymised and numbered (although they did not ask to be). The exception is Paul Flynn MP, who was also interviewed but is named because he is identifiable as the author of *How to Be an MP*, which is quoted.

Political sociology: Discourses, norms, structures

The interviews represent reflexive, discursive rationalisations on the part of parliamentarians on how parliamentary security politics works and why. They are part of a shared parliamentary discourse, which contains similarities and differences. Foucault describes discourses as expressions of 'forms of knowledge' and 'norms of behaviour' which are implicated in the 'constitution of the subject's mode of being'.[11] In Foucaultian terms, a discourse is not a single theory or principle. It is a system of meaning: a discursive space encompassing a range of statements, problems, solutions and practices. He argues:

> To one single set of difficulties, several responses can be made. Moreover, most of the time different responses actually are proposed. But what must be understood is what makes them simultaneously possible: it is the point in which their simultaneity is rooted; it is the soil that can nourish them all in their diversity and sometimes in spite of their contradictions.[12]

Foucault's emphasis on discourses and 'what makes them simultaneously possible' means that it is not enough to only look at the content of what people say. What is important is the wider *dispositif* of which their statements are an expression (see Chapter 3). This is not only discursive but includes other elements and artefacts. Here these are, inter alia, formal parliamentary rules, historical norms and power structures. However, to capture these we need to briefly part company with Foucault. Parliamentary politics is highly structured and institutionalised, and this is not what Foucault developed his method and approach to tackle. What is needed is a way of understanding the discourses, norms and practices of actors in the context of parliamentary power relationships. To this end, the chapter considers the sociological turn in the securitisation literature, and then the work of sociologist Pierre Bourdieu.

In contrast to the Copenhagen School's emphasis on speech acts and their 'grammar', the sociological turn in the securitisation literature draws on the work of Bourdieu to place more emphasis on practices, social context, power relations and the constitution of different 'audiences'.[13] This is helpful for analysing parliamentary security politics because legislatures are complex social settings, riven by power relationships, peculiar practices, and speakers and 'audiences' that can be constituted and disaggregated in numerous ways, for example, parties, upper and lower houses, ministers and backbenchers, committees and so on.

Three of the key scholars in this literature, Thierry Balzacq, Holger Stritzel and Mark Salter, stress the need to understand the socially situated nature of security discourse and practice. They emphasise the 'iterative, political process between speaker and audience' and the differential power positions of the actors involved.[14] For example, Stritzel criticises the overly 'textual' focus of the Copenhagen School, arguing that it is not enough to emphasise the security content of speech acts because meaning is generated not in isolation but in dynamic social and linguistic contexts.[15] Similarly, drawing on Bourdieu's writings on symbolic power, Balzacq has challenged the speech act approach. He argues that it is not the 'almost magical power' of utterances that mobilises legitimacy behind security policies and practices, but rather the 'belief in the legitimacy of words and those who utter them'.[16] This latter point is particularly important in the operation of parliamentary deference to the executive, as we will see.

This 'sociological' approach is helpful in avoiding the 'Hobbesian trap' described in Chapter 1, in which security scholarship slips all too easily into assuming and reproducing executive dominance in the security field and thus assuming and reproducing the marginalisation of other political actors. Although executive dominance is a feature of security politics, the aim in this chapter is to avoid taking this as a 'conceptual axiom' and instead understand how and why it has operated, particularly from the perspective of parliamentarians.[17] The chapter shows, for example, that parliamentarians themselves have helped to reproduce executive dominance through their recognition of its security prerogatives and their self-exclusion from security debates.

What is less helpful about the sociological strand of the securitisation literature is its continuing adherence to the terminology of the Copenhagen School. For example, parliamentarians can indeed be understood as a series of differently constituted 'audiences' who judge the claims of securitising speakers. This is true, for example, when ministers make the case for war through parliamentary speeches. Balzacq analyses the social mechanisms through which this audience judgement may work, conceiving of securitisation as a 'strategic (pragmatic) practice' that works through 'persuasion'.[18] However, parliamentarians are more than an 'audience' for the claims of the executive; they are actors in their own right and constituted in a variety of ways.

More generally, although the historical norms of security politics in the UK resemble much of what is assumed in securitisation theory – such as curtailed democratic debate, narrowed circles of decision making, and executive dominance (and, more rarely, forms of formal legal and constitutional exceptionalism) – this book does not aim to analyse securitisation and the 'social construction of security' as such, but rather the changing forms and practices of security politics.[19] Rather than stick with the securitisation terminology, therefore, it is more appropriate to use this as an opening to the work of Bourdieu.

What is important about Bourdieu for the purposes of this chapter is his conceptualisation of the relationship between agency, structure and power. This offers a way to account for the reproduction of historical norms and power structures without reducing the strategic agency of the actors involved. Actors' actions and choices may be shaped by norms and structures, but those actions and choices are often in harmony with those norms and structures and even play a part in reproducing them. Williams explains that the Bourdieusian schema

> provides a means of overcoming the divide between strategy as pure instrumentality, and visions of culture as 'embedded', norm- or rule-governed action that lack a sense of the strategic action of agents.[20]

In other words, actors can be strategic, rational and even utility-maximising, but at the same time and without contradiction their practices and choices may be the product of historical norms and power structures. This is true of parliamentary security politics.

Scholars in this Bourdieusian debate consider that although actors are capable of reflective and strategic thought, for the most part their social interactions and strategies are a product of practical reason.[21] This is, as Vincent Pouliot puts it, an 'inarticulate know-how' based more on common sense than calculation.[22] For example, in social, political and institutional settings, success often depends on actors internalising the 'rules of the game'.[23] This implies an implicit and instinctive understanding of what is expected and reasonable on the one hand, and what would be frowned upon, deemed unacceptable or have other negative consequences on the other. Bourdieu calls this *doxa*: a 'sense of investment in the game and the outcome, interest in the game, [and] commitment to the presuppositions . . . of the game'.[24] This shapes and defines action in terms of 'things to do or not to do, things to say or not to say'.[25] For Bourdieu, the 'rules of the game' are 'embodied history, internalized as a second nature and so forgotten as history'.[26] They are 'principles which generate and organize practices'.[27]

This aspect of the Bourdieusian theoretical framework is expressed in the concept of *habitus*. This is a way of conceptualising the entangled relationship between the internalised dispositions of individual actors and the naturalised intersubjective dispositions expressed by groups.[28] In other words, *habitus* expresses the way that actors come to exhibit shared dispositions, collective common senses, durable assumptions, collective 'schemes of perception, thought and action' and habitual ways of acting and not acting.[29]

Habitus should not be considered as a singular, homogeneous, determining structure. For example, although arguably there is a parliamentary *habitus* in the sense of shared historical norms and practices, a full-scale Bourdieusian sociological analysis would need to investigate the multiple and overlapping *habitus** of individuals and groups, such as their social class, professional background and

---

* The plural of *habitus* is also *habitus*.

so on, which would shape the symbolic and social capital they possess and thus their authority and recognition in social and political life. This study does not go that far, sticking predominantly to the analytical framework developed in previous chapters. However, the concept of *habitus* is helpful in capturing the shared historical norms of parliamentary security politics, their durability and their reproduction.

In Bourdieu, the concept of *habitus* is paired with that of 'field'. Field is a way of conceptualising the structuring effects of power relations. The CASE Collective explains that to employ 'the notion of field [in security studies] is . . . to invite scholars to explore the relations among security agencies, their status, roles, activities and institutional settings'.[30] Although the CASE Collective refers here to agencies, the implications are similar for individuals and other groupings such as committees. According to this understanding, fields generate the interests and strategies of competing actors according to their positions and relationships.[31] This does not discount agency or the possibility of strategic thinking, but rather reformulates these as embedded forms of rationality that are products of those relationships. Anna Leander explains that 'A field is defined by the fact that those who are in it share an understanding (often unarticulated) of the rules of the game or "stakes at stake" in that given area of social activity'.[32]

Didier Bigo's 'Paris School' approach to the study of security is an influential example of this approach. Bigo opened a debate on the 'professionalisation' of the management of (in)security in the proliferating security agencies and industries at work in Europe and beyond, focusing on the power dynamics and systems of meaning that develop within the relational field of security professionals.[33] Parliament is not a field in the Bourdieusian sense – it is an institution, an 'arena' for an array of discourses and practices and a host of other things mentioned above. A full-scale Bourdieusian analysis of professional politics as a field would need to range further than parliament and to study power relations between actors beyond a single institution. However, the field concept is a productive opening to understanding the effects of the overlapping power structures and the 'stakes' involved in parliamentary politics.

The relationship between field and *habitus* offers a way to explain action and inaction. It accounts for the power relationships in which actors are enmeshed and actors' subjective investment in those relationships.[34] Bourdieu describes this investment as a willingness to play the game, saying that '[actors] are not cynical (or far less and far less often than one might believe) . . . they are absorbed in the game and . . . they really believe in what they are doing'.[35] In terms of parliamentary security politics, for ordinary members of parliament, this 'game' has traditionally involved a subordinate relationship to the executive, which was – and to a large extent still is – symbolically, institutionally and constitutionally dominant. Yet this 'game' has not been without struggle. Many parliamentarians and external commentators have been problematising the relationship between the executive and parliament on security for years, particularly on democratic oversight of the intelligence services.[36]

Unequal parliamentary power relationships

Let us now turn back to parliament with these conceptual points in mind. Unequal power relations shape parliamentary politics. Parliamentary actors are at a disadvantage to the executive on multiple fronts. The executive has command of the machinery of government with all the bureaucratic, informational and symbolic advantages that bestows. In the UK system, the government also controls much of parliamentary business. The legislature has little coercive power to exercise in response. And because parliament is dominated by party, the freedom of action of individual members is constrained in other ways too. In the Commons, there are costs for members who rebel against their party whips, especially for those who are also members of the government or potential members of a future government. Some are happy to accept life on the backbenches in return for more independence, but for those motivated by a desire to enter government, career advancement depends on patronage and promotion up party and government ranks.[37] They have the option of rebelling against their party and this happens increasingly often, but it remains something of a blunt instrument and its impact depends on how the parliamentary arithmetic falls at the time.[38] These unequal power relationships can be understood in Bourdieusian terms as part of the 'rules of the game'.

Despite these conditions, it is not enough to understand parliamentary politics in terms of a naked calculus of power. To do so would lead to the conclusion that legislatures are irrelevant beyond the working majority of votes they give the government. It would then be simple to conclude that parliament is weak and poorly performs one of its key constitutional functions of holding the executive to account. Members of parliament would be, in Max Weber's mocking terms, little more than 'lobby fodder'.[39]

In reference to the UK, Matthew Flinders and Alexandra Kelso argue that this view is 'highly dubious' and fails 'to take account of the real complexities of parliament'.[40] They make the point that the 'executive-legislative relationship . . . is more balanced, or at the very least respectful, than many academic and journalistic accounts would entertain'.[41] Thus, to focus on the outward structure of parliamentary power relations distracts from the importance of 'unobserved control mechanisms' such as backchannels between the executive and backbenchers and the role of internal party and government politics.[42] Although these mechanisms are difficult to discern methodologically, the academic consensus is that legislatures work through influence, not direct power.[43] Much of this is based on 'anticipated reactions', negotiations and avoidance of direct confrontation.[44] For example, Bochel et al. write:

> A number of scholars have argued that Parliament can serve to keep issues off the agenda, as a government's anticipation of an adverse reaction in Parliament or detailed scrutiny by a parliamentary committee may be sufficient to ensure that certain policies or proposals are never pursued.[45]

Outright confrontation, publicly visible rebellion or a breakdown in party unity is often a sign that these behind-the-scenes mechanisms have broken down. This is significant for the 'arena migration' of security issues discussed in Chapter 3, because it hints that the appearance or absence of issues in the parliamentary arena may be due to a variety of reasons. For example, in simple terms, absence may be the result of a deliberate government strategy to keep issues away from parliament, as with secret intelligence or covert operations. Conversely, the appearance of an issue in parliament may be the result of deliberate action by a parliamentarian or committee. However, if we extend this to the potential breakdown of 'unobserved control mechanisms', issues may migrate into the parliamentary arena as a result of unplanned breakdowns in the tacit agreements and historical norms that worked to keep issues out of open parliamentary activity. The 2013 Syria example discussed later involves an increase in parliamentary activity and critical questioning on intelligence, which resulted from the breakdown in trust of executive security prerogatives caused by the Iraq War ten years earlier.

Although the 'unobserved control mechanisms' of executive-legislative relations are difficult to observe, the key point is that the most important functions and practices of parliament are not necessarily those which are overt. One implication is that although the UK parliament was never designed as a constitutional 'check and balance' on executive power, it is not simply a 'rubberstamp' either.[46] And even when appearing to act only passively and acquiescently, parliaments perform a powerful legitimating function that is central to democratic and even non-democratic government.[47] In a study of the Brazilian parliament, Robert Packenham argued that the most important function of legislatures is a 'latent legitimation' derived from the mere fact of existing and meeting regularly.[48] The UK parliament does more than that, but the point is that legislatures do not have to perform independently, overtly or even actively in the policy process to be vital to the legitimacy of government itself.

The power relationships and norms of security politics

Informational imbalance
Historically, 'security' has compounded the unequal power relationship between parliament and government. For example, few

parliamentarians are privy to secret intelligence, on which the executive has a monopoly. Drawing on Bourdieu, we could argue that this concentrates 'symbolic power' in the hands of the executive at the expense of the legislature; this is the 'power of making people see and believe, of predicting and prescribing, of making known and recognized' (and this of course is one of the core features of the securitisation literature).[49]

As a result, parliamentarians are at a disadvantage in any symbolic struggle with the executive or intelligence community over the nature of security threats. While there is plenty of information in the public domain that parliamentarians could deploy, this is not comparable to the intelligence claims that governments can use to justify their legislation, policies and actions. Parliamentarians may have access to other sources of knowledge such as security experts, and a few may have an inside view through their membership of the Intelligence and Security Committee, yet the enduring structures of recognition of the sovereign security prerogative mean that the executive and other security 'insiders' are able to make the strongest claim to authority. In an interview, one member of the House of Lords with a security-related brief said:

> It's very very very hard for a scrutineer to challenge the government, or to challenge people working around government, like the reviewer of terrorism legislation [Lord Alex Carlile at the time] . . . How does someone like me challenge the sometimes explicit, always implicit, 'We know better than you. There's things we can't tell you'? That's very very hard. I haven't found a way to do it properly yet.[50]

The Joint Committee on Human Rights (JCHR) problematised this in 2010, when they complained that parliamentarians suffer a lack of access 'to information about the scale and nature of the threat posed by terrorism in order to be able to make judgements about the necessity and proportionality of the responses'.[51] As Steven Durno of the Law Society told the Lords Constitution Committee, without access to intelligence, legislators 'do not have any way of testing the arguments'.[52] Similarly, the above peer complained that on security 'You have much less access to officials'.[53]

To put this differently, parliament is expected to take the word of the executive on trust. Christopher Andrew, official historian of MI5, calls this 'the traditional doctrine that parliament has simply to trust Ministers "to discharge their responsibilities faithfully"'.[54]

Deference

It is not simply that the executive has all the information on security and the legislature has none. It is also that the government benefits from historic conventions of deference and recognition from parliament on security matters. The parliamentarians interviewed all expressed the principle that security is the first responsibility of government. This is quite plainly a Hobbesian principle. In their discourse this was connected to the seriousness of security issues and the importance of tackling them for the legitimacy of government and the safety of citizens. A longstanding Labour backbencher said:

> There's a little bit more mystique attached to [security policy] and therefore perhaps people are less rigorous in challenging it because it's wrapped up in the security of the nation; there's things we might not know, and it's better not to ask.[55]

This is one reason why the unequal symbolic power relations on security have been self-perpetuating. They have been reproduced not simply by the symbolic dominance of the executive, but also by the embedded recognition and legitimation performed by parliamentarians.

Governments are of course sensitive about revealing intelligence and its sources. This is claimed to be for operational and tactical reasons, since informants and officers in sensitive or dangerous positions could be compromised. These considerations are understood and largely respected in parliament. A former minister explained:

> From the point of view of efficient operation of intelligence, [and] of course from the point of view of protecting the security and lives of the intelligence officers themselves, it is accepted [in parliament] that this is an area where . . . there are serious issues at stake.[56]

Historically, it was parliamentary convention not to ask difficult questions about security in the first place and there are still difficulties in doing so.[57] One former Conservative MP interviewed by Bochel et al. said that in the 1970s asking such questions was 'almost unpatriotic' and 'not done'.[58] A smaller party MP interviewed for this book expressed it similarly: 'There is a sort of unwritten law that you don't say things in the chamber that could be of use to people of ill will towards the UK.'[59] We can relate this directly to Bourdieu's notion of 'things to do or not to do, things to say or not to say'.[60] Florence Sutcliffe-Braithwaite points out that deference may be as much a product of necessity as a 'conviction of the rightness of deference to authority', and this describes parliamentary deference on security, where lack of access, information, opportunity and expertise prevented engagement with security, but where many also thought that strong and secretive executive leadership on security was right and proper.[61]

Arguably, for many decades these were conventions largely supported within parliament. Christopher Andrew considers that parliament helped to maintain them and 'there was no serious challenge to them until the 1980s'.[62] Yet this does not discount the presence of struggle; Bochel et al. disagree with Andrew and point out that some parliamentarians did find ways to ask awkward questions of the government in an attempt to break the silence on intelligence.[63] So, deference was a historical norm rather than a blanket rule. One interviewee noted: 'There have always been probing politicians . . . but they tended to be exceptions.'[64]

Exclusion and lack of opportunity

This unequal symbolic power relationship has been historically reproduced by mutually reinforcing rules and practices. Erskine May's parliamentary rulebook historically ruled parliamentary questions about the security services to be inadmissible. The 1964 edition reads, 'there are certain matters, of their nature secret, such as relating to the security services and to security, and questions on these matters are not in order.'[65] This or similar wording appeared in subsequent editions until 1989, after which it disappeared to coincide with the Security Service Act 1989 that put MI5 on a statutory footing. Furthermore, the government would refuse to answer any such questions other than with the standard response 'the government does not comment'.[66]

Historically, MPs did not have many opportunities to ask security-related questions anyway. For example, Bochel et al. write, 'The passage of the Interception of Communications Act in 1985 offered Parliament the first potential opportunity for substantive debate on the activities of the intelligence and security agencies.'[67] (Prior to the creation of a statutory basis for MI5 and MI6 in 1989 and 1994 respectively, this Act 'outlined the circumstances and procedures under which the interception of communications might be authorised', correcting the unsatisfactory situation under which the executive had used such powers for centuries with only vague legal authority.[68]) Under interview, one senior Liberal Democrat MP said,

> It's not often that parliament speaks about security as such. And that's part of the problem. It's very rare ... There are almost no people in the Commons who speak broadly about security, and there are almost no occasions when they might do so.[69]

Parliamentarians do now have more opportunities to debate intelligence specifically than in the past, with debates on the reports of the Intelligence and Security Committee for example, but these opportunities are often not widely taken up. Bochel et al. observe that each ISC debate has attracted between fifteen and twenty-six speakers in the Commons and between seven and eight in the Lords.[70] The debates themselves have been 'dominated by ISC members', current and former.[71] The Lib Dem interviewee agrees, saying:

> When it comes to intelligence, latterly I would say the debates on the annual report of the ISC have been pretty thinly attended and the main speakers have been current or former members of the committee.[72]

However, seen in the context of general MP specialisation, this may not be so unusual. Most parliamentarians have specialist interests on which they speak, such as the plight of a particular disadvantaged group or an area on which they have expertise from a previous career such as medicine or law (a prior *habitus*). In this sense, security and, in particular, intelligence are specialist areas like any other. One former minister said,

> Every MP decides where they're going to develop their activities; it might be on pensions or it might be on Europe or whatever . . . Naturally those people will tend to be those who've held office . . . I wouldn't say that's particularly unusual for security as opposed to MPs in other areas.[73]

He continued:

> The number of people involved in [a specialist] debate in the House is relatively low, normally less than twenty, that would be the people who've really thought about it, and that includes security . . . You can go in on any subject and you can see the usual suspects who are there and talk about it a lot.[74]

In parliament, security is a specialist subject, and more specialist than most.

Self-exclusion

One problem is that many MPs have felt that security is beyond their remit and competence, which leads to a process of silencing and self-selection. By dint of the rarity of prior experience of security, the topic poses barriers to participation. Another former minister said: '[Security is] damn difficult. They are difficult concepts, difficult areas . . . People tend to shy away from them.'[75] It is an inaccessible subject for all but a few who happen to have some kind of specialist knowledge. Our smaller party MP says that on security

> There are plenty of people who are willing, but in this place you get to know things on a need-to-know basis and unless you are privy to at least some of the stuff that crosses the desk of the [Intelligence and] Security Committee, you can't hope to be doing a reasonable job.[76]

Bochel et al. argue that parliamentarians

> have little experience of the activities, or indeed the role of the intelligence and security agencies . . . [T]hose involved may be approaching their subject from a much lower knowledge base than for some policy areas, [and] the development of expertise may involve a rather steeper learning curve than in other areas of legislative scrutiny.[77]

Deference towards the executive, therefore, has not simply been about rendering unto Caesar that which is Caesar's, that is, deferring to the executive – even if war powers do derive from the ancient powers of the monarch. Rather, it is because most parliamentarians have not felt competent to speak. This links back to informational imbalance. As our smaller party MP put it,

> I don't think anybody's shying away from it, it's just that there's no point making points that you don't really know whether are true or not, or are dreamt up. Clearly, you've got to have some degree of proof before you start discussing these things, and we don't have the avenue to get that proof.[78]

The peer mentioned above said something similar:

> By definition there isn't much that you can get at in the public domain to brief yourself on it. [Thus] there's no doubt an actual reluctance on some people's part, although they may be interested, to get involved.[79]

The effect is the reproduction of executive dominance on security in a circular fashion. Bochel et al. pose this as a central question in their study of parliamentary intelligence oversight, asking 'whether the principal barrier to [greater oversight] is continued secrecy on the part of the government and the [intelligence] agencies, or a lack of resources, interest or understanding with parliament itself'.[80]

Bourdieu stresses the importance of passivity in the workings of symbolic power.[81] Power can depend on the choices of actors to go along with received wisdom and not to challenge recognised sources of authority, conventions or institutional practices. We can see how these choices are produced by structures in the first place. This favours reproduction rather than reflexive alteration. Bourdieu writes that 'power often resides in the – entropic – choice not to do, not to choose'.[82] This is important for explaining the durability of historical norms in parliamentary security politics.

Another way of illustrating how this aspect of deference works is to look at how the judiciary has practised and reproduced it. Judges have maintained that they have neither the capacity nor the competence to decide whether a government declaration of threat or emergency is reasonable or not.[83] They upheld this convention, for example, in a 2004 ruling on the detention without trial of terrorist suspects in Belmarsh prison.[84] The court refused to rule on whether or not there was a 'threat to the life of the nation' (the key facilitating legal term) as asserted by the Home Secretary, claiming that this was beyond its competence. Instead, it ruled on whether the policy had been properly applied within the terms of the law (it found that the policy contravened the 1998 Human Rights Act (HRA) because it discriminated against foreigners). However, this may be another area where conventions are changing. A former minister involved in struggles with the courts over security and human rights said,

> To the extent [deference] ever was true, and some judges tell me it was true, I don't think it is true now . . . The idea that courts are deferential in these areas really is an outdated one. What is true is that courts are more confident since the HRA.[85]

This is also true in parliament. As the next chapter will show, the 1998 HRA and the related creation of the Joint Committee on Human Rights created a rationale, remit and forum for parliamentary challenges to the government on security matters.

Political survival, moral pressure, loyalty, habit
Going against the conventions of parliamentary security politics poses political dangers: threats to 'political survival' rather than 'existential survival', as discussed in Chapter 1. For example, in September 2012 Paul Flynn MP was ejected from the Commons

chamber for accusing Defence Secretary Philip Hammond of lying over soldiers' deaths in Afghanistan. As a symbolic act it got some attention, but *The Sun* newspaper wrote:

> As if facing death from the Taliban wasn't enough, our Forces have to face snipers back home. Labour MP Paul Flynn accuses Our Boys of committing 'atrocities in the name of the British people'.[86]

When British soldiers are in the field, criticism of security policy risks being construed as disloyalty. Such criticism may be seen as questioning the value of British soldiers' 'sacrifices' and result in the accusation of giving succour to terrorists. No MP wants to suggest that a grieving army husband, wife or parent lost their loved one for nothing. When interviewed for this book, Flynn said, 'If you're going to survive, there is a limit to how far you can go and how far you can expose yourself to attack.'[87] MPs have to consider how much criticism they can take before their political life is threatened. MPs do speak out on security, but it takes courage. They might be able to absorb one or two attacks from the press, but an excoriating tabloid story might be the only thing a disengaged constituent remembers about their MP.

Particularly in the aftermath of a terrorist attack, there are also other ways parliament discourages dissent. One interviewee said: 'The moral pressure in the House is such that you're a brave person to speak against . . . the sense that something must be done.'[88] In Bourdieusian terms we can see this as an institutionalised common sense.[89] Our smaller party MP expresses it like this:

> When we get worked up [on security issues] and there's a bit of emotion coming in, you always stop short; something in the back of your mind says you're being disloyal here to the body politic, this isn't what you should be doing.[90]

At work in this tendency is a mix of moral responsibility and political risk calculation:

> When you're talking about taking a risk with people's lives, and you know that there are organisations which are proceeding on the basis

that they're ready to take people's lives, then nobody's very keen to take a risk on those issues, precisely because the responsibility of behaving in a way that might make such individuals or organisations more likely to proceed is one that most politicians would want to avoid.[91]

This implies high political stakes for the politicians involved and may translate into quietude, caution and, again, deference to the government, at least in public.

The Bourdieusian framework also captures other historically repetitive aspects of parliamentary security politics where parliamentarians often appear to express collective common senses and 'natural' ways of thinking and acting. For example, in the immediate aftermath of a security 'event' such as a bombing, parliamentarians tend to see it as 'natural' to support the emergency and security services and not to ask difficult operational or political questions; they consider the time for that to be later. One MP explained,

> The political system naturally responds in human ways to something like that ... [T]he political system wants answers as to whether it was handled well, although there is a tendency to start from the assumption that the emergency services did very very well, because almost certainly there would have been indications of courageous action by the emergency services. It's usually some time later that the mistakes begin to emerge and so the system sets up a process to find out what really happened and learn lessons from it.[92]

Another example is the habitual practice of legislating in response to acts of political violence.[93] As one commentator giving evidence to a parliamentary committee inquiry observed, 'very often in the aftermath of a terrorist atrocity, politicians must be seen to be doing something'.[94] One MP thought that this had been the pattern since 'the peak of IRA atrocities'.[95] This is another aspect of what Bourdieu would call 'a world of already realized ends – procedures to follow, paths to take'.[96] Vincent Pouliot describes an 'inarticulate know-how that makes what is to be done self-evident or commonsensical'.[97] However, the decades-old habit of post-attack legislating may be coming to an end: attacks in London and Manchester in 2017 did not result in the government tabling new legislation, although this may be because Brexit was dominating political and governmental agendas.

Suspension of partisanship

We should not assume that all parliamentarians want to speak out against the government on security but choose not to. Many support strong security policies, regardless of their party affiliation. The 'rules of the game' of parliamentary security politics have often manifested as suspended partisanship on security. One interviewee said: 'it is the one thing [where] as much as possible ... you restrain your party-political instincts ... Because it's the right thing to do.'[98] A former minister said,

> Because security issues, for example dealing with terrorism or the IRA, more recently Al Qaeda or whatever, has potential [implications] for our responsibilities to citizens, there is an intrinsic greater likelihood of cross-party agreement about how to proceed.[99]

In the same vein, when asked at a public lecture about the relationship between security and politics, former deputy prime minister Lord Hattersley simply said: 'MPs always act in the national interest.'[100] This is debatable, but it expresses the sense that security is meant to be above politics. This convention has often been invoked in parliament; for example, former head of MI5 Eliza Manningham-Buller said in her maiden speech to the Lords: 'national security should, as far as possible, be above party politics, as it has been for most of my career.'[101]

However, no politician interviewed for this research thought that security politics was truly depoliticised. 'Nothing escapes politics entirely,' one said.[102] The governing party still has to make policy and ministers may have to implement that policy by pushing legislation through parliament, where they will face scrutiny and challenge. One former minister said:

> National security is all supposed to transcend party politics. [But] when you're a minister that's not always the case, in that you've got a programme, you'll have some manifesto commitments, and you'll have to react to events. There was a requirement for me to get my legislation through.[103]

Despite the norms and conventions discussed above, there may still be robust debate about the proportionality and constitutional propriety of security policies. One peer said, 'There's a very strong feeling that we shouldn't play politics with it, [but] that's not to say the policy is correct.'[104] Similarly, one MP said, 'The argument may well be whether something is illiberal but also about whether it's necessary or efficacious. So that makes the politics slightly different.'[105] The partisan game may be suppressed, but the parliamentary aspect of the policy-making process is still at work. One MP said of their select committee work, 'There may be on the public side more deference. But there are much more robust exchanges on the private side with ministers.'[106] And while it is understandable that the government feels under pressure to make policy in response to perceived security problems, opposition parties experience similar pressures:

> We daren't look weak, so we must support these particular safeguards, or we mustn't disagree with the government . . . Those are slightly different from the factors that divide the parties most of the time.[107]

So, suspension of partisanship does not mean suspension of politics. Neither are attitudes on security uniform across parties. One Labour MP thought that the Liberal Democrats had a 'more sceptical starting point' as part of their 'ideology', that the 'Tory Party are by inclination more supportive' and that the Labour Party is 'quite ambivalent and swings about quite dramatically'.[108] A Lib Dem MP said that security politics does not divide on an axis of right/left but rather authoritarian/libertarian and as a result individual politicians are likely to find allies on security matters in other parties and opponents in their own party.[109]

With parliamentarians expressing a reluctance towards partisanship on security, it is more a case of trying to make best use of the parliamentary system to prevent mistakes being made in the pursuit of security, all the while supporting security as a legitimate policy aim. This might mean hindering or amending unworkable, ill-judged or disproportionate legislation, arguing against policies that damage the constitutional fabric of the country, or speaking out for disproportionately affected minority groups. Simply put, even though parliamentarians all agree that security is the first responsibility of government and that they should not 'play politics' with security, this does not mean they believe the government is infallible on security or incapable of acting disproportionately or counter-productively.

The dilemma of bad faith

The unequal power relations of security politics present parliamentarians with a dilemma. There is an opportunity for the executive to take advantage of its symbolic dominance to manipulate security discourses for political ends. For example, securitisation theory holds that political elites exercise their representative power to define security threats in order to legitimise security policies and responses. Huysmans writes: 'Securitization is characterized by a circular logic of defining and modulating hostile factors for the purpose of countering them politically and administratively.'[110] Rita Floyd argues that this can lead to 'agent-benefitting' and 'insincere' securitisation.[111]

Another way to look at this is that the circular legitimation of security policies may conceal a partisan political struggle. This is Bourdieu's concept of a 'double game', at once a symbolic struggle and a political struggle, where the former may conceal the latter.[112] In other words, security may well be a problem to be solved or a discourse to be constructed and contested, but potentially it is also a concealed weapon in ongoing political struggles where the stake is not only security but also politics. For example, how can parliamentarians be sure the executive really does know the nature of the threat and is not merely asserting so for opportunistic political advantage? How do they know if 'security' really is at stake, or whether the struggle is in fact partisan? How do they know if security politics is being practised in good faith or bad? This dilemma is compounded by the historic recognition of the security prerogatives of the executive. In the wake of major acts of political violence in particular, the executive is virtually assured recognition of its monopolistic position.

In its thirteen years in power, ten under Tony Blair, the Labour Party pursued a relentless agenda of counter-terrorism legislation, from the Criminal Justice (Terrorism and Security) Act 1998 (its response to the Omagh bombing), to the troubled Counter-Terrorism Act 2008 under Gordon Brown. An uncharitable interpretation is that the primary aim was a political one: not to be outflanked by the Tories in toughness on terrorism. One senior Liberal Democrat MP described this as a 'fear of looking weak' and the kind of practice that can lead to accusations of playing politics with security.[113] The MP described the example of

> a party pushing through and voting for a draconian measure not because they really believed that it was strictly necessary in security terms, but because it looked tough, it looked like a response, and that has happened in my view on a number of occasions.[114]

Many of the Labour government's policies were legally and politically controversial, such as a regime of detention without trial for foreign 'terrorist suspects' and the system of 'control orders' that followed it. Arguably this 'politicisation' of security policy (in the qualitative sense discussed in Chapter 3) produced a political reaction. Labour backbenchers, allying with members from other parties, subjected the legislation that facilitated these policies to large rebellions. A backbench MP commented that one issue in particular – a legislative proposal for ninety-day detention without charge of terrorist suspects – 'contributed to changing our attitude a bit'.[115]

The Labour government security agenda also created an opportunity for opposition parties to position themselves against the growth of a 'national security state'. For example, spurred by an emergent libertarian wing, the Tories fought the 2010 election against what they called Labour's 'unprecedented attack' on 'Britain's historic liberties'.[116] One former Labour minister suggested that this was a perverse outcome, saying that 'the Conservatives as the law and order party have moved to being a civil liberty party, very uneasily . . . They're in a very confused place.'[117] Unsurprisingly, the same former minister was more reluctant to concede that his party had shifted on security:

> Have Labour moved? I suppose some would say we've moved from being libertarian to being more security based. Maybe that's true. Maybe it's just the pressure of being in government when we had security threats of a different dimension.[118]

These party shifts may signal a decline of the convention of suspended partisanship on security, which the former minister thought had become 'less true recently . . . but certainly was the case for a long time'.[119]

Returning to the problem of bad faith, it is not only that security politics can be practised in good faith or bad, but rather that parliamentarians would struggle to know the difference, given their weak symbolic position and their convention of recognising the security prerogatives of the executive. It is difficult for anyone else to know if the executive has genuine knowledge of the threat or not. The key point is that its security authority is recognised, institutionalised and part of common sense.[120] Yet, parliamentarians face the dilemma that this recognition may not be deserved. It may be what Bourdieu calls 'misrecognition'.[121]

For example, on apparently new security problems, the executive may know the nature of the threat no better than anyone else, but nevertheless it still receives recognition as an authority on security. In a public lecture in 2009, the Director General of MI5, Jonathan Evans, said,

> After 9/11 the UK and other western countries were faced with the fact that the terrorist threat posed by Al Qaida was indiscriminate, global and massive. Now, 8 years on, we have a better understanding of the nature and scope of Al Qaida's capabilities *but we did not have that understanding in the period immediately after 9/11* [emphasis added].[122]

This may be a reasonable, innocent and genuine account of the situation the British intelligence agencies found themselves in, but it may also suggest an opportunity for the executive and its security agencies to take advantage of the recognition they receive. Although the executive must be careful not to stretch the bounds of credibility, parliamentarians have a limited ability to authoritatively challenge or know the true stakes of the struggle.

There are examples where the government has jealously asserted its security prerogatives for what turn out to be reasons of political survival or convenience rather than national security. One member of the Home Affairs Committee said that, often, 'Ministers want to hide behind security . . . Security is a very convenient hook to use.'[123] The committee member gave an example of a minister invoking security in order to not answer a committee question about whether or not the Home Office was holding the passport of an absconding terrorist suspect, calling this 'a minister with an inconvenient answer looking to use security to save face'.[124] Even a former security-related minister thought this was one of the dangers of security politics:

> The threat from outside or inside a country has always been used by regimes of all kinds in order to be able to either see off an opponent or get something through that otherwise wouldn't be acceptable and that's why we have to be alert to that.[125]

Secrecy offers governments an opportunity to spin, manipulate, suppress or even fabricate intelligence, which is then difficult for parliamentarians (and indeed the judiciary, media and public) to challenge authoritatively.

In another example, governments may invoke sensitive intelligence-sharing relationships with third countries as a reason for secrecy, but again the dilemma of bad faith applies. David Miliband used this intelligence-sharing argument when Foreign Secretary in early 2010.[126] He had redacted a court judgement on the case of UK resident Binyam Mohamed, whom the Pakistani intelligence service had tortured on behalf of the US government.[127] The ruling contained CIA text sent to British intelligence which proved British collusion. The Foreign Secretary claimed that publishing this would damage the US/UK intelligence-sharing relationship. The Court of Appeal rejected this argument and the redacted paragraphs were published.[128] The question was whether Miliband was trying to hide government wrongdoing rather than protect national security.[129]

In another example, the UK and US governments both have mechanisms for setting an official 'threat level'.[130] These have been criticised and satirised for the way that, without empirical substantiation, raising the threat level from 'substantial' to 'severe' is a symbolic gesture without content.[131] Whether changes in the threat level are 'true' or not is difficult to verify. Without public access to intelligence, it is difficult to judge if such moves are made in good faith or bad, particularly if there have been no outward changes in circumstances such as new attacks. The executive could simply modulate the threat level for political advantage.

In 2003 the UK government seemingly tried to depoliticise this issue by creating an independent Joint Terrorism Analysis Centre (JTAC) responsible for setting the threat level. Yet in 2010 it became apparent that there was no connection between the official JTAC 'threat level' and the ongoing government claim that there was a 'public emergency threatening the life of the nation'. This claim justified the UK's derogation from Article 5 of the European Convention on Human Rights in 2001 in order to detain foreign 'terrorist suspects'. Even when the courts forced the government to drop the policy, it did not drop the 'threat to the life of the nation' claim. When questioned by the JCHR, a security minister stated that this claim would not change, 'even if the threat level as assessed by JTAC was at "moderate" or "low"'.[132] In its subsequent report, the JCHR expressed concern that

> the Government's approach means that in effect there is a permanent state of emergency, and that this inevitably has a deleterious effect on public debate about the justification for counter-terrorism measures.[133]

Interestingly, a former minister reflected on this mismatch between the symbolic power of the executive and independent intelligence assessments with some regret:

> Where we, ten years ago, eleven years ago, probably slightly overdid it as a government was to give the impression – I don't mean overtly, but subliminally – that the nation as a whole was under

serious threat, and it was partly because in order to be able to opt out of particular parts of the ECHR you have to say that the nation's under threat, so it was the terminology, as opposed to what you and I would call the substantive reality.[134]

Nevertheless, despite the potential for political manipulation of security discourses, we should not assume that the executive always cynically takes advantage of these power imbalances. There is an acceptance among parliamentarians that the special prerogatives of security are often necessary. One interviewee gave the example of Northern Ireland:

> At the height of the Northern Ireland peace process, at very delicate stages of the process, security may have been used as a convenient way of not revealing too much about what was going on. Funnily enough, that was a quite beneficial use of that behaviour because I think it probably was necessary to have a high degree of secrecy about the moves and various steps that were taken in trying to stitch together what was quite a difficult, complex and fraught process.[135]

Counter-intuitively, the dilemma also poses a problem for the executive side of the relationship. When interviewed for this book, more than one former security-related minister relayed their experience of a reputational dilemma of not being believed in their representation of the security threat.[136] As ministers, they are given threat assessments by the intelligence services that they have little means of verifying or challenging themselves. One former minister said:

> When you're dealing with an issue you really don't know at the time whether everything you're being told is true. You just don't. You've got to make a judgement based on your instinct, on your experience, on your rational thinking skills, in terms of weighing what you're being told and questioning it.[137]

Another former minister put this problem in more political terms, saying,

Conservative opposition behaved scandalously on the basis that they didn't really think there was a terrorist threat, that we were making it up. I thought that was terrible, and still think it's terrible.[138]

Interestingly, then, the dilemmas of security politics may apply as much to ministers as to the wider arena of politicians. Ministers have few means of demonstrating the truth of their claims and the necessity of their policies other than through assertions that cannot be tested. This goes some way to explaining why recognition and trust have been so important in security politics.

Habitus and the House of Lords

The analysis so far has been premised on the assumption that most parliamentarians are in a structurally similar position on security. Although they widely see their unequal symbolic power relations with the executive on security as problematic, they nevertheless reproduce them because of the structural position and informational disadvantage in which they find themselves. Of course, parliamentarians are not homogeneous, and while the discussion above has taken some account of differences between parties and between backbench MPs and current and former security 'insiders' such as ministers and members of the ISC, there are other ways to analytically subdivide the House. The House of Lords warrants a closer look in this regard.

Members of the House of Lords are of course not elected. Although many do take a party whip, they are generally beyond the coercive power of their parties and do not have much more to receive by way of party patronage, having already been made peers. For example, when asked what it means for a peer to rebel against their party, one peer said, 'It doesn't mean a great deal. It doesn't mean what it means in the Commons.'[139] Peers play the 'political game' differently, but party groupings do matter. The peer continued,

> You could lose the whip but that doesn't make much difference . . . It's much more about how things are negotiated in the group, and about how you're regarded within the group relationship . . . It's nuanced and sensitive, it's not a matter of big drama.[140]

Although many peers are political appointees, others have been appointed in recognition of their expertise, success and influence in other fields. As such, they can draw on alternative *habitus* and forms of symbolic capital in addition to their membership of parliament. In particular, the many lawyers, former government ministers and former senior military personnel possess a symbolic capital that can accord them the recognition to authoritatively challenge the government on security. As such, they can play an important role in security politics. A former minister (who has not been elevated to the Lords) explained:

> The Lords sees itself as the guardian of the rights of the citizen. In the Lords you not only have a number of senior lawyers who are genuinely very clever and understand the law very well but also a number of people who exercise serious legal authority, former home secretaries, foreign secretaries and even prime ministers. There are [also] some former permanent secretaries who know about security issues. There's a weight of opinion and experience there that doesn't exist in the Commons and a weight of legal expertise that also doesn't exist in the Commons.[141]

Mostly this is manifested through struggles over the law, human rights and the constitution, with this former minister suggesting that 'the number of lawyers in the House of Lords compared to the number of police officers and security people in the House of Lords [is] probably a factor of about fifteen or twenty'. Anticipated reactions will play a role here too; it may be enough for ministers to know that illiberal or legally contentious policies will be challenged in the Lords for them not to proceed with their plans.

It is less common that struggles occur directly on security grounds, rather than on legal or constitutional matters, but it has happened. For example, with a short maiden speech in the House of Lords, former head of MI5 Baroness Eliza Manningham-Buller singlehandedly undermined the counter-terrorism policy of Prime Minister Gordon Brown on the issue of forty-two-day pre-charge detention for terrorist suspects. Making front-page news, she said: 'I don't see on a practical basis, as well as a principled one, that these proposals are in any way workable.'[142] She then reminded her audience of having 'been fortunate in my career to have dealt with national security'.[143] At the time of writing, Manningham-Buller is the only former head of an intelligence service to have become a peer.

Even with this potentially important role in security politics, the House of Lords still shares practices and attitudes with the Commons and this includes a sense of caution on security matters. One peer thought that on security, 'There is not a huge appetite to question. There's less questioning of the executive [on security] than many other things.'[144]

The breakdown of trust and deference

The chapter to this point has described and analysed the power structures, norms and dispositions of security politics in parliament. These are characterised by a number of factors that make them different from the politics of other issue areas. The parliamentarians interviewed offered similar views on the responsibilities, challenges and constraints they faced on security issues. The dozen interviews conducted in 2012–13 represent a temporal snapshot. The interviewees were all experienced members with at least fifteen years in parliament. Mainly they reflected on the experience of the Blair years, with some looking back to the struggle with the IRA in the 1980s and before. There were one or two hints of how things might be changing, with shifts of party position and increased scepticism. Later chapters will take a more historical view to analyse change. Before that, there are two milestones to discuss: Iraq and Syria. These relate not to the widening meaning and application of security, but to two of the most traditional aspects: war and secret intelligence.

Iraq 2003

Trust on security was seriously damaged by the 2003 Iraq War and particularly the issue of weapons of mass destruction. The Blair government's case for war was contentious and attracted huge public opposition. Robin Cook resigned from the cabinet over the issue then campaigned for an unprecedented parliamentary vote on the war, a demand to which the government conceded. This was a significant constitutional departure, despite the vote not being legally binding. Paul Flynn suggests that cynicism played a part in the government allowing this vote; he writes, 'In the almost certain knowledge that he had a majority in the House, Tony Blair surrendered to demands for a vote.'[145] Indeed, Blair had a huge majority and the support of the main opposition party on most of his foreign and security policies. He could absorb rebellions, even to the extent of using this as a parliamentary tactic to demonstrate a principled or tough stance.

Despite considerable wrangling, parliament ultimately supported the war. A total of 139 Labour members rebelled; eighty Labour doubters were persuaded to support the government. Flynn gives an account of this in his book: 'The whips tried everything including the threat that Blair would resign and call a General Election. The prospect of P45s on the horizon is a potent fear.'[146] This chimes with the imperative for political survival discussed earlier and in Chapter 1: many Labour MPs felt beholden to Blair for their seats. James Strong writes, 'Ultimately a majority preferred to overthrow Saddam Hussein than to overthrow Tony Blair.'[147]

Bochel et al. note that the Blair government's public use of intelligence to make the case for a policy was a historical first.[148] Indeed, this was the executive itself breaking the convention of intelligence secrecy. Flynn argues that MPs trusted the intelligence assessments even if not all were persuaded of the case for war: 'Many [MPs] were persuaded that advice from the secret services was infallible. "After all," one told me, "the Prime Minister would not lie."'[149] An MP from a smaller party says: 'The executive decided that they would feed a line and we as parliamentarians were meant to swallow it hook, line and sinker. Fortunately, many of us didn't but the majority did.'[150]

It is now known that these intelligence assessments were wrong, misleading or at least insufficiently caveated. The *Review of Intelligence on Weapons of Mass Destruction* – an official investigation led by former cabinet secretary Robin Butler (now Lord Butler of

Brockwell) – demonstrated forensically how intelligence assessments never designed for public consumption were subtly manipulated and shorn of the difficult intelligence-gathering context by the government. Butler also criticised the intelligence community for being too willing to accommodate political demands.[151] The Chilcot report published twelve years later supported these conclusions (John Chilcot himself had been one of Butler's five-member review committee).[152]

Iraq and the weapons of mass destruction issue is the biggest single factor in changing the historical norms of parliamentary security politics. One MP said there is a 'wider air of scepticism now . . . and this crosses party lines . . . There is instinctively and traditionally more deference . . . but I think now there is much less trust and that is increasingly evident.'[153] Another described Tony Blair's presentation of 'his best evidence for the war on Iraq' as the 'lowest point in the relationship' between parliament and the executive on security, and, as a result, 'Trust has broken down utterly . . . Trust was hugely damaged by that one event.'[154] This is Flynn's take:

> Voting on joining Bush's Iraq War in 2003 was probably the most important decision that MPs took in the last century . . . Many MPs judge the value of their entire political lives by the decision that they took on that March day in 2003. There is bitter regret from the majority of Labour's eighty doubters. They are haunted by the belief that they failed their sternest test.[155]

Our smaller party MP confirms this view, saying,

> Many are now struggling with their consciences over the fact that they believed the Prime Minister and his advisors and couldn't really think that they were being misled on such an important issue, and they were.[156]

Syria 2013

The 2013 parliamentary vote on Syria demonstrated what a formative experience the Iraq War was. Like Blair, Prime Minister David Cameron made a case for military intervention by invoking intelligence assessments, although it was for a much smaller-scale intervention. Unlike Blair, he lost the vote. The parliamentary mood showed a lasting bitterness and the debate was as much about Iraq in 2003 as Syria in 2013. This time, Bochel et al. note, 'Parliament was less accepting of the evidence.'[157] James Strong writes: 'Distrust bred during debates over Iraq led many to speak out against the case for a further military engagement based primarily on evidence from secret intelligence.'[158] This has been evident in other debates too, as one MP explains:

> The relationship of trust between parliament and the executive hasn't recovered, because during the debate on Libya, for example, some people who had been more or less cheerleaders for Iraq were, to put it mildly, reticent about moving forward.[159]

In more general terms, another MP noted that increased scepticism is 'manifest in the way questions are phrased and the way ministers are challenged, and the way that security is no longer a convenient "get out" for a minister'.[160]

In the event of the 2013 Syria vote, Prime Minister David Cameron's government was defeated by 285 to 272 on a motion to join US air strikes.[161] Yet although parliament spoke on Syria, it is not clear what it said and whether this was for noble reasons or not. Kaarbo and Kenealy write:

> Given that the vote came less than two years after MPs (the same set of MPs) backed the UK's intervention in Libya it may be far-fetched to read the 2013 vote as an abandonment of the UK's global role and interventionism because of the ghosts of Iraq in 2003. Rather, it seems that the complexity of the specific case and the shadow cast by Iraq combined to prevent Cameron from winning the vote at that time.[162]

Furthermore, although Cameron lost, Leader of the Opposition Ed Miliband did not exactly win. The outcome of the vote had much to do with the hung parliament, the arithmetical weakness of the government's parliamentary position and a lack of political reconnaissance by the Tory whips because of the last-minute parliamentary recall from the summer recess.[163] The backroom processes that usually smooth the way for the government's parliamentary business had broken down.

The outcome also followed the decision of Miliband not to follow the traditional deferential stance of consensus. This was controversial precisely because it challenged the old conventions. In the debate, Conservative MP Nadhim Zahawi cried: 'Any reasonable human being would assume that he is looking to divide the House for political advantage. What has happened to the national interest?'[164]

In the wake of the vote, journalist Matthew Holehouse argued that many MPs no longer trusted the word of the Joint Intelligence Committee.[165] This was even though the official role of the JIC is not to make a case for action or support the government position, but to synthesise intelligence from the different services and present it to the government for a judgement. Indeed, Hansard shows that in the Syria debate many MPs openly questioned JIC assessments and demanded to see the intelligence themselves. For example, Richard Ottaway, then Chairman of the Foreign Affairs Select Committee, said,

> On the intelligence, those of us who were here in 2003, at the time of the Iraq war, felt they had their fingers burnt. The case for war was made and Parliament was briefed on the intelligence, but we were given only part of the story and, in some cases, an inaccurate story. A summary of the intelligence [on Syria] has been published, but it is the bare bones, and I urge the Government in the following days to consider how more intelligence can be provided.[166]

He went on to call for the security-cleared members of the Intelligence and Security Committee to be shown the intelligence and in turn report to the House. However, a member of the ISC pointed out that 'If the intelligence cannot be shared nationally, I am not sure that simply sharing it with the ISC would necessarily resolve that problem'.[167]

Members questioned why only the Prime Minister could see the full intelligence account, thus contesting the traditional executive monopoly on intelligence. A few MPs even put forward their own interpretations of events in Syria based on public information. For example, Bernard Jenkin said,

> There is a clear motive for Assad to have done this. He has used chemical weapons on five previous occasions, testing the west to see if it was going to respond. He has lost control of Aleppo airport, Homs is still under rebel control and rebels are fighting in the suburbs of Damascus. Assad is getting desperate and that is why he used chemical weapons. There is no question of any circumstantial evidence that points to anyone else.[168]

It is not the lost vote itself that is so significant for the development of parliamentary security politics, but what the attendant debate reveals about the change in parliamentary attitudes. Many MPs will no longer trust the word of the Prime Minister alone on such matters. James Strong's analysis of the debate finds Roger Godsiff MP (Lab.) saying he 'would never again believe one single solitary assurance given by any Prime Minister' and Cheryl Gillan MP (Con.) saying she would not 'be duped again'.[169]

However, although arguably parliament has become more of an independent security actor as a result – with a precedent seemingly established for it to have a say on military interventions – this in itself does not represent a solution to any of the problems of security politics discussed above.[170] The Syria vote represents a rejection of deference and self-exclusion on the part of some MPs, but it does not change the underlying structural conditions. Parliament has arrived at a situation in which many MPs feel they have the right to see the same intelligence as the government, make their own judgements and act accordingly. Strong writes: 'MPs now expect ministers to prove that the threats they describe exist.'[171] There are two problems with this. First, the intelligence services will not release raw intelligence to the House (and thus the public). Their position is that it would expose their sources and methods, give away a tactical advantage and put intelligence officers and agents at risk. Second, access to intelligence would not necessarily give MPs the means to analyse and interpret that intelligence. One aspect of the historical recognition of executive security authority is not simply that the government possesses secret intelligence, but that it is served by an extensive apparatus for intelligence interpretation. The JIC is a central part of this apparatus.

To consider why this is a problem we can look back to Iraq. Arguably, MPs who demand incontrovertible proof before giving their assent to action have failed to learn the intelligence lessons of the Iraq War, as articulated by Butler and subsequently Chilcot. Butler essentially argued that the problem with Blair's case for war was that it presented intelligence as truth, without any of the usual caveats attached by the JIC. His inquiry – despite being controversial at the time for its limited membership and remit – has come to be seen by the intelligence community as an important explanation of the nature and use of intelligence. Its main point can be summed up in the following extract: 'Intelligence merely provides techniques for improving the basis of knowledge. As with other techniques, it can be a dangerous tool if its limitations are not recognised by those who seek to use it.'[172] The report also quotes Clausewitz – arguably the most important strategic thinker of the modern age – to make the same point:

> Much of the intelligence that we receive in war is contradictory, even more of it is plain wrong, and most of it is fairly dubious. What one can expect from an officer, under these circumstances, is a certain degree of discrimination, which can only be gained from a knowledge of men and affairs and from good judgement.[173]

Perhaps this is why David Cameron adopted a position quite different to Blair in his Syria speech. He seemed to echo Clausewitz's emphasis on judgement when he said:

> I am not standing here and saying that there is some piece or pieces of intelligence that I have seen, or the JIC has seen, that the world will not see, that convinces me that I am right and anyone who disagrees with me is wrong. I am saying that this is a judgement; we all have to reach a judgement about what happened and who was responsible.[174]

From the perspective of the Butler report and indeed Clausewitz, Cameron's position was nuanced. It expressed the need for human judgement rather than asserting a privileged truth. Nevertheless, despite explicitly presenting his case for action in different terms to Blair, Cameron did not win the argument.[175] If he assumed that some of the traditional trust and deference given to prime ministers on matters of war and security would attach to him, he was wrong. Although MPs did not openly question his integrity or sincerity, the relationship between parliament and the government on security had changed.

Notes

1. Hammerstad and Boas, 'National Security Risks?'; HM Government, 'A Strong Britain in an Age of Uncertainty'; Crowcroft, 'A War on "Risk"?'.
2. Foucault, *The Government of Self and Others*, p. 158.
3. Ibid. pp. 159–60; Bigo, 'Security and Immigration'; Aradau and Munster, *Terror and the Politics of Catastrophe*; Huysmans, *The Politics of Insecurity*; Walt, 'The Renaissance of Security Studies'.
4. Wæver, 'Politics, Security, Theory', p. 473.
5. Neal, 'Legislative Practices', 'Terrorism, Lawmaking and Democratic Politics' and 'Normalization and Legislative Exceptionalism'; Bright, 'In Search of the Politics of Security'.
6. Kalyvas, *Democracy and the Politics of the Extraordinary*, p. 6.
7. Buzan, Wæver and de Wilde, *Security*, pp. 4–5.
8. Wright, *Doing Politics*, p. 167.
9. Kelso, *Parliamentary Reform at Westminster*, p. 15.
10. Strong, 'Why Parliament Now Decides on War'; Mello, 'Curbing the Royal Prerogative to Use Military Force'.
11. Foucault, *The Government of Self and Others*, pp. 2–5.
12. Foucault and Rabinow, 'Polemics, Politics and Problematizations', p. 389.
13. Salter, 'Securitization and Desecuritization' and 'When Securitization Fails'; Balzacq, 'A Theory of Securitization', p. 1, and 'The Three Faces of Securitization'; Stritzel, 'Towards a Theory of Securitization'.
14. Salter, 'Securitization and Desecuritization', p. 321.
15. Stritzel, 'Towards a Theory of Securitization', p. 371.

16. Balzacq, 'A Theory of Securitization', p. 3; Bourdieu, 'On Symbolic Power', p. 170.
17. Ciută, 'Security and the Problem of Context', p. 321.
18. Balzacq, 'The Three Faces of Securitization', p. 172.
19. McDonald, 'Securitization and the Construction of Security'.
20. Williams, *Culture and Security*, p. 3.
21. Bourdieu, *Practical Reason*.
22. Pouliot, 'The Logic of Practicality'.
23. Bourdieu, *The Logic of Practice*, p. 56.
24. Ibid. p. 66.
25. Ibid. p. 53.
26. Ibid. p. 56.
27. Bourdieu, *Language and Symbolic Power*, p. 53.
28. Bourdieu, *The Logic of Practice*, pp. 52–65.
29. Ibid. p. 54.
30. CASE Collective, 'Critical Approaches to Security in Europe', p. 458.
31. Bourdieu, *Language and Symbolic Power*, p. 171.
32. Leander, 'Habitus and Field'.
33. Bigo, 'Globalized (in)Security' and 'Security and Immigration'.
34. Bourdieu, *Practical Reason*, p. vii.
35. Bourdieu, *Language and Symbolic Power*, p. 216.
36. Gill, 'The Intelligence and Security Committee and the Challenge of Security Networks' and 'Intelligence, Threat, Risk and the Challenge of Oversight'; Gill, Marrin and Phythian, *Intelligence Theory*; 'Report of a Committee of Privy Counsellors, Review of Intelligence on Weapons of Mass Destruction, HC 898'; Andrew, Aldrich and Wark, *Secret Intelligence*; Bochel, Defty and Kirkpatrick, *Watching the Watchers*; Hennessy, *The New Protective State*; Omand, *Securing the State*; Phythian, 'Still a Matter of Trust' and 'The British Experience with Intelligence Accountability'; Schulhofer, *The Enemy Within*.
37. Wright, 'What Are MPs For?'; Norton, *Parliament in British Politics*, p. 48.
38. Cowley, *Revolts and Rebellions* and *The Rebels*.
39. Weber, 'The Profession and Vocation of Politics', p. 343.
40. Flinders and Kelso, 'Mind the Gap', p. 257.
41. Ibid. p. 258.
42. Ibid. p. 257.
43. Crick, *The Reform of Parliament*, p. 80.
44. Friedrich, *Constitutional Government and Politics*; Arter, 'The Nordic Parliaments', p. 68; Kalitowski, 'Rubber Stamp or Cockpit?';

Norton, *Does Parliament Matter?*, pp. 80–1; Blondel, 'Legislative Behaviour'.
45. Bochel, Defty and Kirkpatrick, *Watching the Watchers*, p. 18.
46. Kalitowski, 'Rubber Stamp or Cockpit?'.
47. Kelso, *Parliamentary Reform at Westminster*, p. 15; Judge, *The Parliamentary State*, p. 2.
48. Packenham, 'Legislatures and Political Development'.
49. Bourdieu, 'Political Representation', p. 181.
50. Interviewee 3.
51. Joint Committee on Human Rights, 'Counter-Terrorism Policy and Human Rights (Seventeenth Report)', p. 9.
52. House of Lords Select Committee on the Constitution, 'Fast-Track Legislation', p. 15.
53. Interviewee 3.
54. Andrew, *Secret Service*, p. 703.
55. Interviewee 6.
56. Interviewee 7.
57. Bochel, Defty and Kirkpatrick, *Watching the Watchers*, p. 30.
58. Ibid.
59. Interviewee 9.
60. Bourdieu, *The Logic of Practice*, p. 53.
61. Sutcliffe-Braithwaite, *Class, Politics, and the Decline of Deference in England*, p. 8.
62. Andrew, *The Defence of the Realm*, p. 1900.
63. Bochel, Defty and Kirkpatrick, *Watching the Watchers*, pp. 33, 46.
64. Interviewee 6.
65. May, *A Treatise on the Law, Privileges, Proceedings and Usage of Parliament*, 17th edn, p. 328; May, *A Treatise on the Law, Privileges, Proceedings and Usage of Parliament*, 21st edn, p. 292; Zehfuss, 'Forget September 11'.
66. Bochel, Defty and Kirkpatrick, *Watching the Watchers*, p. 27.
67. Ibid. p. 49.
68. Ibid. pp. 49, 51.
69. Interviewee 2.
70. Bochel, Defty and Kirkpatrick, *Watching the Watchers*, p. 94.
71. Ibid.
72. Interviewee 2.
73. Interviewee 7.
74. Interviewee 7.
75. Interviewee 8.
76. Interviewee 9.

77. Bochel, Defty and Kirkpatrick, *Watching the Watchers*, p. 5.
78. Interviewee 9.
79. Interviewee 3.
80. Bochel, Defty and Kirkpatrick, *Watching the Watchers*, p. 26.
81. Bourdieu, *In Other Words*, p. 112.
82. Bourdieu, *Language and Symbolic Power*, p. 219.
83. Dyzenhaus, 'An Unfortunate Outburst of Anglo-Saxon Parochialism'; Tierney, 'Determining the State of Exception'.
84. Law Lords, *Opinions of the Lords of Appeal for Judgment in the Cause, a (Fc) and Others (Fc) (Appellants) V. Secretary of State for the Home Department (Respondent)*.
85. Interviewee 7.
86. Sun SAYS, 'Editorial'.
87. Interviewee 4 (Paul Flynn MP, Lab.).
88. Interviewee 6.
89. Bourdieu, *The Logic of Practice*, p. 53.
90. Interviewee 9.
91. Interviewee 7.
92. Interviewee 2.
93. Neal, 'Terrorism, Lawmaking and Democratic Politics'.
94. Professor Brice Dickson giving evidence to the House of Lords Select Committee on the Constitution, 'Fast-Track Legislation: Constitutional Implications and Safeguards', p. 18.
95. Interviewee 6.
96. Bourdieu, *The Logic of Practice*, p. 53.
97. Pouliot, 'The Logic of Practicality', p. 257.
98. Interviewee 5.
99. Interviewee 7.
100. Hattersley, 'John P. Mackintosh Memorial Lecture: "What Are MPs For?"', University of Edinburgh, 2013.
101. Manningham-Buller, 'Lords Hansard Text'.
102. Interviewee 2.
103. Interviewee 1.
104. Interviewee 3.
105. Interviewee 2.
106. Interviewee 5.
107. Interviewee 2.
108. Interviewee 6.
109. Interviewee 2.
110. Huysmans, *The Politics of Insecurity*, p. 61.
111. Floyd, 'Extraordinary or Ordinary Emergency Measures', p. 687.

112. Bourdieu, 'Political Representation', p. 183.
113. Interviewee 2.
114. Interviewee 2.
115. Interviewee 6.
116. Conservative Party, *Invitation to Join the Government of Britain: The Conservative Manifesto 2010*, p. 79.
117. Interviewee 7.
118. Interviewee 7.
119. Interviewee 7.
120. Bourdieu, 'On Symbolic Power', p. 170.
121. Bourdieu, *In Other Words*, p. 112.
122. Evans, 'Defending the Realm', cited in Joint Committee on Human Rights, 'Counter-Terrorism Policy and Human Rights (Seventeenth Report)', p. 10.
123. Interviewee 6.
124. Interviewee 6.
125. Interviewee 8.
126. Miliband, 'House of Commons Hansard Debates'.
127. BBC News, 'Binyam Mohamed Torture Appeal Lost by UK Government'.
128. Ibid.
129. Stafford-Smith, 'Tortuous Evasions on Torture'; Press Association, 'Miliband Loses Attempt to Block Binyam Mohamed Torture Case Evidence'.
130. See Home Office, 'Current Threat Level'; Department of Homeland Security, 'Homeland Security Advisory System'.
131. Brooker, 'Home Office Raises Current Terrorism Threat Level to "Severe"'.
132. Joint Committee on Human Rights, 'Counter-Terrorism Policy and Human Rights (Seventeenth Report)', p. 9.
133. Ibid.
134. Interviewee 8.
135. Interviewee 6.
136. Interviewees 7 and 8.
137. Interviewee 8.
138. Interviewee 7.
139. Interviewee 3.
140. Interviewee 3.
141. Interviewee 7.
142. Manningham-Buller, 'Lords Hansard Text'.
143. Ibid.

144. Interviewee 3.
145. Flynn, *How to Be an MP*, p. 211.
146. Ibid. pp. 211–12.
147. Strong, 'Why Parliament Now Decides on War', p. 610.
148. Bochel, Defty and Kirkpatrick, *Watching the Watchers*, p. 1.
149. Flynn, *How to Be an MP*, p. 212.
150. Interviewee 9.
151. Lord Butler of Brockwell, *Review of Intelligence on Weapons of Mass Destruction*, p. 14.
152. Sir John Chilcot, 'Iraq Inquiry: Executive Summary', p. 130.
153. Interviewee 6.
154. Interviewee 9.
155. Flynn, *How to Be an MP*, p. 211.
156. Interviewee 9.
157. Bochel, Defty and Kirkpatrick, *Watching the Watchers*, p. 1.
158. Strong, 'Interpreting the Syria Vote', p. 1131.
159. Interviewee 9.
160. Interviewee 6.
161. BBC News, 'Syria Crisis: Cameron Loses Commons Vote on Syria Action'.
162. Kaarbo and Kenealy, 'No, Prime Minister', p. 41.
163. Ibid. pp. 40–1.
164. House of Commons, 'Syria and the Use of Chemical Weapons, House of Commons Hansard Debates for 29 Aug 2013', column 1446.
165. Matthew Holehouse to <blogs.telegraph.co.uk>, 2013.
166. House of Commons, 'Syria and the Use of Chemical Weapons, House of Commons Hansard Debates for 29 Aug 2013', column 1460.
167. George Howarth, in ibid., column 1509.
168. In ibid., column 1467.
169. Strong, 'Interpreting the Syria Vote', p. 1131.
170. For more on the implications of the Syria vote and the changing foreign policy role of parliament, see Kaarbo and Kenealy, 'No, Prime Minister'; Strong, 'Why Parliament Now Decides on War' and 'Interpreting the Syria Vote'; Gaskarth, 'The Fiasco of the 2013 Syria Votes'.
171. Strong, 'Interpreting the Syria Vote', p. 1131.
172. Lord Butler of Brockwell, *Review of Intelligence on Weapons of Mass Destruction*, p. 14.
173. Ibid. p. 7; Clausewitz, *On War*, vol. 1, book 1, chapter 6.

174. House of Commons, 'Syria and the Use of Chemical Weapons, House of Commons Hansard Debates for 29 Aug 2013', column 1432.
175. Kaarbo and Kenealy, 'No, Prime Minister', p. 41.

5. Can One Person Make a Difference? Fearless Speech vs. Security Politics

On 12 June 2008, Conservative MP David Davis resigned his parliamentary seat in protest at the Labour government's security policies. His act came the day after the government narrowly won a Commons vote on its 2008 Counter-Terrorism Bill. The legislation was the last in a long line of counter-terrorism laws passed by Labour before it lost the 2010 election. Its main purpose was to extend the amount of time the police could hold and question terrorism suspects for before charging them with an offence. The maximum period of pre-charge detention would have gone from twenty-eight days – already long by EU standards – to forty-two days. The measure was all the more contentious because the government was revisiting ground on which it had already been defeated. On this occasion, the government offered no new evidence that an extension in pre-charge detention was needed on security grounds or that the police or security services had called for one.[1] Many parliamentarians and commentators suspected that the government was legislating in bad faith for purely political reasons, or even that this was a cynical attempt to establish the security credentials of Gordon Brown, the new prime minister.[2] Since 2001 the government had suffered repeated backbench rebellions on counter-terrorism laws, in particular in 2005 on its efforts to extend the pre-charge detention period to ninety days.[3] In the 2008 vote, the government suffered another rebellion and strong opposition from other parties. A heavily watered-down bill was only passed in the Commons with the support of the Democratic Unionist Party, a Northern Irish right-wing party with hard-line views on counter-terrorism.

Davis made his resignation speech on the steps outside parliament, having been refused permission to do so in the chamber on the grounds that he was no longer an MP.[4] Referring to a long list of encroachments by the security state on historic British civil liberties, he said: 'This cannot go on, it must be stopped, and for that reason today I feel it is incumbent on me to take a stand.' He cited the Magna Carta, *habeas corpus*, an assault on the justice system and the arbitrary and excessive use of state power. Although it was an unusual speech for a Tory to make, nothing in it was incompatible with British conservatism, with the emphasis very much on the threat to British traditions rather than, for example, universal human rights or vulnerable minorities. Nor did it reveal anything new, such as state secrets or a grubby backroom deal. Davis was not well regarded as an orator, with some commentators arguing that a bad party conference speech had cost him his bid for the leadership in 2005.[5] However, it was the act rather than the rhetoric of his resignation that was important. It allowed Davis to stake his career on what he saw as the truth of the situation: 'the slow strangulation of fundamental British freedoms by this government'.[6] His act came at great personal cost but changed little in policy terms.

By resigning as an MP, Davis forced a by-election in his constituency, which he then contested. The other main parties did not field candidates. The Liberal Democrats were the first opposition party to respond to the resignation, saying they would not field a candidate against Davis because they supported his position.[7] The Labour Party, after some initial confusion about what had actually happened, followed the Lib Dems' lead by not standing against him. The Home Office Minister Tony McNulty called Davis's act a 'vain stunt'.[8] This denied Davis the opportunity to debate the issues with the other main parties in hustings, although a record twenty-five candidates from fringe parties and single-issue groups stood against him.[9] Davis won comfortably.

Nick Robinson, the BBC's political editor at the time, called it 'an extraordinary move almost without precedent in British politics'.[10] Many commentators and fellow politicians found Davis's act difficult to understand. They recognised it as a principled stand against objectionable policies but struggled to make sense of the political reasoning behind it for three main reasons. First, the detention measure presented in the Counter-Terrorism Bill was likely to be rejected by the House of Lords, as indeed it was four months later.[11] Second, Davis was shadow home secretary in a party that was favourite to win the next election (which it did in 2010, albeit without a full majority). Davis had every chance of becoming the home secretary in the next government. In this position he would have had considerable scope to change security policies to something more agreeable to him and the increasingly animated civil liberties lobby. Third, Davis was already successfully influencing the civil liberties policy of his party and he risked throwing that influence away. For example, *The Telegraph* was of the opinion that Davis had 'free rein' on its home affairs brief and that he had persuaded his party leader (and future prime minister) David Cameron to oppose the forty-two-day detention policy in the 2008 vote, despite the measure being popular with the public.[12] A Liberal Democrat politician interviewed for this book credited Davis with leading the Conservative Party to a libertarian position that was not its 'natural' stance, being more traditionally associated with hard-line measures on justice and policing.[13] In short, Davis's resignation did not make sense as an act of political calculation.

Because of the sensation his resignation caused, Davis discussed his decision in the press for months afterwards. In contrast to how his peers saw it, a striking theme in his comments was the extent to which he saw his choice as a rational calculation. For example, he said,

> I'm more cold blooded than some about crises ... Every decision you make has got an analytical bit and an emotional bit to it and I work very hard getting the analytical bit right and that makes the emotional bit easier ... I did that calculation, I sat and I spent whole weekends thinking about this literally just non-stop.[14]

Although the decision was rational in Davis's view, it did not fit the prevailing rationality of the political game. Many in Westminster and the commentariat tried to impart more expected forms of political calculation to the act, speculating for example that it was the first step in a new leadership campaign in case Cameron lost the general election.[15] Davis explained this away by saying, 'The Westminster village does not respond well to things it has never seen before. The collective view is "what is the ulterior motive here?"'[16]

To make sense of these expectations, we can turn to Bourdieu, who argues that the 'rules of the game' of politics (or any field) structure the beliefs, dispositions and expectations of the actors involved:

> Because native membership in a field implies a feel for the game in the sense of a capacity for practical anticipation of the 'upcoming' future contained in the present, everything that takes place in it seems *sensible*: full of sense and objectively directed in a judicious direction.[17]

In other words, politicians and political commentators are disposed to see a political rationale behind any parliamentary act. These may not always be nakedly partisan but should at least make sense in terms of the political game, such as supporting or opposing the government through speeches and questions, aiming to improve policy through the scrutiny and oversight process, or speaking up for constituency or other group interests.

With this in mind, it is striking that Davis's peers could not make sense of his actions. His close party colleague Andrew Mitchell MP is reported to have been overheard shouting to him 'You're nuts!' on learning of his decision.[18] Another unnamed shadow cabinet colleague said Mr Davis was 'stark, staring bonkers. There is no sane, rational reason for this.'[19] *The Independent*, a newspaper with an interest in civil liberties, was also scathing about the contradictions in Davis's reasoning:

> While we agree entirely with his analysis of the Government's sorry record, and hugely admire his heroic, if rather Quixotic, stand in defence of traditional British liberties, Mr Davis's decision to resign from the Commons to fight a by-election cannot be interpreted as anything other than an act of reckless egotism.[20]

Davis had stepped outside the 'rules of the game' of parliamentary politics. While his resignation was regarded as an act of genuine principle, as a tactic it appeared flawed and costly. *The Independent* concluded: 'it was unquestionably his own party that felt the sting of this resignation most keenly. And we fear that, ultimately, the biggest loser will be Mr Davis himself.'[21]

Davis had a reasoned response to most of the arguments offered against his decision. He knew that he might damage his party and that parties that appear divided are historically not favoured by the electorate.[22] Yet he decided that Cameron had enough of a poll lead that his resignation would not cause him a problem.[23] Of the alternative courses available to him he says:

> I suppose you might calculate that forty-two days would have died anyway, or alternatively that I could have done a better job at defeating it if I was home secretary not shadow home secretary now, which presumably would have happened in due course, but again I did the calculation.[24]

It also seems that Davis believed (wrongly) that the government would invoke the Parliament Act, which would allow it to bypass the House of Lords in order to pass the bill, which he mentions in his resignation speech and in subsequent interviews.[25] With this in mind, he says, 'I couldn't think of any other way to stop this thing in its tracks than by resigning and making as huge an issue of it as I could.'[26] Invoking the Parliament Act would have been a rare and controversial move, having only been done seven times since its creation in 1911, and would have taken some time procedurally.[27] However, while we can judge the veracity of his reasoning with the benefit of hindsight, the point is less whether he was right or wrong in his assessment of the political situation and more that he believed in the truth of his calculation enough to stake his career and reputation on it. He talks about the decision 'taking all his nerve', being 'scared' and how he 'didn't want particularly to sacrifice the remainder of [his] career'.[28] His calculation was that 'the public would see this as an important stand' which would eclipse the negative sides to the story and he would ultimately be vindicated. Although it is not clear how far his resignation contributed to the government eventually dropping the forty-two-day measure, some of his peers credited him with that political success when it happened.[29]

Davis's resignation was a minor episode in the politicisation of security after 9/11 and the Iraq and Afghanistan wars, in both senses discussed in Chapter 3: increasing (qualitative) controversy and increasing (quantitative) mobilisation of activity in the parliamentary arena (and indeed civil society). This period led to a greater willingness of parliamentarians to critically engage with security issues, with mixed results, as seen by the parliamentary debates on interventions in Iraq, Syria and, later, Libya.[30] In the 2010 election, a civil-liberties-based backlash on security policy featured prominently in the manifestos of the main opposition parties.[31] This could also be seen in a greater number of backbench rebellions and other struggles on security legislation and more extensive committee activity (which the next chapter will discuss).[32]

Although Davis's act must be seen in this context, it stands out for its individualism. It raises questions about the limits and indeed the wisdom of an individual taking a stand when parliamentary politics is to a large extent a team game in a highly structured environment. Individual parliamentarians face difficulties in directly challenging government security policy and the 'rules of the game' of security politics, as we heard from several interviewees in the previous chapter. Although security politics has been changing over the past two decades to increasingly resemble 'normal politics' as opposed to 'exceptional politics', the structural and norm constraints that the 'institutionalised securitisation' of traditional security politics places on politicians still exist.[33] These include executive secrecy and parliamentary marginalisation, and often take the form of lack of access to intelligence and a corresponding inability of parliamentarians to 'test the arguments'.[34] The previous chapter argued that these constraints are not only the product of government prerogative, but are also a product of parliamentary deference to the executive, self-exclusion from security debates, suspension of partisanship, loyalty to the police and security services, and respect for the fears of the public.

If individual politicians wish to challenge the norms and constraints of security politics, they face not only structural challenges such as being able to claim authoritative knowledge, but also the risk of being seen as irresponsible, unpatriotic, egotistical, as did Davis. As argued in Chapter 1, although in stable liberal democracies politicians may not face many risks to their existential survival, their political survival is at stake. They may not endanger their life or liberty by speaking out, but they risk their seats, careers and reputations. Some parliamentarians earn the authority and credibility to speak on security – public lawyers and former security chiefs in the House of Lords, for example – but often these actors do not face the problem of re-election or jeopardising their future careers. In the Commons, those towards the end of their parliamentary careers – perhaps having already served in government – may have the weight to speak on security, although not necessarily the inclination.

In light of the parliamentary structures and dilemmas explored in the previous chapter, this chapter asks: what if an individual wants to challenge and go beyond the 'rules of the game'?[35] As we will see, although Davis was not successful in an immediate tactical sense, his action can be seen as a problematisation of security politics and an exception that proves the rule. His act, in its creativity, also problematises aspects of structuralist (Bourdieusian) and performative (securitisation) theories of security politics. To make sense of this, we will now turn again to Foucault.

Parresia and its problematisations

While Davis's act did not change much except the course of his own career, its exceptionality highlights and problematises the structures and norms of security politics, specifically their silencing and marginalising effects. In this sense, Davis's act can be understood though the lens of Foucault's work on *parresia*, the ancient Greek practice of 'truth-telling' or 'free-spokenness'. For Foucault, *parresia* is an act of freely speaking out, when a speaker steps out of the regular agonistic game and puts themselves at risk.[36] In its individualism, *parresia* represents a different perspective to the Bourdieusian account of politics, defying its pathways of expected behaviour in the political field. And in the way the *parrhesiastic* speaker binds themselves and their fate to their statement of 'truth' in a risky act of free-spokenness, *parresia* represents a different kind of truth claim to securitising speech acts that mobilise an existing logic of security in securitisation theory.[37]

Foucault sees *parresia* as an act that problematises the power relations surrounding the ability to freely speak truth. For example, in the court of a tyrant, speaking truth may result in death if it displeases the tyrant. In a democratic assembly riven by jealous rivalries or a cacophony of competing opinions, speaking a truth that is disagreeable to the majority or to powerful factions may result in ostracism or worse. Security politics presents specific relations of power and truth with similar dilemmas.

In simple terms, Davis's resignation can be seen as an act of *parresia*. When Davis tied his 'truth-telling' to his own political fate and went beyond the expected 'rules of the game' of parliamentary politics, he became a modern-day *parrhesiast*. It was a freely chosen, individual act of speaking out, a means of stepping outside the agonistic game of politics to claim a special right to speak the truth. It was not an exercise in skilled rhetoric to persuade an audience of a particular position or goal, nor a recognisable move in an institutionalised dialogical process. Rather, it was an enactment and embodiment of a personal truth expressed through a costly gesture: a risky act with an uncertain outcome. However, viewed in more complex terms, Davis's *parrhesiastic* resignation can be seen as a problematisation of several aspects of security politics: its structures and norms, the possibility of political opposition, and the status and production of the 'truth' about threats.

Before going further, a methodological clarification is needed. In keeping with the Foucaultian methodology outlined in Chapter 2, this chapter approaches *parresia* not as a strictly definable concept to be applied to different examples, but rather as a problematisation. Problematisations are not constant but appear in different forms in different political contexts. In Foucault's work, they are invariably heterogeneous and discontinuous.[38] We can see this discontinuity in the structural movement of the lectures in which *parresia* appears, where *parresia* as a problematisation never stays the same for more than a few pages. In each instance *parresia* is different.[39] Unlike in much of social science where definitions are central to the rigorous identification and analysis of phenomena (as with securitisation theory), from a Foucaultian perspective one does not ask the general analytical question of how to identify *parresia* when one sees it. As with the discussion of how to identify 'security' in Chapter 2, one can only ask the question 'what is the problematisation of *parresia* here?'. Or in other words, what is the problem of 'truth-telling' in this particular historico-political circumstance?

Let us now consider Foucault's work on *parresia* in more detail. Foucault presented this in his final two years of Collège de France lectures and in a shorter six-lecture version he presented at Berkeley.[40] While retaining the qualification that *parresia* is a heterogeneous problematisation that is not consistent across times and places, Foucault outlines a number of its features in the ancient Greek examples he examines. *Parresia* is a particular kind of free speech that is not simply the exercise of the right to speak freely, but an exceptional outspokenness or frankness that embodies a particular kind of 'truth'. It is a mode of speech by which the speaker removes themselves from the regular agonistic rhetorical game to assert a special kind of authentic truth. *Parresia* is an act of freedom in which an individual chooses to come forward to speak.[41] It is characterised by this freedom rather than by the status of the speaker or the content of the speech.[42] The speaker constitutes themselves as a speaker of truth in the very act of freely speaking out. Foucault argues:

> *Parresia* involves the way in which by asserting the truth, and in the very act of this assertion, one constitutes oneself as the person who tells the truth, who has told the truth, and who recognizes oneself in and as the person who has told the truth.[43]

The word *parresia* occurs frequently in Greek texts, but Foucault makes a distinction between the simple occurrence of the term and its problematisation.[44] Furthermore, his interest in *parresia* is not simply as the right to speak freely that was held by every citizen in democratic Athens, which goes by the different name of *isegoria*, but rather as a specific kind of 'frankness, the profession of truth'.[45]

Parresia is thus an individualised practice of truth in the political realm. It may relate to politics in different ways, either directly in the political arena, through lobbying the powers that be in the name of justice, by offering counsel to the Prince or by embodying a philosophical life of truth that exists in relation to the life of illusion perhaps found in politics.[46] It is, in its many forms, a practice of speaking truth to power, but is also related to the exercise of power through the speaking of truth.[47]

In the context of Foucault's wider research, *parresia* is a continuation of his concern with the constitution of subjecthood: 'the different forms by which the individual is led to constitute him or herself as subject'.[48] And in keeping with his general methodology as discussed in Chapter 2, Foucault does not aim to derive a general theory of the subject from his inquiries, but rather to understand heterogeneous, historically situated practices of subjectivity.

Foucault also says that his interest in *parresia* is part of a 'genealogy of politics as game and experience', a concern which only appears as distinct from Foucault's problematisation of government in his final years. As mentioned in earlier chapters, his aim is to understand 'the political game, its rules and instruments, and ... the individual who engages in it'.[49] For this 'game' he uses the Greek term *dunasteia*, which is a different set of problems to that of the classical Aristotelian *politeia* that concerns the question of the correct political constitution and laws.[50] Foucault is also at pains to distinguish his concern with 'politics' from a concern with 'the political'; he says:

> Nothing seems more dangerous to me than that much vaunted shift from politics (*la politique*) to the political (*le politique*), which in many contemporary analyses seems to me to have the effect of masking the specific problem and set of problems of politics, of *dunasteia*, of the practice of the political game.[51]

Foucault's point is that the category of 'the political' makes politics into something quasi-transcendent, rather than a distinct set of human practices. This is significant for debates about security, where there has been a trend of understanding 'the political' as a transcendent category of political life. This is displayed, for example, in the revival of the work of Carl Schmitt, who made the mortal distinction between friends and enemies into a defining criterion of 'the political', and whose work on sovereign exceptionalism shaped securitisation theory.[52] In contrast, Foucault is concerned with practices of politics, not the ontology of 'the political' or the right and legitimacy of constitutional arrangements.

Nevertheless, the problem of truth is a common thread across these debates. In the work of Schmitt, the production of the 'truth' of security and insecurity is a function and expression of sovereign power, expressed in Schmitt's assertion 'Sovereign is he who decides on the exception'.[53] In Foucaultian terms, this sovereign nominalism must be seen as just one of many practices of truth or 'modes of veridiction'.[54]

Parresia is for Foucault yet another form of 'true discourse in the political realm'.[55] In our present, we live with many forms of truth production or veridiction. 'Positivist' or 'scientific' understandings of truth represent only one branch.[56] Other examples include the adversarial judicial system which aims at proclaiming the 'truth' of guilt or innocence, the dialogical process in parliamentary democracies, and the public inquiries conducted in the UK on matters of exceptional public interest such as the Iraq War or Bloody Sunday.

Parresia is notable in the way it differs from other modes of truth production. It is a thoroughly individualistic mode of veridiction through which an actor claims truth not on an epistemological, evidential or dialogical basis, but through the risky act of speaking itself. One who speaks with *parresia* does so by constituting themselves as a truth-teller, a subject bound to 'truth'. From the outset, therefore, we must think of *parresia* as a truth claim based on the specific qualities of the act of speaking, rather than the content of the speech as such. *Parresia* does not produce 'the truth' in the singular, nor a truth that can or should be verified by external standards. It is a truth claim tied to the one who speaks: an ontological rather than epistemological truth claim.[57]

Parresia *and performativity*

Parresia has implications for securitisation theory and specifically its basis in performative speech act theory. Foucault explicitly contrasts *parresia* with speech acts or performative utterances, which he calls 'exactly the opposite of parresia'.[58] Performative speech acts depend on 'felicity conditions' such as authority and context. They attempt to effectuate the known qualities of an established discourse, as with securitising speech acts invoking the prior 'logic' of security that includes urgency, necessity and exceptionality. In contrast, *parresia* does not simply effectuate a known discourse, but steps outside prevailing discursive rules in order to claim a special kind of truth through the risky act of speaking out.

In the lectures, Foucault is clearly referring to the speech act theory of J. L. Austin (their timing pre-dates Judith Butler's work on performativity). Foucault sums up the concept of the 'performative utterance' as being defined by an 'institutionalized context, [and] an individual who has the requisite status or who is in a well-defined situation'.[59] This is familiar as the 'felicity conditions' discussed in the securitisation literature.[60] An utterance is performative when it 'effectuates the thing stated', such as the designated chair of a meeting declaring it to be open, or indeed an actor securitising an issue.[61] Foucault accepts that many instances of *parresia* in Greek texts also take place in an institutionalised context, such as a democratic assembly or the sovereign's court.[62] The difference is that while the effects a performative utterance is meant to bring about are 'known and ordered in advance', the effects of *parresia* are uncertain.[63] For example, in securitisation theory, a successful securitising utterance is one that performs the 'grammar' of security under the right 'felicity conditions' and brings about intended securitised outcomes, as with the construction of a security threat and the legitimation of a mitigating policy. In contrast, Foucault argues that the effects of *parresia* are not codified or known in advance.[64] *Parresia* is an opening up, not the performance of an established code:

> What makes it parresia is that the introduction, the irruption of the true discourse determines an open situation, or rather opens the situation and makes possible effects which are, precisely, not known.[65]

It is this uncertainty that creates a risk for the speaker, because they do not know how their audience will react to their assertion of truth. The speaker does not perform an established discourse with an outcome already expected by the regularities of the political game, but rather interrupts normalised discourse by invoking truth in a particular way. In this way, *parresia* is a kind of discursive exception:

> In a sense, therefore, it is the opposite of the performative, in which the enunciation of something brings about and gives rise to a completely determined event as a function of the general code and institutional field in which the utterance is made. Here, on the contrary, it is a truth-telling, an irruptive truth-telling which creates a fracture and opens up the risk: a possibility, a field of dangers, or at any rate, an undefined eventuality.[66]

Butler's formulation of 'performativity' also demonstrates this key difference with *parresia*. Although Butler's performative discourses of gender and sexuality constitute the identity of a speaker, just as *parresia* constitutes the identity of the speaker as a truth-teller, performativity is the rehearsal and embodiment of socially embedded gender norms rather than their interruption.[67]

To reiterate, the key difference between performativity and *parresia* is that the former effectuates a known discourse while the latter makes a radical break. As such, the 'truth' of the *parrhesiastic* statement is not determined by demonstrable analytical standards, nor by its reaffirmation of accepted norms, nor by the audience's acceptance of what the speaker says, and nor is it a function of status or office. The 'truth' of *parresia* is expressed in the speaker binding themselves to what they have said, constituting themselves as a truth-teller in the process. Taking this further, Foucault argues that *parresia* presents a double-level truth, the first level being the statement itself and the second being the affirmation of identity between the speaker and the truth of the speech, whereby the speaker in effect says: 'I tell the truth, and I truly think that it is true, and I truly think that I am telling the truth when I say it.'[68]

Parresia and context

For Foucault, *parresia* is a practice that appears differently according to specific problems of 'truth' in different political contexts. To this end, Foucault discusses many forms of *parresia* across the historical life of ancient Greece, from the founding of Athenian democracy to its decline and absorption into the Roman Empire. For example, one *parrhesiastic* problematisation is the question of who speaks 'the truth' in a democracy where all citizens have the right to free speech. Again, this is not an epistemological question, but an ontological and political one. Who embodies the truth? Who may speak 'the truth' against the majority, or against the relative and partial opinions of the many? And how may truth be distinguished from the rhetoric and flattery of the political game?[69] Yet no sooner does this problem appear in the founding myths of Athenian democracy than it is already disappearing, being challenged, presenting difficulties and being practised in quite different ways. For example, Foucault moves quickly from a discussion of Pericles as *parrhesiast* in the texts of Euripides and Thucydides to a situation of 'bad *parresia*' in the texts of Isocrates. In the latter, the condition of Athenian democracy has become so bad that truthful speech is no longer possible. Democracy in the political arena has been consumed by flattery and self-serving rhetoric (parallels could certainly be drawn with today's 'post-truth' era of 'fake news').[70] Later, Foucault discusses the practice of *parresia* by philosophers in the court of a despot, who are at risk of punishment by death.[71] Autocracy thus poses the question of *parresia* differently: who may speak truth to the Prince without being punished? Who may counsel him? It also poses an ethical question: what should the role and life of the philosopher, the lover of truth, be in these circumstances? How may the philosopher live a life of truth?

For Foucault, the *parresia* that appears in democratic assemblies is a specific problematisation of speaking out that he terms 'political *parresia*'.[72] This stems from a 'technical, political problem' posed by the right of free speech itself: if all citizens can speak freely, who can and will speak out? Foucault asks: 'Who in fact will speak and actually be able to bring his influence to bear on the decisions of others . . . proffering what he judges to be the truth?'[73] The free speech of all may in fact be a threat to truth:

'Not everybody can tell the truth just because everybody may speak.'[74] Rather than truth emerging from a dialogical process, it may be subsumed under the noise of chatter and rhetoric. If anyone can say anything they please, then rather than striving for truth and the good of the city, people may speak merely 'to ensure their own safety and their own success by pleasing their listeners, by flattering their feelings and opinions'.[75] Foucault thus notes the emergence of a paradox in certain Greek texts on democracy. The very agonism and contestation of egalitarian free speech that is meant to allow the truth to surface rather than be repressed under tyranny may also be a threat to truth. In a democracy, people may fear speaking out against the majority, against more skilled rhetorical rivals, or against flatterers and populists who tell people what they want rather than need to hear.[76]

Parresia in democracies comes with specific risks. Not necessarily death at the hands of a tyrant, but a risk of resentment from rivals or a loss of credibility. In claiming to speak the truth, the *parrhesiast* presents themselves as a truth-teller and not simply as another voice in the political game. For this reason, *parresia* represents an assertion of 'ascendancy' over one's peers in a democratic assembly.[77] While all have the right to speak, *parresia* is a special claim to be heard; it introduces difference into the 'formal egalitarianism' of free speech, presenting a risk to the speaker because the crowd may not accept that difference.[78] Consider the charge of 'reckless egotism' levelled at Davis.[79] The *parrhesiast* may face 'the jealousy of rivals who cannot tolerate one of them advancing and assuming ascendancy over the others'.[80] For example, by speaking out as an individual, the *parrhesiast* rejects collective voice such as that of their party. For these reasons, *parresia* requires courage; this is the 'Fearless Speech' and 'Courage of Truth' in the publication titles of two of these lecture series.[81]

The problematisation of truth in security politics

Let us now consider the problem of truth in security politics. As discussed in earlier chapters, two mechanisms keep most parliamentarians in a position of tutelage on security matters.

First, governments use systems of official secrecy and executive prerogative to restrict security knowledge. Second, parliamentarians reinforce their own ignorance through trust or self-exclusion, deferring to the right of the executive to hold security secrets for the purposes of national security, or simply resigning to their powerlessness because of their lack of knowledge and experience. There are practical and political reasons for this deference, such as not wanting to force the government to reveal the existence of sensitive security programmes, which might expose covert operatives to danger or undermine the tactical advantage of the security agencies over its targets, and the desire for national unity or to avoid the potentially dangerous and cynical politicisation of security.

The previous chapter discussed how the symbolic structures of security are open to abuse or bad faith. There are many examples of governments and their agencies using secrecy to hide wrongdoing, avoid embarrassment, stretch their legal remit, use their powers in ways that were never intended or foreseen by those who granted them, and perhaps even alter the fundamental constitutional relationship between governors and the governed through new technologies of surveillance and control. These abuses – real, imagined, perceived and contested – have prompted some security practitioners to become whistle-blowers, breaking their contract of secrecy to publicly reveal the truth of what they consider to be wrong, exposing themselves to the danger of prosecution in the process. Several scholars have argued that the whistle-blower can be considered a contemporary *parrhesiast*, Edward Snowden being the most prominent example in recent years.[82] However, the whistle-blower is not the same as the political *parrhesiast*. The whistle-blower has a secret to reveal and the politician does not (unless perhaps they are a minister resigning from office, but ministers do not generally become whistle-blowers). As such, David Davis can be considered a *parrhesiast*, but not a whistle-blower.

Snowden, although not himself a politician, did re-problematise the question of truth in security politics. After his revelations, many democracies struggled with the question of the proper constitutional balance between democratic transparency and operational secrecy. In the US, questions were raised about whether the head of the NSA James Clapper lied to Congress about the existence of surveillance programmes.[83] In the UK, where the response to Snowden's revelations was muted in comparison to other countries, there was nonetheless a public debate about democratic oversight of the intelligence agencies.[84]

The current UK parliamentary intelligence oversight body, the Intelligence and Security Committee, was already undergoing reform before Snowden's leaks and afterwards faced a stern test of whether it would either act as an apologist for the intelligence services or effectively hold them to account.[85] There was strong public and political pressure to reveal the truth of what Snowden had apparently exposed. Yet a question remains over whether the closed sessions of the ISC are the correct place to produce such truths and whether it is still appropriate to entrust such a responsibility to a group of insiders who are arguably too close to security officials.[86] Often they are not disinterested, with several having been ministers with security-related responsibilities in previous governments. This can lead to the peculiar situation where they may find themselves overseeing decisions they made themselves in their previous ministerial careers.[87] However, intelligence oversight is a debate for elsewhere; the concern of this book is not with security insiders but with the rest of the political arena.

The Snowden leaks compelled some politicians to say where they stood on security matters. Some expressed continuing trust in the security services; others warned of a distorted relationship between democracy, liberty and security.[88] Others simply stayed away from the debates. Yet if parliamentarians are to take a greater role in speaking on security, this raises *parrhesiastic* questions. Who can be trusted to speak out? What credibility do they have? How can we be sure that freer political speech on security will not result in an irresponsible and incoherent politicisation of sensitive security matters? As one Conservative MP asked in a parliamentary debate on the Snowden leaks: 'Does my hon. Friend agree that the very people about whom he is talking [intelligence officers] have been put under grave threat by some of the reporting, particularly by *The Guardian* newspaper, of the leaks?'[89] If security is becoming a more normal feature of the political game, as this book argues, how can 'truth' be practised? What form will it take? And what problems will it pose? Foucault, reviewing a scene from Plato's *Republic*, observes:

> In the hubbub of all the orators arguing with each other and trying to seduce the people and seize control of the helm . . . who will be listened to, approved, followed, and loved? It will be those who please the people, say what they want to hear, and flatter them. The others, those who say or try to say what is true and good, and not what pleases the people, will not be listened to. Worse, they will provoke negative reactions, irritation, and anger. And their true discourse will expose them to vengeance or punishment.[90]

Our modern notions of truth are not the same as those of the ancient Greeks, but they still pose *parrhesiastic* problems. The arts of political rhetoric still have no necessary connection with truth, being concerned with strategically persuading others of 'truths' that speakers themselves do not have to believe in (although genuine belief may help with the impression of sincerity).[91] Furthermore, as discussed under the Bourdieusian schema of the previous chapter, politicians are unavoidably engaged in a partisan struggle to defeat their opponents and persuade the public of their particular conception of political reality. The *parrhesiastic* slant on this is that when all parliamentarians have the right of free speech and are engaged in an agonistic game to defeat their opponents and secure electoral approval for their particular representation of the world, truth becomes a relative and partial notion towards which the public are understandably cynical. Extending this to security, although parliamentary convention has it that security is meant to be above politics, it is difficult to know if this is ever the case; as one interviewee cited in the previous chapter put it, 'Nothing escapes politics entirely.'[92] The necessary compromises of politics lead to a cynicism towards political truth claims. The traditional structural exclusions of security politics compound this.

Parresia as a rejection of the rules of the game

Foucault saw *parresia* as a practice for actors to cut through these problems of truth, power and politics. Yet although *parresia* is an irruption in discursive structures, it is not *ex nihilo* or without context – quite the contrary. Each instance of *parresia* that Foucault selects for examination is specific to particular political structures and circumstances. Acts of *parresia* are notable and meaningful only in relation to them. For example, Foucault relates the story of Dion, a disciple of Plato, in the court of the tyrant Dionysius.[93] Dion is the tyrant's brother-in-law. He enjoys privilege and high status in the city and does not wish to take the throne himself since he has all the honour and wealth that he needs.[94] Dion's truth-telling to Dionysius on the nature of his tyranny is not motivated by gain or, Foucault explains, by a desire to persuade, teach or discuss.[95] Rather it comes from a desire or obligation to speak the truth, whatever the personal risk or cost. What is notable in the story of Dion is that he went along with the 'game' of courtly life at his own personal benefit, and could have continued to do so, until the point when he chose not to. His *parresia* against Dionysius was for the sake of truth itself.

Foucault argues that '*Parresia* is a particular way of telling the truth'. He distinguishes this from the way discourses 'are usually analyzed either in terms of the structure of the discourse itself or in terms of the purpose of the discourse'.[96] We might map the first of these two 'usual' analytical options on to securitisation theory, which looks for the security 'grammar' or 'logic' in securitisation speech acts, and the second on to forms of rational choice theory, which assume that speech and action must be power-seeking or utility-maximising. *Parresia* is neither of these. This does not mean it is without purpose or intent, but rather that its meaning is to be found in the act itself. Acts of *parresia* problematise structures of discursive power and the dilemmas of speech, silence and risk they pose to individuals. By extension, they problematise wider societal and political structures of inclusion, exclusion and power.

Some of the basic tensions of British parliamentary politics rest upon these sorts of problems. British parliamentarians in fact have a greater right to free speech than the rest of us because of parliamentary privilege. They cannot be sued for libel, slander or defamation for what they say on the parliamentary estate.[97] This does not mean they speak freely all the time of course. Aside from specific issues relating to security, there are many reasons why they do not, such as demonstrating party loyalty, ambition for a government career and the fact that they play the political game not simply as individuals but as representatives of constituents and members of political parties engaged in a continuous electoral struggle. The British parliamentary system – where members of the government are drawn from the legislature and continue to hold seats there – is built on the premise that once an MP has taken a government position they will no longer speak freely but instead speak for the government and accept collective responsibility for its policies. Additionally, all new ministers are bound by the Official Secrets Act 1989 because they may need to be made aware of sensitive security-related matters, whatever their area of government.[98] (The members of the Intelligence and Security Committee face a similar dilemma of free speech. In effect they exchange access to the intelligence services for public silence on the details they hear.)

Free political speech thus represents a dilemma for MPs, who often have to weigh up the desire to join a current or future government to exercise power on the one hand and to defend their own political values, causes and consciences on the other. Often there may be no contradiction between these positions. But sometimes a desire to speak on pressing political issues such as security and civil liberties may be difficult to reconcile with government or party policy. Former MP Chris Mullin captures this dilemma perfectly in his memoirs, reflecting on his ill-considered choice to leave a prominent position in parliament as chair of the Home Affairs Select Committee – under which the committee had pressed the government for a greater parliamentary oversight of intelligence – for a lowly ministerial post that in effect silenced him.[99] At the time the political journalist Andrew Rawnsley wrote: 'Since he became a junior minister, Mr Mullin has been buried as effectively as if he had been fitted with concrete overshoes and dropped into the Thames.'[100]

The practice of ministerial resignation is one way to cut through these problems once one is in government. This is something the political game recognises and understands. It even has its own discourse of euphemisms, such as the classic 'resigning to spend more time with my family'.[101] Ministerial resignation is usually enacted through a letter or speech in which the resigning minister publicly rejects the official government discourse, especially if the speaker has no desire to maintain the goodwill of their former political masters. One of the most famous resignation speeches in British political history is that of Geoffrey Howe, deputy prime minister to Margaret Thatcher, who spoke out against her Europe policy. Like Davis's resignation speech, Howe's was not regarded as great oratory. But unlike Davis's speech, it had an effect: it was the 'kiss of death' to the PM, who resigned nine days later.[102] Howe later claimed that this was not his intention.[103] The special attention and personal cost attached to the act of ministerial resignation makes it notable in the game of parliamentary politics, but it is a practice that is understood within the rules of the political game, in contrast to Davis's apparently nonsensical act. In this sense, ministerial resignation fits Foucault's understanding of the 'performative' because it effectuates a known discourse. However, it does also invoke a *parrhesiastic* problem of political speech: when a minister chooses to resign on a matter of principle, it means they feel they can no longer speak for the government.[104] By leaving the government for the backbenches they reclaim their right to speak freely.

Davis was in a different situation, being in opposition rather than in government. He was in a position of some leadership and influence within the Conservative Party on security and civil liberties. But instead of playing along with the 'game', Davis seems to have felt that the encroachment of the security state on British liberties was such an important 'truth' that it needed to be expressed in an exceptional, individualised way, exhorting his peers and the public to see the true nature of security policies and their implications for liberty, democracy and society. Seen as an act of *parresia*, his resignation problematised the 'rules of the game' of security politics and rejected collective mechanisms of opposition. Instead of succumbing to the frustrations expressed by many backbench politicians on security, as explored in the previous chapter, Davis chose to act creatively in a way that was not comprehensible within the expectations of parliamentary politics. In taking a personal risk, Davis also rejected the 'rule' of political survival by staking his political career on his resignation. Although it was likely that he would win his re-election battle in a constituency where he had a reasonable majority, the implications for his reputation and career were less predictable. In his resignation speech he refers to the risk of not being returned to parliament: 'I [may] have made my last speech to the House.' Later, on the night of his re-election and having already been replaced in the shadow cabinet, he said: 'When I went into this I knew I was risking not just my shadow cabinet position but possibly my cabinet career.'[105] The BBC's political correspondent at the count concluded that, 'while he won the by-election, and continues to argue the debate on forty-two days, Mr Davis may have lost his position in the front rank of British politics for the foreseeable future'. In the event, although he did win his seat back, his act came at the cost of his shadow cabinet position and the likely office of home secretary in the 2010 David Cameron government. (In 2016, after the Brexit referendum, Davis was recalled from the backbenches to make a political comeback as Brexit Secretary, a post from which he resigned in July 2018. In 2008, when Davis resigned the first time, none of this was a foreseeable future.)

Davis's individual act of truth-telling also rejected three collective mechanisms of political veridiction through which he could have continued alongside his parliamentary colleagues to try to make the 'truth' of government security policies manifest. Many parliamentary practices can be understood as mechanisms for pursuing or producing different kinds of 'truth', such as the debate, the committee inquiry and the urgent parliamentary question, but Davis implicitly rejected three in particular: first, voting against the government in collusion with backbench Labour rebels; second, influencing the internal policy formation process of his party; and third, making security central to the impending general election campaign. It was widely understood that Davis was already making headway in all these areas, but he still chose to dramatically act in an individualistic way that was outside the political comprehension of peers and commentators. Indeed, those expressing consternation at Davis's act did not question the truth that he spoke but rather the means by which he spoke it. Arguably it was his choice to act so individualistically – when democracy is by nature a collective and dialogical process – that left Davis open to the charge of egotism. Let us now look more closely at these three rejected mechanisms.

First, the backbench rebellion. This is an established parliamentary practice whereby MPs vote against their own party line. In the 2008 vote on the Counter-Terrorism Bill, Davis's party and the Lib Dems were already opposing the government and had been joined by enough rebel Labour MPs to remove the chance of the government winning the vote with a majority from its own ranks. The government only got the bill through with support from the DUP, and this was a sign that the veracity of its policies was under serious question. It was not the first time the government had suffered a rebellion on this issue. We could say that a large proportion of the political arena considered that the government's account of the necessity of the measures in the bill was not 'truthful'; or, to use securitisation terminology, the government's securitising 'speech' that aimed to construct the necessity and legitimacy of the policy had not convinced its audience. For example, the Home Secretary's claim that the police had requested more counter-terrorism powers was not supported by evidence given to a parliamentary committee by the chief constable of the Metropolitan Police.[106] There was widespread suspicion that the government was pushing ahead with the bill for symbolic political reasons rather than operational need.

The parliamentary rebellion is not, however, a pure means of veridiction in politics. It remains couched in parliamentary arithmetic and political compromise. Although it has been a common trope for commentators to excoriate parliament for not resisting the government enough, in fact parliament has become increasingly rebellious over time.[107] However, frequently rebelling can be as damaging to an MP's democratic credibility and influence as never rebelling. When weighing up the dilemmas of loyalty versus principle, Chris Mullin refers disparagingly to serial rebels as the 'Usual Suspects', and not wanting to be one of them.[108] (These 'usual suspects' would have included Jeremy Corbyn, current leader of the Labour Party, with a record of being the most rebellious Labour MP of all.[109] His rebellions had come at little cost to himself, having held a safe seat and with no desire to join government. However, his track record has made it harder for him to expect party loyalty now he is leader.) In the case of the 2008 Counter-Terrorism Bill vote, Davis could have simply stayed in parliament and continued to work with Labour rebels, who indeed came close to defeating the government. Although during the first and second Labour terms under Blair, it could have been argued that the government had such a big majority and so much control over parliament that a coordinated rebellion would have been ineffectual, this was not the case under the smaller majority of the third Labour term. This was one reason why Davis's act seemed so inexplicable to his peers.

Second, Davis rejected his party and the collective voice of the shadow cabinet, even though on the face of it they agreed on security and civil liberties policy. His shadow cabinet colleague Liam Fox said, 'Many of us feel very similarly to David but his way of highlighting it, calling a by-election, was a personal decision, it wasn't something that was taken in consultation with the shadow cabinet.'[110] The party can be seen as a mechanism of veridiction in the sense that it produces policies through an internal dialogical process. Of course, the internal mechanisms and politics of this can vary and be contentious. The Labour government under Blair was often criticised for 'control freakery', with a central party elite exercising too much control over party policy. In contrast, the Liberal Democrats have an institutionalised mechanism of internal democracy, with the grassroots party approving policy at its annual conferences. The Soviet system would be the extreme example of the party as a mechanism of veridiction. Here, the party as the 'vehicle of the masses' was by definition a producer of truth; public 'self-criticism' was a practice in Communist countries whereby individuals renounced their mistaken 'subjective' views and deferred to the 'objective' truth of the party.[111]

It was not, however, that Davis believed his party had come to the wrong view and that he had to resign to assert the truth as an individual. As mentioned, Davis had been largely responsible for pushing his party to its policy position in the first place. In making such an individualistic gesture he rejected the collective voice of his party, not its version of the truth. His resignation also put the Conservative leadership in an awkward position. David Cameron came out as publicly supportive of Davis, later even visiting his constituency to campaign for him, but at the same time the Tory leader distanced himself from Davis's move, calling it 'a personal decision, a decision that he has made'.[112] Cameron did not keep Davis's shadow home secretary position open for him, replacing him the very night of the resignation. Perhaps their common position on civil liberties did not run very deep. Given also the comments from his closest peers about the 'insanity' of his act, Davis had seemingly touched a nerve regarding parliamentary convention and party discipline.

Third, Davis rejected the general election as a mode of veridiction, even though it was likely to vindicate his stance on civil liberties. The general election is arguably the most important means of veridiction in a democratic system, being the moment when the public decide which party's representation of the truth they prefer. Indeed, the etymology of 'manifesto' stems from the Latin 'to make public', 'clear' or 'obvious': a manifestation of the party's version of the truth that will be acted upon if and when they become the next government. Indeed, Bourdieu describes a central aspect of the political game as 'a struggle over the specifically symbolic power of making people see and believe, of predicting and prescribing, of making known and recognized'.[113] Parties and election campaigns are organised means of doing this. Davis could simply have said his piece and waited until the general election, which was only two years away. When the election came, the main opposition parties made unusually strong pledges on civil liberties in their manifestos, promising to roll back some of the most controversial of the Labour government's security measures. Given that the Conservative Party campaigned on a civil liberties platform that was largely of Davis's own making, his implicit rejection of the general election in favour of his own personal by-election was all the more exceptional.

Conclusion: 'Nevertheless, in spite of everything'

Parresia is a discursive practice that we might recognise in many areas of social and political life. While in Foucault's works the examples he chooses are heterogeneous, their common thread is the problematisation of structures of discursive power in particular political contexts. In this sense, Foucault's work on *parresia* follows the double-level method of problematisation outlined in Chapter 2: on one level it identifies and describes historically situated problematisations as found in discursive materials, in which contemporary actors saw a particular issue or situation as a problem, and on a second level it intervenes in those problematisations and amplifies them in a critical move which is directed at theories and assumptions in the present. This chapter followed the same method. Having used Bourdieu to set out the structures of security politics in Chapter 4, Chapter 5 has identified and described an episode in the recent history of the politicisation of security that worked to problematise those structures. At the same time, it has used that episode to further problematise present theoretical assumptions about security politics. While much of Bourdieu and securitisation theory holds true about security politics in the UK, the increasing politicisation of security is bringing the old institutionalised structures and conventions of security politics into question. As explained in previous chapters, the aim is not to refute those theories but to date them and explore their limits.

In short, the interest of this chapter in *parresia* is as a problematisation of security politics. Foucault asks of *parresia*: 'Where can this right, or possibility, or risky obligation to tell the truth be accommodated in a given regime?'[114] In parliamentary democracies, our representatives have a privileged right to speak out on anything, but for many reasons they hold back on security. This is largely for structural reasons as discussed in Chapter 4. It is not only coerced but also voluntary, conventional and explicable in terms of the 'rules of the game' of security politics. Politicians generally aim to be cautious and responsible in their handling of security matters. They may feel they do not have the competence, knowledge or expertise to speak on specialised security matters. In contrast, *parresia* is an example of when individuals do speak out, in spite of everything. It speaks to Weber's problematisation of the vocation of politics discussed in Chapter 1, in which the only way for a politician with a true calling to continue in the face of so many obstacles is to say '"Nevertheless" in spite of everything'.[115]

Parresia in parliamentary security politics is a problematisation of free speech in the political game. It questions how that game might meaningfully accommodate 'truth'. The problem for the political game, and the cynicism often attached to it, is that it involves tactics, compromise and the institutionalisation of differences over truths through the party system.[116] This always tempers the possibility that statements of 'truth' might be uncorrupted and authentic. As Weber pointed out, particularly when politics is a game played by professionals, a gulf emerges between the democratic authenticity of political representation and the necessary compromises of daily tactical struggles.[117] Whereas for Weber it was only heroic leader figures who could rise above the fray to 'seize the spokes of the wheel of history', Foucault does not look to a special kind of human to overcome the compromises of the political game, but rather to a special kind of act.[118]

So what does *parresia* mean in security politics? It means taking a risk to remove oneself from convention to invoke a different kind of truth that might be seen as more authentic as a result. Although we could judge *parrhesiastic* speech in the performative terms of securitisation theory by analysing the status of the speaker, the grammar of the statement, the response of the audience and the success or failure of policy outcomes, this would be to miss its significance. *Parresia* is not a performative speech act that invokes an established 'grammar' in order to construct a particular framing of 'security' as an intersubjective political 'truth'. Rather, it is a form of discourse in which the speaker is constituted as 'truthful' in the risky and costly act of speaking.

Judged in terms of Davis's intention 'to stop this thing in its tracks', his dramatic act of resignation was a failure. He failed to stop the Commons passing the legislative measure he was trying to defeat. Then four months later the House of Lords decisively defeated the forty-two-day detention measure anyway, as many had predicted.[119] All of this would have probably happened without Davis resigning. He damaged his credibility among his peers and gave himself a reputation as a 'reckless egotist'.[120] It removed his chance of wielding real power over security and civil liberties policy in the likely future office of home secretary. As a tactical move in the parliamentary game it was a bad one and Davis's retrospective justifications seem misjudged. However, his act had other effects. In keeping with Foucault's interest in *parresia* as a practice of subject constitution, for a time it further constituted Davis as a prominent voice in the wider campaign for civil liberties against security policy. As a senior politician and a Conservative, he lent cross-party credibility and weight to a campaign that was otherwise dominated by the liberal left, for example by appearing frequently alongside Liberty director Shami Chakrabarti (who subsequently became a Labour peer and shadow attorney general). Furthermore, his departure from the Conservative frontbench added to the momentum of party political opposition to Labour security policy and the politicisation of security generally. The 2010 Conservative-Liberal Democrat coalition agreement promised to implement 'a full programme of measures to reverse the substantial erosion of civil liberties under the Labour Government and roll back state intrusion', much of which it achieved (although Home Secretary Theresa May extended security policy in other ways, most notably through changes to the Prevent policy).[121] In 2011 the government allowed the legal time limit for pre-charge detention of terrorist suspects to lapse to fourteen days.[122] Ultimately, however, Davis's quixotic act tested the limits of possibility for individual action on security politics in the parliamentary arena. The next chapter examines a very different avenue for action: select committee inquiries, which draw on collective voice, common purpose, cross-party compromise and expert evidence.

Notes

1. See Neal, 'Normalization and Legislative Exceptionalism'.
2. BBC News, 'David Davis Resigns from Commons'.
3. BBC News, 'Blair Defeated over Terror Laws'.
4. For a comprehensive report on Parliamentary Labour Party rebellions in the 2001–5 parliament, see Cowley and Stuart, 'Dissension amongst the Parliamentary Labour Party, 2001–2005'.
5. Percival, Summers and agencies, 'Tories in Turmoil as David Davis Resigns over 42-Day Vote'.

6. Davis, 'Why I Am Resigning | Opinion'.
7. BBC News, 'David Davis Resigns from Commons'.
8. Swaine, 'Haltemprice By-Election: David Davis to Continue Civil Liberties Campaign'.
9. Ibid.
10. BBC News, 'David Davis Resigns from Commons'.
11. Watt, 'Brown Abandons 42-Day Detention after Lords Defeat'; Wintour and Watt, 'Desperate Brown Scrapes Through'.
12. Porter, 'David Davis to Resign from Shadow Cabinet and as MP'.
13. Interviewee 2.
14. BBC, 'David Davis MP, Desert Island Discs – BBC Radio 4'.
15. Kite, 'David Davis – "I'm Not Plotting – I No Longer Want to Be Conservative Party Leader"'.
16. Ibid.
17. Bourdieu, *The Logic of Practice*, p. 66.
18. Kite, 'David Davis – "I'm Not Plotting – I No Longer Want to Be Conservative Party Leader"'.
19. Ibid.
20. *The Independent*, 'Leading Article: Laudable Principle, Reckless Egotism'.
21. Ibid.
22. BBC, 'David Davis MP, Desert Island Discs – BBC Radio 4'.
23. Kite, 'David Davis – "I'm Not Plotting – I No Longer Want to Be Conservative Party Leader"'.
24. BBC, 'David Davis MP, Desert Island Discs – BBC Radio 4'.
25. Davis, 'Why I Am Resigning | Opinion'; BBC, 'David Davis MP, Desert Island Discs – BBC Radio 4'.
26. 'David Davis MP, Desert Island Discs – BBC Radio 4'.
27. Wikipedia, 'Parliament Acts 1911 and 1949'.
28. BBC, 'David Davis MP, Desert Island Discs – BBC Radio 4'.
29. Ibid.
30. Kaarbo and Kenealy, 'No, Prime Minister'; Strong, 'Interpreting the Syria Vote'; Gaskarth, 'The Fiasco of the 2013 Syria Votes'.
31. Conservative Party, *Invitation to Join the Government of Britain*, p. 79; Liberal Democrats, 'Liberal Democrat Manifesto 2010: Change that Works for You', in *Building a Fairer Britain*, p. 87.
32. 'The 2005–2010 Parliament easily goes down as the most rebellious in the post-war period': Cowley and Stuart, 'End of Parliament Stats – Stage 1'; see also Cowley and Stuart, 'Dissension amongst the Parliamentary Labour Party, 2001–2005'.
33. See Chapter 3.

34. House of Lords Select Committee on the Constitution, 'Fast-Track Legislation', p. 15.
35. Balzacq, 'The Three Faces of Securitization' and *Securitization Theory*; Bigo and Tsoukala, *Terror, Insecurity and Liberty*; Bigo, 'Security and Immigration'.
36. Foucault, *The Government of Self and Others*, p. 66.
37. Ibid. p. 67. See also Walters, 'Drone Strikes, Dingpolitik and Beyond'.
38. Dreyfus and Rabinow, *Michel Foucault*, p. 106.
39. Arguably, the same shifting internal structure can be found in all of Foucault's works. See Neal, 'Foucault'.
40. Foucault, *Fearless Speech*, *The Government of Self and Others* and *The Courage of Truth*.
41. Foucault, *The Government of Self and Others*, p. 66.
42. Ibid.
43. Ibid. p. 68.
44. Ibid. pp. 187–8.
45. Ibid. p. 188.
46. Ibid. pp. 6, 132, 354.
47. Ibid. p. 133.
48. Ibid. p. 5.
49. Ibid. pp. 159–60.
50. Ibid. p. 158.
51. Ibid. p. 159.
52. See Neal, *Exceptionalism and the Politics of Counter-Terrorism*; McDonald, 'Securitization and the Construction of Security', p. 578; Williams, 'Words, Images, Enemies', p. 512; Wæver, 'Politics, Security, Theory', p. 470.
53. Schmitt, *Political Theology*, p. 5.
54. Foucault, *The Government of Self and Others*, p. 4.
55. Ibid. p. 6.
56. Ibid.
57. Ibid. p. 42.
58. Ibid. p. 61.
59. Ibid.
60. Balzacq, 'The Three Faces of Securitization'.
61. Foucault, *The Government of Self and Others*, p. 61. Rita Floyd has pointed out that this 'illocutionary' reading renders the 'audience' superfluous in securitisation theory, because it is the performative act that does the work, not its acceptance by an 'audience'; see Floyd, 'Extraordinary or Ordinary Emergency Measures'.

62. Foucault, *The Government of Self and Others*, p. 62.
63. Ibid.
64. Ibid.
65. Ibid.
66. Ibid. p. 63.
67. Butler, *Gender Trouble*.
68. Foucault, *The Government of Self and Others*, p. 64.
69. Ibid. p. 193.
70. Ibid. p. 182.
71. Ibid. p. 56.
72. Ibid. p. 154.
73. Ibid. p. 188.
74. Ibid. p. 183.
75. Ibid.
76. Ibid. p. 184.
77. Ibid. p. 382.
78. Ibid.
79. *The Independent*, 'Leading Article: Laudable Principle, Reckless Egotism'.
80. Foucault, *The Government of Self and Others*, p. 300.
81. Foucault, *Fearless Speech* and *The Courage of Truth*.
82. See for example Mansbach, 'Keeping Democracy Vibrant'; Garrido, 'Contesting a Biopolitics of Information and Communications'; Seitz, 'Truth Beyond Consensus'; Carlson, 'Nietzsche's Snowden'.
83. Nelson, 'Lock Him Up?'.
84. Anderson, 'A Question of Trust'; Royal United Services Institute for Defence and Security Studies, *A Democratic Licence to Operate*; Intelligence and Security Committee of Parliament, 'Privacy and Security'; Raab, 'Security, Privacy and Oversight'.
85. Royal United Services Institute for Defence and Security Studies, *A Democratic Licence to Operate*, p. 95.
86. Ibid.
87. Ibid.
88. House of Commons, 'Westminster Hall, Backbench Business, Intelligence and Security Services, House of Commons Hansard Debates for 31 Oct 2013 (Pt 0001)'.
89. Julian Smith, in ibid.
90. Foucault, *The Courage of Truth*, p. 37.
91. Foucault, *The Government of Self and Others*, pp. 330, 370; Bourdieu, *Language and Symbolic Power*, p. 216.
92. Interviewee 2.

93. Foucault, *The Government of Self and Others*, pp. 47–57.
94. Ibid. p. 51.
95. Ibid. pp. 54–7.
96. Ibid. p. 52.
97. See UK Parliament, 'Parliamentary Privilege – Glossary Page'.
98. The Official Secrets Act 1989 'creates offences connected with the unauthorised disclosure of information in six specified categories by Government employees. These are: security and intelligence, defence, international relations, information which might lead to the commission of crime, foreign confidences, and the special investigation powers under the *Interception of Communications Act 1985* and the *Security Services Act 1989*.' Everett, Maer and Bartlett, 'The Official Secrets Acts and Official Secrecy'.
99. Mullin, *A View from the Foothills*, p. 106.
100. Ibid. p. 121.
101. See for example *The Guardian*, 'Spending More Time with the Family'.
102. Staff Blogger, *New Statesman*, 'Geoffrey Howe, 1990'.
103. Geoffrey Howe, *Conflict of Loyalty*.
104. In what claims to be 'the first fully quantified analysis of ministerial resignations in Britain in the postwar period', Keith Dowding and Won-Taek Kang report that in the period 1945–97, the majority of Labour government ministerial resignations were for matters of principle, but for Conservative governments less than half were, with as many taken up by sex scandals, financial scandals and professional errors. Dowding and Kang, 'Ministerial Resignations 1945–97'.
105. BBC News, 'Did David Davis Keep His Dignity?'.
106. For more details see Neal, 'Normalization and Legislative Exceptionalism'.
107. Cowley, *The Rebels*.
108. Mullin, *A View from the Foothills*, pp. 231, 558.
109. Cowley, *The Rebels*, p. 51.
110. Kite, 'David Davis – "I'm Not Plotting – I No Longer Want to Be Conservative Party Leader"'.
111. Larson points out that the practice served many other social functions; see 'Deviant Dialectics'.
112. BBC News, 'David Davis Resigns from Commons'.
113. Bourdieu, 'Political Representation', p. 181.
114. Foucault, *The Government of Self and Others*, p. 52.
115. Weber, 'The Profession and Vocation of Politics', p. 369.

116. Crick, *In Defence of Politics*, p. 4.
117. Weber, 'The Profession and Vocation of Politics'.
118. Ibid. p. 352.
119. Cockcroft, 'Timeline: How the 42 Day Detention Plan Was Dropped'.
120. *The Independent*, 'Leading Article: Laudable Principle, Reckless Egotism'.
121. BBC News, 'Full Text: Conservative-Lib Dem Deal'.
122. Green, 'Pre-Charge Detention Will Revert to 14 Days – GOV.UK'.

6. Security as Normal Politics: The Rise of Security in Parliamentary Committees

Historically, conceptually and institutionally, 'security' has been understood as existing in a pathological relationship to politics. 'Security' is of course political, but its conventions, practices and effects have been understood as inimical to the 'normal' practice of politics. The constitutional structures of states have traditionally reflected this. For example, governments have kept secretive security agencies at arm's length from open democratic scrutiny and have jealously guarded their Hobbesian security prerogatives. Yet responsibility for the anti-political qualities of security cannot be laid solely at the feet of government. As Chapter 4 noted, in the UK there has been a convention of parliamentary deference to the security state, based on a sense of propriety, responsibility and a lack of knowledge and expertise, although elements of this convention may now be falling away due to a post-Iraq breakdown in trust.

Against these historical conventions and structures, the central argument of this book is that the relationship between 'security' and professional politics is changing. In the UK, in demonstrable ways, security has been migrating out of its exceptional, institutionalised, anti-political 'black box' at the dark heart of the state. To invert the words of the Copenhagen School, security is becoming part of the 'normal run of the merely political', which by their definition is not where it is supposed to be.[1] This change is not primarily because the black box of security has been opened, although compared to the 1980s it has a little, with the creation of a limited parliamentary intelligence oversight mechanism in

1994 and further reform in 2013. Rather, it is because the meaning and scope of 'security' have broadened to include more and more areas of government and politics. This has created opportunities for professional political activity on security where there was little before.

This chapter uses the rise in parliamentary committee engagement with 'security' over time as an empirical indicator of the migration of 'security' into 'normal politics'. It examines Westminster select committees since 1979, the year the current system of departmental select committees was created. It presents a mostly quantitative analysis over time, analysing a trend of increasing security activity. This approach sacrifices some qualitative depth; for example, it does not investigate the reasons why every committee chose to inquire into the topics it did, which would require considerable time and resources.

The analysis finds that the cumulative number of committees to have substantively engaged with 'security' has grown from six in the 1980s to twenty-five in the present day. This is from a current total of about 100 committees. There are different ways to count the number of committees; this particular count does not include bill committees but does include House business committees. Also, the number of committees has increased over time. Committee engagement with security has grown from a very low base to the current situation in which 'security' appears in multiple committee contexts. This is symptomatic of the trend described by this book: the migration of 'security' into 'normal politics', which makes the old anti-political assumptions about security appear out of date.

The methodology employed here draws on that which was set out in Chapters 2 and 3. Identifying committee activity on security means invoking the question 'how do we know security when we see it?'. As Chapter 2 set out, this book aims to 'know security' not on the basis of an ahistorical, static and universal criterion, but, following Foucault, by identifying the problematisations expressed by contextual actors in discourse and practice. As discussed, although this method is primarily driven by contextual discourses, it is not an entirely 'actor-led' contextual hermeneutics along the lines proposed by Felix Ciută.[2] There are situations in which historical discourse does not speak for itself, and there are limits in 'seeing things their way'.[3] For example, an external analyst may have access to information that contextual actors did not have; they have a different historical and contextual vantage point; they may see systems of meaning in which contextual actors did not realise they were enmeshed; and they have the benefit of hindsight to see the implications and consequences of particular choices. Moreover, while the Foucaultian methodology developed by this book rests upon empirical validity, it is not based on (mythical) observational neutrality. Rather, it identifies and amplifies contextual problematisations on the basis of their critical implications for assumptions in the present, which here is the assumption that security is a form of anti-politics.

In this chapter, the content of problematisations is less important than the fact of their presence in the institutional 'arena' of 'normal politics', taken here as parliament. This follows the conceptual framework developed in Chapter 3 regarding the 'migration' of issues into particular institutional arenas as a form of politicisation. Translating this method practically, the analysis in this chapter looks at committee activity on 'security' as an indicator of this. Note that it is an indicator of the trend and not a comprehensive analysis of all parliamentary activity on security. Analyses of different parliamentary activities would also be possible, such as legislative activity, early day motions or parliamentary questions.[4] The analysis here includes select committees of the Commons and the Lords, and also the Intelligence and Security Committee (which until 2013 was not technically a parliamentary committee, and it still differs in being a statutory committee, but it is obviously significant in this context). The analysis excludes bill committees and other ad hoc committees unless directly relevant.[5]

In order to identify relevant committee activity, an initial keyword search was conducted on electronic archives of select committee reports from 1979 to the present day. This used the search terms 'security', 'intelligence', 'defence', 'terror/ist/ism', 'war', 'conflict' and 'arms'. Next, a manual search was undertaken of the same archive, using the report titles (and in cases of ambiguity the report content too) to identify substantive problematisations of 'security' that were missed by the initial search (for example, the 1985 Foreign Affairs Committee report on the British sinking of the Argentine battleship *General Belgrano* in the Falklands War is unhelpfully titled 'The Events Surrounding the Weekend of 1–2 May 1982'). Committee activity on security was interpreted as 'substantive' if the issues under consideration appeared to be wholly or mostly meaningful to the contextual actors as problematisations of 'security'. This excluded mere passing mentions of the word 'security' or similar. This criterion of contextual meaningfulness to the actors was also gleaned from secondary historical sources, particularly where the authors had interviewed contextual actors or conducted archival research themselves.[6] For the most part, therefore, the analysis was 'actor-led' along the lines set out by Ciută. However, it is the Foucaultian angle that allows for a historical analysis.

This is a genealogical analysis that treats problematisations of security as a historically moving target. The scope of what security meant in the mid-1980s and its range of governmental application was considerably narrower than what it means and how it is applied today. For example, although 'energy' has recently been problematised in security terms, in the 1980s it was not, at least not in the activities of parliament. This historical problematisation-based approach has three implications: first, the fact that an issue was not problematised in security terms until a particular time does not mean that it did not exist materially or in an alternately problematised way beforehand. For example, in the 1970s, industrial states faced an energy crisis because of political instability in the Middle East and oil price fixing by OPEC. This may have had grave implications for the 'national security' of those states, but nevertheless the energy crisis was not problematised as a 'security' problem in the activities of parliament. Second, this kind of Foucaultian historical analysis precludes the retrospective application of current meanings of security and insecurity. To take a methodological counter-example, while it is an important and legitimate political and analytical project to argue that women have always faced profound insecurities, to do so depends on a gendered problematisation of 'insecurity' that did not exist until at least the 1980s.[7] This would be incompatible with the methodology of this book, which is to identify when and in which political arena particular problematisations of security appeared. Third, the book's methodology precludes saying 'this is not really security'. This goes against the Copenhagen School position which, as discussed in Chapter 2, argues that 'The analyst can . . . intervene to countersay actors in relation to the use of the *word* security'.[8] In contrast, under this methodology, if the UK government chooses to include flooding in its 2010 National Security Strategy, whether or not this is 'really security' does not come into it; analytically it counts as a problematisation of security that should be dated to a particular time and place.

The stakes of committee politics: Democratic legitimacy and executive oversight

Parliamentary committees may not at first glance be the most exciting place to look for the politics of security. In a way that is the point, because security research is all too often drawn towards the dramatic and the 'exceptional'. Even in political science, interest in parliaments, let alone their committees, is a niche concern. In the media, specialist political programmes such as the BBC's *Today in Parliament* feature only highlights of committee activity, such as confrontations with ministers defending failing or contentious policies, heads of executive agencies defending poor performance, or business executives subjected to public humiliation for their tax avoidance practices. Most of what parliamentary committees do is little noticed beyond those with a direct interest. But this is the point: what could be more 'normal' than this kind of political work?[9] If 'security' is increasingly found here, then this challenges the assumption that security is a form of anti-politics.

Some background on the nature of the committee system in the UK is necessary. The Westminster parliament has used committees for hundreds of years for scrutiny, oversight, advice and inquiry, but the current system of permanent committees shadowing government departments dates from 1979.[10] These departmental select committees number twenty-one at the time of writing (twenty-three if we include Scottish and Welsh Affairs), but their number and form vary in line with the creation and reorganisation of government departments.[11] However, these amount to less than a quarter of the total number of committees.[12] Other committees have 'cross-cutting' remits that cover broader sweeps of government, such as the Public Administration and Public Accounts committees, or they look at specific issues, such as the Joint Committee of Human Rights and the Environmental Audit Committee. Others are concerned with parliament itself, its business, rights, standards, structures and administration (and these matters can be contentious, such as the role that parliament plays in the decision to take the country to war). The House of Lords has its own select committees, which in general aim not to replicate those of the Commons but rather focus on broader thematic areas, namely 'Europe, science, economics, communications, the UK constitution and international relations'.[13] Parliament sometimes sets up temporary committees for specific purposes, either independently or at the behest of government, such as to investigate the implications of a specific issue (where relevant these have been included in the analysis).

The Intelligence and Security Committee is an outlier in the committee system: although it was created as a 'committee of parliamentarians' in 1994, it was until recently more a creature of the executive than of parliament. It was not made into a parliamentary committee until 2013. Unlike the others it is a 'statutory committee' established by law. It still operates under special rules, as will be discussed later.

Unusually in comparative international terms, the select committees of Westminster are mainly for oversight of the executive; detailed legislative scrutiny is done through a separate system of non-permanent 'public bill committees' that are assembled ad hoc for each bill.[14] These are not included in the analysis. If they were, they too would indicate increased parliamentary activity on security, given the amount of terrorism legislation created since the late 1990s, for example. However, because their activity is entirely a product of the legislative programme of government, this would not reveal as much as the more independent activity of select committees (which still follows the activity of government to an extent). Occasionally, select committees or specially constituted

Table 6.1 Parliamentary Committees of the United Kingdom in 2018

Commons	Departmental	Business, Energy and Industrial Strategy; Communities and Local Government; Defence; Digital, Culture, Media and Sport; Education; Environment; Exiting the European Union; Food and Rural Affairs; Foreign Affairs; Health; Home Affairs; International Development; International Trade; Justice; Northern Ireland Affairs; Political and Constitutional Reform; Science and Technology; Scottish Affairs; Transport; Treasury; Welsh Affairs; Work and Pensions
	Topical	Arms Export Controls; Environmental Audit; European Scrutiny; Petitions; Public Accounts; Public Administration and Constitutional Affairs; Regulatory Reform; Statutory Instruments; Women and Equalities
	General	Delegated Legislation Committee; European Committees; Grand Committee; Legislative Grand Committee; Northern Ireland; Panel of Chairs; Public Bill Committee; Scottish Grand Committee; Welsh Grand Committee
	Internal	Administration; Backbench Business; Finance; Liaison; Members' Expenses; Privileges; Procedure; Selection; Standards; Works of Art
Lords	Topical	Communications; Constitution; Delegated Powers and Regulatory Reform; Economic Affairs; European Union; International Relations; Science and Technology; Scrutiny; Secondary Legislation
	Private Business	Hybrid Instruments; Internal: House; Liaison Committee; Privileges and Conduct; Procedure; Selection; Standing Orders
	Domestic	Administration and Works; Information; Refreshment; Works of Art
Joint	Select	Consolidation, etc. Bills; Human Rights; National Security Strategy; Palace of Westminster; Statutory Instruments
Statutory	Commons	House of Commons Commission (Administration Estimate Audit, Members Estimate, Members Estimate Audit); Public Accounts Commission; Speaker's Committee on the Electoral Commission; Speaker's Committee for the Independent Parliamentary Standards Authority
	Joint	Ecclesiastical Committee; Intelligence and Security

Source: Wikipedia.

committees do engage in legislative activity, such as 'pre-legislative scrutiny' of a bill in addition to the usual legislative stages, or occasionally 'post-legislative' scrutiny to review the operation of legislation.[15] In the Commons, pre-legislative scrutiny committees are often set up at the behest of the government, but select committees are free to review legislation on their own initiative if they wish.[16] There are important examples of this in the analysis below, and indeed it accounts for much of the increase in activity after 11 September 2001.

UK parliamentary committees have few formal powers, unlike, for example, US congressional committees. They have the power to 'send for persons, papers and records' but little else.[17] On traditional security matters such as secret intelligence, the government can and often does refuse.[18] The tasks of select committees were left largely undefined until recently, which was in part to maintain their freedom to set their own agendas.[19] After consultation in the early 2000s, the House of Commons Liaison Committee published a list of ten core committee tasks, which included examining policy proposals and emerging areas of policy; scrutiny of departmental expenditure, administration, appointments and documentation; and producing reports 'suitable for debate in the House'.[20] These remain guidelines only. As Brazier and Fox point out, the system 'enshrines the right of committees to hold as many inquiries as they wish, when they wish, on whatever issues are of interest to them providing they fall within the broad purview of departmental activity'.[21] This is important because, as we will see, some committees have used this freedom to engage with security in unexpected ways.

The committee system was boosted by the 'Wright reforms' of 2010, which increased their profile and legitimacy.[22] Although committee membership continues to reflect the balance of parties in parliament, the reforms have made committees more independent of party and executive influence. Reforms included internal parliamentary elections for chairmanships with additional salaries, and more transparent processes for selecting members.

The reforms have made committee chairmanships more desirable and prestigious. Some former senior ministers have taken these up, bringing experience and authority to the role. Recent examples include former Labour minister Margaret Hodge, outspoken chair of the Public Accounts Committee from 2010 to 2015, and former deputy Labour leader Harriet Harman, currently chair of the Joint Committee on Human Rights. Other MPs who for various reasons were never likely to hold government posts have used the committee system as an alternative career path, such as the Conservative MP and prominent Eurosceptic Bernard Jenkin, chair of the Public Administration Committee since 2010 (which in 2015 became the Public Administration and Constitutional Affairs Committee).

Unlike the wider partisan game, the main struggle of select committees is between parliament and the executive.[23] At stake is not victory over the other side, but rather the legitimacy and effectiveness of parliament in holding the government to account. As Rogers and Walters explain, consensus-seeking rather than partisanship is the norm in select committees, because they have little authority if their cross-party membership does not speak with a united voice: 'Even on highly contentious issues, select committees have a long history of operating in a consensual rather than an adversarial way.'[24] While the partisan considerations of committee members may play a part in choosing what topics to pursue, the decision is ultimately consensual, and for maximum credibility it is highly desirable that the ensuing report is too.[25]

However, it would be wrong to assume that partisan politics plays no role in committees, or that consensus-seeking is a straightforward or apolitical process. The internal workings of committees have remained rather mysterious until recently, and the traditional institutionalist methodology of parliamentary studies was not suited to peering inside. Marc Geddes has pioneered the use of ethnography to examine the interaction between committee members, clerks and the external witnesses who provide written and oral evidence to committee inquiries, revealing complex 'webs of scrutiny'.[26] He argues that 'a consensual report is not necessarily based on evidence but what is politically feasible', and that a 'committee inquiry is inherently political'.[27] This may lead, for example, to the avoidance of topics where there may be strong partisan divisions.

In the UK, the select committee system is widely regarded as a success.[28] Yet in light of their broad and unfixed tasks and their lack of formal constitutional powers, measuring that success is not straightforward. Benton and Russell, following a long line of literature, point out that empirical measures of committee influence or effectiveness are problematic.[29] For example, although select committees make recommendations to government, it is not possible to simply count which of them are adopted in order to assess 'influence'.[30] The government may have implemented such changes anyway without the suggestion of the committee, recommendations may be formally accepted but not ultimately implemented, or the government may formally reject recommendations only to implement them in another form later on.[31] Tracing causal influence is also problematic. For example, interest groups may simultaneously lobby the government and give evidence to committees on the same policies, making it difficult to isolate the influence of committee recommendations.[32] Benton and Russell nevertheless conclude that select committees are influential, but their most important forms of influence are indirect and intangible. They argue that these include influencing the 'direction' of policy debate, gathering and publishing evidence, 'drawing attention to overlooked issues', 'exposing wrongdoing or poor decision-making' and 'generating fear (anticipated reactions)'.[33] They add that the last of these – 'anticipated reactions', when ministers and civil servants are influenced by 'the threat of future evidence sessions and inquiries' – is probably the most important but also the most difficult to discern (see also Chapter 4).[34]

This all has implications for understanding committee engagement with security. For example, some of the committee norms described above may be amplified on security topics. A desire to serve the national interest or a sense of responsibility can make partisan contention within committees even less likely. For these reasons, the Defence Committee has never divided on one of its reports (meaning that it has always managed to reach internal consensus and avoid an internal vote or a minority report from disagreeing members).[35] The same is apparently true of the ISC according to one former member, although it does not publish its internal voting records (presumably because to do so could unduly politicise a security issue if there was a non-unanimous vote).[36]

In some ways, committee activity on security counteracts some of its traditional anti-political effects. Compared to individual MPs, committee members are less encumbered by deference or a lack of expertise. They become part of a group that transcends party, has institutional memory and is animated by shared purpose. They can launch their own inquiries, commission specialist advice, call for evidence and invite witnesses. In so doing they constitute themselves as an alternative authority that may be able to challenge the executive on security matters. Committees thus offer a chance for parliamentarians to practise security politics more creatively and proactively. By taking the initiative to launch their own inquiries, for example, they can problematise security in novel ways and even attempt to securitise issues. If they do so in committees that do not have a traditional security remit, they may implicitly bring into question the traditional authority structures and prerogatives of 'security'.

Noting these considerations for understanding committees, the analysis will now investigate their pattern of activity on security over time. What follows is a narrative discussion of parliamentary security politics from 1979 to 2017, based on archival analysis of committee activity and secondary sources. The sections are organised roughly into decades, although a strict periodisation would serve little purpose.

The 1980s as 'traditional' security politics and the beginnings of change

The history of parliamentary security politics before the 1980s is not uneventful but is more or less stable and unchanging. Taking the 1980s as an analytical starting point does not refer to a precise date in the history of security politics but is significant for three reasons. The first is Ole Wæver's semi-rhetorical question, mentioned in previous chapters. He asks: 'Did securitization theory maybe appropriately capture only the politics of security of 1995 or 1985?'[37] This book answers yes, and so looks to the

1980s to substantiate that answer (empirically there is no great difference between 1985 and 1995, as we will see). The second (related) reason is that in this book's extended UK case study, the 1980s represent the historical norms of security politics rather well. In the 1980s we find an institutionalised form of securitisation represented by a constitutionally 'exceptional' security black box at the heart of the state and almost complete parliamentary marginalisation from security issues. Here it could indeed be said that security was an anti-politics. Of course, this does not mean that security was not 'political'. As the analysis will show, some security-related issues were contentious, particularly for the left, such as the status and activities of MI5. Nevertheless, the political centre held around the convention that security was in effect a special kind of politics, as discussed in Chapter 4. The third reason is merely practical: the current departmental select committee system was created in 1979 and it is convenient to take an analysis of committee activity back to here, even though the analysis covers further types of committee.

At this point it is worth discussing the main secondary accounts relating to parliamentary security politics in this period, namely those of Bochel et al. and Christopher Andrew. Bochel et al. are primarily concerned with parliamentary oversight of intelligence rather than 'security' more broadly. Andrew is the official historian of MI5. Bochel et al. cite Andrew to describe the historical position of the intelligence services in the British constitution until the mid-1980s. This was governed by two conventions that were only partly codified: first, the intelligence agencies did not officially exist and would be treated as such by the government, and second, by extension, the intelligence agencies would not be subject to 'external scrutiny or regulation'.[38] Bochel et al. point out that the agencies were in fact subject to ministerial scrutiny (which was technically external to the agencies but not the executive), although in some cases ministers and prime ministers apparently preferred to keep the agencies at arm's length.[39] These conventions were practised and enforced in a number of ways, including Erskine May's parliamentary rulebook deeming any questions about the security services to be out of order, the clerks refusing to table such questions and the government refusing to answer them, or at least answering with only the standard line 'the government does not comment' (which is the British version of the famous US 'Glomar response' of 'neither confirm nor deny').[40] UK security politics did indeed resemble the narrow and exclusive form of decision making with limited dialogue and choice that securitisation theory describes.

There had been several slips in the edifice of secrecy over the decades, usually when prime ministers were forced to comment on events. From these events and comments, the existence of secret intelligence, intelligence officers and intelligence agencies could be inferred. Examples include Prime Minister Stanley Baldwin's 1927 reading out in parliament of intercepted Soviet telegrams to explain a diplomatic schism with Moscow, and in the 1960s and 1970s the handling of difficult questions about the Cambridge spy ring by Prime Ministers Harold Macmillan and Edward Heath.[41]

Change began to occur in the mid-1980s. Bochel et al. point to the 1985 Interception of Communications Bill as a significant moment in the history of parliament's relationship with the intelligence agencies. Tony Benn MP noted in the legislative debate: 'it is one of the few occasions – I cannot recall another one – when we have had a debate on the security services.'[42] Bochel et al. think it is the first debate.[43] Although at no point did the government acknowledge the existence of MI5, other speakers referred to MI5 with no apparent controversy.[44] Evidently MI5 was not so much a taboo but a legal anomaly and an open secret that the government policy of non-acknowledgement was designed to accommodate. The resulting legislation put the surveillance powers of the intelligence agencies into law for the first time, although not the existence of the agencies themselves (it did not mention them by name). It also created a commissioner to handle complaints from individuals who thought they had improperly had their communications intercepted.

In the eight-hour debate on the bill there was clearly an appetite among parliamentarians to discuss not only its provisions but also the activities of MI5 itself.[45] There were frequent references to a contemporaneous television documentary based on the claims of an MI5 whistle-blower, Cathy Massiter, who alleged surveillance of the CND, trade unions and civil liberties organisations, which reinforced the suspicions held by some Labour members. Andrew argues, 'Many Opposition MPs believed that the Security Service had become a political tool of the right.'[46] In terms of the historical norms of security politics this episode displays much that is familiar from the security literature: complaints about discretionary definitions of national security (or frustration with the symbolic security prerogative of the executive and its potential for abuse), caution against handing too many powers to the executive and uncertainty about the ideological persuasions of future governments who may use those powers.[47]

However, Andrew argues that 'The most influential attack on the traditional taboos came . . . from the courts' rather than parliament.[48] The European Court of Human Rights had ruled that phone tapping by an unspecified UK agency had no basis in law.[49] It was this that forced the UK government to create a statutory basis for surveillance powers in the 1985 Interception of Communications Act.[50] Cases such as these made the policy of intelligence deniability increasingly untenable for two reasons: first, it was difficult to legally defend the actions of agencies and officers that did not officially exist, and second, the powers of the agencies had no legal basis, they had fallen foul of the European Convention on Human Rights and they would continue to do so.[51] According to Andrew, it was the security services themselves who were first convinced of the need to legalise their own existence and they lobbied the reluctant Thatcher government to do so.[52]

Bochel et al. support the view that court proceedings had this effect, including a failed government legal attempt to prevent former MI5 officer Peter Wright from publishing his memoir *Spycatcher*.[53] However, they also note several openings for change.[54] For example, after the Falklands War the government commissioned a review by a committee of privy counsellors (who swear an oath of secrecy to the Crown, and many of whom are MPs) into the conflict and associated intelligence failures, which led to the 'Franks Report' (which is not strictly a parliamentary committee inquiry and so has not been included in the count below).[55] The Foreign Affairs Committee also conducted a Falklands inquiry, specifically on the sinking of the Argentine battleship *General Belgrano*.⁵⁶ The government allowed both committees to have access to intelligence material under special arrangements. Bochel et al. argue that this established a principle of parliamentary oversight and set a precedent for sharing intelligence with committees – two developments that fuelled the demand for fuller parliamentary oversight of intelligence and security.⁵⁷

An examination of select committee activity in the 1980s supports the narratives of Bochel et al. and Andrew. Although these authors are respectively concerned with intelligence oversight and the intelligence agencies themselves (rather than 'security' more broadly), the conclusions to be drawn on this decade are similar. Simply put, there was little parliamentary engagement with 'security' in the 1980s. Only five Commons select committees undertook any substantive security-related work, six if the count includes the report by the Committee on Privileges on 'Speaker's Order of 22 January 1987 on a Matter of National Security', which related to the right of the Commons Speaker to prevent parliamentary speech on national security matters. The five committees were Defence, which published several reports a year on a range of military matters; Foreign Affairs, which published a smaller number of security-related reports on, for example, 'The Economic and Political Security of Small States', contemporary wars such as 'Current UK Policy towards the Iran/Iraq Conflict' and the Falklands inquiry mentioned above; Public Accounts, which published regular reports on defence budgets and procurement (and also a 1988 inquiry into 'computer security', which must be one of the first parliamentary examples of this particular problematisation); Transport, which regularly inquired into airport and rail security; and Home Affairs. This last was active on race relations, immigration and policing, but these topics were not often explicitly associated with 'security' until the 2000s (although the roots of this policy linkage go back to the 1980s).⁵⁸ Its only substantive security-related engagement in the 1980s was an inquiry into 'Special Branch', the opening paragraph of which offers an insight into the mutually reinforcing dynamic of exclusion and self-exclusion discussed in previous chapters:

> Our inquiries into the special branches of the police force have inevitably been severely restricted by what we recognised from the start as the need to avoid any disclosure of matters which could damage national security. Because of the close relations which exist between the special branches and the security services we have been inhibited from investigating individual complaints and cases. To have done so, or to have investigated special branch working methods, could have cast light on the activities and methods of the security services and assisted those who are opposed to the safety of the state. For this reason we agreed at the start of the inquiry that no questions would be allowed which dealt with matters of national security, and that all our evidence would be heard in public.[59]

Perhaps surprisingly, the Northern Ireland Affairs Committee published nothing explicitly related to security in the 1980s, being concerned only with 'normal' policy areas such as housing, education and social security (welfare). It could be argued that these areas were all 'institutionally securitised' to an extent, because every aspect of social, economic and political life was implicated in sectarian divisions in Northern Ireland, and for the most part still is. However, the committee's activities in the 1980s do not meet the criterion of substantive problematisations of security.

The 1990s: Intelligence oversight and post-Cold War security issues

In the 1990s there is little change from the pattern of the 1980s. The most significant event in the relationship between parliament and security is the creation of the Intelligence and Security Committee (ISC) in 1994. The 1989 Security Service Act had put the existence of MI5 into law and created the first form of external oversight in the form of a commissioner and a tribunal. Bochel et al. point out that the bill preceding the 1989 Act had been the first opportunity for parliament to debate the intelligence agencies since the 1985 Act discussed above.[60] In the debate, several members called for the creation of a system of democratic intelligence oversight, but it was not until the Intelligence Services Act 1994 that the government conceded (the Act also put MI6 and GCHQ

Table 6.2 Substantive committee engagements with 'security' in the 1980s

Committees	Reports
Defence	[Examples of many] 1984 'The Physical Security of Military Installations in the United Kingdom' 1985 'Security at Royal Ordnance Factories and Nuclear Bases' 1989 'The Physical Security of Military Installations in the United Kingdom'
Foreign Affairs	1984–85 'The Economic and Political Security of Small States' 1985 'The Events Surrounding the Weekend of 1–2 May 1982' [*Belgrano* inquiry] 1987 'Current UK Policy towards the Iran/Iraq Conflict'
Home Affairs	1984–85 'Special Branch'
Privileges	1987 'Speaker's Order of 22 January 1987 on a Matter of National Security'
Public Accounts	[Examples of many] 1984–85 'Maintenance of Major RAF Equipments [*sic*]' 1985–86 'Production Costs of Defence Equipment' 1987–88 'Computer Security in Government Departments'
Transport	1985 and 1998 'Airport Security'

Source: Cumulative total number of committees to have engaged substantively with 'security' = 6.

on a statutory footing, as the 1989 Act had done for MI5).[61] However, as with developments in the 1980s, Bochel et al. argue that parliament could not be given much credit for this:

> In contrast to a number of other states, most notably the US, where legislation for intelligence oversight and reform was forced upon governments by revelations of intelligence agency abuse, legislation in the UK was not the result of sustained pressure from within Parliament or beyond, and came at a time when the agencies themselves felt reform would be beneficial.[62]

Security as Normal Politics

The ISC, until its reform by the Justice and Security Act 2013, was not a parliamentary select committee but an unusual 'committee of parliamentarians'. It was not housed on the parliamentary estate but in the Cabinet Office, which sits at the organisational heart of government, thus placing 'security' literally outside the arena of parliament and inside the arena of government. The unusual constitution of the ISC reflected its sensitive remit and the continuing predominance of the executive in security matters. ISC members were selected by, and answered to, the prime minister, who had, and still has, the power to redact ISC reports before they are laid before parliament. Even after the Justice and Security Act 2013 reformed the ISC into a 'committee of parliament', many parliamentarians continued to see the ISC as being too close to the security establishment and acting as its cheerleader rather than overseer.[63] ISC members are aware of this dilemma. As a former ISC member interviewed for this book put it, although the ISC may be 'less partisan' (as in its lack of internal politics), it risks being 'more partisan towards the agencies'.[64]

The closed forum of the ISC does not give members a platform for grandstanding or pursuing personal ambitions in public, unlike other committees or parliamentary venues where evidence sessions may be broadcast, for example.[65] This is one reason why the partisan struggle is suspended here to a greater extent than anywhere else.[66] The former member explained: 'It's not that it's not political, but that we all agree.'[67] This may be a reflection of ISC membership selection, which is controlled by the executive and favours senior parliamentarians, especially those with ministerial experience of security policy and of working with the intelligence agencies from the Foreign, Defence and Home departments, and excludes those who may be ideologically suspicious of the agencies and their work. One recent exception was Scottish National Party Westminster leader Angus Robertson MP, appointed to the ISC after the SNP became the third largest party in a landslide victory of Scottish Westminster seats at the 2015 general election. Robertson was a longstanding critic of UK security and defence policies and of course an advocate of Scottish independence. It is impossible to know if his appointment unsettled the traditional harmony of the committee. His membership of the ISC did not appear to make him less strident and he continued to pose oral and written questions to ministers about civil and military nuclear policy and procedure.[68] This little experiment came to an abrupt end when Robertson lost his seat in the 2017 snap general election.

In 1994, the creation of the ISC represented a limited opening up of the 'black box' of state security. As well as allowing a select few senior parliamentarians inside, Bochel et al. argue that it created new opportunities for parliament to debate intelligence matters where there had been almost none before, for example with parliamentary debates on ISC annual reports. Andrew Defty argues that the gradual turnover of ISC membership has led to a growing number of former ISC members remaining in parliament who bring experience and a willingness to speak on intelligence matters, and so has increased the collective intelligence expertise of parliament.[69] However, Bochel et al. consider that the pace of change and learning has been slow, and that the existence and work of the ISC has not significantly led the wider body of parliamentarians to increase their interest or expertise in intelligence matters.[70] For example, debates on ISC reports continue to suffer from low attendance, with the speakers usually limited to current and former members of the ISC itself.[71] Bochel et al. argue – based on interviews with many parliamentarians – that as a result the ISC remains a source of tension and frustration regarding the role of parliament in intelligence oversight.[72] Nevertheless, despite the constitution of the ISC being a compromise between government secrecy and parliamentary accountability, Bochel et al. consider that the annual reports of the ISC have shone light on the practices of the intelligence agencies.[73] Indeed, by all accounts the ISC is hard working, meets at least weekly and spends long hours in close contact with the intelligence agencies.[74]

Perversely, the creation of the ISC also had an effect opposite to this limited opening up: governments have frequently used the existence of the ISC as a reason to prevent other committees from gaining access to intelligence or from hearing evidence from intelligence agency staff.[75] In the second half of the 1990s the relationship between the ISC and other select committees became a source of tension. The Defence, Foreign Affairs and Home

Affairs Committees considered themselves to have an interest in the work of the intelligence services because MI5 reports to the home secretary, MI6 and GCHQ report to the foreign secretary, and (in theory at least) the Defence Intelligence agency reports to the defence secretary.[76]

The Home Affairs Committee stance was notable compared to its lack of engagement with 'security' in the 1980s: in the 1990s the Committee constituted itself as an active player in parliamentary security politics. For example, in 1999 under chair Chris Mullin it conducted an inquiry into the 'Accountability of the Security Service'.[77] This was a direct challenge to the intelligence oversight arrangements that had been set up only five years earlier, which the Home Affairs Committee described as 'merely transitional'.[78] The Intelligence Services Act 1994 was meant to have established that MI5 was accountable to the ISC and not to the Home Affairs Committee. The committee's report highlighted many of the inadequacies of the ISC discussed above and called for many of the changes that were eventually made in 2013, such as making the ISC a true parliamentary committee, having it meet on the parliamentary estate, and giving it greater investigative powers and more independence from the executive.[79] The report also describes a pattern of refusal from the government to select committee requests for access to intelligence and intelligence officials.[80]

Bochel et al. note that the committees of Trade and Industry and Foreign Affairs made similar complaints around this time.[81] The Trade and Industry Committee conducted an inquiry into possible arms exports to Iran by the British company BMARC in contravention of a ban. Its report noted: 'intelligence material is the one area where we have not obtained evidence we requested during present inquiry.'[82] It was the same with a 1999 Foreign Affairs Committee report on events in Sierra Leone (preceding UK military intervention in 2000), with complaints that the Foreign Secretary had refused them access to intelligence reports: '[he] told us that the Intelligence and Security Committee (ISC) set up under the Intelligence Services Act 1994 was the appropriate committee to examine the work of the SIS [Secret Intelligence Service – MI6].'[83] The Foreign Secretary also refused access of the type arranged for the committee's 1984 inquiry into the sinking of the *Belgrano*, which he claimed was a one-off, not a precedent.[84] In 2000, the Liaison Committee (a parliamentary business committee made up of the chairs of all the select committees) commented on these tensions in a report on the relationship between select committees and the executive, which included a section on 'Accountability of the intelligence and security services'.[85] This noted what was already known: 'The Government has been reluctant to provide information about these [intelligence] agencies to select committees, or to allow members of the agencies to give evidence.'[86]

Beyond intelligence access, in terms of broader select committee activity on security in the 1990s, there was not a significant increase compared to the 1980s. The Home Affairs Committee produced a report on 'The Private Security Industry' in 1994 that somewhat pre-empts current academic debates on the issue, although it only relates to domestic security contractors (everything from nightclub door staff to CCTV operators) rather than, for example, private military companies.[87] The Trade and Industry Committee conducted the 1996 BMARC inquiry mentioned above. The Defence, Foreign Affairs and Public Accounts Committees continued their regular work, including inquiries into the costs of contemporary conflicts such as the Gulf War and the former Yugoslavia.

Some change occurred with the 1997 election of a Labour government under Tony Blair. The Northern Ireland peace process saw the Northern Ireland Affairs Committee begin to directly address security-related matters, starting with an inquiry into the 'Composition, Recruitment and Training of the RUC [Royal Ulster Constabulary]' in 1997. The incoming government created the Department for International Development (DfID), and as a matter of course an International Development select committee was created to shadow it. The committee produced a number of security-related reports from the beginning, including 'Conflict Prevention and Post-Conflict Reconstruction' in 1998, 'Kosovo: The Human Crisis' in 1999 and 'The Future of Sanctions' in 2000. The year 1999 also saw the creation of the Quadripartite Committee, renamed the Committee on Arms Export Controls in 2008. This is not a true committee (and hence has not been included in the count below) but rather a forum for four committees with an interest in arms controls to work together: Defence, Foreign Affairs, International Development, and Trade and Industry (which after several name changes to reflect department reorganisations is currently called the Business, Energy and Industrial Strategy Committee). The Transport Committee became less active on security in the 1990s and did not produce the reports on transport security that it had in the 1980s (from 1997 to 2001 it became the Environment, Transport and Regional Affairs Committee, which may have given it less time to focus on transport security).

The Labour government passed the landmark Human Rights Act 1998, which fully incorporated the European Convention on Human Rights into British law. This was accompanied by the creation of a new Joint Committee on Human Rights which took a strong interest in security issues, although it did not convene until 2001. Arguably, the Human Rights Act emboldened parts of parliament, including the JCHR, to challenge government security prerogatives.[88] The House of Lords European Union select committee also became active on security because of the development of the EU's Common European Policy on Security and Defence from the late 1990s. The committee created a new sub-committee that reported on developments annually, publishing its first report in July 2000.[89]

Away from the select committees, parliament was becoming more active on security in other ways. The Labour government passed extensive new counter-terrorism legislation beginning with the Criminal Justice (Terrorism and Conspiracy) Act 1998 in response to the Omagh bombing. It then passed the Terrorism Act 2000 which – after a long drafting and consultation process – rationalised and normalised UK terrorism law in light of the Northern Ireland peace process. This was meant to end the decades-old habit of creating knee-jerk legislation in the wake of a terrorist attack (of which the 1998 Act is an example), but that did not last long after the 11 September 2001 attacks.[90] The events of 9/11 prompted copious legislation and parliamentary committee activity on security, as the next section will discuss.

For most of the 1990s, parliamentary security politics resembles the institutionalised securitisation and marginalised democratic politics described by the Copenhagen School. The birth of limited parliamentary intelligence oversight in 1994 entrenched this tradition as much as reformed it, because it maintained the principle and practice of a security 'black box' at the heart of government. At the same time, this spurred demands from other committees for more access. In particular, the Home Affairs Committee established its interest in security matters, and many of its demands for intelligence oversight reform were eventually implemented in the Justice and Security Act 2013.

Change only began to occur in the security/politics relationship towards the end of the decade. The change of government in 1997 created new areas of governmental and parliamentary activity related to security, such as international development and human rights. This mirrored a broadening of the meaning of 'security' itself in international policy and academic circles, such as the rise of 'human security' discourses and common EU security policies. The growth of liberal interventionism under Blair, including interventions in Sierra Leone and Kosovo, also created work for security-interested parliamentary committees. The Northern Ireland peace process had the perverse effect of allowing the Northern Ireland Affairs Committee to engage with security issues directly for the first time. The 1990s sees the cumulative number of committees to have substantively engaged with 'security' rise from six to twelve (including the unusually constituted ISC).

The 2000s: Post-9/11 politicisation

The 2000–2001 session of parliament began on 6 December 2000, while in terms of analytical significance the 2000s really began on 11 September 2001. In the ten months before that, committee activity on security proceeded as before, with the Northern Ireland Committee continuing its new engagement with security by publishing a report on 'Relocation Following Paramilitary Intimidation', and the Lords European Union Select Committee

Table 6.3 Substantive committee engagements with 'security' in the 1990s (including the 1999–2000 parliamentary session which ended on 30 November 2000)

Committees	Reports
Defence	[Example of many] 1995 'Reconnaissance, Intelligence, Surveillance and Target Acquisition'
Foreign Affairs	1994 'UK Policy on Weapons Proliferation and Arms Control in the Post-Cold War Era' 1999 'Sierra Leone'
Home Affairs	1994 'The Private Security Industry' 1999 'Accountability of the Security Service'
Intelligence and Security	1995–2000 Annual Reports 1996 'Report on Security Service Work against Organised Crime' 1999 'Sierra Leone'
International Development	1998 'Conflict Prevention and Post-Conflict Reconstruction' 1999 'Kosovo: The Human Crisis'
Liaison Committee	2000 'Shifting the Balance: Select Committees and the Executive'
House of Lords European Union Select Committee (sub-committee on EU Common Foreign and Security Policy)	2000 'The Common European Policy on Security and Defence'
Northern Ireland Affairs	1997 'Composition, Recruitment and Training of the RUC'
Public Accounts	[Examples of several] 1992 'The Costs and Receipts Arising from the Gulf Conflict' 1996 'Management of the Military Operations in the Former Yugoslavia'
Trade and Industry	1996 'Export Licensing and BMARC' 1997 'Aspects of Defence Procurement and Industrial Policy'

Source: Cumulative total number of committees to have engaged substantively with 'security' (including Transport and Privileges from previous) = 12.

sub-committee on EU Common Foreign and Security Policy continuing its work.

The events of 9/11 and the start of the 'war on terror' prompted a big increase in governmental activity on security and a corresponding increase in parliamentary activity. From that point onwards, security moved further out of its traditional 'black box' and into the arena of 'normal' parliamentary politics, although arguably under a general discourse of emergency.[91] The first development was the Anti-Terrorism, Crime and Security Bill 2001, through which the government proposed new counter-terrorism powers. The powers were controversial, such as detention without charge of foreign terrorist suspects, but so was the bill itself, being exactly the kind of post-terrorist-attack legislation that the 2000 Terrorism Act was supposed to end.[92] Several committees took a direct interest. Although departmental select committees do not often scrutinise legislation, two chose to do so in this case, namely Home Affairs and Defence. Two non-departmental committees that do have a legislative role – the Lords Constitution Committee and the new Joint Committee on Human Rights – also inquired into the bill.

At the same time, the Foreign Affairs Committee began what would become an annual series of reports on the 'Foreign Policy Aspects of the War against Terrorism', which amounted to seven reports published between 2001 and 2006. In other committee work relating to counter-terrorism and what Jason Burke calls the '9/11 Wars', the Commons Science and Technology Committee inquired into 'The Scientific Response to Terrorism' in 2003.[93] This examined the best ways to harness scientific expertise to detect and counter threats from chemical, biological, radiological and nuclear weapons, following the appearance of weapons of mass destruction on political agendas. The International Development Committee reported on 'The Humanitarian Crisis in Afghanistan and the Surrounding Region' in 2001, and on 'Preparing for the Humanitarian Consequences of Possible Military Action against Iraq' in 2004.

Throughout the decade, strong governmental security agendas in the UK, EU and US continued to drive committee activity. Much of this was on draft legislation. The Lords Constitution Committee published reports in 2005 on the Terrorism Bill, Identity Cards Bill and Prevention of Terrorism Bill, in 2006 on the Armed Forces Bill, in 2008 on the Counter-Terrorism Bill and in 2010 on the Crime and Security Bill. It also conducted broader inquiries on 'Waging War: Parliament's Role and Responsibility' in 2006, 'Fast-Track Legislation: Constitutional Implications and Safeguards' in 2009 and 'Surveillance: Citizens and the State', also in 2009. The Lords Delegated Powers and Regulatory Reform Committee examined the Iraq War Inquiry Bill and Counter-Terrorism Bill in 2008. The Justice Committee – a departmental select committee created when the Ministry of Justice was spun off from the Home Office in 2007 – also inquired into the Counter-Terrorism Bill in 2008.

Beyond legislation, other committee activity was concerned with counter-terrorism policies more generally. The Lords EU committee looked at the EU/US Passenger Name Record (PNR) Agreement in 2007 and 2008 (a transatlantic policy that increased data sharing on international travel after 9/11). The Committee also inquired into 'Money Laundering and the Financing of Terrorism' in 2009. And because under Labour the Department for Communities and Local Government led the 'Prevent' strand of the CONTEST counter-terrorism strategy, its corresponding departmental select committee became engaged with security policy when it inquired into 'Preventing Violent Extremism' in 2010. The Northern Ireland Committee continued its security-related activity, some of which mirrored wider themes in the 'war on terror', such as its 2002 report on 'The Financing of Terrorism in Northern Ireland'.

The UK and international counter-terrorism agenda alone does not explain every aspect of the growth in committee activity on security in the 2000s. Other aspects reflect a more general broadening of the meaning and practice of 'security'. Examples include the Trade and Industry Committee report on 'Security of Energy Supply' in early 2001, anticipating what is now an established energy security agenda with a rather different meaning of security; the Environment, Food and Rural Affairs Committee report on 'Climate Change, Water Security and Flooding' in 2003; the Lords Science and Technology Committee's report on 'Personal Internet Security' in 2007; and the Innovation, Universities, Science and

Skills Committee report on 'Biosecurity in UK Research Laboratories' in 2008 (a short-lived committee that replaced the Science and Technology Committee for two years because of departmental reorganisations). The 2009 Lords Constitution Committee inquiry 'Surveillance: Citizens and the State' – mentioned above – fits into this category of broadened security too. The Scottish Affairs Committee made its first engagement with security-related issues in 2008, on the topic of 'Employment and Skills for the Defence Industry in Scotland'.

It is difficult to conclude anything other than 11 September 2001 being a turning point in parliamentary activity on 'security'. In some ways it is obvious that this should be the case: governmental security agendas became so broad that they spilled into multiple policy areas and hence multiple areas of parliamentary activity, drawing in committees such as Communities and Local Government and Science and Technology. It is also the case that 'security' became politicised in the qualitative sense of becoming more salient and controversial, arousing public and parliamentary interest. Whereas in the 1980s only six committees had any substantive engagement with 'security' (at a time when it had a narrower meaning and policy scope), and by the 1990s a cumulative total of twelve committees had engaged as the concept began to broaden, the 2000s saw the total rise to twenty-two.

These engagements were driven by two forces: first, the qualitative politicisation and increasing public salience of traditional areas of security, such as secret intelligence and executive prerogative powers; and second, the continuing broadening in meaning and application of 'security' across further areas of social, political and economic life and government activity. In one sense, more areas and issues were constructed as having security implications, which could be loosely described as 'securitisation', but this did not result in what the Copenhagen School theory of securitisation would expect: an 'extreme politicization' that damages 'normal politics' by shifting security issues out of 'normal' political deliberation and bargaining. The effect was the opposite, bringing 'security' into the 'normal' political arena.

Security as Normal Politics

Table 6.4 Substantive committee engagements with 'security' in the 2000s (up to and including the 2009–2010 parliamentary session)

Committees	Reports
Constitution (Lords)	2005 Terrorism Bill 2005 Identity Cards Bill 2005 Prevention of Terrorism Bill 2006 Armed Forces Bill 2006 'Waging War: Parliament's Role and Responsibility' 2008 'Counter-Terrorism Bill: The Role of Ministers, Parliament and the Judiciary' 2009 'Fast-Track Legislation: Constitutional Implications and Safeguards' 2009 'Surveillance: Citizens and the State' 2010 Crime and Security Bill
Communities and Local Government	2010 'Preventing Violent Extremism'
Defence	[Example of many] 2001 'Changes in Jurisdiction Proposed under the Anti-Terrorism, Crime and Security Bill 2001'
Delegated Powers and Regulatory Reform Committee (Lords)	2008 Iraq War Inquiry Bill 2008 Counter-Terrorism Bill
Environment, Food and Rural Affairs	2003 'Climate Change, Water Security and Flooding'
Energy and Climate Change Committee (created 2008)	2009 'Securing Food Supplies up to 2050: The Challenges Faced by the UK'
European Union (Lords)	2004 'EU Security Strategy' 2005 'European Defence Agency' 2007, 2008 EU/US Passenger Name Record (PNR) Agreement 2009 'Money Laundering and the Financing of Terrorism'
Foreign Affairs	[Examples of many] 2001 'Foreign Policy Aspects of the War against Terrorism' 2002 'The Decision to Go to War in Iraq'
Home Affairs	[Example of many] 2001 'First Report on the Anti-Terrorism, Crime and Security Bill 2001'
Intelligence and Security	2002 'Inquiry into Intelligence, Assessments and Advice prior to the Terrorist Bombings on Bali' 2003 'Iraqi Weapons of Mass Destruction – Intelligence and Assessments' 2005 'The Handling of Detainees by UK Intelligence Personnel in Afghanistan, Guantanamo Bay and Iraq' 2006 'Report into the London Terrorist Attacks on 7 July 2005' 2007 'Rendition' 2009 'Review of the Intelligence on the London Terrorist Attacks on 7 July 2005'

Table 6.4 *Continued*

Committees	Reports
International Development	[Examples of many] 2004 'Preparing for the Humanitarian Consequences of Possible Military Action against Iraq' 2005 'Darfur, Sudan: The Responsibility to Protect' 2006 'Conflict and Development: Peacebuilding and Post-Conflict Reconstruction'
Joint Committee on Human Rights	[Example of many] 2001 'Anti-Terrorism, Crime and Security Bill 2001'
Northern Ireland Affairs	2002 'The Financing of Terrorism in Northern Ireland' 2008 'Policing and Criminal Justice in Northern Ireland: The Cost of Policing the Past' 2009 'The Omagh Bombing: Access to Intelligence' 2010 'The Omagh Bombing: Some Remaining Questions'
Public Accounts	[Examples of many] 2002 'Ministry of Defence: Combat Identification' 2003 'Ministry of Defence: Building an Air Manoeuvre Capability: The Introduction of the Apache Helicopter' 2007 'Recruitment and Retention in the Armed Forces' 2008 'The Privatisation of QinetiQ' 2009 'Defence Information Infrastructure'
Public Administration	2007 'Reserve Forces' 2009 'The Iraq Inquiry'
Science and Technology (including Innovation, Universities, Science and Skills Committee which replaced the committee from 2008 to 2009)	2003 'The Scientific Response to Terrorism' 2008 'Biosecurity in UK Research Laboratories'
Science and Technology (Lords)	2007 'Personal Internet Security'
Scottish Affairs	2008 'Employment and Skills for the Defence Industry in Scotland'
Transport Committee (reconstituted after being subsumed into the Environment, Transport and Regional Affairs Committee from 1997 to 2001)	2005 'UK Transport Security – Preliminary Report' 2006 'Piracy'
Trade and Industry	2002 'Security of Energy Supply'

Source: Cumulative total number of committees to have engaged substantively with 'security' (including Liaison and Privileges from previous) = 22.

2010 onwards

In 2010 there was a change of government from Labour to a Conservative/Liberal Democrat coalition. The next chapter discusses how this new government distanced itself from the legislative security agenda and foreign policy adventurism of the Blair and Brown administrations, and how its 'austerity' agenda eclipsed the symbolic dominance of 'security' of the post-9/11 years. In terms of committee activity there were fewer new committee engagements with security than in the previous decade. No notably new meanings or applications of 'security' come into usage (at the time of writing the decade is not yet finished, and the remainder is likely to be dominated by Brexit). Overall committee activity on security also appears lower. One notable new area was on the security implications of potential Scottish independence in the run-up to the 2014 referendum. For example, in 2014 the Scottish Affairs Committee published a report entitled 'The Referendum on Separation for Scotland: A Defence Force for Scotland – A Conspiracy of Optimism?', and other committees with a more established security remit also examined the Scottish question, such as Defence and Foreign Affairs.

The first new committee engagement with security was the Public Administration Committee. In 2010 it launched an inquiry into the government formulation of 'strategy'. This was in the context of the Strategic Defence and Security Review and National Security Strategy, which the new government was about to publish. The Committee's report 'Who Does UK National Strategy?' asked critical questions about the nature and scope of 'security' and how the more general 'direction' of government and the country are set. It said:

> The central contention of our Report is that Government has lost the capacity to think strategically. The burden of expert evidence we received was that short termism and reaction to events predominate in recent Whitehall practice. The ability to articulate our enduring interests, values and identity has atrophied. Strategy is too often thought of as a plan for action or a document rather than a process which needs to be articulated constantly and updated regularly.[94]

In terms of UK constitutional traditions on national security, this represents an activist and even impertinent departure for a parliamentary committee, especially one with no established security remit.

The second new engagement was by the Political and Constitutional Reform Committee, which existed from 2010 to 2015. This was established in part to examine the work of Deputy Prime Minister Nick Clegg as leader of the junior coalition party, the Liberal Democrats.[95] The committee inquired into 'Parliament's Role in Conflict Decisions' in 2011 and 2014, the latter prompted by the August 2013 parliamentary vote on Syria.[96] This topic was also of interest to other parliamentary committees, with the Lords Constitution Committee addressing it in 2006 with an inquiry entitled 'Waging War: Parliament's Role and Responsibility', and again in 2013 with 'Constitutional Arrangements for the Use of Armed Force'.

The third new engagement arose from the establishment of a Joint Committee on the National Security Strategy (JCNSS) in 2010, to coincide with the publication of a National Security Strategy and creation of a National Security Council (discussed at length in the next chapter). A JCNSS member suggested that it had been slow to gain respect in parliament.[97] Reasons suggested included the fact that it meets only quarterly, unlike other committees which meet weekly, and it has a fairly narrow remit: not national security as such, but the National Security Strategy specifically. The interviewee also suggested that the chairs of the other security-related select committees had not wanted their authority diluted by the new committee, although this is difficult to confirm.[98] Since 2012, the JCNSS has published one report a year, the first three of which were simply reports on its work on the 2010 NSS. In 2015 and 2016 its reports focused on the subsequent edition of the NSS and Strategic Defence Review (which were combined in 2015, whereas previously they had been separate). In 2017 it started branching out and published its first thematic report, on the 'Conflict, Stability and Security Fund', a central fund created by the government for departments to use for projects relating to peace and stability.[99]

Security as Normal Politics

Two other developments in committee activity are worth noting in the period 2010 to 2017. The first is ISC reform. With the Justice and Security Act 2013, the ISC became a parliamentary committee rather than a committee of parliamentarians. It was given new powers, such as being able to require rather than merely request evidence from the security services, and to inspect their facilities. In addition to these reforms, the ISC also expanded its own mandate, openness and workload unilaterally.[100] For example, it has become more outward facing, undertaking a number of firsts including a (largely symbolic) public evidence session with the three intelligence service heads, a public call for written evidence for an inquiry into communications surveillance, and the publication of interim statements about its ongoing work.[101] It now meets in the Palace of Westminster rather than the Cabinet Office, bringing it physically into the arena of parliament. In its 2015–17 guise under chair Dominic Grieve MP it has been more robust towards the government. For example, an ISC press release announcing its report into 'UK Lethal Drone Strikes in Syria' said:

> This failure to provide what we consider to be relevant documents is profoundly disappointing. Oversight depends on primary evidence: the Government should open up the ministerial decisionmaking process to scrutiny on matters of such seriousness.[102]

Despite this profoundly undeferential stance, the ISC is still unavoidably shaped by the compromises involved in the democratic oversight of secret intelligence: it still does most of its work in secret and its reports are still subject to executive redaction. The selection process for ISC members has changed but is in effect still controlled by the prime minister.[103]

The second development is the increasing use of draft bill committees for security matters. This technically falls outside the scope of this chapter, but it does represent significant parliamentary activity in terms of security entering the arena of 'normal politics'. Draft bill committees are a form of 'pre-legislative scrutiny' first introduced by the Labour government in 1997.[104] This is when draft legislation is scrutinised by committee (either existing select committees or specially constituted ones) before going through its main legislative stages on the floor of the House, rather than after them by bill committees as in the formal 'committee stage' of the legislative process. There is no discernible pattern as to when pre-legislative scrutiny is used and the decision to do so is largely in the hands of government parliamentary business managers.[105]

Before 2010 the only security-related bill to have been treated in this way was the Counter-Terrorism Bill 2008. Since 2010 the use of this process on security topics has grown, with a Joint Committee on the Draft Detention of Terrorist Suspects (Temporary Extension) Bills in 2011, a Joint Committee on the Draft Communications Data Bill and a Joint Committee on the Draft Enhanced Terrorism Prevention and Investigation Measures Bill in 2012, and a Joint Committee on the Draft Investigatory Powers Bill in 2015–16.

The significance of the increasing use of these draft bill committees warrants further research as it may have implications for security politics, but there is no space to undertake this here.[106] For example, pre-legislative scrutiny can arguably improve the quality of a bill.[107] Instead of the partisanship of legislative debates on the floor of the House, or rubberstamping by public bill committees, more independent-minded cross-party joint committees with specialist expertise can call for written and oral evidence from experts and interest groups. While there is limited evidence, it seems that pre-legislative scrutiny can have specific effects on security-related legislation. For example, one frequent complaint is that the arguments put forward by ministers for new security laws and powers are made on the basis of privileged information and therefore compound the symbolic power imbalance between the executive and parliament. Ministers may make claims about necessary responses to security threats which can only be proved with secret intelligence, or claims about the operational needs of the police or security services which have only been communicated to ministers in private. However, when security legislation is put into pre-legislative scrutiny the arguments can be better tested by calling witnesses such as senior police officers, security experts and so on. This can have the effect of diluting the informational and symbolic advantages held by the executive.

A good example is the Counter-Terrorism Bill 2008, which was put into pre-legislative scrutiny seemingly as a government depoliticisation strategy to overcome criticism that it had too often rushed security legislation through parliament.[108] However, no witnesses called to give evidence supported the arguments made by Home Secretary Jacqui Smith about the police needing extended forty-two-day pre-charge detention for 'terrorist suspects'.[109] This was part of the episode that led the Shadow Home Secretary David Davis to resign his seat, as discussed in Chapter 5. If creating a draft bill committee was a depoliticisation strategy, it was not successful.

Conclusion: The migration of security into the political arena

A quantitative analysis of committee engagement with security as offered by this chapter is not an entirely straightforward exercise, particularly when looking at a period of nearly four decades. The meaning and scope of 'security' is a moving target. So are the lives of the committees themselves, with new committees created and old ones replaced. Nor can this broad historical sweep hope to delve into the reasons why each committee conducted the inquiries they did, beyond those offered in committee reports and what may be apparent from the wider context. To do so would require a different methodology altogether, such as the ethnography of Geddes, and would necessarily sacrifice breadth for depth. It would also be difficult to investigate historical inquiries when the members have long since departed.

Even with this caveat there is a clear pattern. In the 1980s the number of select committees to have substantively engaged with security was six, roughly what it was for many years before and several years after. In 2017, the cumulative number of committees to have substantively engaged with security at least once in their institutional existence was twenty-five. This cannot decisively tell us whether 'security' has been entirely normalised in qualitative terms to become like any other policy area, but it does suggest that 'security' has extensively entered the 'arena' of 'normal politics'.

Table 6.5 Substantive committee engagements with 'security' from 2010 to 2017 (parliamentary session began 25 May 2010)

Committees	Reports
Business, Innovation and Skills	2012 'Scrutiny of Arms Exports Controls' 2014 'Scrutiny of Arms Exports Controls' 2016 'The Use of UK-Manufactured Arms in Yemen' (joint inquiry with International Development Committee)
Constitution Committee (Lords)	2010 Terrorist Asset Freezing etc. 2011 Terrorism Prevention and Investigation Measures Bill 2012 Justice and Security Bill 2013 'Constitutional Arrangements for the Use of Armed Force' 2014 Data Retention and Investigatory Powers Bill 2016 Investigatory Powers Bill
Defence	[many examples – business as usual]
Energy and Climate Change Committee	2011 'The UK's Energy Supply: Security or Independence?'
Foreign Affairs	[selected examples] 2011 '1st Report – Future Inter-Parliamentary Scrutiny of EU Foreign, Defence and Security Policy' 2013 'Foreign Policy Considerations for the UK and Scotland in the Event of Scotland Becoming an Independent Country' 2014 'The Use of Diego Garcia by the United States' 2015 'The Extension of Offensive British Military Operations to Syria' 2016 'The UK's Role in the Economic War against ISIL'
Home Affairs	[selected examples] 2010 Counter-Terrorism Measures in British Airports 2011 'New Landscape of Policing' 2012 'Olympics Security' 2013 'Counter-Terrorism' 2014 'Regulation of Investigatory Powers Act 2000' 2015 'Counter-Terrorism: Foreign Fighters' 2016 'Radicalisation: The Counter-Narrative and Identifying the Tipping Point'
Intelligence and Security	2013 Access to Communications Data by the Intelligence and Security Agencies 2013 Foreign Involvement in the Critical National Infrastructure 2013 GCHQ's Alleged Interception of Communications under the US PRISM Programme 2014 Report on the Intelligence Relating to the Murder of Fusilier Lee Rigby 2015 Report on Women in the UK Intelligence Community 2015 Report on Privacy and Security 2016 Report on Draft Investigatory Powers Bill 2017 Report on UK Lethal Drone Strikes in Syria

Table 6.5 *Continued*

Committees	Reports
International Development	[example] 2013 'Global Food Security'
Joint Committee on Human Rights	[example] 2016 'Counter-Extremism'
Joint Committee on the National Security Strategy	2012 'First Review of the National Security Strategy 2010' 2013 'The Work of the Joint Committee on the National Security Strategy in 2012' 2014 'The Work of the Joint Committee on the National Security Strategy in 2013–14' 2015 'The Next National Security Strategy' 2016 'National Security Strategy and Strategic Defence and Security Review 2015' 2017 'Conflict, Stability and Security Fund'
Northern Ireland Affairs	2014 'Downey Disclosure Papers' 2015 'The Administrative Scheme for "On-the-Runs"'
Political and Constitutional Reform Committee (existed from 2010 to 2015)	2011 'Parliament's Role in Conflict Decisions' 2014 'Parliament's Role in Conflict Decisions: A Way Forward'
Public Accounts	[example] 2014 'Army 2020'
Public Administration and Constitutional Reform, replaced by Public Administration and Constitutional Affairs from 2015	2011 'Who Does UK National Strategy?'
Science and Technology Committee (Commons)	2012 'Devil's Bargain? Energy Risks and the Public' 2015 'Investigatory Powers Bill: Technology Issues'
Scottish Affairs	2012 'The Referendum on Separation for Scotland: Terminating Trident – Days or Decades?' 2013 'The Referendum on Separation for Scotland: How Would Separation Affect Jobs in the Scottish Defence Industry?' 2014 'The Referendum on Separation for Scotland: A Defence Force for Scotland – A Conspiracy of Optimism?'
Transport	2013 'Land Transport Security – Scope for Further EU Involvement?' 2014 'Security on the Railway'

Source: Cumulative total number of committees to have engaged substantively with 'security' = 25.

In the 1980s and early to mid-1990s the meaning of 'security' was narrow, relating mainly to defence and intelligence. It broadly reflected the meaning of security used in 'traditional security studies', as discussed in earlier chapters.[110] The governments of the time and indeed the Commons Speaker actively sought to limit parliamentary engagement with 'security', first through a blanket taboo on parliamentary questions about intelligence and security that lasted until the late 1980s, and then by treating the ISC as the exclusive arena for such discussions.

In the late 1990s committee engagements with security started to increase. New committees covered the activities of government that were implicated with security in different ways, such as international development. This mirrored the rise of new security agendas such as 'human security' and 'humanitarian intervention'. At the same time, select committees demanded more access to intelligence and the agencies. Security further spilled out of its traditional 'black box' and into other policy areas when government departments became newly involved in security policy, such as the 'Prevent' counter-radicalisation policy led by the Department for Communities and Local Government (until 2010, when the Home Office took over).

Despite academic calls to 'forget 9/11', in the four-decade period under analysis, it is difficult to avoid the conclusion that the attacks of 11 September 2001 are the most significant event in the growth of committee activity on 'security'.[111] Committees responded to government security policy initiatives and what they perceived as increased public interest. The controversial way Labour ministers invoked secret intelligence to justify their policies in the post-9/11 era, such as the decisions to go to war and to detain 'terrorist suspects', also politicised security in the qualitative sense.

Aside from the drama of 9/11 there may be other factors at work in the full period under analysis. Meg Russell and Philip Cowley have drawn on several large datasets to analyse parliamentary trends over the past half-century, including backbench rebellions, defeats of the government in the Lords, bill amendments and select committee influence; they conclude: 'Changes in parliamentary organization, behaviour, and resources mean that its influence has almost certainly increased over the past half-century.'[112] This is likely to be reflected in its engagements with security too. It is also striking that committee activity on security mirrors the appearance of new topics in academic security studies and in international policy agendas. The trend is the same whichever correlations and possible explanations are given weight: 'security' has been migrating into the 'arena' of 'normal politics'.

Notes

1. Buzan, Wæver and de Wilde, *Security*, p. 5.
2. Ciută, 'Security and the Problem of Context'.
3. Skinner, *Visions of Politics*, vol. 1, pp. 1–7.
4. See the discussion of other metrics in Bochel, Defty and Kirkpatrick, *Watching the Watchers*, pp. 128–55.
5. Note that the limitations of the digitised parliamentary archives for the 1980s meant that it was only possible to search the activities of the permanent Commons and Joint select committees in this period, and not Lords committees and other ad hoc committees in the earliest part of the timeframe under analysis. However, other primary and secondary sources offer no indication that this resulted in the exclusion of anything significant.
6. Bochel, Defty and Kirkpatrick, *Watching the Watchers*.
7. Buzan and Hansen write of 'the writings on gender, peace and security that first materialized in the early 1980s': *The Evolution of International Security Studies*, p. 139. See also, to name but a few, Sylvester, 'Tensions in Feminist Security Studies' and *Feminist Theory and International Relations in a Postmodern Era*, vol. 32; Tickner, *Gender in International Relations*; Hudson, '"Doing" Security as though Humans Matter'; Wibben, *Feminist Security Studies*.
8. Buzan, Wæver and de Wilde, *Security*, p. 47, fn. 9, their emphasis.
9. Freeman, 'Political Work: Inaugural Lecture', University of Edinburgh, 2015; Leigh and Freeman, 'Teaching Politics after the Practice Turn'.
10. Rogers and Walters, *How Parliament Works*, p. 346.
11. Wikipedia, 'Parliamentary Committees of the United Kingdom'.
12. Rogers and Walters, *How Parliament Works*, p. 347.

13. UK Parliament, 'Select Committees'; Rogers and Walters, *How Parliament Works*, p. 378.
14. Benton and Russell, 'Assessing the Impact of Parliamentary Oversight Committees', p. 772.
15. Law Commission, *Post-Legislative Scrutiny*; Kelly, 'Pre-Legislative Scrutiny – Commons Library Briefing'.
16. Rogers and Walters, *How Parliament Works*, p. 355.
17. Kelly, 'Select Committees: Evidence and Witnesses – Commons Library Briefing'.
18. Bochel, Defty and Kirkpatrick, *Watching the Watchers*, pp. 173–5.
19. Brazier and Fox, 'Reviewing Select Committee Tasks and Modes of Operation', p. 356.
20. Ibid. p. 357, citing para. 13 of House of Commons Liaison Committee, 'Select Committee on Liaison First Report'.
21. Brazier and Fox, 'Reviewing Select Committee Tasks and Modes of Operation', p. 357.
22. Russell, '"Never Allow a Crisis to Go to Waste"'.
23. For discussion of the 'political game', see the examination of Bourdieu in Chapter 4; Bourdieu, *The Logic of Practice*, p. 66.
24. Rogers and Walters, *How Parliament Works*, p. 181.
25. Geddes, *Dramas at Westminster*.
26. Geddes, 'Building Webs of Scrutiny'.
27. Ibid. p. 15.
28. Fisher, 'The Growing Power and Autonomy of House of Commons Select Committees'; Marsh, 'The Commons Select Committee System in the 2015–20 Parliament', p. 96; Bates, Goodwin and McKay, 'Do UK MPs Engage More with Select Committees since the Wright Reforms?'.
29. Benton and Russell, 'Assessing the Impact of Parliamentary Oversight Committees', p. 773.
30. Ibid. p. 775.
31. Ibid.
32. Rogers and Walters, *How Parliament Works*, p. 374.
33. Benton and Russell, 'Assessing the Impact of Parliamentary Oversight Committees', p. 792.
34. Ibid. p. 793.
35. Interviewee 5.
36. Interviewee 1.
37. Wæver, 'Politics, Security, Theory', p. 473.
38. Bochel, Defty and Kirkpatrick, *Watching the Watchers*, p. 27; Andrew, *The Defence of the Realm*, p. 753.

39. Bochel, Defty and Kirkpatrick, *Watching the Watchers*, pp. 36–7.
40. Ibid. p. 30; May, *A Treatise on the Law, Privileges, Proceedings and Usage of Parliament*, 21st edn, p. 292. See for example Hansard 1803–2005, 'Points of Order (Hansard, 4 November 1987)'. The response is still standard today; see for example UK Parliament, 'Sellafield: Written Question – HL1269'; Wikipedia, 'Glomar Response'.
41. Bochel, Defty and Kirkpatrick, *Watching the Watchers*, pp. 31–4.
42. House of Commons, 'Interception of Communications Bill (Hansard, 12 March 1985) Vol. 75 Cc151-244'.
43. Bochel, Defty and Kirkpatrick, *Watching the Watchers*, p. 49.
44. House of Commons, 'Interception of Communications Bill (Hansard, 12 March 1985) Vol. 75 Cc151-244'.
45. Ibid.
46. Andrew, *The Defence of the Realm*, p. 1912.
47. See for example Neocleous, *Critique of Security*; Loader and Walker, *Civilizing Security*; Neal, *Exceptionalism and the Politics of Counter-Terrorism*.
48. Andrew, *The Defence of the Realm*, p. 1906.
49. Ibid. p. 1907.
50. Ibid.
51. Ibid. pp. 1912–27.
52. Ibid. p. 1931.
53. Bochel, Defty and Kirkpatrick, *Watching the Watchers*, p. 43.
54. Ibid.
55. Ibid. p. 44; Franks and Privy Council, 'Falkland Islands Review'.
56. Foreign Affairs Committee, 'Third Report from the Foreign Affairs Committee, Session 1984–85: Events Surrounding the Weekend of 1–2 May 1982'.
57. Bochel, Defty and Kirkpatrick, *Watching the Watchers*, p. 45.
58. See Huysmans, *The Politics of Insecurity*, p. 71.
59. Home Affairs Committee, 'Special Branch: Fourth Report from the Home Affairs Committee, Session 1984–85'.
60. Bochel, Defty and Kirkpatrick, *Watching the Watchers*, p. 56.
61. Ibid. pp. 56–61.
62. Ibid. pp. 71–2.
63. Interviewee 1. See also Rifkind, 'Intelligence Oversight in the UK: The Intelligence and Security Committee'.
64. Interviewee 1.
65. Interviewee 1.
66. Alan Beith, quoted in Bochel, Defty and Kirkpatrick, *Watching the Watchers*, p. 81.

67. Interviewee 1.
68. See *The Scotsman*, 'MP Raises Questions over 266 Fires on Nuclear Subs'; Acronym Institute, 'Angus Robertson Asks if MoD Will Place the Defence Nuclear Executive Board's Risk Register for the Nuclear Programme in the Library'.
69. Defty, 'Educating Parliamentarians about Intelligence'.
70. Bochel, Defty and Kirkpatrick, *Watching the Watchers*, p. 102. See also Bochel and Defty, 'Parliamentary Oversight of Intelligence Agencies'.
71. Bochel, Defty and Kirkpatrick, *Watching the Watchers*, p. 102.
72. Ibid. pp. 126–7.
73. Ibid. p. 17.
74. Ibid. p. 88.
75. Ibid. pp. 173–4.
76. Ibid. pp. 112–13.
77. Home Affairs Committee, 'Accountability of the Security Service'.
78. Ibid. para. 48.
79. Ibid.
80. Ibid. para. 3.
81. Bochel, Defty and Kirkpatrick, *Watching the Watchers*, pp. 112–13.
82. Trade and Industry Committee, 'Export Licensing and BMARC, Third Report of 1995–96', para. 167.
83. Foreign Affairs Committee, 'House of Commons – Foreign Affairs – Second Report', para. 105.
84. Bochel, Defty and Kirkpatrick, *Watching the Watchers*, p. 113.
85. See UK Parliament, 'Role – Liaison Committee'.
86. House of Commons Liaison Committee, 'Select Committee on Liaison First Report', para. 92.
87. Home Affairs Committee, 'The Private Security Industry'.
88. Interviewee 7.
89. European Scrutiny Committee, 'Fifteenth Report, House of Commons Session 1999–2000'.
90. For a discussion of security law making in relation to the wider themes and concepts of security politics, see Neal, 'Normalization and Legislative Exceptionalism' and 'Terrorism, Lawmaking and Democratic Politics'.
91. See Neal, 'Normalization and Legislative Exceptionalism'.
92. See Neal, 'Terrorism, Lawmaking and Democratic Politics'; Lord Lloyd of Berwick, 'Inquiry into Legislation against Terrorism, Cm. 3420'.
93. Burke, *The 9/11 Wars*.

94. House of Commons Public Administration Select Committee, 'Who Does UK National Strategy?', p. 3.
95. See UK Parliament, 'Political and Constitutional Reform Committee – Role'.
96. Political and Constitutional Reform Committee, 'Parliament's Role in Conflict Decisions: A Way Forward'.
97. Interviewee 11.
98. Interviewee 11.
99. Joint Committee on the National Security Strategy, 'Conflict, Stability and Security Fund'.
100. Rifkind, 'Intelligence Oversight in the UK: The Intelligence and Security Committee'.
101. Bochel, Defty and Kirkpatrick, *Watching the Watchers*, p. 99.
102. Intelligence and Security Committee of Parliament, 'Press Release – 26 April 2017 – UK Lethal Drone Strikes in Syria'.
103. Peto and Tyrie, 'Neither Just Nor Secure', p. 87.
104. Kelly and Parry, 'Pre-Legislative Scrutiny under the Coalition Government'.
105. Ruth Fox, Director of the Hansard Society, author interview, 2013.
106. See Neal, 'Normalization and Legislative Exceptionalism'.
107. Fox and Korris, *Making Better Law*.
108. House of Commons, 'House of Commons Hansard Debates for 01 Apr 2008 (Pt 0009)'.
109. Neal, 'Normalization and Legislative Exceptionalism'.
110. For example Walt, 'The Renaissance of Security Studies'.
111. Toros, '"9/11 Is Alive and Well"'; Zehfuss, 'Forget September 11'.
112. Russell and Cowley, 'The Policy Power of the Westminster Parliament', p. 134.

7. Security as a Whole-of-Government Project: Risk, Economy, Politics

This chapter departs from others in this book by focusing on government as a site of politics. Earlier chapters considered professional politics as an activity that takes place within a particular institutional arena, that of parliament. They questioned what it means for politicians who do not hold government office to practise security politics, and to do so in a field dominated by government. In contrast, this chapter examines security politics within government. It finds the same trend at work: 'security' migrating out from a 'black box' at the dark heart of the state and into the wider reaches of government, potentially entering all policy areas and all departments. The chapter argues that central to this trend is the rise of a risk-based rationality. This supplants the existential necessity of the traditional threat-based security logic with one based on possibilities. It also allows security to become subordinate to other policy goals such as economic growth.

The chapter focuses on three developments in UK government in the past decade: austerity, the creation of a National Security Council and the publication of a largely risk-based National Security Strategy. When in office at the head of a coalition government from 2010 to 2016, Prime Minister David Cameron and Chancellor George Osborne led an economic political project of austerity. In the name of this project, they used the security machinery of government to promote economic aims. While it has always been a core task of MI6 to exercise its functions 'in the interests of the economic well-being of the United Kingdom', austerity seemed to subordinate security concerns to potential economic gains.[1]

Cameron and Osborne's economic-political project coincided with two developments in UK security governance: first, the creation of a National Security Council (NSC), which represented a reform in the security machinery of central government; and second, the government's embrace of a rationality of 'risk' in its National Security Strategy (NSS). Austerity, the creation of the NSC and the embrace of 'risk' in the NSS were not causally related or necessary to each other, but they were mutually facilitating. The NSC created strategic and practical links between 'security' and other policy areas in the machinery of government, particularly economic policy. The effect was to dilute the traditional 'institutionalised securitisation' and black-boxing effect that made security an exception to normal policy. It facilitated the balancing of security with other political priorities. The embrace of risk had the same effect. It diluted the traditional imperatives of threat in favour of a more hedged policy stance towards the multiple possibilities of risk. Together, these developments facilitated a shift whereby 'security' came to serve 'political economy'. This displaced, but did not destroy, the older rationalisation of security as existential threat. Because of this, the politics of austerity and risk worked to undo the traditional pathological opposition between security politics and normal politics.

The chapter begins with an account of two controversies that concerned the appropriate balance between security and economy. The subsequent section considers the literature on risk and security. Then, the second half of the chapter explores the politics of austerity, the NSC and risk from three angles: first, as a form of governmental centralisation and policy linkage that altered the traditional configuration of the security state; second, as a reform that 'normalised' security policy as a corrective to the perceived security 'exceptionalism' of the previous government; and third, as a vehicle for a politics of economy.

Osborne goes to China: The NSC, risk assessment and balance

On site at a nuclear power facility in China on 17 October 2013, the Chancellor George Osborne announced that Chinese nuclear companies would be allowed to invest in the British nuclear industry, starting with a new reactor at Hinkley. Reiterating the economic narrative of his government, Osborne said: 'It means the potential of more investment and jobs in Britain, and lower long-term energy costs for consumers.'[2] The deal would allow Chinese nuclear companies, mostly or wholly owned by the Chinese state, to take a stake in British nuclear plants. This would be a minority holding at first but allowed to grow to full ownership in the future. The move was controversial because it appeared to place economic interests above potential security risks. Labour MP Alan Whitehead, a member of the Energy and Climate Change Committee, said: 'There is clearly an issue of national security about a Chinese government stake in and possible control of the building and operation of a British nuclear power plant.'[3] In a climate of austerity, the nuclear investment decision seemed to pit economy against security.

Although there is no objective measure of what makes something a security threat, the Chinese nuclear deal had symbolic connections with existing security discourses.[4] In nuclear weapons states – including China and the UK – there is invariably a link between civil and military nuclear programmes.[5] Chinese state-ownership structures in particular meant that the deal created an indirect link to the Chinese military. Nuclear safety was an implied concern too. Although China has a good civil nuclear safety record and the UK has tightly regulated nuclear safety standards, nuclear power carries an inevitable association with danger, which had been heightened since the Fukushima disaster in March 2011. Further political disquiet about the UK building a close economic relationship with China stemmed from the latter's poor human rights record and its widely suspected involvement in industrial espionage. For all these reasons, Chinese investment in critical national infrastructure (CNI) appeared to be in tension with traditional conceptions of national security.[6]

The nuclear deal was not the first controversial Chinese investment in UK CNI. In 2011 it emerged that in 2005, British Telecom had contracted the Chinese company Huawei to carry out national IT infrastructure works. This prompted an inquiry by the Intelligence and Security Committee, which published a report in

June 2013. Based on oral evidence from MI5 among others, the ISC said that the risk from Chinese involvement in the UK's IT infrastructure came from the possibility of hidden 'backdoors' or vulnerabilities in Huawei software and hardware that could be exploited for espionage or even to disrupt the network itself.[7] (We know from the Snowden revelations that the UK intelligence agencies and their 'Five Eyes' intelligence allies also exploit such backdoors and vulnerabilities.[8]) The ISC noted that similar concerns had prompted the Australian government to prevent Huawei from carrying out comparable network upgrade work there.[9] And in the US, an investigation by the House Permanent Select Committee on Intelligence concluded that 'the risks associated with Huawei and ZTE's provision of equipment to US critical infrastructure could undermine core US national-security interests'.[10] In contrast to Australia and the US, UK inward investment policy represented a more relaxed attitude towards potential security concerns.

Piecing the Huawei backstory together, the ISC said that although BT had informed the UK government of the day about the deal, officials had not passed this information to ministers for consideration. Even if they had, it was not clear that the government would have had the power to block the deal on national security grounds, at least not without facing the possibility of judicial review and paying compensation for the commercial losses incurred.[11] The ISC concluded that it had unearthed 'a disconnect between the UK's inward investment policy and its national security policy'.[12]

On the nuclear investment issue, the government had appeared to weigh economic interests above security risks. In contrast, the Huawei issue was about a historic lack of diligence towards security risk assessment. The government gave the same response to both cases. In an official response to the ISC, it rebutted the charge that it held an inappropriate balance between inward investment policy and national security and said it had put robust procedures in place to assess national security risks when it created the National Security Council:

> The government has put in place an approach which enables it to assess the risks associated with foreign investment and develop strategies to manage them. The NSC ... brings together the

economic and security arms of the government and is the forum that ultimately balances the risks and opportunities of inward investment decisions.[13]

The response also invoked the NSC to rebuff the criticism that national security considerations had been disconnected from other policy decisions on the Huawei case:

> The Government accepts the Committee's conclusion that the processes of considering national security issues at the time of the BT/Huawei case in 2003–06 were insufficiently robust. In particular with hindsight, we agree that Ministers should have been informed.
>
> The Government does not agree with the Committee's statement that there have been no improvements since then or that national security issues are overlooked. Indeed the National Security Council (NSC), which was not in existence at the time of the BT/Huawei contract, can and does consider similar issues today in order to ensure that *HMG's* approach balances economic prosperity and commercial competitiveness with national security.[14]

Central to the response was the idea of having a mechanism to properly 'balance' economy and security (although it did not clarify whether the risk assessment procedures had been properly followed). Indeed, this is how the risk assessment model of the NSC and NSS works: by balancing possibilities and policy concerns. The implication is that national security is no longer dominated by the imperatives of threat. Security becomes one concern among many – a relative consideration.

When former prime minister Tony Blair gave evidence to the Chilcot inquiry into the Iraq War, he said that Saddam Hussein's Iraq had not suddenly become more dangerous after 9/11, but that 'our calculus of risk' had changed.[15] Under Tory-led austerity, it seemed that the 'calculus of risk' moved in the other direction, making certain perceived security risks appear less risky, or at least a risk worth taking in relation to potential economic gains. As Hammerstad and Boas argue: 'The language of risk serves rhetorical purposes, but also reveals shifts in security elites' perception of the nature of the UK's external security environment.'[16] The NSC and NSS have become vehicles for the government's 'calculus of risk'.

Threat and risk in the National Security Strategy

The government created the National Security Council on its first day in office in May 2010. This was symbolically important, marking a break with the security politics of the previous government. The NSC has an institutional formalism that contrasts with the widely perceived informality and personalisation of security policy under Prime Minister Tony Blair. However, the NSC does not represent a complete break with the past. In many ways it is a return to tradition, restoring a constitutionally appropriate relationship between the political (ministerial) and bureaucratic (civil service) parts of government. A simple aspect of this is that the NSC is a cabinet committee, which follows a century-old tradition of using cabinet committees for foreign and defence matters.[17]

NSC membership is a subset of the full cabinet and is chaired by the prime minister. Its membership is itself revealing of the policy areas the government deems to be important to security; it includes the chancellor, foreign secretary, home secretary, defence secretary, energy and climate change secretary, international development secretary and one or two others depending on the make-up of the wider cabinet at the time. Other ministers, intelligence chiefs and defence chiefs attend as required by the matters under consideration.[18]

The NSC has its own lead official – the National Security Advisor (NSA) – and a dedicated secretariat of approximately 200 staff. Formally it does not make policy; that responsibility remains with ministers and their departments. Rather, it coordinates policy delivery across government and is responsible for overall 'strategy', which in current government parlance seems to refer to overarching government policies that transcend individual policies.[19] In so doing, the NSC creates a new central linkage between government departments, policy areas, ministers and officials.

A key expression of the NSC risk rationality is the National Security Strategy (NSS). Although the innovation of publishing an NSS belongs to the previous government, the 2010 version was the first to publish an accompanying risk-based methodology, which it calls 'national security risk assessment'.[20] The NSC and the NSS are not mirrors of each other: while the NSC is a dynamic and evolving committee, a published policy document such as the NSS is fixed in time until updated. The 2010 NSS signalled the direction and intent of security reforms under the Cameron government and was an important expression of its risk rationality. As we will see, it was also a demonstration of how a new rationality can exist alongside and rearticulate the old. Let us now turn to the literature to explore the difference between the rationalities of 'security' and 'risk' and their relationship to policy.

The NSC and NSS are officially vehicles for 'strategy', so it makes sense to begin considering risk as a form of military-strategic rationality. Mikkel Vedby Rasmussen uses the term 'rationality' in the Weberian sense of 'the way actions make sense to the agents who carry them out'.[21] Here, at its simplest, 'risk' is a different rationality to 'threat'. Rasmussen argues that a threat is a 'specific danger which can be precisely identified', whereas a risk is a hypothetical 'scenario' that only has the possibility to become real.[22] Threat belongs to a 'means-ends rational framework' in which policy is directed towards a threat to defeat or contain it.[23] Recall that for Clausewitz, the most important thinker in the Western strategic tradition, 'war is nothing but the continuation of policy by other means', where policy and war are simply different means to pursue rationally identified ends.[24] We can see a similar strategic rationality at work in securitisation theory, where securitisation is the legitimation of a policy to deal with a (constructed) security threat.[25]

Unlike threats, which in security discourses necessitate specific mitigating policies, risk is a shifting terrain of possibilities.[26] If traditional strategic rationality is defined by hypothetical imperatives ('if you want x, do y'), under a risk rationality all choices are relative. This implies that a security strategy based on risk must be a constantly modulated balance of stances towards different possibilities that can never be entirely mitigated. As such, Rasmussen argues, 'Strategy is no longer a question of defeating concrete threats in order to achieve perfect security; it has instead become a way of managing risks.'[27] The strategic implications of risk are therefore less concrete, less necessitarian, more plural and call for more hedged policy stances. In this context, traditional means-ends policy making is a blunt tool. Yet although the probabilistic aspect of risk implies that risks can be 'weighed', for Rasmussen risk implies a politics of value judgement rather than rational calculation: 'Policy-makers must choose which risks they most need to prevent and which they have to accept.'[28]

In a thorough work of discourse analysis, Hammerstad and Boas examine UK strategic documents from 1998 to 2011 to chart the rise of 'risk' therein. Their assessment supports Rasmussen's framing in which threats are 'known and specific' while 'risks' are less certain possibilities.[29] They agree that risk implies that a certain level of insecurity can be lived with because not every probability can be foreseen or prevented, and that 'risk' permits a wider range of policy stances, unlike the singular imperatives of 'threat'.[30] Hammerstad and Boas argue that while a shift from 'threat' to 'risk' is certainly under way in these documents, it is not total or complete. Much like this book's Foucaultian argument that new problematisations do not necessarily cancel the old but come to exist alongside them, they argue that in these documents the new language and rationality of risk exists alongside older discourses of threat.[31] In the earlier documents, Hammerstad and Boas find that 'risk' and 'threat' are used somewhat interchangeably, but by 2010 the distinction has become clearer.[32] 'Threat' is used to invoke 'drama', 'urgency' and 'danger' in keeping with the traditional 'grammar' of security described by securitisation theory.[33] 'Risk' on the other hand is used to discuss emerging possibilities, vulnerabilities and preventative strategies.[34] The 2010 NSS does not therefore represent a complete shift away from more traditional threat-based understandings of national security policy, but is a significant rearticulation.[35]

The foreword of the 2010 NSS document signed by Cameron and Deputy Prime Minister Nick Clegg – the most 'political' part of the document – demonstrates these discursive tensions by starting out in a more traditional 'security' style. It declares:

> the National Security Council has overseen the development of a proper National Security Strategy, for the first time in this country's history . . . This National Security Strategy and the Strategic Defence and Security Review mobilise the whole of Government behind the protection of this country's security interests.[36]

'Mobilise' is of course a war metaphor, but we need to treat this with caution; Hammerstad and Boas write: 'Individual quotes . . . may be striking, but are not necessarily symptomatic of deeper shifts in conceptualizations of security.'[37] They argue that this more traditional security 'grammar' serves a particular purpose: 'The more urgent and dangerous sounding "threat" seems to be chosen when the aim is to grasp attention and establish the pressing nature of the document's message.'[38] This is an apt characterisation of this foreword. Beyond this attention-grabbing language, the NSS document signals less eye-catching but more important institutional and strategic changes. Rather than enacting an all-encompassing security mobilisation, it is more accurate to say that the NSC and NSS have created an overarching risk rationality and new security policy linkages within government.

The NSS's strategic openness towards different possibilities has prompted criticisms. Robert Crowcroft sees incoherence in its stated aim to protect 'our people, economy, infrastructure, territory and way of life from all major risks'.[39] He argues that this and its tiered list of risks in effect encompass 'everything': 'the challenges are sometimes so different from each other that literally all that connects them is that they can be filed under the terminology of "threat" and "risk".'[40] But this is precisely the point. It is not that a risk-based security strategy is incoherent, but that it is, to invoke Rasmussen again, a different kind of rationality to the means-ends thinking of traditional strategic thought – one based on a hedged stance towards a plurality of possibilities. In a similar vein, the 2010 Public Administration Select Committee report 'Who Does UK National Strategy?' complained that 'we have all but lost the capacity to think strategically. We have simply fallen out of the habit, and have lost the culture of strategy making.'[41] It called for the new machinery of the NSC to rekindle some of this capacity. Cornish and Dorman – similarly to Rasmussen – argue that traditionally minded criticisms such as these, which demand the government articulate a clear national strategy, misunderstand the meaning of a risk-based strategy. They argue that risk is not about means and ends, but more about understanding, preparing for and balancing different possibilities, including the choice 'to prepare for some contingencies and not for others'.[42]

In this way we can see how the pluralisation of possibilities expressed by risk facilitates policy linkage. If risks can arise in any area of social, political and economic life, then they have implications for any area of government or policy. As Rasmussen argues: 'The concept of risk as the new guiding principle of strategy makes it possible to connect a number of events, policy initiatives and technological developments, which would otherwise seem random and unconnected.'[43] To put it another way, risk rationality takes security policy away from being the 'exception' it once was – an institutionalised securitisation isolated from other policy areas in a 'black box' at the heart of the state. Rasmussen writes: 'the strategic agenda has become much more like "normal" policy areas than it used to be.'[44] Tara McCormack comes to the same conclusion: 'Effectively, security has become normalised – it is no longer the core existential area of state policy protected from the normal political procedures but something subject to the same stresses that other aspects of policy are.'[45] As we will see, this goes some way to explaining how under Cameron and Osborne security could become subservient to austerity.

Risk as depoliticisation?

Some scholars have argued that risk rationality is a form of depoliticisation, and this is obviously relevant for this book. For example, Karen Lund Petersen argues that a form of 'practical risk analysis' inspired by economics is used by large businesses, consultancies and some governments for a rationalised form of decision making.⁴⁶ Traditionally this uses statistical methods to quantify probable risks, particularly in the insurance industry.⁴⁷ We could say that it follows the tenet described by Weber in *Science as a Vocation*: 'that there are in principle no *mysterious, incalculable powers at work,* but rather one could in principle master everything through *calculation*'.⁴⁸ Or as Luis Lobo-Guerrero puts it via François Ewald, the purpose of this kind of risk analysis is to make 'uncertainty governable'.⁴⁹ At first glance, this could be seen as the kind of reasoning used in the NSS, but it is not the case, as we will see.

Hagmann and Dunn Cavelty offer a different critique of risk rationality in their work on 'national risk registers'. Risk registers aim to be 'comprehensive inventories of public dangers . . . to provide secure foundations for public policymaking, security-related resource allocation and policy planning'.⁵⁰ They are a form of expert knowledge that scores risks along two axes: likelihood and impact.⁵¹ Hagmann and Dunn Cavelty explain that this impact/likelihood methodology derives from hard sciences such as engineering, a discipline with established methods to quantify these variables based on extensive empirical data.⁵² It is also the basic methodology of the insurance industry.⁵³ This is ostensibly how the UK's 'national security risk assessment' methodology works, as detailed in Figure 7.1, from the 2010 NSS.⁵⁴

Hagmann and Dunn Cavelty are critical of these risk assessment techniques, arguing that they hide a lack of knowledge under scientistic language. In the security field in particular, given the uncertainty and infrequency of 'events' and the sheer number of contextual variables, 'risk assessment' depends not on historical data but on estimates from intelligence agencies and other 'experts'.⁵⁵ Hagmann and Dunn Cavelty's concern is that this is not a genuine form of probabilistic risk assessment, but rather an all too human form of judgement that only borrows the scientific authority of probabilistic risk assessment methods. They argue that the calculative and 'scientific' language of risk projects scientific authority even though its actual scientific basis is unsound; security risk assessment amounts to an

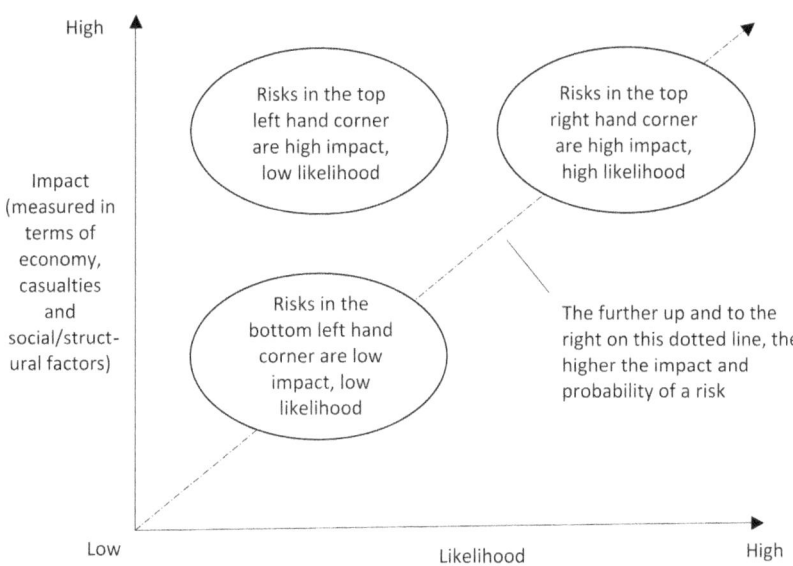

Figure 7.1 National security risk assessment methodology.

'expert-generated knowledge that is actively used to mask non-knowledge'.[56] It replaces uncertainty with a depoliticising rationalisation, 'cloaked in apolitical and technocratic language'.[57] Hammerstad and Boas come to a similar view about the basis of scientific authority in the NSS, arguing that 'National Security Risk Assessment aims to justify hard choices with scientific reasoning to reassure citizens that the government remains capable of responding'.[58]

Traditional statistical risk assessment techniques are based on known historical data. Yet, another problem is that historical data cannot account for that which has not been seen before and has not yet happened. For this reason, much of the critical literature on this topic concerns the problem of incalculable or difficult-to-quantify risks, including 'high-impact low-probability' events such as large-scale acts of terrorism or systemic crises.[59] Something that has never happened before will always fall beyond the bell curve of probability in models that expect the future to be like the past. This is the basis of Nassim Taleb's critique of 'black swan' events, and also Mark Blyth's related critique of the failure of risk assessment models in the banking sector preceding the 2008 financial crisis.[60] As Blyth puts it:

> Such models see the future only as a normally distributed replication of the past. This makes big, random, game-changing events impossible to foresee, when in fact they are all too common. Such technologies give us, as Taleb says, the illusion of control.[61]

These various critiques of risk management differ in their political conclusions. Taleb, for example, has become associated with centre-right political thought, including that of David Cameron and the British Conservative Party. He urges a politics of less top-down control and a greater openness and resilience towards uncertainties.[62] Hagmann and Dunn Cavelty are more concerned with how risk assessment practices favour an expert technocracy. Their concerns echo the fear of bureaucracy expressed by Max Weber.[63] As Sheldon Wolin writes of this Weberian theme: 'The bureaucratic ideal asserts, somewhat paradoxically, that the bureaucrat can be both "neutral" and a staunch believer that the common good is realizable through objective thinking based on expert knowledge.'[64] For Hagmann and Dunn Cavelty, the scientism of risk assessment 'downplay[s] . . . crucial questions of a political, ethical and normative nature'.[65] This is a depoliticisation in which technocratic rationalisation displaces public choice.

In Hagmann and Dunn Cavelty's interpretation, the way risk analysis favours experts also has implications for traditional security politics. Its scientificity undermines the sovereign decisionism traditionally associated with security because it hinders the symbolic leeway of political leaders to represent threats and risks. Because the authority of risk is built upon seemingly 'scientific' language, 'political leaders feel constrained in their own articulation of public danger narratives'.[66] To put it another way, once security policy is written down and rationalised through a risk methodology, its meaning is less dependent on the securitising speech acts of leaders or other elites. Hagmann and Dunn Cavelty see a form of depoliticisation at work in the authority 'risk' gives to experts at the expense of politicians.

Aradau and van Munster's Foucaultian 'critical governmentality' interpretation also sees 'risk' as depoliticising. For them, like Rasmussen, risk is a departure from traditional strategic rationality, distinct from the sovereign decision and exceptionalism traditionally associated with 'security'.[67] Like Hagmann and Dunn Cavelty, their concern is that the techniques of government associated with 'risk' equate to a technocratic and depoliticising management of issues that should rightly belong to the realm of public politics and deliberation:

> The infinity of risk does not lead to a democratic politics that debates what is to be done, but to intensified efforts and technological inventions on the part of the risk managers to adjust existing risk technologies or to supplement them.[68]

For Aradau and van Munster, it is not so much that politics has been abolished, but that it has been displaced to a collection of technologies, experts and private risk management mechanisms such as insurance. This echoes the concerns of the growing literature on depoliticisation discussed in Chapter 3: democratic authorities have outsourced their responsibilities and competences to experts and arm's-length agencies, hollowing out public deliberation and accountability.[69] Unlike Hagmann and Dunn Cavelty, however, Aradau and van Munster ultimately see risk as an extension of security logics. Olaf Corry points out that despite their theorisation of the difference between risk management techniques and sovereign decision, they see the use of 'risk' *in extremis* as a tool in service to 'sovereign decision on dangerousness'.[70] Corry adds: 'Although the original idea was that security had changed, risk is thus seen essentially as a multiplication of securitisation.'[71]

These critiques of risk management as depoliticising technocracy do not quite capture the politics of risk and economy in the NSC and NSS. Here, risk assessment does rely on expert judgements provided by the NSC secretariat, intelligence agencies and occasionally outside experts.[72] And this does lead to a reduction in sovereign nominalism. But this does not necessarily hand authority from politicians to technocrats. Risk assessment adds another dimension to the policy process but does not supplant it.

The NSC and NSS remain within the arena of democratic government in the analytical sense used in this book. They also remain under the control of the 'political' or 'ministerial' side of government, rather than the 'officialdom' that concerned Weber so much. Moreover, as the next section discusses, the NSC is a reform of government that increases policy coordination from the centre rather than shifting it to arm's-length agencies. It does this not by increasing executive power in the Schmittian sense, but by using a rationalising discourse of 'risk assessment' and 'balance' to link policy areas and bring them under an overarching political-economic project. So, although invested in a rationality of risk, this is not a depoliticisation of the kind that removes responsibility from politicians and hands it to apolitical technocrats. On the contrary, it is a reform that has allowed the government's political-economic priorities to permeate national security policy.

Security as not Blair: Security from the joined-up centre

There was a different kind of depoliticisation at work in the creation of the NSC. This sought to reduce the controversy of security policy and restore public confidence after the security excesses of former prime minister Tony Blair.

It was in opposition that the Conservative Party developed its policy to create a National Security Council. It first mooted the idea in a 2006 policy paper written by Dame Pauline Neville-Jones, formerly a diplomat, defence civil servant, and Chair of the JIC. Published a year after the 7 July 2005 London bombings, and while the Iraq invasion was still raw, the paper was critical of foreign and security policy under Blair. Its opening paragraph argued that British actions overseas in Iraq had led to domestic radicalisation, leaving the country less safe: 'The fact that the bombers were radicalised in part by events outside the United Kingdom forced us to recognise that foreign affairs have become domestic affairs.'[73] According to the paper, not only was UK participation in the Iraq intervention overambitious, highly risky and insufficiently independent from US foreign policy, it also demonstrated a lack of joined-up thinking about foreign and domestic events and a failure to make connections between policy areas. Neville-Jones called into question 'the adequacy of the security policy making process itself' and declared that 'it would be an early task of an incoming Conservative government to restore confidence in the integrity of the policy process'.[74] This must be seen in light of the Butler report of 2004, mentioned in Chapter 4, which criticised the public presentation of intelligence material by the Blair government.[75] The Conservative policy paper proposed to create an NSC to address these failings. This was a conscious political reaction against the controversy in foreign and security policy that Blair had created:

> What is needed is a mechanism within which those responsible for action across Government – the Foreign and Home Offices, DfID, the Ministry of Defence, the Intelligence Agencies and the Cabinet Office – supported by a dedicated cross-departmental staff – can ensure that, from the start, policy adopted in any of these areas is coherent in the sense that it takes fully into account the likely consequences at home and abroad.[76]

This envisaged model is exactly what has been put into place. The NSC encourages input from a range of senior cabinet ministers and considers security policy in relation to other policy priorities. Cameron defended this principle in his 2014 evidence to the JCNSS when he said: 'I think it joins up Prime Minister, Foreign Secretary, Chancellor, Home Secretary and others in a way in which perhaps they have not been joined up in the past.'[77] He went on to give the example of visa rules to demonstrate the NSC's 'joined-up thinking', referencing an economy/security balance:

> When we decide about visa rules and visa waivers for countries, you have to weigh up the prosperity agenda with the security agenda and make sure that you are making the right decision. In the past, visa decisions were made by the Home Office, prosperity decisions were made by the Treasury, and 'never the twain shall meet'. We now discuss and

debate them around the table: 'Well, we have important economic relations with this country and, frankly, the visa restrictions are getting in the way. Is the national security really being threatened?'[78]

In a sense, the NSC has formalised security policy making to mark a break with its perceived informality and imprudence under Blair. It represents a comparatively different style of governing. It meets weekly in the Cabinet Room with a regular core membership. It follows formal procedures in terms of having civil servants present, following agendas, circulating papers and having minutes taken. This is distinct from security decision making under Blair, who is said to have preferred ad hoc groups of advisors who were 'on side' rather than going through formal cabinet procedures.[79] Lord Richard Wilson – Cabinet Secretary from January 1998 to September 2002 – told the Chilcot inquiry into the Iraq War that foreign and security policy was highly personalised under Blair, who had a fear that going through cabinet committees would lead to obstruction:

> He knew what he thought, he knew what he wanted and his job was to devise a strategy. He took full responsibility for it and his job was to drive it through . . . He wanted meetings . . . of people who were directly involved and implicitly on side. If you have a Cabinet Committee meeting you may have all sorts of people who are going to get in the way, who are going to slow you down.[80]

If security policy under Blair was personalised, under Cameron it became a committee affair. This facilitated policy linkage and coordination between ministries. Significantly, the 'political' members of the NSC – the ministers – were to contribute not only in the name of their departments, but also as part of collective political decision making. Again, this was the intention. As Neville-Jones wrote in the 2006 policy paper:

> Better integrated decision making should not undermine what remains of genuine collective cabinet responsibility by leading to more concentration of power at the centre. The present government has failed to use properly the Cabinet committee system which

underpins cabinet government and the Prime Minister and the department he has effectively created has instead exercised excessive control. The cabinet committee system needs revival.[81]

The way Blair and Brown jealously guarded their own policy fiefdoms has been well documented.[82] Of course, their schism was in part personal, but also an effect of the personalisation of foreign and security policy under Blair: if security policy was kept out of cabinet committees, then this kept the treasury out of security policy too. In contrast, Chancellor George Osborne has apparently been actively engaged in the NSC. Devanny and Harris of the Institute for Government write:

> Chancellor George Osborne's interventions at NSC meetings, in particular his questioning of senior military officers on the rationale behind Afghanistan policy, his argument for reducing expenditure on counter terrorism activities and increasing cyber security investment, and his engagement in NSC discussions of possible responses to the Ukraine crisis, have led one journalist to label him the 'imperial chancellor'.[83]

They also quote an anonymous NSC source who told them:

> Osborne has personally engaged a great deal, but this seems to be as the prime minister's strategist, speaking accordingly, rather than as Chancellor per se. Discussion of resources has featured little if at all.[84]

There was probably some element of personality in Osborne's role, given his closeness to Cameron politically and socially. But his involvement is also an effect of the NSC structure which formalises the political and ministerial input of the chancellor and other ministers.

On the civil service side, the creation of the NSC, the NSC secretariat and the post of National Security Advisor (NSA: the civil servant heading the NSC) represents a formalised institutional structure after a decade of frequent reorganisations of the intelligence and security machinery under Blair. Such reorganisations are not unusual historically, but the years from 2001 onwards saw several different configurations tested alongside increased counter-terrorism efforts, including the creation of the CONTEST strategy, the Joint Terrorism Analysis Centre (JTAC) and the Office for Security and Counter Terrorism (OSCT) in the Home Office.[85] Between 2002 and 2010 there were four senior national security posts between the cabinet office and the prime minister's office, with several changes of title and role. In 2010 the new government reduced this to just two: the National Security Advisor and Chair of the Joint Intelligence Committee.[86] Several other posts and heads of office have been subordinated to the NSA, including a Deputy NSA for Foreign and Defence Policy and another for Intelligence, Security and Resilience.[87] Devanny and Harris argue that

> The move towards a more over-arching national security machine can be seen as an attempt to provide greater stability, seniority and more coherence to areas of overlap that the centre had struggled to coordinate effectively.[88]

Indeed, from 2011 the government continued to enhance the 'lead driver' role of the NSC, including having the NSC set the agenda of the JIC and putting other units and agencies such as the JTAC and Defence Intelligence 'more directly at [its] disposal'.[89]

Again, an element of this formalisation is an effort to restore a sense of 'business as usual' after the tumult of Blair. Although the NSC was new in 2010, its structure is not entirely novel in historical terms. The NSC is ultimately descended from the Committee of Imperial Defence of the early 1900s, which was replaced by the Defence Committee in 1947.[90] These committees comprised small groups of ministers and officials. They often had various sub-committees and offshoots, such as the Joint Intelligence Committee (JIC) established in 1936 which exists to this day.[91] Thus Devanny and Harris describe the NSC as 'the latest iteration of over a century of prime ministerial efforts to coordinate national security issues from the centre'.[92]

The NSC also resembles the streamlined 'war cabinets' UK governments created for decision making in extraordinary circumstances in the First and Second World Wars.[93] Devanny and Harris suggest that the NSC 'attempts to emulate the intensity and coherence of such extraordinary measures in normal business'.[94] However, in the context of critical security debates about 'exceptionalism' we need to treat this characterisation with caution.[95] The NSC does not work to perpetuate a sense of threat, urgency and crisis. Although its language does veer into this traditional 'grammar' of security, its modus operandi is to use the more balanced language of risk.[96] The NSC in operation, formality and regularity of meetings represents a normalisation of security policy, not in the sense that it normalises exceptionalism, but rather that it makes security policy more like other policy areas.[97]

This 'war cabinet' model has a parallel in recent history. In 2008 Prime Minister Gordon Brown convened a National Economic Council (NEC) to deal with the financial crisis.[98] Former Labour government special advisor Dan Corry argues that the NEC was set up 'in a period of extreme danger for the economy' and was 'in a sense an Economic War Council'.[99] The centre of the UK government – in the form of No. 10 and the Cabinet Office – is institutionally quite small in comparison to that of other national governments, and as a result, Corry explains, 'The view then was that new machinery was needed at the heart of government to reflect these new and urgent priorities.'[100] The NEC met at first twice weekly and then weekly.[101] Corry argues that its strength came not simply from the fact of meeting but because 'everyone knew it was the key committee of the day', the Prime Minister was 'fully committed', it required preparatory work from departments in advance of the meetings, it created a cross-departmental sense of involvement in a collective effort, and by joining up policy areas it loosened the traditional grip of the treasury on economic matters, despite resistance from treasury ministers and officials.[102] Corry concludes his reflections on the NEC with a prescient suggestion that its model could become a permanent feature of government and not just an ad hoc crisis response mechanism.[103] This is exactly what the NSC represents. Devanny and Harris note five close parallels between the NEC and the NSC (see Figure 7.2).

Prime ministerial commitment – in both cases the prime minister chaired the committee
High-level senior attendance by ministers, including key political players
Participation of officials in discussions – the NSC provides a platform for the security services, and senior economic officials participated in the NEC
Lead departments being prepared to 'cede sovereignty' on issues under discussion
High-powered, activist and well-resourced secretariats

Figure 7.2 Similarities between the National Economic Council and the National Security Council
Source: Devanny and Harris, 'The National Security Council', p. 36.

To sum up this section, the NSC was born of a specific politics, that of restoring public confidence in security policy after the controversies of Blair. This represents a kind of depoliticisation, but not of the technocratic 'arena shifting' kind discussed in Chapter 3.[104] Rather it is a qualitative de-controversialisation enacted through institutional reform within government. It also represents a limited form of 'arena migration' within government, in the sense that it reduced the informal dominance of the prime minister in security policy in favour of a wider and more formal cabinet and civil service structure. The NSC is thus a reform that increases governmental coordination of security policy from the centre, draws more ministers and departments into the process, but reduces the executive prerogative power vested in the prime minister. It does this by balancing political leadership, collective cabinet responsibility, coordination between departments, and expert input and implementation by officials. This is only partly a bureaucratic rationalisation in the Weberian sense. It also represents a particular politics as a corrective to the politicised perception of irresponsibility, imprudence and hubris in Blair. The NSC harks back to historical forms of central security governance in the British state, in some sense restoring the 'norm' after the 'exception' of the Blair years. What is new is the increased role for a risk rationality. This has facilitated the joining up of policy areas and the 'normalisation' of security policy in the sense articulated by Rasmussen and McCormack. The next section will discuss how, in turn, this facilitated a politics of economy that put the security machinery of government at the service of a particular political-economic vision: austerity.

Security, risk and political economy

The economic political priorities and choices that went into the NSS are no secret. Many commentators see these in terms of austerity. For example, on publication of the NSS, the International Institute for Strategic Studies commented: 'This is a document explicitly predicated on the need to deal with a fiscal deficit.'[105] Similarly, Hammerstad and Boas argue that the risk discourse of the NSS favours the politics of austerity:

> Risk language suits the austerity message of the recent NSS discourse well. Adopting a financial language of quantification and prioritisation, the National Security Risk Assessment aims to justify hard choices with scientific reasoning to reassure citizens that the government remains capable of responding to both financial and security challenges ... A key goal for the 2010 NSS was to justify austerity cuts in defence spending.[106]

While this may be true in one sense, this chapter argues that the economic-political aims of the Cameron government were about more than the implementation of cuts. Cuts alone do not make a political strategy, and unjustified cuts in security and defence spending would have been seen as irresponsible. This was indeed the case for many traditional defence commentators when the Conservative Party flirted with cutting defence below the NATO-stipulated two per cent of GDP before the election, to great furore within their ranks.[107] Furthermore, it is not accurate to say that the NSS is entirely based on cuts. There were spending increases in some areas, notably £860m for a new National Cyber Security Programme, a policy attributed to Osborne.[108]

Cameron and Osborne pursued a particular political-economic vision, in part through the NSC and NSS. This implies that security is no longer just a Hobbesian guarantee of safety, or the threat modulation implied by securitisation, but a policy area tied to wider political-economic aims. The UK cyber security strategy is a prime example, its first objective being to make the UK 'one of the most secure places in the world to do business in cyberspace'.[109] Cameron made the economic priorities of his government's security strategy clear in his 2014 evidence to the Joint Committee on the NSS:

> I do not have to look at a bit of paper to tell us what our strategy is: it is to restore Britain's economic strength, it is to tie us to the fast growing parts of the world, it is to refresh and enhance the great alliances that we have, it is to tackle the threats that could threaten our country – and it is to make sure that we do this right across government and it is not just the Foreign Office fighting for us abroad but every single bit of government working together. That is the strategy.[110]

In the government's security strategy, economy came first. 'Tackling threats' was still there, but further down the list. What kind of politics is this? It is a politics validated by economy. It is a politics of economy pursued through the machinery of government, including its security machinery. It implies a particular stance towards perceived risks and rewards, as seen with the example of Chinese CNI investment. Its elements include expert risk assessment, cabinet committees, secretariats, trade and investment deals, policy documents and a public political-economic narrative. To explore this subordination of security to a politics of economy, or even its transformation into a politics of economy, we will now turn again to Foucault.

In his lecture series 'Security, Territory, Population', Foucault introduces an understanding of security that is quite different to the traditional Hobbesian sovereignty-based version. 'Security' in Foucault's non-standard terms is not a form of direct power and control over a territory, but a measured stance towards the processes and possible events that occur in a population and its environment. This is akin to 'risk' as discussed earlier, as we see here: 'The specific space of security refers then to a series of possible events; it refers to the temporal and uncertain.'[111]

In this discourse of 'security', these processes and events have an independent existence that needs to be respected: they are 'taken to be necessary, inevitable processes, as natural processes in the broad sense'.[112] Any attempts to intervene to influence these processes and possibilities will have to be based upon a knowledgeable understanding of this nature, judicious and – ideally – indirect.[113] So instead of the direct and symbolic exercise of power on a territory, this version of 'security' is less direct: 'The apparatus of security, by contrast . . . "lets things happen".'[114]

What is interesting about this unusual understanding of 'security' – as well as its similarity to 'risk' – is its correlation with economic liberalism. Foucault contrasts it with the traditional rationality of the sovereign state: *raison d'état*, which is a form of reason that justifies the state and its actions in reference to the state itself, and not to some higher moral authority, purpose or law. In Foucault's terms *raison d'état* involves

> identifying what is necessary and sufficient for the state to exist and maintain itself in its integrity if, in the event of it being damaged, it is necessary to re-establish this integrity.[115]

This is in keeping with the traditional security rationality discussed above; it is the traditional prerogative of the state to define and tackle threats to its own 'national security'. In contrast, economic liberalism does not define everything in terms of the state. It conceives of the economy as having a separate existence and nature to that of the state. Economic liberalism 'isolates the economy as a specific domain of reality'.[116]

Taking this up in his lectures of the following year, Foucault argues that the core concern of 'political economy' is not that of increasing the power and wealth of the state, as was the case with *raison d'état* and mercantilism.[117] Rather, as a system of knowledge that posits the natural existence of economic 'phenomena, processes and regularities', the defining problematisation concerns the positive or negative effects of government on the economy.[118] Too much government or the wrong kind of intervention could be bad for the economy.[119] Thus the rationality of political economy is a rationality of limited government. From this perspective,

'A government is never sufficiently aware that it always risks governing too much.'[120]

This liberalism of 'limited' or 'frugal' government sets a different standard of judgement to that of *raison d'état*.[121] Instead of judging the government according to the strength or 'national security' of the state, it is the market that judges whether government policy is good or bad. Foucault calls this a mechanism of veridiction (which we first encountered in Chapter 5).[122] To put it differently, in the *raison d'état* of traditional security politics, it is the state that 'tells the truth' of the nature of threats to the state and what must be done about them (as in Hobbes and securitisation theory). In economic liberalism, 'The market must tell the truth; it must tell the truth in relation to governmental practice.'[123]

This also means that the dangers posed by government itself are different. In *raison d'état* and traditional understandings of security, the danger is that the state may go beyond what is necessary for security and do self-defeating damage to its politics or civil society, as discussed in Chapter 1. In economic liberalism, the danger is that government may exceed what is acceptable to the market and damage the economy.[124] As Foucault puts it: 'The fundamental question of liberalism is: What is the utility value of government and all action of government in a society where exchange determines the true value of things?'[125] Turning to the politics of economy and risk in the NSC and NSS under Cameron and Osborne, we could say that their guiding rationality was to ensure that government did not govern too much in the name of security at the expense of the economy. This is a problematisation that consists in asking: does this or that security policy damage the economy? For example, Cameron demonstrated exactly this with his comments on visa policy above.

Conclusion: Security as economy, security as politics

This chapter has argued that the NSC, the NSS and their risk rationality have altered the traditional position of security within government and politics. The NSC does not represent a root and branch transformation of the UK security architecture. Its structure resembles that of many earlier cabinet committees. Its agendas are often concerned with traditional foreign and security policy. And it often employs the discourse of security and threat alongside the more recent discourse of risk. But through a risk rationality that links possibilities and policy areas, and by boosting security coordination from the governmental centre but not increasing the prerogative security powers of the prime minister, it has altered the relationship between politics, security and economy.

Contrary to what security theory might assume, this centralisation has not had the effect of lending more power to a Schmittian sovereign 'who decides the exception' or even to a Weberian charismatic leader figure. Rather, this centralisation, combined with formalisation and policy linkage, has reduced the scope for executive security improvisation, but increased the scope for using the security machinery of government for other political aims. The UK government, through the NSC and NSS, displaced security as an 'anti-politics' and supplanted it with a politics validated by economy. The NSC and NSS do not represent a depoliticisation through expert technocracy, as explored by the critical risk literature. Although experts and technology (such as the techniques of risk assessment) play a role in the NSC, they remain at the service of the government. The position of these security experts is different to those favoured few who 'whispered in the Prince's ear' under Blair.[126] Instead, they help to 'develop and implement' the government's policies, as is their traditional constitutional role.[127]

Didier Bigo argues that the rise of professional managers of security and insecurity has displaced the traditional political arena.[128] For Bigo, security politics exists, but it is not where it is supposed to be. Instead of being located among the democratic public or its elected representatives, it takes place among security experts and professionals. However, in the NSC, NSS and the UK government's economic policy, politics *is* where it is supposed to be. Between economic policy, the NSC and the NSS, there is a form of cabinet government at work, as opposed to the sovereign exceptionalism feared by critical approaches to security. The NSC publishes policies which must be publicly defended by ministers before parliament. In the NSC, the civil service serves the political aims of the elected government, as is their constitutional role. And the whole austerity project was democratically validated by the general election victory in 2015, much to the despair of many British citizens (although since the Brexit vote and the 2017 general election the case for austerity has been falling apart). In short, this is a case of 'security politics' that is neither the simultaneous hyperpoliticisation/depoliticisation represented by securitisation, nor the depoliticising governmentality of risk management and technocracy.

This conjunction of austerity, institutional security reform and risk rationality represents a modification of the traditional structures, grammars and prerogatives of security. The shifts of emphasis from 'security' to 'economy' and from 'threat' to 'risk' follow an underlying logic whereby imperatives are replaced by possibilities. This distinction between 'threat' and 'risk' is well understood in the security literature.[129] The addition of 'economy' to the equation holds the government to a different standard of judgement for its security policies: not whether it protects its citizens or manages potential sources of risk, but whether the market responds favourably and economic growth is encouraged.

This new rationality does not replace the old logic of 'security'. The Hobbesian guarantee of security from the fear of violent death remains a background responsibility of government. On some issues and in some parts of government – for example the counter-terrorism policies led by the Home Office – the old logic prevails. Rather, the new rationality develops alongside the old. In their co-articulation, 'economy' and 'risk' put 'security' into a relative balance with other policy considerations. This undermines the traditional 'institutionalised securitisation' of security policy and facilitates its subservience to political-economic aims. So, although keeping the country 'secure' remains an undisputed principle for those who play the political game, risk alters the Hobbesian contract, because the state can no longer provide such a guarantee. The NSS states: 'we cannot prevent every risk as they are inherently unpredictable.'[130] As Louise Amoore argues, the contingencies of risk offer economic opportunities but undermine sovereign control:

> The necessary unknowability of the future – so central to profit, speculation, Adam Smith's invisible hand, the figure of *Homo economicus* – appears as anathema to the sovereign founder of the law, right, and the monopoly of legitimate violence.[131]

Once security gets hedged in this way and the economy takes precedence, the door is opened to the possibility of balancing 'security' with other policy priorities. From 2010 to 2016, at least until the interruption of the Brexit vote and the ensuing policy confusion, the economy was the government's highest priority.

As argued throughout the chapter, risk makes security more like other policy areas. Because a risk rationality entails multiple possibilities and contingencies, as opposed to the singular imperatives of threat, it favours the balancing of policy options. The effect is that risk relativises possible policies and outcomes. These may be presented through a veneer of expert-calculated likelihoods and impacts, but in the UK case they are ultimately a matter of political judgement. Given how politicised austerity has been in the UK, it seems perverse to call this 'normal politics', but in line with the terminology used throughout this book, and compared to the 'exceptionalism' of traditional security logics, that is what it is. Andrew Gamble describes austerity under Osborne as 'statecraft'.[132] Over and above economic arguments about the merits of austerity, and aside from the success or otherwise of the Chancellor meeting his targets for cuts and growth, Gamble argues that the aim of this government was primarily political: 'to make their version of what has happened to the economy the dominant one . . . to define the nature of the crisis'.[133] For Gamble, this was at root 'an important step in developing a winning electoral strategy for the next election', which the Tories duly did in May 2015, increasing their number of MPs and winning an overall majority.[134] Ironically, then, while the government in effect 'desecuritised' security by reducing its exceptionality and making it more like other kinds of policy, its ministers were not above co-opting traditional security discourse to service the politics of economy; like Gordon Brown 'saving the world' with his economic 'war cabinet', Osborne at times defined the austerity as a 'national emergency'.[135] However, the elected government was not waging economic war. It was using the governmental tools of a reformed security state to conduct politics.

Notes

1. Intelligence Services Act 1994.
2. *The Telegraph*, 'Chinese Companies to Buy Big Stake in Next Generation of British Nuclear Power'.
3. Broomby, 'Questions about UK Scrutiny of Chinese Nuclear Tie-Up'.
4. Buzan, Wæver and de Wilde, *Security*, p. 30.
5. Simpson, *The Independent Nuclear State*, pp. 131–2.
6. The UK defines critical national infrastructure as 'certain "critical" elements of infrastructure, the loss or compromise of which would have a major, detrimental impact on the availability or integrity of essential services, leading to severe economic or social consequences or to loss of life'. Centre for the Protection of National Infrastructure, 'Critical National Infrastructure | CPNI | Public Website'.
7. Intelligence and Security Committee, 'Foreign Involvement in the Critical National Infrastructure'; Zajko, 'Security against Surveillance', p. 40.
8. Zajko, 'Security against Surveillance', p. 44.
9. Intelligence and Security Committee, 'Foreign Involvement in the Critical National Infrastructure', p. 6.
10. Ibid.
11. Ibid. p. 8.
12. Ibid.
13. HM Government, 'Foreign Involvement in the Critical National Infrastructure: Government Response', p. 6.
14. Ibid. p. 3.
15. Norton-Taylor and Watt, 'The Blair Defence: September 11 Changed the "Calculus of Risk"'.
16. Hammerstad and Boas, 'National Security Risks?', p. 3.
17. Devanny and Harris, 'The National Security Council', p. 7.
18. GOV.UK, 'National Risk Register for Civil Emergencies – 2015 Edition'.

19. Devanny and Harris, 'The National Security Council', pp. 40–1.
20. HM Government, 'A Strong Britain in an Age of Uncertainty', p. 37. The government published a new version in 2015.
21. Rasmussen, *The Risk Society at War*, p. 5.
22. Ibid. pp. 1–2.
23. Ibid. p. 2.
24. Ibid. p. 6; Clausewitz, *On War*.
25. Wæver, 'Securitization and Desecuritization', p. 54. See also the critique of the Copenhagen School/Clausewitz link by Howell, 'The Global Politics of Medicine', pp. 968–9.
26. Rasmussen, *The Risk Society at War*, p. 4.
27. Ibid. p. 11.
28. Ibid. p. 4.
29. Hammerstad and Boas, 'National Security Risks?', p. 2.
30. Ibid. p. 8; Rasmussen, *The Risk Society at War*, p. 4.
31. Hammerstad and Boas, 'National Security Risks?', p. 2. See for example Foucault, *The Birth of Biopolitics*, p. 28.
32. Hammerstad and Boas, 'National Security Risks?', pp. 7–8.
33. Ibid. p. 8.
34. Ibid.
35. Ibid. p. 2.
36. HM Government, 'A Strong Britain in an Age of Uncertainty', pp. 5–7.
37. Hammerstad and Boas, 'National Security Risks?', p. 2.
38. Ibid. p. 8.
39. HM Government, 'A Strong Britain in an Age of Uncertainty', p. 10.
40. Crowcroft, 'A War on "Risk"?', p. 173.
41. House of Commons Public Administration Select Committee, 'Who Does UK National Strategy?', p. 3.
42. Cornish and Dorman, 'Fifty Shades of Purple?', p. 1194; Rasmussen, *The Risk Society at War*, p. 10.
43. Rasmussen, *The Risk Society at War*, p. 4.
44. Ibid. p. 9.
45. McCormack, 'The British National Security Strategy', p. 14.
46. Petersen, 'Risk Analysis', p. 698.
47. Ibid.
48. Weber, 'Science as a Vocation', p. 13.
49. Lobo-Guerrero, *Insuring Security*, p. 78; Ewald, 'Insurance and Risk'.
50. Hagmann and Dunn Cavelty, 'National Risk Registers', p. 80.

51. Ibid. p. 84.
52. Ibid. p. 81.
53. See Lobo-Guerrero, *Insuring Security*, p. 97.
54. The UK also has a national risk register for civil emergencies that is separate from the National Security Strategy, and a series of specific local risk registers. See GOV.UK, 'National Risk Register for Civil Emergencies – 2015 Edition'.
55. Hagmann and Dunn Cavelty, 'National Risk Registers', pp. 84–5.
56. Ibid. p. 81.
57. Ibid. p. 87.
58. Hammerstad and Boas, 'National Security Risks?', p. 11.
59. Petersen, 'Risk Analysis', p. 698.
60. Taleb, *The Black Swan*, p. 6; Blyth, *Austerity*, p. 44.
61. Blyth, *Austerity*, p. 37.
62. See Corry, 'Whispering Risk in the Prince's Ear'.
63. Weber, 'Parliament and Government in Germany under a New Political Order', p. 159.
64. Wolin, 'Agitated Times', p. 7.
65. Hagmann and Dunn Cavelty, 'National Risk Registers', p. 91.
66. Ibid. p. 88.
67. Aradau and van Munster, 'Governing Terrorism through Risk'.
68. Ibid. p. 108.
69. Burnham, 'New Labour and the Politics of Depoliticisation'; Wood, 'Depoliticisation, Resilience and the Herceptin Post-Code Lottery Crisis'; Flinders and Wood, 'Depoliticisation, Governance and the State'.
70. Aradau and van Munster, 'Governing Terrorism through Risk', p. 107; Corry, 'Securitisation and "Riskification"', p. 245.
71. Corry, 'Securitisation and "Riskification"', p. 245.
72. Joint Committee on the National Security Strategy, 'Uncorrected Transcript of Oral Evidence, Rt Hon David Cameron MP, Sir Kim Darroch, KCMG', p. 11.
73. Neville-Jones, 'Security Issues: Interim Position Paper', p. 1.
74. Ibid. pp. 14, 5.
75. Lord Butler of Brockwell, *Review of Intelligence on Weapons of Mass Destruction*, p. 79.
76. Neville-Jones, 'Security Issues: Interim Position Paper', p. 2.
77. Joint Committee on the National Security Strategy, 'Uncorrected Transcript of Oral Evidence, Rt Hon David Cameron MP, Sir Kim Darroch, KCMG', p. 3.
78. Ibid. p. 9.

79. Devanny and Harris, 'The National Security Council', p. 20.
80. Lord Wilson of Dinton, 'Oral Evidence', p. 88.
81. Neville-Jones, 'Security Issues: Interim Position Paper', p. 15.
82. Powell, *The New Machiavelli*, pp. 156–7; Corry, 'Power at the Centre', p. 465.
83. Devanny and Harris, 'The National Security Council', p. 37. They cite James Forsyth, 'The Risks for Osborne Now He's Back on Top'.
84. Devanny and Harris, 'The National Security Council', p. 37.
85. Ibid. p. 14.
86. Ibid. p. 13. The JIC remains separate from the NSC in order to maintain the independence of intelligence assessments following the recommendations of the 2004 Butler report.
87. Ibid.
88. Ibid. p. 15.
89. Cabinet Office, 'Supporting the National Security Council (NSC)', p. 1.
90. Devanny and Harris, 'The National Security Council', pp. 7–8.
91. Ibid. p. 8.
92. Ibid. p. 4.
93. Ibid. p. 16.
94. Ibid. p. 43.
95. Huysmans, 'The Jargon of Exception'; Neal, *Exceptionalism and the Politics of Counter-Terrorism*; Prozorov, 'X/Xs: Toward a General Theory of the Exception'; Walker, 'Sovereignties, Exceptions, Worlds'; Buzan, Wæver and de Wilde, *Security*.
96. Hammerstad and Boas, 'National Security Risks?'; Buzan, Wæver and de Wilde, *Security*.
97. McCormack, 'The British National Security Strategy', p. 14.
98. Devanny and Harris, 'The National Security Council', p. 36.
99. Corry, 'Power at the Centre', pp. 462–3.
100. Ibid. pp. 459, 462; Powell, *The New Machiavelli*, p. 29.
101. Corry, 'Power at the Centre', p. 467.
102. Ibid. pp. 462–8.
103. Ibid. p. 468.
104. Burnham, 'New Labour and the Politics of Depoliticisation'.
105. Cited in House of Commons Library, 'UK Defence and Security Policy', p. 19.
106. Hammerstad and Boas, 'National Security Risks?', pp. 11, 13.
107. Swinford, 'Tories Would Need £8bn to Protect Defence Spending'; BBC News, 'Nato 2% Defence Spending Target Should Be Met, MPs Say'.

108. HM Treasury, Government Communications Headquarters and George Osborne, 'Chancellor's Speech to GCHQ on Cyber Security'.
109. Cabinet Office, 'The UK Cyber Security Strategy', p. 21.
110. Joint Committee on the National Security Strategy, 'Uncorrected Transcript of Oral Evidence, Rt Hon David Cameron MP, Sir Kim Darroch, KCMG', p. 7.
111. Foucault, *Security, Territory, Population*, p. 35.
112. Ibid. p. 68.
113. Ibid. p. 38.
114. Ibid. p. 67.
115. Ibid. p. 339.
116. Ibid. p. 143.
117. Foucault, *The Birth of Biopolitics*, pp. 1–22.
118. Ibid. p. 15.
119. Ibid. p. 16.
120. Ibid. p. 17.
121. Ibid. p. 28.
122. Ibid. p. 32.
123. Ibid.
124. Ibid. p. 40.
125. Ibid. p. 46.
126. Corry, 'Whispering Risk in the Prince's Ear'.
127. 'The Civil Service helps the government of the day develop and implement its policies as effectively as possible': GOV.UK, 'Civil Service'.
128. Bigo, 'Security and Immigration', p. 83.
129. Corry, 'Securitisation and "Riskification"'; Petersen, 'Risk Analysis'; Rasmussen, *The Risk Society at War*.
130. HM Government, 'A Strong Britain in an Age of Uncertainty', p. 25. See also Rasmussen, *The Risk Society at War*, p. 4.
131. Amoore, *The Politics of Possibility*, p. 5.
132. Gamble, 'Austerity as Statecraft'.
133. Ibid. p. 44.
134. Ibid. p. 43.
135. Ibid. p. 49.

Conclusion: More Security, More Politics

Professional politicians – in this case parliamentarians – are more active on security than ever before. Parliamentary politics is deeply unfashionable among critical scholars, but it is precisely this unfashionableness that makes it so important in this context. If 'security' can increasingly be found in this most 'normal' of political arenas, then we cannot seriously maintain that security is inherently exceptional and anti-political. If security is increasingly part of normal politics, and not a damaging exception to it, then we need to rethink our very understanding of security. The exclusions, prerogatives, taboos, boundaries, hierarchies and symbolic inequalities that elevated security above normal politics have been diluted by new security practices and problematisations. As these have proliferated, they have spilled into the political arena and the activities of politicians. More security does not mean less politics, it means more.

'More security' means security as a practice, not security as a condition of being secure. It means more security laws, more security policies, and a greater footprint in government and society for their development and implementation. It means that more areas of social, political and economic life have been problematised in security terms. 'More security' also means more security practices conducted by actors and agencies beyond central government, including private companies, sub-state forms of government and arm's-length agencies.[1] This does not go unnoticed in the political arena.

'More politics' means more political activity in the traditional arena of liberal democratic politics, taken here as the UK parliament. As discussed from the outset, this is not the entirety of politics.

Nor is it an ideal form of politics. Nor a statement on what could or should be taken as political. Rather, it is a significant form of politics that has experienced a shift from almost complete marginalisation from security in the 1980s to extensive activity on security today. Whatever the merits and failings of parliamentary politics, it embodies the 'normal politics' from which 'security' is assumed to be a pathological deviation in securitisation theory and critical security studies more generally.[2] In the wider orbit of politics outside parliament, 'more politics' also means more public interest, more politicisation in the qualitative sense of controversy and contestation, and increased mobilisation for and against security policies by NGOs, campaigners and community groups. These wider developments feed into parliamentary activity as it channels public concerns, hears from expert witnesses, responds to controversy, publishes reports and votes on legislation. Yet, much of the increase in parliamentary activity on security is not dramatic or controversial but routine.

It has never been an aim of this book to refute securitisation theory. A huge literature has already picked apart its every facet. Rather, the aim has been to date it. In turn, this reveals profound change in security politics. The historical angle provided by Michel Foucault has been central here. A Foucaultian approach encourages us to see all ideas, theories, discourses and practices in their historical context, instead of in axiomatic terms (as the positivist heritage of much international relations theory would have us do). To put it simply, securitisation theory was a product of its time. That time was the 1980s and early 1990s. It is for this reason that securitisation theory offers a good historical account of UK security politics. Not every detail fits, but as Wæver points out, theories are not meant to be mirrors of reality.[3]

Securitisation theory conceives of security as a 'special kind of politics or . . . above politics' that favours 'the empowerment of a smaller elite'.[4] This was certainly the case in the UK in the 1980s. Security favoured government at the expense of parliament. More specifically, it favoured the highest pinnacles of government and ultimately the prime minister. In fact, the key concept for understanding the historical UK is not 'securitisation' – which relates to a specific kind of social construction of threat – but rather 'institutionalised securitisation', a condition in which security rationales have become implicit, legitimacy is assumed, and certain responses are expected.[5]

In this era, security was a constitutionally exceptional policy area resting on de facto legitimation derived from ancient royal prerogatives and practices. The intelligence agencies did not officially exist. They and their forebears had been created by the secret wartime decisions of prime ministers. Until the Interception of Communications Act 1985 their surveillance powers had no legal basis. Neither were the counter-terrorist activities of the police special branch discussed in parliament. Counter-terrorist powers were authorised by 'temporary' emergency laws that parliament repeatedly renewed. Some of these applied only to the constitutionally exceptional province of Northern Ireland. Parliamentary rules forbade questions 'relating to the secret services and to security', which were 'of their nature secret'.[6] The government would refuse to answer anyway. Most parliamentarians agreed it was wrong to ask in the first place.[7] Not everyone felt the same way, of course, as attested by the Faslane peace camp, the British Irish community, leftist MPs and trade unionists.[8]

The interviews with parliamentarians presented in Chapter 4 revealed something of why institutionalised securitisation in the UK worked. It is true that state secrecy and parliamentary rules prevented debate on security. The security policy area was also narrow at the time. It included intelligence and defence and little else, creating few opportunities for parliamentary engagement. But it is also true that certain norms of security deference pervaded parliamentary life. Asking difficult questions about national security was deemed disloyal, irresponsible and something only MPs on the political fringes would do. The first responsibility of government is security, the interviewees said, and it was not their role to make that grave task more difficult. Even if they wanted to, they faced considerable obstacles due to lack of information and expertise.

Deference to the security state was in effect a constitutional pillar. It was based on trust. Most parliamentarians accepted the premise that there was little in the security realm that governments could share without endangering intelligence sources and giving away a tactical advantage. This created an obvious temptation for government to use national security secrecy in bad faith or to hide wrongdoing. As long as most parliamentarians trusted this was not happening, or could live with the possibility that it was, the system more or less worked. Scandals such as the BMARC arms to Iran affair, and intelligence whistleblowers such as Cathy Massiter, animated the left and led to calls for parliamentary intelligence oversight, but did not damage the whole edifice. Parliament in general deferred to the government on intelligence and national security.

The Iraq War destroyed this trust. Before the unprecedented political misuse of intelligence on weapons of mass destruction, most MPs trusted the security authority vested in prime ministers. Afterwards, trust was broken. This was a much bigger issue than loss of trust in Prime Minister Tony Blair. The unwritten constitutional edifice could no longer work. The reasons for deference still exist today, parliamentarians still appreciate the seriousness of national security, and they still find it hard to challenge the executive on intelligence. Many parliamentarians continue to trust prime ministers on security, particularly if they are of the same party, but that is not enough. Some others will never trust a word any government says on security again, as is evident from the Syria debate in 2013. Most have become sceptical rather than cynical. They want evidence. They want to be persuaded. On matters hinging on intelligence this is impossible. As Robin Butler pointed out via Clausewitz, intelligence is not evidence, it is inherently imperfect information couched by professionals in delicate terms to help ministers decide.[9] This is one reason why the system rested on trust, secrecy and deference in the first place.

Today, the institutionalised securitisation that characterised the UK is becoming a historical relic. Most security policies are no longer 'of their nature secret'.[10] Nor are they constitutionally exceptional or siloed in special departments or agencies. The constitutional place and structure of security governance has changed. While sovereign exceptionalism and executive prerogative still exist, they are not the defining feature of the security policy or the policy-making process.

Security is now pursued with 'an integrated, whole-of-government approach'.[11] This is not an exercise on paper only. The UK National

Security Council and Secretariat represent a reorganisation of security policy making at the heart of central government, with mechanisms for cross-departmental policy coordination at the highest level. The government's March 2018 National Security Capability Review proposed to extend intra-governmental and extra-governmental security integration through the declaration of a so-called 'Fusion Doctrine', which calls for better use of capabilities and sources of information from 'outside traditional national security departments' and beyond.[12] These reforms allow for a balancing of security risks with other policy considerations such as cost and economic opportunity, challenging the idea that security is based on narrow existential choices and necessitous decisions.

There are thus two main drivers of the migration of security into the arena of normal politics. The first driver is the widening scope and reach of security policy and practice. As further areas of social, political and economic life have been problematised in security terms by government, academics, activists and indeed parliamentarians, they have correspondingly appeared in the activities of parliament. Examples include counter-extremism, anti-terrorist finance, and forms of risk management relating to systems of supply, circulation and infrastructure. Yet, parliament itself should not be regarded as the primary driver of this widening process. Most parliamentary activity on security is a response to government policies, proposed or existing legislation, failings in government agencies or the need for periodic review of security governance in various sectors. Parliamentarians may fuel or dispel security problematisations initiated elsewhere. Sometimes it may follow and other times it may lead. However, rarely is parliament itself the source of new security problematisations.

The second driver is declining deference among parliamentarians towards governmental security authority. The Iraq and Syria episodes are 'cusps and conjugate' points in this process.[13] But declining deference is also 'the permanent course of the political curve', and not just on security.[14] It is a wider trend that has been noted for decades in post-industrial societies.[15] This is associated with increasing individual freedom, declining class structures, successive crises in elites, and more tolerance and celebration of minorities. Parliamentarians reflect these societal changes, even if they lag behind in looking and sounding like the people they represent.

The normalisation of security politics does not mean the end of the *Leviathan*, however. Although the traditional black box of the security state has been prised open a little by leaks, parliamentary struggle, reforms and increased democratic oversight, it has not been abolished. For example, the Intelligence and Security Committee is still hindered by the government in its efforts at oversight, most recently in its investigation of British involvement in 'extraordinary rendition'.[16] Neither is the modest opening of the security black box the main reason for the increasing presence of security in normal politics. Most parliamentary activity on security does not relate to secretive aspects of security practice, but rather to the wider security problematisations mentioned above.

Despite this normalisation, there are still security exceptions in play today, including cruel and inhumane practices of bad faith and dubious legality. With the advent of peace in Northern Ireland, 'exceptional' counter-terrorism laws were not scrapped but rather extended to the whole UK, and then extended further after 9/11.[17] The government still has many exceptional security powers at its disposal, some of which apply only at state borders or to 'terrorist suspects' designated by the home secretary.[18] Some are misused by 'petty sovereign' civil servants aiming to meet targets for migrant expulsions.[19] The government even has the power to declare a full-scale 'state of emergency' under the Civil Contingencies Act 2004, but it has never done so.

The concept of a 'state of exception' crystallised in the post-9/11 period as a shorthand for the security logics behind the so-called 'war on terror'. These led to the Guantanamo Bay detention camp, intended as an exceptional space beyond the reach of US law. The same exceptional logics lay behind torture, 'extraordinary rendition' and, arguably, 'targeted killings' by drones.[20] The Italian philosopher Giorgio Agamben – tracing a genealogy via Schmitt, Hobbes and Roman forms of constitutional dictatorship – described the 'state of exception' as a condition in which the exception becomes generalised, creating a legal and judicial void in which sovereign power becomes unlimited.[21] The Copenhagen School follows a similar genealogy, placing a more limited exceptionalism at the heart of its definition of security.²²

Yet, demonstrably, the extension of security problematisations throughout social, political and economic life does not mean the rise of exceptional, securitising logics everywhere. We do not live in a state of exception. As security problematisations have proliferated they have become normalised. Exceptionalism has not been abolished, but most security problematisations are today assembled and implemented through normal policy processes. Practices of exceptionalism are still possible, but they describe little of the increasing political activity on security discussed in these pages.²³

This book has argued against the assumption that security is a special kind of rarefied, limited and exceptional politics that distorts and damages normal democratic politics. Most of the political activity explored here is unexceptional by any measure. It is rarely hindered by executive secrecy, it is not expedited, and it is not legally or constitutionally unusual. Although discourses of exception and emergency do emerge in the wake of major security events, these do not characterise most professional political activity on security in the past thirty years. The topics and policies may still be problematic, objectionable or controversial, but they are not necessarily urgent and exceptional. At a minimum, this activity may mean routine scrutiny of policies or budgets by select committees. More fully, it might mean the choice of parliamentarians to problematise security via a variety of parliamentary activities such as early day motions, private members' bills, all-party parliamentary groups or committee inquiries. It may even mean dramatic confrontations with the government over security policy. All this is part of normal politics.

Do these developments make us more secure? This is difficult to answer. The security literature has long since established that being more secure and feeling more secure are two different things with no necessary connection and with no agreed metrics of measurement. Even leaving this essential problem aside, answering the question would require a methodology that somehow correlated increased levels of political activity on security to incidences or non-incidences of security events, or more amorphously to the hypothetical possibilities presented by risks. This would be methodologically dubious with terrorist attacks, for example, which are so rare as to make statistical analysis almost meaningless. Risks cannot be assessed in such binary terms because by definition they are not things that happen or do not, but possibilities to be managed.[24] While assessing the effect of policies may be possible with large-scale population governance problems such as road safety or health, there is nothing on a comparable statistical scale in security governance.[25]

More fundamentally, to ask if more political activity on security makes us more or less secure is itself a politicised question that invokes the exceptionalism at the heart of traditional security politics. It invokes securitisations in which security actors demand fewer political constraints on action because of existential necessity. It also invokes struggles between governments and legislatures (and others) over the necessity and proportionality of security powers. In other words, to accept the premise that too much parliamentary activity on security may hinder a government that needs to act decisively is to accept the premise of the exceptionalism behind Guantanamo Bay, torture and rendition. It is also to accept the dubious premise that democratic legislatures are somehow less keen on security than governments, which feeds into claims about democratic (or liberal) peace that go back to Kant.[26] This book has found no evidence for parliamentary dovishness in the UK. Parliament in all its aspects, from whipped partisan votes to committee inquiries, is not pro- or anti-security. Individual parliamentarians may be, but others occupy all points in between. Parliamentary processes have resulted both in stronger security powers for government and in stronger limits on them.

In asking such a question, we have to consider what parliament is for. Unlike the US Congress, the UK parliament is not and never was intended to be a check or balance on executive government. Neither does it have its roots in republican or democratic ideals, but rather in the legitimation of sovereign power. Kelso argues that 'Parliament's fundamental role has been to facilitate legitimate government. Consequently, any notion that parliament exists primarily to promote democracy and democratic processes is historically inaccurate.'[27] The UK parliament website says its main functions are to: 'Check and challenge the work of the Government (scrutiny); Make and change laws (legislation); Debate the important issues of the day (debating); Check and approve Government spending (budget/taxes)'.[28] Taken together, this means that parliament may at times hinder government but is also a tool of government. In a majoritarian system such as that of the UK, it is rare that a government is blocked when it acts through parliament. Numbers matter, and while minority views may be heard, they usually remain marginal. In the Lords, where numbers and votes matter less, it is a constitutional convention to respect the manifesto commitments of the governing party. Ultimately, the parliamentary process, which includes the government, has to find a way to get business done. Although there have been parliamentary rebellions on counter-terrorist powers, and these have on occasion defeated the government, it is more likely that parliamentary influence happens in subtler ways.[29] With greater parliamentary engagement with security topics, there is greater breadth of discussion, greater representation of sectional interests and minority concerns, greater ability to test arguments to destruction, and a greater degree of wisdom brought to bear on policies. Ideally, this should mean better policy and fewer mistakes. However, parliamentary politics is a messy business, not a council of experts.

Parliamentary politics does influence security policy. This remains difficult to measure, but criticisms heard in the House or published in committee reports do shape policy even if governments are loath to admit it. One example is the Prevent counter-radicalisation policy, which was heavily criticised under Labour from across the political spectrum for trying to encourage 'moderation' but in effect tainting community relations policy with security suspicions. When the government changed, Prevent was brought into the Home Office and made into more of a system for apprehending 'extremism'. This addressed some of the old problems, but of course introduced many new ones.[30]

Ultimately, if we do not like the extension of security problematisations throughout society, parliament is not going to be our salvation. Parliament is both for and against security. It is a site of tradition and creativity, conservatism and progressivism, elite interest and democratic voice. There is no such thing as parliament as a whole.[31] It has hindered many unwise security policies, such as extended pre-charge detention for terrorist suspects, but it also passes the government's security laws and gives its policies democratic legitimacy.

What does increased parliamentary activity mean for security oversight? This question usually relates to parliamentary oversight of the intelligence agencies. The Snowden revelations in particular raised serious questions about the effectiveness of the Intelligence and Security Committee: if they knew what the agencies were doing, why did they not sound the alarm? If they did not know, what kind of overseers were they anyway? The growth of parliamentary politics on security does not solve this problem. Apart from ministers, ex-ministers, privy counsellors and ISC members, what parliament knows is what the public knows. Things are either secret or they are not. Parliamentarians, journalists, academics and activists are still struggling to uncover them. Perhaps they are getting better at it.[32]

However, as this book has argued throughout, this is a narrow way to think about security. Security policy is now everywhere, in all policy areas. As such, we need to rethink what oversight means. Intelligence oversight may have improved only incrementally, but parliament now oversees a much fuller spectrum of security policy that is mostly not secret. Parliament can question ministers and officials, call for evidence and papers, and launch inquiries on topics as diverse as the National Security Strategy, immigration policy, border management, counter-extremism, energy security, algorithms, surveillance, data retention, military restructuring, arms exports, terrorist attacks, the security implications of Scottish independence or Brexit or indeed anything it likes. While government is not always as cooperative as it could be, neither does it prevent this kind of everyday parliamentary work. Previous generations of parliamentarians may have been reluctant to engage with security topics, but there is decreasing evidence of that now.

Some scholars may argue that much of this new political activity is not really 'security'. They may argue that parliamentary inquiries on food or energy security have little to do with what Patrick

A. Mello and Dirk Peters called, in a recent special issue on parliaments and security, '"hard" security issues related to war involvement, military operations, and the use of force'.[33] In their definition little has changed from Stephen Walt's 1991 stand against the conceptual broadening of the meaning of security, when he wrote that 'security studies may be defined as the study of the threat, use and control of military force, [and the] specific policies that states adopt in order to prepare for, prevent, or engage in war'.[34] Methodologically and empirically, these traditionalist definitions are increasingly arbitrary and untenable. They imply that much of what governments now do under the banner of security is not really security. In the UK, this would exclude much of the National Security Strategy, including 'public health' and 'major natural hazards', which the 2015 edition ranks as 'Tier One priority risks'.[35] While war may remain a scourge for succeeding generations, to use this to define the limits of 'security' results in analytical restriction and the creation of political blind spots. Whatever the merits of the NSS and similar comprehensive security projects globally, if we want to understand the evolution of security governance and its relationship to politics then we should not dismiss such developments by analytical fiat.

It was in the same vein that the Copenhagen School reserved the right to use its 'strict criteria' to call out 'sloppy talk' of security.[36] We should not rule out the possibility of actors using security discourses lazily or in bad faith, nor should we take every elite utterance of security seriously. However, to insist on the priority of strict criteria over actors' contextual discourses comes at too great a cost: it jettisons the ability to track changes in the meaning and practice of security over time. This is why securitisation theory – by Wæver's own admission – is dated. This book began by answering 'yes' to his rhetorical question: 'Did securitization theory maybe appropriately capture only the politics of security of 1995 or 1985? Was it more accurate for 1955 than for 2015?'[37] For security politics in the UK, there is little difference between 1955, 1985 and even 1995; 2015, however, looks very different. New meanings and practices of security have proliferated, including risk, resilience, surveillance, algorithms and so on, as they have globally. While these developments have been charted and analysed extensively, their relationship to the traditional political arena has not.

To address these analytical problems, the book used a methodological approach to the study of security politics based on Michel Foucault's understanding of problematisations. Foucault described his method as a 'critical analysis in which one tries to see how the different solutions to a problem have been constructed'.[38] This is deceptively simple. Problematisation as method implies a radical constructivism that dispenses with fixed definitions of phenomena. It is a form of historical empiricism that examines through discourses and other artefacts the changing ways that actors speak, write and organise around what they see in different ways as problems. The methodological argument of the book thus dispensed with outdated 'hard' and 'strict' criteria of security. Although it entertained the 'contextualist' approach to security proposed by Felix Ciută, it concluded that this did not reflect enough on the critical role of the analyst. Foucault's work on genealogy tells us there is no neutral point where we can stand outside the political struggles and problematisations of our age.[39] In short, we cannot maintain the illusion of objectivity or interpretive neutrality. Analytical choices are inevitably political and historically situated. However, following Robert Castel, this does not give us licence to create analytical fictions for political ends.[40] Problematisation as method is still based on empirical validity. Its legitimacy comes from its historical sensibility and the critical-political aim of describing changing historical problematisations and then amplifying them in order to challenge prevailing theoretical and political assumptions.

This book set out to rethink the relationship between politics and security. The idea that security is a form of anti-politics – an issue area that favours executive power and reduces political choice – has been central to the study of security. It is present in Hobbes, with the *Leviathan* towering over the land and guaranteeing civic life by the sword. It is implicit in the study of international relations with its focus on statecraft and war, and its reduction of domestic politics to a mere variable. Most importantly, the anti-politics of security is a foundational concern for critical security studies, with its aspirations to unmake egregious security practices and draw attention to the insecurities of the downtrodden. However, although critical security studies was built on a deep understanding of change and the emergence of new security problematisations in the dying days of the Cold War, its proponents never rethought its foundational premise of security as an anti-politics.

This book has shown that while the anti-politics of security made sense in the 1980s and 1990s, it no longer describes the political life of security. Professional politicians, the political class, parliamentarians, legislators – whatever we call them – are increasingly active and engaged with security. It is part of everyday political life. It is part of normal politics. This does not mean the normalisation of security is complete. Security exceptionalism still exists. The executive security prerogatives of secrecy and decision still exist. Parliamentarians and the public are still excluded from their inner workings. Yet this is now only one part of security governance. Rightly or wrongly, security problematisations now reach far and wide. New concepts and practices have emerged that are not off limits to parliamentarians. Though these may have extra gravity, parliamentarians handle them like any others, debating them, calling for evidence, publishing reports and asking questions. Whether they do it well is another question. The point is that they do it at all.

What does all this mean for the concept of security? Primarily that it is not a pathology of politics. It can be, but it is not necessarily so. One of the key dilemmas in the development of securitisation theory was how to accommodate the widening and deepening of security without losing analytical coherence. As Huysmans put it, if 'the difference between a security question and a non-security question . . . cannot be established, security will be a trivial concept; it will be everywhere'.[41] Today, security *is* everywhere. The policy, politics and practice of security have been indifferent to scholars' efforts to maintain analytical coherence in the face of change. Security has been – to use Bartelson's phrase – 'performing new tricks behind our backs'.[42] Demonstrably this does not mean the extension of securitisation or exceptionalism everywhere. But what does it mean? It means the dilution of security, but not to the point of triviality. Urgency, necessity and existential peril are not so firmly embedded in its meaning as they once were, yet they have not disappeared and can still be invoked with deleterious effects. But talk of water, food or energy security – for example – rarely has such connotations. In rich countries at least, these are risks to be managed where catastrophic failure is only the most extreme hypothetical possibility. Problematising such issues in security terms does not securitise them but brings them into balance with other security priorities and choices: how much risk is tolerable? What resources should be allocated to their management? What are the social, political and economic costs of failing to prevent flooding, for example, compared to failing to prevent terrorist attacks? These are not easy choices, but it is clear that not every threat or risk can be treated as an urgent and exceptional priority. Even the more dramatic threat-based security topics such as terrorism, drone strikes, surveillance powers and decisions to go to war are handled through normal governmental and political processes in a way they were not thirty or even fifteen years ago. Security policy making increasingly resembles policy making in other areas. Security, for better or worse, is an increasingly everyday practice. Security is increasingly part of normal politics.

Notes

1. Abrahamsen and Williams, 'Securing the City'; Amoore, 'Algorithmic War'; Haggerty and Ericson, 'The Surveillant Assemblage'; Ragazzi, 'Countering Terrorism and Radicalisation'; Heath-Kelly, 'The Geography of Pre-Criminal Space'; Balzacq et al., 'Security Practices'.
2. Buzan, Wæver and de Wilde, *Security*, pp. 4–5.
3. Wæver, 'Politics, Security, Theory', p. 467.
4. Buzan, Wæver and de Wilde, *Security*, p. 23; Wæver, 'Politics, Security, Theory', p. 469.
5. Buzan, Wæver and de Wilde, *Security*, pp. 27–8.
6. May, *A Treatise on the Law, Privileges, Proceedings and Usage of Parliament*, 21st edn, p. 292.
7. Bochel, Defty and Kirkpatrick, *Watching the Watchers*, p. 27; Andrew, *The Defence of the Realm*, p. 753.

8. Buzan, Wæver and de Wilde, *Security*, p. 27.
9. Lord Butler of Brockwell, *Review of Intelligence on Weapons of Mass Destruction*, p. 7.
10. May, *A Treatise on the Law, Privileges, Proceedings and Usage of Parliament*, 21st edn, p. 292.
11. UK Government, 'National Security Strategy and Strategic Defence and Security Review 2015'.
12. UK Government, 'National Security Capability Review (NSCR)'.
13. Bagehot, *The English Constitution*, p. 17.
14. Ibid.
15. Nevitte, *The Decline of Deference* and 'The Decline of Deference Revisited'; Scammell and Semetko, 'Election News Coverage in the UK'.
16. Cobain and MacAskill, 'Criticism Mounts over UK's Post-9/11 Role in Torture and Rendition'.
17. Neal, 'Normalization and Legislative Exceptionalism'.
18. *The Guardian*, 'Glenn Greenwald's Partner Detained at Heathrow Airport for Nine Hours'.
19. Maddox, 'Windrush Cases Expose Arbitrary Immigration Targets'; Butler, *Precarious Life*, p. 65.
20. Intelligence and Security Committee of Parliament, 'Press Release – 26 April 2017 – UK Lethal Drone Strikes in Syria'; Schwarz, 'Prescription Drones'; Kindervater, 'The Emergence of Lethal Surveillance'.
21. Agamben, *State of Exception*, p. 40.
22. Williams, 'Securitization as Political Theory', p. 19.
23. Buzan, Wæver and de Wilde, *Security*, p. 33.
24. Rasmussen, *The Risk Society at War*, pp. 1–2.
25. Hagmann and Dunn Cavelty, 'National Risk Registers', pp. 84–5.
26. As any serious democratic peace literature will point out, democracies are not peaceful (usually the contrary), they are just more peaceful with each other. See Doyle, 'Kant, Liberal Legacies, and Foreign Affairs, Part 2'.
27. Kelso, *Parliamentary Reform at Westminster*, p. 15.
28. UK Parliament, 'Parliament's Role'.
29. Russell and Cowley, 'The Policy Power of the Westminster Parliament'.
30. NUS Black Students, 'Preventing Prevent'; Heath-Kelly, 'The Geography of Pre-Criminal Space'; Spiller, Awan and Whiting, '"What Does Terrorism Look Like?"'.
31. Wright, *Doing Politics*, p. 167.

32. For example, see Raphael et al., 'Tracking Rendition Aircraft as a Way to Understand CIA Secret Detention and Torture in Europe'.
33. Mello and Peters, 'Parliaments in Security Policy', p. 5.
34. Walt, 'The Renaissance of Security Studies', p. 212.
35. UK Government, 'National Security Strategy and Strategic Defence and Security Review 2015', p. 87.
36. Buzan, Wæver and de Wilde, *Security*, p. 47, fn. 9.
37. Wæver, 'Politics, Security, Theory', p. 473.
38. Foucault and Rabinow, 'Polemics, Politics and Problematizations', p. 389.
39. Veyne, 'Foucault Revolutionizes History' and *Foucault*; Dreyfus and Rabinow, *Michel Foucault*; Foucault, 'Nietzsche, Genealogy, History'.
40. Castel, '"Problematization" as a Mode of Reading History'.
41. Huysmans, 'Revisiting Copenhagen', p. 491.
42. Bartelson, *A Genealogy of Sovereignty*, p. 55.

Bibliography

Abrahamsen, Rita, 'Blair's Africa: The Politics of Securitization and Fear', *Alternatives* 30, no. 1 (2005): 55–80.

Abrahamsen, Rita, and Michael C. Williams, 'Securing the City: Private Security Companies and Non-State Authority in Global Governance', *International Relations* 21, no. 2 (2007): 237–53.

Ackerman, Bruce, 'The Emergency Constitution', *The Yale Law Journal* 113, no. 5 (2004): 1029–91.

Acronym Institute, 'Angus Robertson Asks if MoD Will Place the Defence Nuclear Executive Board's Risk Register for the Nuclear Programme in the Library', <http://www.acronym.org.uk/old/parliamentary-records/201501/angus-robertson-asks-if-mod-will-place-defence-nuclear-executive-boards-risk-register-nuclear-progr> (last accessed 6 September 2018).

Adey, Peter, 'Security Atmospheres or the Crystallisation of Worlds', *Environment and Planning D: Society and Space* 32, no. 5 (2014): 834–51.

Adey, Peter, and Ben Anderson, 'Anticipating Emergencies: Technologies of Preparedness and the Matter of Security', *Security Dialogue* 43, no. 2 (2012): 99–117.

Agamben, Giorgio, *State of Exception*, trans. Kevin Attell, Chicago and London: University of Chicago Press, 2005.

Alker, Hayward, 'Emancipation in the Critical Security Studies Project', in Ken Booth (ed.), *Critical Security Studies and World Politics*, Boulder: Lynne Rienner, 2005, pp. 189–214.

Amoore, Louise, 'Algorithmic War: Everyday Geographies of the War on Terror', *Antipode* 41, no. 1 (2009): 49–69.

Amoore, Louise, *The Politics of Possibility: Risk and Security Beyond Probability*, Durham, NC: Duke University Press, 2013.

Amoore, Louise, and Marieke de Goede, *Risk and the War on Terror*, London: Routledge, 2008.

Amoore, Louise, and Rita Raley, 'Securing with Algorithms: Knowledge, Decision, Sovereignty', *Security Dialogue* 48, no. 1 (2017): 3–10.

Anderson, David, 'A Question of Trust: Report of the Investigatory Powers Review', London: HMSO, 2015.

Andrew, Christopher, *The Defence of the Realm: The Authorized History of MI5*, London: Penguin Books Limited, 2012.

Andrew, Christopher, *Secret Service: The Making of the British Intelligence Community*, London: Heinemann, 1985.

Andrew, Christopher, Richard J. Aldrich and Wesley K. Wark, *Secret Intelligence: A Reader*, Abingdon: Taylor & Francis, 2009.

Aradau, Claudia, 'The Promise of Security: Resilience, Surprise and Epistemic Politics', *Resilience* 2, no. 2 (2014): 73–87.

Aradau, Claudia, 'Security and the Democratic Scene: Desecuritization and Emancipation', *Journal of International Relations and Development* 7 (2004): 388–413.

Aradau, Claudia, and Tobias Blanke, 'The (Big) Data-Security Assemblage: Knowledge and Critique', *Big Data & Society* 2, no. 2 (2015): 1–12.

Aradau, Claudia, and Rens van Munster, 'Governing Terrorism through Risk: Taking Precautions, (Un)Knowing the Future', *European Journal of International Relations* 13, no. 1 (2007): 89–115.

Aradau, Claudia, and Rens van Munster, *Terror and the Politics of Catastrophe: Risk, Security and Modernity*, London: Routledge, 2009.

Aradau, Claudia, Andrew W. Neal, Jef Huysmans and Nadine Voelkner (eds), *Critical Security Methods: New Frameworks for Analysis*, Abingdon: Routledge, 2014.

Arter, David, 'The Nordic Parliaments: Patterns of Legislative Influence', *West European Politics* 8, no. 1 (1985): 55–70.

Bagehot, Walter, *The English Constitution, and Other Political Essays*, New York: D. Appleton, 1930.

Balzacq, Thierry, 'The "Essence" of Securitization: Theory, Ideal Type, and a Sociological Science of Security', *International Relations* 29, no. 1 (2015): 103–13.

Balzacq, Thierry (ed.), *Securitization Theory: How Security Problems Emerge and Dissolve*, Prio New Security Studies, Abingdon: Routledge, 2011.

Balzacq, Thierry, 'A Theory of Securitization: Origins, Core Assumptions and Variants', in Thierry Balzacq (ed.), *Securitization Theory: How Security Problems Emerge and Dissolve*, Abingdon: Routledge, 2011, pp. 1–30.

Balzacq, Thierry, 'The Three Faces of Securitization: Political Agency, Audience and Context', *European Journal of International Relations* 11, no. 2 (2005): 171–201.

Balzacq, Thierry, Tugba Basaran, Didier Bigo, Emmanuel-Pierre Guittet and Christian Olsson, 'Security Practices', in Robert A. Denemark (ed.), *The International Studies Encyclopedia*, Blackwell Reference Online: Blackwell Publishing, 2010.

Bartelson, Jens, *A Genealogy of Sovereignty*, Cambridge: Cambridge University Press, 1995.

Bates, Stephen, Mark Goodwin and Stephen McKay, 'Do UK MPs Engage More with Select Committees since the Wright Reforms? An Interrupted Time Series Analysis, 1979–2016', *Parliamentary Affairs* (April 2017).

BBC, 'David Davis MP, Desert Island Discs – BBC Radio 4', 2008.

BBC News, 'Binyam Mohamed Torture Appeal Lost by UK Government', <http://news.bbc.co.uk/1/hi/uk/8507852.stm> (last accessed 6 September 2018).

BBC News, 'Blair Defeated over Terror Laws', <http://news.bbc.co.uk/1/hi/uk_politics/4422086.stm> (last accessed 6 September 2018).

BBC News, 'David Davis Resigns from Commons', <http://news.bbc.co.uk/1/hi/uk_politics/7450627.stm> (last accessed 6 September 2018).

BBC News, 'Did David Davis Keep His Dignity?', <http://news.bbc.co.uk/1/hi/uk_politics/7501110.stm> (last accessed 6 September 2018).

BBC News, 'Full Text: Conservative-Lib Dem Deal', <http://news.bbc.co.uk/1/hi/8677933.stm> (last accessed 6 September 2018).

BBC News, 'MI5 "Secretly Collected Phone Data" for Decade', <http://www.bbc.co.uk/news/uk-politics-34729139> (last accessed 6 September 2018).

BBC News, 'Nato 2% Defence Spending Target Should Be Met, MPs Say', <https://www.bbc.com/news/uk-politics-31857044> (last accessed 6 September 2018).

BBC News, 'Syria Crisis: Cameron Loses Commons Vote on Syria Action', <https://www.bbc.co.uk/news/uk-politics-23892783> (last accessed 6 September 2018).

Behnke, Andreas, 'No Way Out: Desecuritization, Emancipation and the Eternal Return of the Political – a Reply to Aradau', *Journal of International Relations and Development* 9 (2006): 62–9.

Bellanova, Rocco, 'Digital, Politics, and Algorithms: Governing Digital Data through the Lens of Data Protection', *European Journal of Social Theory* (2016), <https://doi.org/10.1177/1368431016679167>.

Benton, Meghan, and Meg Russell, 'Assessing the Impact of Parliamentary Oversight Committees: The Select Committees in the British House of Commons', *Parliamentary Affairs* 66, no. 4 (2012): 772–97.

Biebricher, Thomas, 'Genealogy and Governmentality', *Journal of the Philosophy of History* 2, no. 3 (2008): 363–96.

Bigo, Didier, 'Globalized (in)Security: The Field and the Ban-Opticon', in Didier Bigo and Anastassia Tsoukala (eds), *Terror, Insecurity and Liberty: Illiberal Practices of Liberal Regimes after 9/11*, London: Routledge, 2008, pp. 10–48.

Bigo, Didier, 'Security and Immigration, toward a Critique of the Governmentality of Unease', *Alternatives: Global, Local, Political* 27, no. 1 (2002): 63–92.

Bigo, Didier, and Anastassia Tsoukala, *Terror, Insecurity and Liberty: Illiberal Practices of Liberal Regimes after 9/11*, Routledge Studies in Liberty and Security, London: Routledge, 2008.

Biswas, Shampa, and Sheila Nair (eds), *International Relations and States of Exception: Margins, Peripheries, and Excluded Bodies*, Abingdon: Routledge, 2009.

Blondel, Jean, 'Legislative Behaviour: Some Steps Towards a Cross-National Measurement', *Government and Opposition* 5, no. 1 (1970): 67–85.

Blyth, Mark, *Austerity: The History of a Dangerous Idea*, New York: Oxford University Press, 2015.

Bochel, Hugh, and Andrew Defty, 'Parliamentary Oversight of Intelligence Agencies: Lessons from Westminster', in Andrew W. Neal (ed.), *Security in a Small Nation: Scotland, Democracy, Politics*, Cambridge: Open Book Publishers, 2017, pp. 103–23.

Bochel, Hugh, Andrew Defty and Jane Kirkpatrick, '"New Mechanisms of Independent Accountability": Select Committees and Parliamentary Scrutiny of the Intelligence Services', *Parliamentary Affairs* (2013).

Bochel, Hugh, Andrew Defty and Jane Kirkpatrick, *Watching the Watchers: Parliament and the Intelligence Services*, Basingstoke: Palgrave Macmillan, 2014.

Bonditti, Philippe, Andrew W. Neal, Sven Opitz and Christopher Zebrowski, 'Genealogy', in Claudia Aradau, Andrew W. Neal, Jef Huysmans and Nadine Voelkner (eds), *Critical Security Methods: New Frameworks for Analysis*, Abingdon: Routledge, 2014, pp. 159–88.

Booth, Ken, 'Security and Emancipation', *Review of International Studies* 17, no. 4 (1991): 313–26.

Born, Hans, and Marina Caparini (eds), *Democratic Control of Intelligence Services: Containing Rogue Elephants*, Aldershot: Ashgate, 2013.

Boswell, Christina, 'Migration Control in Europe after 9/11: Explaining the Absence of Securitization', *JCMS: Journal of Common Market Studies* 45, no. 3 (2007): 589–610.

Bourbeau, Philippe, 'Moving Forward Together: Logics of the Securitisation Process', *Millennium – Journal of International Studies* 43, no. 1 (2014): 187–206.

Bourdieu, Pierre, *In Other Words: Essays Towards a Reflexive Sociology*, Cambridge: Polity, 1990.

Bourdieu, Pierre, *Language and Symbolic Power*, ed. John B. Thompson, Cambridge: Polity, 1992.

Bourdieu, Pierre, *The Logic of Practice*, Cambridge: Polity, 1990.

Bourdieu, Pierre, 'On Symbolic Power', in John B. Thompson (ed.), *Language and Symbolic Power*, Cambridge: Polity, 1992, pp. 163–70.

Bourdieu, Pierre, 'Political Representation: Elements for a Theory of the Political Field', in John B. Thompson (ed.), *Language and Symbolic Power*, Cambridge: Polity, 1992, pp. 171–202.

Bourdieu, Pierre, *Practical Reason: On the Theory of Action*, Cambridge: Polity Press, 1998.

Brazier, Alex, and Ruth Fox, 'Reviewing Select Committee Tasks and Modes of Operation', *Parliamentary Affairs* 64, no. 2 (2011): 354–69.

Bright, Jonathan, 'In Search of the Politics of Security', *The British Journal of Politics and International Relations* 17, no. 4 (2014): 585–603.

Brooker, Charlie, 'Home Office Raises Current Terrorism Threat Level to "Severe"', Newswipe, <http://www.youtube.com/watch?v=OxuYt7iBijQ> (last accessed 6 September 2018).

Broomby, Rob, 'Questions about UK Scrutiny of Chinese Nuclear Tie-Up', <https://www.bbc.co.uk/news/uk-politics-30778427> (last accessed 6 September 2018).

Browning, Christopher S., and Matt McDonald, 'The Future of Critical Security Studies: Ethics and the Politics of Security', *European Journal of International Relations* 19, no. 2 (2013): 235–55.

Brundtland, Gro Harlem, 'Our Common Future – Call for Action', *Environmental Conservation* 14, no. 4 (1987): 291–4.

Bubandt, Nils, 'Vernacular Security: The Politics of Feeling Safe in Global, National and Local Worlds', *Security Dialogue* 36, no. 3 (2005): 275–96.

Bull, Hedley, *The Anarchical Society: A Study of Order in World Politics*, London: Macmillan, 1977.

Burchell, Graham, 'Liberal Government and Techniques of the Self', *Economy and Society* 22, no. 3 (1993): 267–82.
Burke, Anthony, 'Security Cosmopolitanism: The Next Phase', *Critical Studies on Security* 3, no. 2 (2015): 190–212.
Burke, Jason, *The 9/11 Wars*, London: Allen Lane, 2011.
Burnham, Peter, 'New Labour and the Politics of Depoliticisation', *The British Journal of Politics and International Relations* 3, no. 2 (2001): 127–49.
Butler, Judith, *Gender Trouble: Feminism and the Subversion of Identity*, 10th anniversary edn, New York and London: Routledge, 1999.
Butler, Judith, *Precarious Life: The Powers of Mourning and Violence*, London: Verso, 2004.
Buzan, Barry, *People, States and Fear: The National Security Problem in International Relations*, Brighton: Wheatsheaf, 1983.
Buzan, Barry, and Lene Hansen, *The Evolution of International Security Studies*, Cambridge: Cambridge University Press, 2009.
Buzan, Barry, and Ole Wæver, *Regions and Powers: The Structure of International Security*, vol. 91, Cambridge: Cambridge University Press, 2003.
Buzan, Barry, Ole Wæver and Jaap de Wilde, *Security: A New Framework for Analysis*, Boulder and London: Lynne Rienner, 1998.
Cabinet Office, 'Supporting the National Security Council (NSC): The Central National Security and Intelligence Machinery', 2011.
Cabinet Office, 'The UK Cyber Security Strategy: Protecting and Promoting the UK in a Digital World', 2011.
Canada, 'Securing an Open Society: Canada's National Security Policy', Ottawa: Privy Council Office, 2004.
Caparini, Marina, 'Controlling and Overseeing Intelligence Services in Democratic States', in Hans Born and Marina Caparini (eds), *Democratic Control of Intelligence Services: Containing Rogue Elephants*, Aldershot: Ashgate, 2007, pp. 1–24.
Carlson, Richard J., 'Nietzsche's Snowden: Tightrope Walking the Posthuman Dispositif', in Debashish Banerji and Makarand R. Paranjape (eds), *Critical Posthumanism and Planetary Futures*, New Delhi: Springer, 2016, pp. 49–74.
CASE Collective, 'Critical Approaches to Security in Europe: A Networked Manifesto', *Security Dialogue* 37, no. 4 (2006): 443–87.
Castel, Robert, '"Problematization" as a Mode of Reading History', in Jan Goldstein (ed.), *Foucault and the Writing of History*, Oxford: Blackwell, 1994, pp. 237–52.

Centre for the Protection of National Infrastructure, 'Critical National Infrastructure | Cpni | Public Website', <https://www.cpni.gov.uk/critical-national-infrastructure-0> (last accessed 7 September 2018).

Chang, Nancy, *The Silencing of Political Dissent*, New York: Seven Stories; London: Turnaround, 2002.

Chilcot, Sir John, 'Iraq Inquiry: Executive Summary', House of Commons, 2016.

Childs, Sarah, *Women and British Party Politics: Descriptive, Substantive and Symbolic Representation*, Routledge Advances in European Politics, Abingdon: Taylor & Francis, 2008.

Chowanietz, Christophe, 'Rallying around the Flag or Railing against the Government? Political Parties' Reactions to Terrorist Acts', *Party Politics* 17, no. 5 (2011): 673–98.

Ciută, Felix, 'Security and the Problem of Context: A Hermeneutical Critique of Securitisation Theory', *Review of International Studies* 35, no. 2 (2009): 301–26.

Clausewitz, Carl von, *On War*, trans. Michael Howard and Peter Paret, Oxford: Oxford University Press, 2007.

Cobain, Ian, and Ewen MacAskill, 'Criticism Mounts over UK's Post-9/11 Role in Torture and Rendition', *The Guardian*, 28 June 2018.

Cockcroft, Lucy, 'Timeline: How the 42 Day Detention Plan Was Dropped', *The Telegraph*, 14 October 2008.

Cohn, Carol, 'Sex and Death in the Rational World of Defense Intellectuals', *Signs: Journal of Women in Culture and Society* 12, no. 4 (1987): 687–718.

Conservative Party, *Invitation to Join the Government of Britain: The Conservative Manifesto 2010*, Conservative Research Department, 2010.

Cornish, Paul, and Andrew M. Dorman, 'Fifty Shades of Purple? A Risk-Sharing Approach to the 2015 Strategic Defence and Security Review', *International Affairs* 89 (2013): 1183–202.

Corry, Dan, 'Power at the Centre: Is the National Economic Council a Model for a New Way of Organising Things?', *The Political Quarterly* 82, no. 3 (2011): 459–68.

Corry, Olaf, 'Securitisation and "Riskification": Second-Order Security and the Politics of Climate Change', *Millennium* 40, no. 2 (2012): 235–58.

Corry, Olaf, 'Whispering Risk in the Prince's Ear: Towards an Ideological Approach to Security and Risk', International Studies Association Annual Convention, San Francisco, 2013.

Cowley, Philip, *The Rebels: How Blair Mislaid His Majority*, London: Politico's, 2005.
Cowley, Philip, *Revolts and Rebellions: Parliamentary Voting under Blair*, London: Politico's, 2002.
Cowley, Philip, and Mark Stuart, 'Dissension amongst the Parliamentary Labour Party, 2001–2005: A Data Handbook', <http://www.revolts.co.uk/DissensionamongsttthePLP.pdf> (last accessed 7 September 2018).
Cowley, Philip, and Mark Stuart, 'End of Parliament Stats – Stage 1', 9 April 2010, <http://revolts.co.uk/?p=517> (last accessed 18 September 2018).
Crick, Bernard, *In Defence of Politics*, London: Bloomsbury Academic, 2013.
Crick, Bernard, *The Reform of Parliament*, London: Weidenfeld & Nicolson, 1968.
Crowcroft, Robert, 'A War on "Risk"? British Government and the National Security Strategy', *The Political Quarterly* 83, no. 1 (2012): 172–6.
Davis, David, 'Why I Am Resigning | Opinion', *The Guardian*, <https://www.theguardian.com/commentisfree/2008/jun/12/speeches> (last accessed 7 September 2018).
Dayan, Colin, *The Story of Cruel and Unusual*, Boston Review Books, Cambridge, MA: MIT Press, 2007.
Dean, Mitchell, *Critical and Effective Histories: Foucault's Methods and Historical Sociology*, London: Routledge, 1994.
Dean, Mitchell, *Governmentality: Power and Rule in Modern Society*, London: SAGE, 1999.
Defty, Andrew, 'Educating Parliamentarians about Intelligence: The Role of the British Intelligence and Security Committee', *Parliamentary Affairs* 61, no. 4 (2008): 621–41.
Department of Homeland Security, 'Homeland Security Advisory System', <https://www.dhs.gov/homeland-security-advisory-system> (last accessed 18 September 2018).
Devanny, Joe, and Josh Harris, 'The National Security Council: National Security at the Centre of Government', Institute for Government & King's College London, 2014.
Dillon, Michael, and Julian Reid, *The Liberal Way of War: Killing to Make Life Live*, London: Routledge, 2009.
Dowding, Keith, and Won-Taek Kang, 'Ministerial Resignations 1945–97', *Public Administration* 76, no. 3 (1998): 411–29.
Doyle, Michael W., 'Kant, Liberal Legacies, and Foreign Affairs, Part 2', *Philosophy & Public Affairs* 12, no. 4 (1983): 323–53.

Dreyfus, Hubert L., and Paul Rabinow, *Michel Foucault: Beyond Structuralism and Hermeneutics*, Brighton: Harvester, 1982.

Duffield, Mark, 'The Liberal Way of Development and the Development–Security Impasse: Exploring the Global Life-Chance Divide', *Security Dialogue* 41, no. 1 (2010): 53–76.

Dunn Cavelty, Myriam, Mareile Kaufmann and Kristian Søby Kristensen, 'Resilience and (in)Security: Practices, Subjects, Temporalities', *Security Dialogue* 46, no. 1 (2015): 3–14.

Dyzenhaus, David, 'An Unfortunate Outburst of Anglo-Saxon Parochialism', *The Modern Law Review* 68, no. 4 (2005): 673–6.

Elbe, Stefan, 'Aids, Security, Biopolitics', *International Relations* 19, no. 4 (2005): 403–19.

Enloe, Cynthia H., *Bananas, Beaches and Bases: Making Feminist Sense of International Politics*, London: Pandora, 1989.

Eriksson, Johan, 'Observers or Advocates?', *Cooperation and Conflict* 34, no. 3 (1999): 311–30.

European Scrutiny Committee, 'Fifteenth Report, House of Commons Session 1999–2000, Hc23-Xv', 1999.

Evans, Jonathan, 'Defending the Realm', public lecture by the Director General of the Security Service, Jonathan Evans, Bristol University, 15 October 2009.

Everett, Michael, Lucinda Maer and Gail Bartlett, 'The Official Secrets Acts and Official Secrecy', <http://researchbriefings.parliament.uk/ResearchBriefing/Summary/CBP-7422> (last accessed 7 September 2018).

Ewald, François, 'Insurance and Risk', in Graham Burchell, Colin Gordon and Peter Miller (eds), *The Foucault Effect: Studies in Governmentality: With Two Lectures by and an Interview with Michel Foucault*, Chicago: University of Chicago Press, 1991, pp. 197–210.

Farson, Anthony S., David Stafford and Wesley K. Wark, *Security and Intelligence in a Changing World: New Perspectives for the 1990s*, London: Frank Cass, 1991.

Fawcett, Paul, and David Marsh, 'Depoliticisation, Governance and Political Participation', *Policy & Politics* 42, no. 2 (2014): 171–88.

Feldman, Allen, *Formations of Violence: The Narrative of the Body and Political Terror in Northern Ireland*, Chicago: University of Chicago Press, 1991.

Fierke, Karin M., *Changing Games, Changing Strategies: Critical Investigations in Security*, Manchester: Manchester University Press, 1998.

Fisher, Lucy, 'The Growing Power and Autonomy of House of Commons Select Committees: Causes and Effects', *The Political Quarterly* 86, no. 3 (2015): 419–26.

Flinders, Matthew, and Jim Buller, 'Depoliticisation: Principles, Tactics and Tools', *British Politics* 1, no. 3 (2006): 293–318.

Flinders, Matthew, and Alexandra Kelso, 'Mind the Gap: Political Analysis, Public Expectations and the Parliamentary Decline Thesis', *The British Journal of Politics and International Relations* 13, no. 2 (2011): 249–68.

Flinders, Matthew, and Matt Wood, 'Depoliticisation, Governance and the State', *Policy & Politics* 42, no. 2 (2014): 135–49.

Floyd, Rita, 'Extraordinary or Ordinary Emergency Measures: What, and Who, Defines the "Success" of Securitization?', *Cambridge Review of International Affairs* 29, no. 2 (2016): 677–94.

Floyd, Rita, 'Towards a Consequentialist Evaluation of Security: Bringing Together the Copenhagen and the Welsh Schools of Security Studies', *Review of International Studies* 33, no. 2 (2007): 327–50.

Flynn, Paul, *How to Be an MP*, London: Biteback, 2012.

Foreign Affairs Committee, 'House of Commons – Foreign Affairs – Second Report', <https://publications.parliament.uk/pa/cm199899/cmselect/cmfaff/116/11610.htm#a37> (last accessed 7 September 2018).

Foreign Affairs Committee, 'Third Report from the Foreign Affairs Committee, Session 1984–85: Events Surrounding the Weekend of 1–2 May 1982: Together with the Proceedings of the Committee, Minutes of Evidence, and Appendices', in *HC (Series) (Great Britain. Parliament. House of Commons)*, London: HM Stationery Office, 1985.

Forsyth, James, 'The Risks for Osborne Now He's Back on Top', *The Spectator*, 22 March 2014.

Foucault, Michel, *The Archaeology of Knowledge*, trans. A. M. Sheridan Smith, London: Routledge, 2002.

Foucault, Michel, *The Birth of Biopolitics: Lectures at the Collège de France, 1978–1979*, trans. Graham Burchell, ed. Arnold Davidson, Basingstoke: Palgrave Macmillan, 2008.

Foucault, Michel, 'The Confession of the Flesh', in *Power/Knowledge: Selected Interviews and Other Writings, 1972–1977*, ed. Colin Gordon, Brighton: Harvester, 1980, pp. 194–228.

Foucault, Michel, *The Courage of Truth: Lectures at the Collège de France, 1983–1984*, Basingstoke: Palgrave Macmillan, 2011.

Foucault, Michel, 'The Discourse on Language', in José Medina and David Wood (eds), *Truth: Engagements Across Philosophical Traditions*, Oxford: Blackwell Publishing, 2005, pp. 315–35.

Foucault, Michel, *Fearless Speech*, Foreign Agents Series, Cambridge, MA: MIT Press, 2001.

Foucault, Michel, *The Government of Self and Others: Lectures at the Collège de France, 1982–1983*, Basingstoke: Palgrave Macmillan, 2010.

Foucault, Michel, 'Governmentality', in *The Essential Works of Michel Foucault, 1954–1984, Vol. 3: Power*, ed. James D. Faubion, London: Penguin, 2002, pp. 201–22.

Foucault, Michel, *History of Madness*, trans. Jonathan Murphy and Jean Khlafa, Abingdon: Routledge, 2006.

Foucault, Michel, 'Interview with Michel Foucault', in *The Essential Works of Michel Foucault, 1954–1984, Vol. 3: Power*, ed. James D. Faubion, London: Penguin, 2002, 239–97.

Foucault, Michel, 'Nietzsche, Genealogy, History', trans. Donald F. Bouchard and Sherry Simon, in *The Foucault Reader*, ed. Paul Rabinow, London: Penguin, 1991, pp. 76–100.

Foucault, Michel, 'Questions of Method', in Graham Burchell, Colin Gordon and Peter M. Miller (eds), *The Foucault Effect: Studies in Governmentality*, London: Harvester Wheatsheaf, 1991, pp. 73–86.

Foucault, Michel, *Security, Territory, Population: Lectures at the Collège de France, 1977–1978*, Basingstoke: Palgrave Macmillan, 2007.

Foucault, Michel, *'Society Must Be Defended': Lectures at the Collège de France, 1975–1976*, trans. David Macey, New York: Picador, 2002.

Foucault, Michel, 'Truth and Power', trans. Colin Gordon, Leo Marshall, John Mepham and Kate Soper, in *Power/Knowledge: Selected Interviews and Other Writings, 1972–1977*, ed. Colin Gordon, New York: Harvester Wheatsheaf, 1980, pp. 109–33.

Foucault, Michel, and Paul Rabinow, 'Polemics, Politics and Problematizations: An Interview with Michel Foucault', in *The Foucault Reader*, ed. Paul Rabinow, London: Penguin, 1991, pp. 381–90.

Fox, Ruth, and Matt Korris, *Making Better Law: Reform of the Legislative Process from Policy to Act*, London: Hansard Society, 2010.

Franks, Oliver, and Privy Council, 'Falkland Islands Review: Report of a Committee of Privy Counsellors', London: HM Stationery Office, 1983.

Frazer, Elizabeth, and Kimberly Hutchings, 'Virtuous Violence and the Politics of Statecraft in Machiavelli, Clausewitz and Weber', *Political Studies* 59, no. 1 (2011): 56–73.

Freeman, Richard, 'Political Work: Inaugural Lecture', University of Edinburgh, 2015, <https://www.ed.ac.uk/arts-humanities-soc-sci/news-events/lectures/inaugural-lectures/archive/inaugural-lectures-2015-2016/richard-freeman> (last accessed 18 September 2018).

Friedrich, Carl J., *Constitutional Government and Politics*, New York: Harper and Brothers, 1937.

Furedi, Frank, *Invitation to Terror: The Expanding Empire of the Unknown*, London: Continuum, 2007.

Gad, Ulrik Pram, and Karen Lund Petersen, 'Concepts of Politics in Securitization Studies', *Security Dialogue* 42, nos. 4–5 (2011): 315–28.

Gamble, Andrew, 'Austerity as Statecraft', *Parliamentary Affairs* 68, no. 1 (2015): 42–57.

Garrido, Miguelángel Verde, 'Contesting a Biopolitics of Information and Communications: The Importance of Truth and Sousveillance after Snowden', *Surveillance & Society* 13, no. 2 (2015): 153–67.

Gaskarth, Jamie, 'The Fiasco of the 2013 Syria Votes: Decline and Denial in British Foreign Policy', *Journal of European Public Policy* 23, no. 5 (2016): 718–34.

Gearty, Conor, '11 September 2001, Counter-Terrorism, and the Human Rights Act', *Journal of Law and Society* 32, no. 1 (2005): 18–33.

Geddes, Marc, 'Building Webs of Scrutiny: How Everyday Practices Shape Select Committee Inquiries in the UK House of Commons', paper presented at the Political Studies Association Annual Conference, Glasgow, 10–12 April 2017.

Geddes, Marc, *Dramas at Westminster: Select Committees and the Quest for Accountability*, Manchester: Manchester University Press, 2019.

Giddens, Anthony, *The Constitution of Society: Outline of the Theory of Structuration*, Berkeley: University of California Press, 1986.

Gill, Peter, 'Evaluating Intelligence Oversight Committees: The UK Intelligence and Security Committee and the "War on Terror"', *Intelligence and National Security* 22 (2007): 14–37.

Gill, Peter, 'The Intelligence and Security Committee and the Challenge of Security Networks', *Review of International Studies* 35, no. 4 (2009): 929–41.

Gill, Peter, 'Intelligence, Threat, Risk and the Challenge of Oversight', *Intelligence and National Security* 27, no. 2 (2012): 206–22.

Gill, Peter, and Michael Andregg, *Democratization of Intelligence*, Abingdon: Taylor & Francis, 2017.

Gill, Peter, Stephen Marrin and Mark Phythian, *Intelligence Theory: Key Questions and Debates*, Studies in Intelligence, Abingdon: Taylor & Francis, 2008.
Gill, Peter, and Mark Phythian, *Intelligence in an Insecure World*, Cambridge: Polity, 2006.
Goffman, Erving, *The Presentation of Self in Everyday Life*, Harmondsworth: Penguin, 1978.
Goldman, Kjell, 'Miljöhot, Migration Och Terrorister I Tokyo-Om Begreppet Säkerhet', *Brobyggare: en vänbok till Nils Andrén* (1997).
GOV.UK, 'Civil Service', <https://www.gov.uk/government/organisations/civil-service> (last accessed 7 September 2018).
GOV.UK, 'National Risk Register for Civil Emergencies – 2015 Edition', <https://www.gov.uk/government/publications/national-risk-register-for-civil-emergencies-2015-edition> (last accessed 7 September 2018).
Green, Damian, 'Pre-Charge Detention Will Revert to 14 Days – GOV.UK', <https://www.gov.uk/government/news/pre-charge-detention-will-revert-to-14-days> (last accessed 7 September 2018).
Guardian, The, 'Glenn Greenwald's Partner Detained at Heathrow Airport for Nine Hours', 18 August 2013.
Guardian, The, 'Spending More Time with the Family', 4 November 2014.
Guzzini, Stefano, 'A Reconstruction of Constructivism in International Relations', *European Journal of International Relations* 6, no. 2 (2000): 147–82.
Haggerty, Kevin D., and Richard V. Ericson, 'The Surveillant Assemblage', *The British Journal of Sociology* 51, no. 4 (2000): 605–22.
Hagmann, Jonas, and Myriam Dunn Cavelty, 'National Risk Registers: Security Scientism and the Propagation of Permanent Insecurity', *Security Dialogue* 43, no. 1 (2012): 79–96.
Hammerstad, Anne, and Ingrid Boas, 'National Security Risks? Uncertainty, Austerity and Other Logics of Risk in the UK Government's National Security Strategy', *Cooperation and Conflict* 50, no. 4 (2014): 1–17.
Hansard 1803–2005, 'Points of Order (Hansard, 4 November 1987)', <https://api.parliament.uk/historic-hansard/commons/1987/nov/04/points-of-order> (last accessed 7 September 2018).
Hansard Society, 'Audit of Political Engagement 14: The 2017 Report', London, 2017.
Hansen, Lene, 'Reconstructing Desecuritisation: The Normative-Political in the Copenhagen School and Directions for How to Apply It', *Review of International Studies* 38, no. 3 (2012): 1–22.

Hattersley, Roy, 'John P. Mackintosh Memorial Lecture: "What Are MPs For?"', University of Edinburgh, 2013.
Hay, Colin, 'Depoliticisation as Process, Governance as Practice: What Did the "First Wave" Get Wrong and Do We Need a "Second Wave" to Put It Right?', *Policy & Politics* 42, no. 2 (2014): 293–311.
Hay, Colin, *Political Analysis: A Critical Introduction*, Basingstoke: Palgrave, 2002.
Hay, Colin, *Why We Hate Politics*, Cambridge: Polity, 2007.
Heath-Kelly, Charlotte, 'Counter-Terrorism and the Counterfactual: Producing the "Radicalisation" Discourse and the UK Prevent Strategy', *The British Journal of Politics and International Relations* 15, no. 3 (2012): 394–415.
Heath-Kelly, Charlotte, 'The Geography of Pre-Criminal Space: Epidemiological Imaginations of Radicalisation Risk in the UK Prevent Strategy, 2007–2017', *Critical Studies on Terrorism* 10, no. 2 (2017): 297–319.
Heath-Kelly, Charlotte, 'Securing through the Failure to Secure? The Ambiguity of Resilience at the Bombsite', *Security Dialogue* 46, no. 1 (2015): 69–85.
Hennessy, Peter, *The New Protective State: Government, Intelligence and Terrorism*, London and New York: A&C Black, 2008.
Hindess, Barry, 'Politics and Governmentality', *Economy and Society* 26, no. 2 (1997): 257–72.
HM Government, 'Foreign Involvement in the Critical National Infrastructure: Government Response', 2013, <https://www.gov.uk/government/publications/foreign-involvement-in-the-critical-national-infrastructure-government-response> (last accessed 18 September 2018).
HM Government, 'A Strong Britain in an Age of Uncertainty: The National Security Strategy', 2010, <http://www.direct.gov.uk/prod_consum_dg/groups/dg_digitalassets/@dg/@en/documents/digitalasset/dg_191639.pdf> (last accessed 18 September 2018).
HM Treasury, Government Communications Headquarters and George Osborne, 'Chancellor's Speech to GCHQ on Cyber Security', <https://www.gov.uk/government/speeches/chancellors-speech-to-gchq-on-cyber-security> (last accessed 7 September 2018).
Hobbes, Thomas, *Leviathan*, ed. Richard Tuck, Cambridge: Cambridge University Press, 1996 [1651].
Holehouse, Matthew, 'How to Be an MP Is the Most Borrowed Book in Parliament', *The Telegraph*, 12 February 2013.
Holehouse, Matthew, 'Ten Years after Iraq, MPs Simply Do Not Trust Our Spies', <blogs.telegraph.co.uk>, 2013.

Bibliography

Holland, Jack, and Lee Jarvis, *Security: A Critical Introduction*, Basingstoke: Palgrave Macmillan, 2014.

Home Affairs Committee, 'Accountability of the Security Service', House of Commons Papers, 1999.

Home Affairs Committee, 'The Private Security Industry', London: House of Commons, 1994.

Home Affairs Committee, 'Special Branch: Fourth Report from the Home Affairs Committee, Session 1984–85, Together with Proceedings of the Committee, Minutes of Evidence, and Appendices', in *Papers*, London: HM Stationery Office, 1985.

Home Office, 'Current Threat Level', <http://www.homeoffice.gov.uk/counter-terrorism/current-threat-level/> (last accessed 7 September 2018).

House of Commons, 'House of Commons Hansard Debates for 01 Apr 2008 (Pt 0009)', <https://publications.parliament.uk/pa/cm200708/cmhansrd/cm080401/debtext/80401-0009.htm> (last accessed 7 September 2018).

House of Commons, 'Interception of Communications Bill (Hansard, 12 March 1985) Vol. 75 Cc151-244', <https://api.parliament.uk/historic-hansard/commons/1985/mar/12/interception-of-communications-bill> (last accessed 7 September 2018).

House of Commons, 'Syria and the Use of Chemical Weapons, House of Commons Hansard Debates for 29 Aug 2013', <https://publications.parliament.uk/pa/cm201314/cmhansrd/cm130829/debtext/130829-0001.htm> (last accessed 7 September 2018).

House of Commons, 'Westminster Hall, Backbench Business, Intelligence and Security Services, House of Commons Hansard Debates for 31 Oct 2013 (Pt 0001)', <https://publications.parliament.uk/pa/cm201314/cmhansrd/cm131031/halltext/131031h0001.htm> (last accessed 18 September 2018).

House of Commons Liaison Committee, 'Select Committee on Liaison First Report', 2002.

House of Commons Library, 'UK Defence and Security Policy: A New Approach? Research Paper 11/10', 2011.

House of Commons Public Administration Select Committee, 'Who Does UK National Strategy? Further Report with the Government Response to the Committee's First Report of Session 2010–11', in *Sixth Report of Session 2010–11*, London: The Stationery Office Limited, 2011.

House of Lords Select Committee on the Constitution, 'Fast-Track Legislation: Constitutional Implications and Safeguards', London: The Stationery Office Limited, 2009.

Howarth, David R., *Discourse*, Concepts in the Social Sciences, Buckingham: Open University Press, 2000.
Howe, Geoffrey, *Conflict of Loyalty*, Great Statesmen, London: Methuen Publishing Ltd, 2007.
Howell, Alison, 'The Global Politics of Medicine: Beyond Global Health, against Securitisation Theory', *Review of International Studies* 40, no. 5 (2014): 961–87.
Howell, Alison, *Madness in International Relations: Psychology, Security, and the Global Governance of Mental Health*, Interventions (Routledge), Abingdon: Taylor & Francis, 2011.
Howell, Alison, and Andrew W. Neal, 'Human Interest and Humane Governance in Iraq: Humanitarian War and the Baghdad Zoo', *Journal of Intervention and Statebuilding* 6, no. 2 (2012): 213–32.
Hudson, Heidi, '"Doing" Security as though Humans Matter: A Feminist Perspective on Gender and the Politics of Human Security', *Security Dialogue* 36, no. 2 (2005): 155–74.
Hudson, Valerie M., *Foreign Policy Analysis: Classic and Contemporary Theory*, Lanham, MD: Rowman & Littlefield Publishers, 2007.
Hutchinson, Robert, *Elizabeth's Spymaster*, London: Orion, 2011.
Huysmans, Jef, 'Defining Social Constructivism in Security Studies: The Normative Dilemma of Writing Security', *Alternatives: Global, Local, Political* 27, no. 1 suppl. (2002): 41–62.
Huysmans, Jef, 'The Jargon of Exception – on Schmitt, Agamben and the Absence of Political Society', *International Political Sociology* 2, no. 2 (2008): 165–83.
Huysmans, Jef, *The Politics of Insecurity: Fear, Migration and Asylum in the EU*, London: Routledge, 2006.
Huysmans, Jef, 'Revisiting Copenhagen: Or, on the Creative Development of a Security Studies Agenda in Europe', *European Journal of International Relations* 4, no. 4 (1998): 479–505.
Huysmans, Jef, *Security Unbound: Enacting Democratic Limits*, Critical Issues in Global Politics, Abindgdon and New York: Routledge, 2014.
Huysmans, Jef, 'What Is in an Act? On Security Speech Acts and Little Security Nothings', *Security Dialogue* 42, nos. 4–5 (2011): 371–84.
Ilgit, Asli, and Audie Klotz, 'How Far Does "Societal Security" Travel? Securitization in South African Immigration Policies', *Security Dialogue* 45, no. 2 (2014): 137–55.
Independent, The, 'Leading Article: Laudable Principle, Reckless Egotism', 13 June 2008.

Bibliography

Intelligence and Security Committee, 'Foreign Involvement in the Critical National Infrastructure', <https://www.gov.uk/government/publications/foreign-involvement-in-the-critical-national-infrastructure-intelligence-and-security-committee-report> (last accessed 7 September 2018).

Intelligence and Security Committee of Parliament, 'Press Release – 26 April 2017 – UK Lethal Drone Strikes in Syria', <http://isc.independent.gov.uk/news-archive/26april2017> (last accessed 7 September 2018).

Intelligence and Security Committee of Parliament, 'Privacy and Security: A Modern and Transparent Legal Framework', London: HMSO, 2015.

Intelligence Services Act 1994, <https://www.legislation.gov.uk/ukpga/1994/13/section/1> (last accessed 18 September 2018).

Jabri, Vivienne, 'Michel Foucault's Analytics of War: The Social, the International, and the Racial', *International Political Sociology* 1, no. 1 (2007): 67–81.

Joint Committee on Human Rights, 'Counter-Terrorism Policy and Human Rights (Seventeenth Report): Bringing Human Rights Back In', London: The Stationery Office Limited, 2010.

Joint Committee on the National Security Strategy, 'Conflict, Stability and Security Fund', 2017, <https://publications.parliament.uk/pa/jt201617/jtselect/jtnatsec/208/20802.htm> (last accessed 18 September 2018).

Joint Committee on the National Security Strategy, 'Uncorrected Transcript of Oral Evidence, Rt Hon David Cameron MP, Sir Kim Darroch, KCMG', 2014, <https://www.parliament.uk/documents/joint-committees/national-security-strategy/PM%20session/JCNSS14-01-30TranscriptCameron.pdf> (last accessed 18 September 2018).

Joseph, Jonathan, 'Resilience as Embedded Neoliberalism: A Governmentality Approach', *Resilience* 1, no. 1 (2013): 38–52.

Judge, David, *The Parliamentary State*, London: SAGE, 1993.

Kaarbo, Juliet, *Coalition Politics and Cabinet Decision Making: A Comparative Analysis of Foreign Policy Choices*, Ann Arbor: University of Michigan Press, 2012.

Kaarbo, Juliet, and Daniel Kenealy, 'No, Prime Minister: Explaining the House of Commons' Vote on Intervention in Syria', *European Security* 25, no. 1 (2016): 28–48.

Kalitowski, Susanna, 'Rubber Stamp or Cockpit? The Impact of Parliament on Government Legislation', *Parliamentary Affairs* 61, no. 4 (2008): 694–708.

Kalyvas, Andreas, *Democracy and the Politics of the Extraordinary: Max Weber, Carl Schmitt, and Hannah Arendt*, Cambridge and New York: Cambridge University Press, 2008.
Kelly, Richard, 'Pre-Legislative Scrutiny – Commons Library Briefing – UK Parliament', London, 2011.
Kelly, Richard, 'Select Committees: Evidence and Witnesses – Commons Library Briefing – UK Parliament', London, 2016.
Kelly, Richard, and Keith Parry, 'Pre-Legislative Scrutiny under the Coalition Government', in *Standard Note: SN/PC/5859*, London: House of Commons Library, 2013.
Kelso, Alexandra, *Parliamentary Reform at Westminster*, Manchester: Manchester University Press, 2009.
Kendall, Gavin, and Gary Wickham, *Using Foucault's Methods*, London: SAGE, 1999.
Kenny, Meryl, *Gender and Political Recruitment: Theorizing Institutional Change*, Gender and Politics, Basingstoke: Palgrave Macmillan, 2013.
Kindervater, Katharine Hall, 'The Emergence of Lethal Surveillance: Watching and Killing in the History of Drone Technology', *Security Dialogue* 47, no. 3 (2016): 223–38.
Kite, Melissa, 'David Davis – "I'm Not Plotting – I No Longer Want to Be Conservative Party Leader"', 14 June 2008, <http://www.telegraph.co.uk/news/politics/2131415/David-Davis-Im-not-plotting-I-no-longer-want-to-be-Conservative-Party-leader.html> (last accessed 18 September 2018).
Krause, Keith, and Michael C. Williams, *Critical Security Studies: Concepts and Cases*, London: UCL Press, 1997.
Larson, Jonathan L., 'Deviant Dialectics: Intertextuality, Voice, and Emotion in Czechoslovak Socialist *Kritika*', in Petre Petrov and Lara Ryazanova-Clarke (eds), *The Vernaculars of Communism: Language, Ideology and Power in the Soviet Union and Eastern Europe*, Abingdon: Routledge, 2014, pp. 130–46.
Latour, Bruno, *Reassembling the Social*, Oxford: Oxford University Press, 2005.
Latour, Bruno, 'Why Has Critique Run out of Steam? From Matters of Fact to Matters of Concern', *Critical Inquiry* 30, no. 2 (2004): 225–48.
Law Commission, *Post-Legislative Scrutiny: A Consultation Paper*, London: The Stationery Office Limited, 2006.
Law Lords, *Opinions of the Lords of Appeal for Judgment in the Cause, a (Fc) and Others (Fc) (Appellants) V. Secretary of State for the Home Department (Respondent)*, London, 2004.

Leander, Anna, 'Habitus and Field', in Robert A. Denemark (ed.), *The International Studies Encyclopedia*, Blackwell Reference Online, 2010.

Leese, Matthias, 'The New Profiling: Algorithms, Black Boxes, and the Failure of Anti-Discriminatory Safeguards in the European Union', *Security Dialogue* 45, no. 5 (2014): 494–511.

Leigh, Darcy, and Richard Freeman, 'Teaching Politics after the Practice Turn', *Politics* (2017), <https://doi.org/10.1177/0263395717693027> (last accessed 7 September 2018).

Leigh, Ian, 'The UK's Intelligence and Security Committee', in Hans Born and Marina Caparini (eds), *Democratic Control of Intelligence Services: Containing Rogue Elephants*, Aldershot: Ashgate, 2007, pp. 177–94.

Liberal Democrats, 'Liberal Democrat Manifesto 2010: Change that Works for You', in *Building a Fairer Britain*, Liberal Democrats, 2010.

Loader, Ian, and Neil Walker, *Civilizing Security*, Cambridge: Cambridge University Press, 2007.

Lobo-Guerrero, Luis, *Insuring Security: Biopolitics, Security and Risk*, Abingdon: Taylor & Francis, 2010.

Locke, John, *Political Writings*, ed. David Wootton, Hackett Classics Series, Indianapolis: Hackett Publishing, 1993.

Lord Butler of Brockwell, *Review of Intelligence on Weapons of Mass Destruction*, London: The Stationery Office Limited, 2004.

Lord Lloyd of Berwick, 'Inquiry into Legislation against Terrorism, Cm. 3420', London: The Stationery Office Limited, 1996.

Lord Wilson of Dinton, 'Oral Evidence', The Iraq Inquiry, 2011.

Lundborg, Tom, and Nick Vaughan-Williams, 'Resilience, Critical Infrastructure, and Molecular Security: The Excess of "Life" in Biopolitics', *International Political Sociology* 5, no. 4 (2011): 367–83.

McCormack, Tara, 'The British National Security Strategy: Security after Representation', *The British Journal of Politics and International Relations* 17, no. 3 (2014): 1–18.

McCormick, John, *Carl Schmitt's Critique of Liberalism*, Cambridge: Cambridge University Press, 1997.

McDonald, Matt, 'Securitization and the Construction of Security', *European Journal of International Relations* 14, no. 4 (2008): 563–87.

Machiavelli, Niccolo, *The Prince*, trans. George Anthony Bull, London: Penguin, 1999.

Maddox, Bronwen, 'Windrush Cases Expose Arbitrary Immigration Targets', <https://www.ft.com/content/41dcc7f0-447d-11e8-803a-295c97e6fd0b> (last accessed 7 September 2018).

Making History, 'Interview with Professor Quentin Skinner', <http://www.history.ac.uk/makinghistory/resources/interviews/Skinner_Quentin.html> (last accessed 7 September 2018).

Mälksoo, Maria, '"Memory Must Be Defended": Beyond the Politics of Mnemonical Security', *Security Dialogue* (2015), <https://doi.org/10.1177/0967010614552549> (last accessed 7 September 2018).

Manningham-Buller, Eliza, 'Counter-Terrorism Bill', House of Lords debates for 8 July 2008, column 647, <https://publications.parliament.uk/pa/ld200708/ldhansrd/text/80708-0004.htm#80708-0004.htm_spnew6> (last accessed 18 September 2018).

Mansbach, Abraham, 'Keeping Democracy Vibrant: Whistleblowing as Truth-Telling in the Workplace', *Constellations* 16, no. 3 (2009): 363–76.

Marsh, Ian, 'The Commons Select Committee System in the 2015–20 Parliament', *The Political Quarterly* 87, no. 1 (2016): 96–103.

May, Thomas Erskine, *A Treatise on the Law, Privileges, Proceedings and Usage of Parliament*, 17th edn, ed. Sir Barnett Cocks, London: Butterworth & Co., 1964.

May, Thomas Erskine, *A Treatise on the Law, Privileges, Proceedings and Usage of Parliament*, 21st edn, ed. Clifford J. Boulton, London: Butterworths, 1989.

Mayall, James, 'Reflections on the "New" Economic Nationalism', *Review of International Studies* 10, no. 4 (1984): 313–21.

Mello, Patrick A., 'Curbing the Royal Prerogative to Use Military Force: The British House of Commons and the Conflicts in Libya and Syria', *West European Politics* 40, no. 1 (2017): 80–100.

Mello, Patrick A., and Dirk Peters, 'Parliaments in Security Policy: Involvement, Politicisation, and Influence', *The British Journal of Politics and International Relations* 20, no. 1 (2018): 3–18.

MI5, Security Service, 'The "Wilson Plot"', <https://www.mi5.gov.uk/the-wilson-plot> (last accessed 7 September 2018).

Miliband, David, 'House of Commons Hansard Debates', UK Parliament, <https://publications.parliament.uk/pa/cm200910/cmhansrd/cm100210/debtext/100210-0004.htm#10021063000006> (last accessed 7 September 2018).

Mill, John Stewart, *'On Liberty' and Other Writings*, Cambridge Texts in the History of Political Thought, Cambridge: Cambridge University Press, 1989.

Bibliography

Miller, Peter, and Nikolas Rose, 'Governing Economic Life', *Economy and Society* 19, no. 1 (1990): 1–31.

Miller, Russell A., *US National Security, Intelligence and Democracy: From the Church Committee to the War on Terror*, Studies in Intelligence, Abingdon: Taylor & Francis, 2008.

Ministerie van Justitie en Veiligheid, 'National Security – Counterterrorism and National Security', <https://www.government.nl/topics/counterterrorism-and-national-security/national-security> (last accessed 7 September 2018).

Ministry of Defence (Finland), 'Security Strategy for Society (Government Resolution 16.12.2010)', Helsinki: Ministry of Defence, 2010.

Mommsen, Wolfgang J., *Max Weber and German Politics, 1890–1920*, Sociology/History/Political Science, Chicago: University of Chicago Press, 1990 [1959].

Morgenthau, Hans J., *Politics Among Nations: The Struggle for Power and Peace*, 5th edn, New York: Knopf, 1978.

Mullin, Chris, *A View from the Foothills: The Diaries of Chris Mullin*, London: Profile Books, 2010.

Neal, Andrew W., 'Cutting Off the King's Head: Foucault's *Society Must Be Defended* and the Problem of Sovereignty', *Alternatives: Global, Local, Political* 4, no. 29 (2004): 373–98.

Neal, Andrew W., '"Events Dear Boy, Events": Terrorism and Security from the Perspective of Politics', *Critical Studies on Terrorism* 5, no. 1 (2012): 107–20.

Neal, Andrew W., *Exceptionalism and the Politics of Counter-Terrorism: Liberty, Security and the War on Terror*, Abingdon and New York: Routledge, 2010.

Neal, Andrew W., 'Foucault', in Jenny Edkins and Nick Vaughan-Williams (eds), *Critical Theorists and International Relations*, London: Routledge, 2009, pp. 161–70.

Neal, Andrew W., 'Legislative Practices', in Mark B. Salter and Can E. Mutlu (eds), *Research Methods in Critical Security Studies: An Introduction*, Abingdon: Routledge, 2012, pp. 125–8.

Neal, Andrew W., 'Normalization and Legislative Exceptionalism: Counterterrorist Lawmaking and the Changing Times of Security Emergencies', *International Political Sociology* 6, no. 3 (2012): 260–76.

Neal, Andrew W., 'Terrorism, Lawmaking and Democratic Politics: Legislators as Security Actors', *Terrorism and Political Violence* 24, no. 3 (2012): 357–74.

Nelson, Steven, 'Lock Him Up? Lawmakers Renew Calls for James Clapper Perjury Charges', *US News & World Report* (2016), <https://www.usnews.com/news/articles/2016-11-17/lawmakers-resume-calls-for-james-clapper-perjury-charges> (last accessed 7 September 2018).
Neocleous, Mark, *Critique of Security*, Edinburgh: Edinburgh University Press, 2008.
Neville-Jones, Pauline, 'Security Issues: Interim Position Paper', National and International Security Policy Group, Conservative Party, 2006.
Nevitte, Neil, *The Decline of Deference: Canadian Value Change in Cross-National Perspective*, Peterborough: Broadview Press, 1996.
Nevitte, Neil, 'The Decline of Deference Revisited', in Russell J. Dalton and Christian Welzel (eds), *The Civic Culture Transformed: From Allegiant to Assertive Citizens*, New York: Cambridge University Press, 2014, pp. 35–58.
Nietzsche, Friedrich, *The Genealogy of Morals*, Dover Thrift Editions, New York: Dover Publications, 2012 [1887].
Norton, Philip, *Does Parliament Matter?*, New York and London: Harvester Wheatsheaf, 1993.
Norton, Philip, *Parliament in British Politics*, Basingstoke: Palgrave Macmillan, 2005.
Norton-Taylor, Richard, and Nicholas Watt, 'The Blair Defence: September 11 Changed the "Calculus of Risk" | UK News', *The Guardian*, 28 June 2010.
Nunes, João, *Security, Emancipation and the Politics of Health: A New Theoretical Perspective*, Abingdon: Routledge, 2014.
NUS Black Students, 'Preventing Prevent: A Student Handbook on Countering the Prevent Agenda on Campus', London, 2015.
Nyman, Jonna, 'What Is the Value of Security? Contextualising the Negative/Positive Debate', *Review of International Studies* 42, no. 5 (2016): 821–39.
Nyman, Jonna, and Anthony Burke, *Ethical Security Studies: A New Research Agenda*, Abingdon: Routledge, 2016.
O'Malley, Pat, Lorna Weir and Clifford Shearing, 'Governmentality, Criticism, Politics', *Economy and Society* 26, no. 4 (1997): 501–17.
Omand, David, *Securing the State*, London: Hurst, 2010.
Packenham, Robert, 'Legislatures and Political Development', in Allan Kornberg and Lloyd D. Musolf (eds), *Legislatures in Developmental Perspective*, Durham, NC: Duke University Press, 1970, pp. 521–2.

Bibliography

Palonen, Kari, *The Struggle with Time: A Conceptual History of 'Politics' as an Activity*, Münster: LIT Verlag, 2006.

Peoples, Columba, and Nick Vaughan-Williams, *Critical Security Studies*, London: Routledge, 2013.

Percival, Jenny, Deborah Summers and agencies, 'Tories in Turmoil as David Davis Resigns over 42-Day Vote', *The Guardian*, 12 June 2008.

Petersen, Karen Lund, 'Risk Analysis – A Field within Security Studies?', *European Journal of International Relations* 18, no. 4 (2012): 693–717.

Peto, Anthony, and Andrew Tyrie, 'Neither Just Nor Secure: The Justice and Security Bill', Centre for Policy Studies (2013), <https://www.cps.org.uk/files/reports/original/130123103140-neitherjustnorsecure.pdf> (last accessed 7 September 2018).

Phythian, Mark, 'The British Experience with Intelligence Accountability', *Intelligence and National Security* 22, no. 1 (2007): 75–99.

Phythian, Mark, 'Still a Matter of Trust: Post-9/11 British Intelligence and Political Culture', *International Journal of Intelligence and CounterIntelligence* 18, no. 4 (2005): 653–81.

Phythian, Mark, '"A Very British Institution": The Intelligence and Security Committee and Intelligence Accountability in the United Kingdom', in Loch K. Johnson (ed.), *The Oxford Handbook of National Security Intelligence*, Oxford: Oxford University Press, 2010, pp. 699–718.

Pinker, Steven, *The Better Angels of Our Nature: The Decline of Violence in History and Its Causes*, London: Allen Lane, 2011.

Pitkin, Hanna F., *Fortune Is a Woman: Gender and Politics in the Thought of Niccolo Machiavelli*, Political Science/Philosophy, Chicago: University of Chicago Press, 1984.

Political and Constitutional Reform Committee, 'Parliament's Role in Conflict Decisions: A Way Forward', 2014, <https://publications.parliament.uk/pa/cm201314/cmselect/cmpolcon/892/89202.htm> (last accessed 18 September 2018).

Porter, Andrew, 'David Davis to Resign from Shadow Cabinet and as MP', *The Telegraph*, 12 June 2008.

Pouliot, Vincent, 'The Logic of Practicality: A Theory of Practice of Security Communities', *International Organization* 62, no. 2 (2008): 257–88.

Powell, J. Enoch, *Joseph Chamberlain*, London: Thames & Hudson, 1977.

Powell, Jonathan, *The New Machiavelli: How to Wield Power in the Modern World*, London: Random House, 2010.

Press Association, 'Miliband Loses Attempt to Block Binyam Mohamed Torture Case Evidence', *The Independent*, 10 February 2010.

Prozorov, Sergei, 'X/Xs: Toward a General Theory of the Exception', *Alternatives: Global, Local, Political* 30 (2005): 81–112.

Raab, Charles D., 'Security, Privacy and Oversight', in Andrew W. Neal (ed.), *Security in a Small Nation: Scotland, Democracy, Politics*, Cambridge: Open Book Publishers, 2017, pp. 77–102.

Ragazzi, Francesco, 'Countering Terrorism and Radicalisation: Securitising Social Policy?', *Critical Social Policy* 37, no. 2 (2017): 163–79.

Ragazzi, Francesco, 'Preventing Radicalisation in the EU: Preemption, Rights and Effectiveness', presentation of the report 'Preventing and Countering Youth Radicalisation in the EU', Access Europe Annual Conference, University of Amsterdam, 2015.

Raphael, Sam, Crofton Black, Ruth Blakeley and Steve Kostas, 'Tracking Rendition Aircraft as a Way to Understand CIA Secret Detention and Torture in Europe', *The International Journal of Human Rights* 20, no. 1 (2016): 78–103.

Rasmussen, Mikkel Vedby, *The Risk Society at War: Terror, Technology and Strategy in the Twenty-First Century*, Cambridge: Cambridge University Press, 2006.

'Report of a Committee of Privy Counsellors, Review of Intelligence on Weapons of Mass Destruction, HC 898', London: House of Commons, 2004.

Rhodes, R. A. W., John Wanna and Patrick Weller, *Comparing Westminster*, Oxford Scholarship Online, Oxford: Oxford University Press, 2009.

Richter-Montpetit, Melanie, 'Beyond the Erotics of Orientalism: Lawfare, Torture and the Racial–Sexual Grammars of Legitimate Suffering', *Security Dialogue* 45, no. 1 (2014): 43–62.

Richter-Montpetit, Melanie, 'Empire, Desire and Violence: A Queer Transnational Feminist Reading of the Prisoner "Abuse" in Abu Ghraib and the Question of "Gender Equality"', *International Feminist Journal of Politics* 9 (2007): 38–59.

Rifkind, Malcolm, 'Intelligence Oversight in the UK: The Intelligence and Security Committee', Royal United Services Institute, London, 16 November 2010, <https://docs.google.com/viewer?a=v&pid=sites&srcid=aW5kZXBlbmRlbnQuZ292LnVrfGlzY3xneDo0OWZlNGE3ZGRhMjdiNmNi> (last accessed 18 September 2018).

Roberts, Dorothy, 'Torture and the Biopolitics of Race', *U. Miami L. Rev.* 62 (2007): 229.

Roe, Paul, 'Is Securitization a "Negative" Concept? Revisiting the Normative Debate over Normal versus Extraordinary Politics', *Security Dialogue* 43, no. 3 (2012): 249–66.

Rogers, Robert, and Rhodri Walters, *How Parliament Works*, London: Pearson Education Limited, 2006.

Rose, Nikolas, *Powers of Freedom: Reframing Political Thought*, Cambridge: Cambridge University Press, 1999.

Royal United Services Institute for Defence and Security Studies, *A Democratic Licence to Operate: Report of the Independent Surveillance Review*, London: Royal United Services Institute for Defence and Security Studies, 2015.

Runciman, David, *Politics: Ideas in Profile*, London: Profile Books, 2014.

Russell, Meg, '"Never Allow a Crisis to Go to Waste": The Wright Committee Reforms to Strengthen the House of Commons', *Parliamentary Affairs* 64, no. 4 (2011): 612–33.

Russell, Meg, and Philip Cowley, 'The Policy Power of the Westminster Parliament: The "Parliamentary State" and the Empirical Evidence', *Governance* 29, no. 1 (2016): 121–37.

Ryan, Barry J., 'Reasonable Force: The Emergence of Global Policing Power', *Review of International Studies* 39, no. 2 (2012): 435–57.

Sabaratnam, Meera, 'Avatars of Eurocentrism in the Critique of the Liberal Peace', *Security Dialogue* 44, no. 3 (2013): 259–78.

Salter, Mark B., 'Passports, Mobility, and Security: How Smart Can the Border Be?', *International Studies Perspectives* 5, no. 1 (2004): 71–91.

Salter, Mark B., 'Securitization and Desecuritization: A Dramaturgical Analysis of the Canadian Air Transport Security Authority', *Journal of International Relations and Development* 11, no. 4 (2008): 321–49.

Salter, Mark B., 'When Securitization Fails: The Hard Case of Counter-Terrorism Programs', in Thierry Balzacq (ed.), *Securitization Theory: How Security Problems Emerge and Dissolve*, Abingdon: Routledge, 2011, pp. 116–31.

Scammell, Margaret, and Holli A. Semetko, 'Election News Coverage in the UK', *The Handbook of Election News Coverage around the World* (2008): 73–89.

Scheuerman, William E., 'Survey Article: Emergency Powers and the Rule of Law after 9/11', *Journal of Political Philosophy* 14, no. 1 (2006): 61–84.

Schmitt, Carl, *The Concept of the Political*, trans. George Schwab, Chicago: University of Chicago Press, 1996 [1932].

Schmitt, Carl, *The Leviathan in the State Theory of Thomas Hobbes: Meaning and Failure of a Political Symbol*, trans. George Schwab and Erna Hilfstein, Westport, CT: Greenwood Press, 1996 [1938].

Schmitt, Carl, *Political Theology: Four Chapters on the Concept of Sovereignty*, trans. George Schwab, Cambridge, MA, and London: MIT Press, 1985 [1934].

Schouten, Peer, 'Security as Controversy: Reassembling Security at Amsterdam Airport', *Security Dialogue* 45, no. 1 (2014): 23–42.

Schulhofer, Stephen J., *The Enemy Within: Intelligence Gathering, Law Enforcement, and Civil Liberties in the Wake of September 11*, New York: Century Foundation Press, 2002.

Schwarz, Elke, 'Prescription Drones: On the Techno-Biopolitical Regimes of Contemporary "Ethical Killing"', *Security Dialogue* 47, no. 1 (2016): 59–75.

Scotsman, The, 'MP Raises Questions over 266 Fires on Nuclear Subs', 9 July 2012.

Secret Intelligence Service, 'Our History', <https://www.sis.gov.uk/our-history.html> (last accessed 7 September 2018).

Secretary of State for the Home Department, 'CONTEST: The United Kingdom's Strategy for Countering Terrorism', London: The Stationery Office Limited, 2011.

Seitz, Sergej, 'Truth Beyond Consensus. Parrhesia, Dissent, and Subjectivation', *EPEKEINA. International Journal of Ontology. History and Critics* 7, nos. 1–2 (2016): 1–13.

Shaw, Tamsin, 'Max Weber on Democracy: Can the People Have Political Power in Modern States?', *Constellations* 15, no. 1 (2008): 33–45.

Simpson, John, *The Independent Nuclear State: The United States, Britain and the Military Atom*, Basingstoke: Palgrave Macmillan, 1983.

Skinner, Quentin, *Visions of Politics: Regarding Method*, vol. 1, Cambridge: Cambridge University Press, 2002.

Smist, Frank J., *Congress Oversees the United States Intelligence Community, 1947–1994*, Knoxville: University of Tennessee Press, 1994.

Spiller, Keith, Imran Awan and Andrew Whiting, '"What Does Terrorism Look Like?" University Lecturers' Interpretations of Their Prevent Duties and Tackling Extremism in UK Universities', *Critical Studies on Terrorism* 11, no. 1 (2018): 130–50.

Squire, Vicki, *The Contested Politics of Mobility: Borderzones and Irregularity*, Abingdon: Routledge, 2010.

Squire, Vicki, 'Desert "Trash": Posthumanism, Border Struggles, and Humanitarian Politics', *Political Geography* 39 (2014): 11–21.
Staff Blogger, *New Statesman*, 'Geoffrey Howe, 1990', <https://www.newstatesman.com/uk-politics/2010/02/geoffrey-howe-1990-speech> (last accessed 7 September 2018).
Stafford-Smith, Clive, 'Tortuous Evasions on Torture', *The Guardian*, 16 June 2009.
Stritzel, Holger, 'Security, the Translation', *Security Dialogue* 42, nos. 4–5 (2011): 343–55.
Stritzel, Holger, 'Towards a Theory of Securitization: Copenhagen and Beyond', *European Journal of International Relations* 13, no. 3 (2007): 357–83.
Strong, James, 'Interpreting the Syria Vote: Parliament and British Foreign Policy', *International Affairs* 91, no. 5 (2015): 1123–39.
Strong, James, 'Why Parliament Now Decides on War: Tracing the Growth of the Parliamentary Prerogative through Syria, Libya and Iraq', *The British Journal of Politics and International Relations* 17, no. 4 (2015): 604–22.
Suganami, Hidemi, 'Reflections on the Domestic Analogy: The Case of Bull, Beitz and Linklater', *Review of International Studies* 12, no. 2 (1986): 145–58.
Sun Says, 'Editorial', *The Sun*, 28 October 2010, p. 8.
Sutcliffe-Braithwaite, Florence, *Class, Politics, and the Decline of Deference in England, 1968–2000*, The Past and Present Book Series, Oxford: Oxford University Press, 2018.
Swaine, Jon, 'Haltemprice By-Election: David Davis to Continue Civil Liberties Campaign', *The Telegraph*, 11 July 2008, <http://www.telegraph.co.uk/news/politics/conservative/2284969/Haltemprice-by-election-David-Davis-to-continue-civil-liberties-campaign.html> (last accessed 15 October 2018).
Swinford, Steven, 'Tories Would Need £8bn to Protect Defence Spending', *The Telegraph*, 19 March 2015.
Sylvester, Christine, *Feminist Theory and International Relations in a Postmodern Era*, vol. 32, Cambridge: Cambridge University Press, 1994.
Sylvester, Christine, 'Tensions in Feminist Security Studies', *Security Dialogue* 41, no. 6 (2010): 607–14.
Szabó, Márton, 'Review Article: The Conceptual History of Politics as the History of Political Conceptualizations – Kari Palonen, *The Struggle with Time: A Conceptual History of "Politics" as an Activity*', *European Journal of Political Theory* 8, no. 2 (2009): 275–84.

Taleb, Nassim Nicholas, *The Black Swan: The Impact of the Highly Improbable*, London: Allen Lane, 2007.

Telegraph, The, 'Chinese Companies to Buy Big Stake in Next Generation of British Nuclear Power', 17 October 2013.

Tickner, J. Ann, *Gender in International Relations: Feminist Perspectives on Achieving Global Security*, New York: Columbia University Press, 1992.

Tierney, Stephen, 'Determining the State of Exception: What Role for Parliament and the Courts?', *The Modern Law Review* 68, no. 4 (2005): 668–73.

Toros, Harmonie, '"9/11 Is Alive and Well" or How Critical Terrorism Studies Has Sustained the 9/11 Narrative', *Critical Studies on Terrorism* 10, no. 2 (2017): 203–19.

Trade and Industry Committee, 'Export Licensing and BMARC, Third Report of 1995–96, HC 87', UK Parliament, London, 1996.

UK Government, 'National Security Capability Review (NSCR)', <https://www.gov.uk/government/publications/national-security-capability-review-nscr> (last accessed 7 September 2018).

UK Government, 'National Security Strategy and Strategic Defence and Security Review 2015', <https://www.gov.uk/government/publications/national-security-strategy-and-strategic-defence-and-security-review-2015> (last accessed 7 September 2018).

UK Parliament, 'Parliamentary Privilege – Glossary Page', <http://www.parliament.uk/site-information/glossary/parliamentary-privilege/> (last accessed 18 September 2018).

UK Parliament, 'Parliament's Role', <https://www.parliament.uk/about/how/role/> (last accessed 7 September 2018).

UK Parliament, 'Political and Constitutional Reform Committee – Role', <https://www.parliament.uk/business/committees/committees-a-z/commons-select/political-and-constitutional-reform-committee/role/> (last accessed 7 September 2018).

UK Parliament, 'Role – Liaison Committee', <https://www.parliament.uk/business/committees/committees-a-z/commons-select/liaison-committee/role/> (last accessed 7 September 2018).

UK Parliament, 'Select Committees', <https://www.parliament.uk/about/how/committees/select/> (last accessed 7 September 2018).

UK Parliament, 'Sellafield: Written Question – HL1269', <https://www.parliament.uk/business/publications/written-questions-answers-statements/written-question/Lords/2015-07-09/HL1269> (last accessed 7 September 2018).

Ullman, Richard H., 'Redefining Security', *International Security* 8, no. 1 (1983): 129–53.

Vasquez, John A., *The War Puzzle*, Cambridge: Cambridge University Press, 1993.
Vaughan-Williams, Nick, *Border Politics: The Limits of Sovereign Power*, Edinburgh: Edinburgh University Press, 2009.
Vaughan-Williams, Nick, '"We Are Not Animals!" Humanitarian Border Security and Zoopolitical Spaces in Europe', *Political Geography* 45 (2015): 1–10.
Veyne, Paul, *Foucault: His Thought, His Character*, Cambridge: Polity, 2010.
Veyne, Paul, 'Foucault Revolutionizes History', in Arnold I. Davidson (ed.), *Foucault and His Interlocutors*, Chicago and London: University of Chicago Press, 1997, pp. 146–82.
Vucina, Naja, Claus Drejer and Peter Triantafillou, 'Histories and Freedom of the Present: Foucault and Skinner', *History of the Human Sciences* 24, no. 5 (2011): 124–41.
Vuori, Juha A., 'Illocutionary Logic and Strands of Securitization: Applying the Theory of Securitization to the Study of Non-Democratic Political Orders', *European Journal of International Relations* 14, no. 1 (2008): 65–99.
Vuori, Juha A., 'A Timely Prophet? The Doomsday Clock as a Visualization of Securitization Moves with a Global Referent Object', *Security Dialogue* 41, no. 3 (2010): 255–77.
Wæver, Ole, 'The EU as a Security Actor: Reflections from a Pessimistic Constructivist on Post-Sovereign Security Orders', in Michael C. Williams and Morten Kelstrup (eds), *International Relations Theory and the Politics of European Integration: Power, Security, and Community*, London: Routledge, 2000, pp. 250–94.
Wæver, Ole, 'European Security Identities', *Journal of Common Market Studies* 31, no. 1 (1996): 103–32.
Wæver, Ole, 'Politics, Security, Theory', *Security Dialogue* 42, nos. 4–5 (2011): 465–80.
Wæver, Ole, 'Securitization and Desecuritization', in Ronnie D. Lipschutz (ed.), *On Security*, New York and Chichester: Columbia University Press, 1995, pp. 46–86.
Wæver, Ole, 'Securitizing Sectors? Reply to Eriksson', *Cooperation and Conflict* 34, no. 3 (1999): 334–40.
Wæver, Ole, 'The Theory Act: Responsibility and Exactitude as Seen from Securitization', *International Relations* 29, no. 1 (2015): 26–32.
Walker, R. B. J., *Inside/Outside: International Relations as Political Theory*, Cambridge: Cambridge University Press, 1993.
Walker, R. B. J., 'Sovereignties, Exceptions, Worlds', in Jenny Edkins, Véronique Pin-Fat and Michael J. Shapiro (eds), *Sovereign Lives:*

Power in Global Politics, New York and London: Routledge, 2004, pp. 239–49.

Walt, Stephen M., 'The Renaissance of Security Studies', *International Studies Quarterly* 35, no. 2 (1991): 211–39.

Walters, William, 'Drone Strikes, Dingpolitik and Beyond: Furthering the Debate on Materiality and Security', *Security Dialogue* 45, no. 2 (2014): 101–18.

Waltz, Kenneth N., *Theory of International Politics*, London: McGraw-Hill, 1979.

Watt, Nicholas, 'Brown Abandons 42-Day Detention after Lords Defeat', *The Guardian*, 13 October 2008.

Weber, Max, *Economy and Society: An Outline of Interpretive Sociology*, Berkeley: University of California Press, 1978 [1922].

Weber, Max, 'Parliament and Government in Germany under a New Political Order', in *Weber: Political Writings*, ed. Peter Lassman and Ronald Speirs, Cambridge: Cambridge University Press, 1994 [1918], pp. 130–271.

Weber, Max, 'Politics as a Vocation', in *From Max Weber: Essays in Sociology*, ed. Hans Heinrich Gerth and C. Wright Mills, Abingdon: Routledge, 1991 [1919], pp. 77–128.

Weber, Max, 'The Profession and Vocation of Politics', in *Weber: Political Writings*, ed. Peter Lassman and Ronald Speirs, Cambridge: Cambridge University Press, 1994 [1919], pp. 309–69.

Weber, Max, *The Protestant Ethic and the Spirit of Capitalism*, Abingdon: Taylor & Francis, 2013 [1920].

Weber, Max, 'Science as a Vocation', in *Max Weber's 'Science as a Vocation'*, ed. Peter Lassman, Irving Velody and Herminio Martins, London: Taylor & Francis, 1989 [1922], pp. 3–31.

Wibben, Annick T. R., *Feminist Security Studies: A Narrative Approach*, Prio New Security Studies, Abingdon: Taylor & Francis, 2010.

Wibben, Annick T. R., 'Opening Security: Recovering Critical Scholarship as Political', *Critical Studies on Security* 4, no. 2 (2016): 137–53.

Wikipedia, 'Glomar Response', <https://en.wikipedia.org/w/index.php?title=Glomar_response&oldid=849959764> (last accessed 7 September 2018).

Wikipedia, 'Parliament Acts 1911 and 1949', <https://en.wikipedia.org/w/index.php?title=Parliament_Acts_1911_and_1949&oldid=799461601> (last accessed 7 September 2018).

Wikipedia, 'Parliamentary Committees of the United Kingdom', <https://en.wikipedia.org/w/index.php?title=Parliamentary_Committees_of_the_United_Kingdom&oldid=801722525> (last accessed 7 September 2018).

Williams, Michael C., 'The Continuing Evolution of Securitization Theory', in Thierry Balzacq (ed.), *Securitization Theory: How Security Problems Emerge and Dissolve*, Abingdon: Routledge, 2011, pp. 212–22.

Williams, Michael C., *Culture and Security: Symbolic Power and the Politics of International Security*, London: Routledge, 2007.

Williams, Michael C., 'Securitization as Political Theory: The Politics of the Extraordinary', *International Relations* 29, no. 1 (2015): 19–25.

Williams, Michael C., 'Words, Images, Enemies: Securitization and International Politics', *International Studies Quarterly* 47 (2003): 511–31.

Wintour, Patrick, and Nicholas Watt, 'Desperate Brown Scrapes Through', *The Guardian*, 11 June 2008.

Wolin, Sheldon, 'Agitated Times', *Parallax* 11, no. 4 (2005): 2–11.

Wood, Matt, and Matthew Flinders, 'Rethinking Depoliticisation: Beyond the Governmental', *Policy & Politics* 42, no. 2 (2014): 151–70.

Wood, Matthew, 'Depoliticisation, Resilience and the Herceptin Post-Code Lottery Crisis: Holding Back the Tide', *The British Journal of Politics and International Relations* 17, no. 4 (2015): 644–64.

Wright, Anthony, *Doing Politics*, London: Biteback, 2012.

Wright, Tony, 'What Are MPs For?', *The Political Quarterly* 81, no. 3 (2010): 298–308.

Zajko, Mike, 'Security against Surveillance: IT Security as Resistance to Pervasive Surveillance', *Surveillance & Society* 16, no. 1 (2018): 39–52.

Zebrowski, Chris, 'The Nature of Resilience', *Resilience* 1, no. 3 (2013): 159–73.

Zebrowski, Chris, *The Value of Resilience: Securing Life in the Twenty-First Century*, Abingdon: Routledge, 2015.

Zehfuss, Maja, 'Forget September 11', *Third World Quarterly: Journal of Emerging Areas* 24, no. 3 (2003): 513–28.

Index

1960s, 109
1980s, 30, 109, 204–5, 230
1990s, 30, 49, 85, 106, 209, 230
1997 election of Labour government, 214, 225
2010 general election, 161, 163, 166
2015 general election, 262–3
2017 general election, 262
7 July 2005 London bombings, 250
9/11, 6, 141, 215, 218, 220, 230

Abrahamsen, Rita, 47, 88
actor network theory, 57
actor-led approach, 50–5
actor/analyst distinction, 63, 94
Agamben, Giorgio, 274
agency, 97
Al Qaida, 141
Amoore, Louise, 262–3
analyst, role of, 43–4, 51–2, 70
Andrew, Christopher, 107, 129–30, 205–8
anonymisation of interviewees, 119–20

anti-politics, 6, 7, 11–13, 15, 33, 42, 49, 62, 69, 84, 91, 205, 260, 280
Anti-Terrorism, Crime and Security Bill 2001, 218
Anticipated reactions, 146, 203
Aradau, Claudia, 3, 12–18, 249
Aradau, Claudia, and Rens Van Munster, 71, 249
archaeology, 61
arena
   arena migrations, 103–5, 107–8, 126, 231, 256
   arena of government, 100–5, 117
   arena, political, 10, 85, 90, 90, 92, 95–110, 117, 196
   arena shifting, 86–7, 89, 92, 102
Arendt, Hannah, 16
assemblages, 60
audience, 121–2
austerity, 223, 236–40, 245, 257, 262–4
Austin, J. L., 172
Australian government, 239

backbench rebellion, 126, 148, 161, 166, 183–4, 230, 277

bad faith, 136–43, 161, 176, 272, 274, 279
Bagehot, Walter, 26, 28
balance between economy and security, 238–40
Baldwin, Stanley, 206
Balibar, Étienne, 13
Balzacq, Thierry, 53, 121–2
Bartelson, Jens, 48, 63, 281
battlefield metaphors, 69–70, 75
Benn, Tony, 206
Benton, Meghan, and Meg Russell, 203
Biebricher, Thomas, 67–8
Bigo, Didier, 3, 26, 102, 124, 260
Birth of Biopolitics, 70–1
Biswas, Shampa, 89
Blair, Tony, 31, 140, 147, 153–4, 183, 214, 240, 242, 250, 252, 256, 271
Blyth, Mark, 247–8
BMARC, 213, 271
Bochel, Hugh, Andrew Defty and Jane Kirkpatrick, 126, 130–3, 148, 150, 206–13
Booth, Ken, 18
Bourbeau, Philippe, 48
Bourdieu, Pierre, 21, 49, 121–6, 133–5, 139, 163, 178, 185–6
Brazier, Alex, and Ruth Fox, 201
Brexit, 182, 262
Bright, Jonathan, 88, 90
Brown, Gordon, 140, 146, 161, 253, 255, 263
Bubandt, Nils, 50
Buller, Jim, 101–2, 104
Burchell, Graham, 66
bureaucracy, 25, 248

Burke, Jason, 218
Butler report *see Review of Intelligence on Weapons of Mass Destruction*
Butler, Judith, 172–3
Butler, Robin, 148, 272

cabinet committees, 241, 252
Cabinet Office, 211, 255
calculus of risk, 240–1
Cambridge School, 52
Cambridge spy ring, 206
Cameron, David, 149, 150, 153–4, 164–5, 182, 184–5, 236–7, 242–3, 245, 248, 251–3, 257–8, 260
Carlile, Alex, 128
CASE Collective, 124
Castel, Robert, 64, 65, 67, 68, 280
Chakrabarti, Shami, 188
Chilcot inquiry/report, 149, 153, 240, 252
Chinese military, 238
Chinese nuclear companies, 238
Church, Frank, 3
CIA, 106–7, 142
Ciuță, Felix, 44, 48–55, 63, 197, 280
Civil Contingencies Act 2004, 274
Clapper, James, 177
Clausewitz, Carl Von, 153–4, 242, 272
Clegg, Nick, 243
Cold War, end of, 45, 62, 281
Committee of Imperial Defence, 254

317

Committee on Arms Export Controls, 215
Common European Policy on Security and Defence, 215
Commons Science and Technology Committee, 218
consensus, 31
consensus-seeking in committees, 202
Conservative Party, 138–40, 181, 185, 248
Conservative-Liberal Democrat coalition, 188, 223, 236
constitution, British, 118
constitutional settlement around security, 62
constructivism, 46, 51–3
CONTEST, 110, 254
contextual hermeneutics, 50–6, 61, 63
contextualist approach, 44, 50–6, 93, 195–6, 280
Cook, Robin, 119, 148
Copenhagen School, 9, 12, 15, 20, 21, 32, 42, 45, 46, 51, 89, 92, 96–7, 106–7, 121–2, 194, 198, 216, 220, 275, 279
Corbyn, Jeremy, 183
Cornish, Paul, and Andrew M. Dorman, 245
Corry, Olaf, 249
Corry, Dan, 255
Counter-Terrorism Bill/Act 2008, 140, 161, 163, 182–3, 226–7
Crick, Bernard, 7, 8, 13
Criminal Justice (Terrorism and Conspiracy) Act 1998, 215

critical approach, 44, 56
critical national infrastructure, 238, 258
critical security studies, 2, 3, 10, 28, 66, 70, 71, 73, 115, 280
Crowcroft, Robert, 244

Davis, David, 161–8, 175–6, 181–8, 227
Dean, Mitchell, 61, 71–2
debates on ISC reports, 212
Defence Committee, 203
deference, 31, 118, 129–30, 136, 148, 153, 176, 204, 271, 273
    judicial, 134
defining politics, 8
definitions, 57–8, 69, 280
Defty, Andrew, 212
democracy, Athenian, 173
democratic politics, 12, 13, 15, 16, 17, 25
Democratic Unionist Party, 161, 182
Department for International Development (DfID), 214
departmental select committees, 195, 198–9
depoliticisation, 10, 91, 95–109, 143, 227, 245–50, 261–2
Derrida, Jacques, 17
desecuritisation, 12, 86, 96
detention of terrorist suspects, 134, 140, 146, 161, 163, 182, 188, 218, 226, 230
Devanny, Joe, and Josh Harris, 253–6
dialogue, 16–17

Dion, 179
Dionysius, 179
Discipline and Punish, 67–8
discourse, 16, 44, 56, 60, 61, 120, 173
dispositif, 60–4, 120
domestic violence, 8, 85, 89, 94
double game, 139
draft bill committees, 225–6
Duffield, Mark, 74
Durkheim, Émile, 92

Easton, David, 92
economic liberalism, 259
economy, 238–40, 249, 251, 255–61
empiricism, 43, 57, 58, 61
Energy and Climate Change Committee, 239
energy security, 197, 219
Eriksson, Johan, 66
Erskine May, 130, 205
ethic of conviction, 24
ethic of responsibility, 24
Euripides, 174
European Convention on Human Rights, 143, 215
European Court of Human Rights, 207
Evans, Jonathan, 141
'everything becomes security trap', 45, 47, 52
Ewald, François, 246
exceptional politics, 9, 12, 16, 17, 28, 32, 42, 84, 237
exceptionalism, 49, 87–9, 99, 237, 254, 262, 272, 275–6, 281

executive-legislative relationship, 126
existential survival, 19
existential threat, 88
expertise, lack of, 186, 204, 271
experts, 14–15, 26, 32, 84, 101–2, 128, 186–92, 218, 246–9, 256, 258, 261, 263, 270

Falklands War, 207
Fawcett, Paul, and Marsh, David, 101
fear of looking weak, 139–40
feminist politics, 8, 85, 94
field, 124–5
Fierke, Karen, 18
'Five Eyes' intelligence alliance, 239
Flinders, Matthew, 99, 101–2, 104, 126
Floyd, Rita, 47, 88, 139
Flynn, Paul, 22, 120, 134, 148–9
Foreign Affairs Committee, 207, 213, 218
foreign policy, 28
foreign policy analysis, 4
'Foreign Policy Aspects of the War against Terrorism', 218
fortuna, 20–1
Foucault, Michel, 11, 23, 43–4, 50, 55–76, 120, 168–188, 195–7, 258–60, 280
Foucault's Eurocentrism, 75
Foucault's final lectures, publication of, 75
Fox, Liam, 184
Franks Report, 207

free speech, 174–80, 187
Fusion Doctrine, 273

Gamble, Andrew, 263
GCHQ, 30, 209–10
Geddes, Marc, 202, 227
genealogy, 61, 67, 69, 75, 197, 280
General Belgrano, 197, 208, 214
general election, 184–5
Giddens, Anthony, 95
Goffman, Erving, 54
government and politics not synonymous, 72
governmentality, 44, 71, 73–4, 115, 262
grammar of security, 46, 47, 53, 187
Greeks, ancient, 75, 173–8
Grieve, Dominic, 225
Guantanamo Bay, 274
Guardian, The, 177
Guzzini, Stefano, 54, 63

habitus, 123–5, 132
Hagmann, Jonas, and Myriam Dunn Cavelty, 246, 248
Hammerstad, Anne, and Ingrid Boas, 240, 243–4, 247, 257
Hammond, Philip, 135
hard security issues, 279
Harman, Harriet, 202
Hattersley, Roy, 137
Hay, Colin, 8, 55, 85–6, 89, 93–104
Heath, Edward, 206
Hindess, Barry, 73

Hinkley Point nuclear power station, 238
historical empiricism, 57, 63, 70, 280
historical methodologies, 64–5, 70, 197–8
history as war, 68–9
History of Madness, 58
history of the present, 57, 65, 94
Hobbes, Thomas, 2, 18–22, 27, 42, 129, 258, 262, 280
Hobbesian trap, 5, 6, 19, 121
Hodge, Margaret, 202
Holehouse, Matthew, 151
Home Affairs Select Committee, 180, 208, 213–14, 218
Home Office, 142
House Permanent Select Committee on Intelligence, 239
How to Be an MP, 22–3
Howe, Geoffrey, 181
Howell, Alison, 48, 89
Huawei, 238–40
Human Rights Act 1998, 134, 215
human security, 218
Huysmans, Jef, 3, 5, 15, 43, 45, 46, 48, 281
hyperpoliticization, 91, 99

independent reviewer of terrorism legislation, 128
Independent, The, 164–5
influence, parliamentary, 126, 203, 231, 277
Inside/Outside, 89

Index

institutionalised securitisation, 105–6, 166, 205, 237, 270–2
intelligence
  interpretation, 153
  oversight, 62, 177, 205, 278
  services, 106–7
  sharing, 142
Intelligence and Security Committee, 30, 128, 131, 151, 177, 180, 199, 203, 209–11, 213, 225, 238, 274
Intelligence Services Act 1994, 106–9, 209–10
Interception of Communications Bill/Act 1985, 131, 206–7, 271
International Development Committee, 218
International Institute for Strategic Studies, 257
international relations, 4, 20, 280
inward investment policy, 238–40
Iraq War, 2003, 62, 119, 127, 147–??, 153, 240, 250–1, 271

Jabri, Vivienne, 75
Jenkin, Bernard, 152, 202
Joint Committee on Human Rights, 128, 134, 215
Joint Committee on the National Security Strategy, 224, 251, 258
Joint Intelligence Committee (JIC), 151, 153, 254
Joint Terrorism Analysis Centre (JTAC), 143, 254

judgement, 153
Justice and Security Act 2013, 30, 211, 213, 216

Kaarbo, Juliet, and Daniel Kenealy, 6, 150
Kalyvas, Andreas, 10, 12, 13, 15, 17, 32, 91
Kelso, Alexandra, 126, 276

Labour Party, 138, 140, 185
Laclau, Ernesto, 91
Latour, Bruno, 57, 59, 61, 73
Leander, Anna, 124
legislating after terrorist attacks, 136
Leviathan, 5, 18, 20, 21, 27, 274, 280
Liaison Committee, 201, 214
liberal democracies, 9, 13, 17
Liberal Democrats, 138, 184–5
liberal government, 72, 73, 74
Libya, 149
Lloyd, Janet, 60
Loader, Ian, 3, 14, 15
Lobo-Guerrero, Luis, 246
Lords Constitution Committee, 199, 218–20
Luhmann, Niklas, 92
Lund Petersen, Karen, 71, 73, 92, 245

McCormack, Tara, 245
McCormick, John P., 27
Machiavelli, Nicolo, 19, 20, 22, 23
Macmillan, Harold, 108, 206
McNulty, Tony, 162

321

Mälksoo, Maria, 91, 99
manifesto, 185
Manningham-Buller, Eliza, 137, 146–7
market, 260
Massiter, Cathy, 206, 271
May, Theresa, 188
Mello, Patrick A., and Dirk Peters, 278–9
Members of Parliament, 22, 23, 104–5, 135
methodology, 196–8
MI5, 30, 55, 107, 130, 205–6, 209–10, 239
MI6, 30, 107, 209–10, 213, 236
migration, 15
Miliband, David, 141–2
Miliband, Ed, 150–1
ministerial resignation, 180–1
ministers, 30, 101, 103–6, 122, 129, 137, 142, 144–6, 150–2, 176–7, 180, 198, 201, 203, 205, 226, 230, 236, 241, 252
misrecognition, 141
Mitchell, Andrew, 164
Mohamed, Binyam, 142
Morgenthau, Hans J., 23
Mullin, Chris, 180, 183, 213

Nair, Sheila, 89
National Cyber Security Programme, 257–8
National Economic Council (NEC), 255
national risk registers, 246
National Security Advisor, 241, 253

National Security Capability Review, 273
National Security Council, 31, 224, 236–50, 256
national security risk assessment, 246–7, 257
National Security Strategy, 4, 31, 50, 62, 109, 115, 198, 223–4, 241–5, 266, 278–9
NATO 2% of GDP spending, 257
necessity, 2, 20, 84, 86, 91, 97, 99, 100, 128, 130, 145, 172, 183, 236, 276, 282
Neocleous, Mark, 3, 13, 14, 15, 16
neoliberalism, 70, 72, 73
Neville-Jones, Pauline, 250–2
Nietzsche, Friedrich, 69
'Nietzsche, Genealogy, History', 67, 70
non-politicised, 96
normal politics, 7, 9, 10, 12, 17–19, 28, 32, 33, 42, 62, 84–6, 90–1, 96, 99, 109, 117, 195, 220, 237, 275, 281–2
normalisation, 274–5, 281
Northern Ireland, 144
Northern Ireland Affairs Committee, 209
Northern Ireland peace process, 214–6
Nyman, Jonna, 18

Office for Security and Counter Terrorism (OSCT), 254
Official Secrets Act 1989, 180
officials, 25–6

Omagh bombing, 215
O'Malley, Pat, Lorna Weir and Clifford Shearing, 72
OPEC, 197
Osborne, George, 236–8, 245, 253, 257, 260, 263–4
Ottaway, Richard, 151

pacifism, 24
Packenham, Robert, 127
Palonen, Kari, 92–5
Paris School, 26
parliament, 22, 30, 31, 117, 125
Parliament Act, 165
parliamentarians, 62, 72, 121–45, 175–9, 204, 275, 281
parliamentary committee system at Westminster, 198–9
parliamentary committees, 31–2, 62, 104–5, 194–231
  powers and tasks, 201
parliamentary systems, 104
parliaments, 6
parresia, 167–88
  bad, 174
  political, 174
partisanship, suspension of, 137
party, 25, 31, 125–6, 137, 145, 187, 272
performative speech acts, 172, 187
Pericles, 174
Plato's *Republic*, 178
polemics, 69
political agency, 74–5
Political and Constitutional Reform Committee, 224
political economy, 259

political game, 76, 116–25, 170, 173, 180, 186
political rationality, 163
political survival, 21, 134
political, the, 170
politicians, 23–6
politicisation, 86, 91, 105–8, 166, 176, 230
  re-, 101
politics
  as an activity, 92–5
  definition of, 85, 90–1, 95
  problematisation of, 74–6
  qualitative aspects of, 87, 89, 92, 100
positive security, 18
post-legislative scrutiny, 201
postcolonial subject, 75
Pouliot, Vincent, 123, 136
Powell, Jonathan, 88
powers of freedom literature, 74
practical reason, 123
practices, 56, 58
Pram Gad, Ulrik, 92
pre-legislative scrutiny, 201, 225
Prevent, 188, 219, 240, 277
privy council, 207
problematisation, 59–60, 63, 64, 67, 70, 75–6, 168
  as method, 43, 44, 70, 75, 168, 186, 280
professional politics, 1–2, 5, 7–8, 9, 11, 18, 21, 23, 27–8, 32–4, 66–7, 72, 76, 84–5, 91, 104–5, 115, 117, 124, 194
proportionality, 138–9
Prozorov, Sergei, 17

Public Administration Select Committee, 223, 244
public bill committees, 199

Quadripartite Committee, 214

raison d'état, 259
Rancière, Jacques, 13
Rasmussen, Mikkel Vedby, 242–5
rational choice theory, 179
rationalisation, 25
rationality of government, 74
rationality, Weberian, 242
Rawnsley, Andrew, 180
realism, 19
recognition, 129, 139, 141, 153
reflectivism, 51
reflexivity, 43
responsibility, 23–8, 101
Review of Intelligence on Weapons of Mass Destruction, 148–9, 153–4, 251
rhetoric, 178
Richter-Monpetit, Melanie, 8
risk, 47, 236–82, 242
risk assessment, 239–40, 246, 250
Robertson, Angus, 211
Robinson, Nick, 162
Roe, Paul, 47, 88
Rogers, Robert, and Rhodri Walters, 202
Rose, Nikolas, 74
Royal prerogative, 119
rules of the game, 23, 90, 116, 119, 123–6, 137, 163, 167, 181, 186

Runciman, David, 21
Russell, Meg, and Philip Cowley, 230

Sabaratnam, Meera, 74
Salter, Mark, 89, 121
Schmitt, Carl, 17, 27–8, 88, 250, 261
Science as a Vocation, 246
Scottish Affairs Committee, 220
Scottish independence, 223
Scottish National Party, 211
secrecy, 142
secret intelligence, 62, 127–9, 148
sectors of security, 46, 51, 90, 92
securitisation, 15, 16, 20, 24, 47, 91, 96, 100, 121, 139, 220, 242, 258, 262
securitisation theory, 7, 16, 24, 28, 44, 46–9, 56, 63, 86, 88, 90–1, 97, 105, 172, 179, 184, 187, 204, 242, 270, 279
securitisation theory, sociological turn, 121–2
Security: A New Framework for Analysis, 90
security, definitions, 42–3, 45–8, 69
security logic, 46, 47, 50, 57, 62, 172
security professionals, 5, 55, 102, 124, 261
Security Service Act 1989, 106–9, 130, 209
Security, Territory, Population, 69, 70, 258

security, widening, 4, 45–7, 50, 273–4, 281
sedimented meanings, 52–3
select committee chairs, 201–2, 214, 224
Sheldon, Wolin, 248
Sierra Leone, 213
Skinner, Quentin, 52–3, 55, 57, 63
Smith, Jacqui, 226
Snowden, Edward, 176–7, 239, 278
societal securitisation, 46
'Society Must Be Defended', 68
Soviet party system, 184
Soviet telegrams, 206
Speaker, Commons, 230
'Speaker's Order of 22 January 1987 on a Matter of National Security', 208
Special Branch, 208–9
speech act, 51, 60; see also performative speech act
spheres of politics, 93–5
Spycatcher, 207
state of exception, 274–5
Strategic Defence and Security Review, 223, 244
strategic studies, 45
strategy, 242–3
Stritzel, Holger, 50, 89, 121
Strong, James, 148, 150, 152
subject constitution, 170
Sun, The, 135
Sutcliffe-Braithwaite, Florence, 130
symbolic capital, 146
symbolic power, 128, 185

Syria debate, 2013, 62–3, 119, 127, 149–53, 272–3
Syria vote, 2013, 119
Szabó, Márton, 93

Taleb, Nassim, 247–8
Taylor, Charles, 51
technocratic politics, 15
Telecommunications Act 1984, 55
Telegraph, The, 183
Terrorism Act 2000, 218
Thatcher, Margaret, 181, 207
The Government of Self and Others, 75–6
The Prince, 19–22
The Profession and Vocation of Politics, 11, 23, 76
threat compared to risk, 242–4, 248
threat level setting, 143
'threat to the life of the nation', 143–4
Thucydides, 174
Today in Parliament, 198
torture, 274
Trade and Industry Committee, 213
traditional approach to security, 45–6, 51–2, 63, 65, 115, 230, 279
Transport Committee, 215
trust, 147–9, 271
truth, 57–9, 64–73, 144–5, 153–4, 162, 167–87, 260
  and power, 67, 170
  production of, 72
  truth-telling see parresia

UK, 3, 4, 5, 6, 28–33, 49, 62–3, 104, 106–7, 109–10

validity, 67, 71
veridiction, 185, 260
Veyne, Paul, 58, 60
violence, 24
visa decisions, 251–2

Wæver, Ole, 7, 9, 16, 24, 43–5, 47–50, 204
Walker, Neil, 3, 14, 15
Walker, R. B. J., 19, 21, 49, 89
Walt, Stephen, 4, 279
war cabinets, 254–5, 264
war on terror, 6, 218
Weber, Max, 8, 11, 23–8, 74, 76, 91–2, 126, 186–7, 242, 246, 248, 250, 256, 261

Weimar Constitution, 27
Welsh or Aberystwyth School, 17–18
Whistle-blowers, 176
Whitehead, Alan, 238
whole of government problem, 109
Wibben, Annick, 66
widening security *see* security, widening
Williams, Michael C., 16–17, 91, 103, 121
Wilson, Harold, 3
Wilson, Richard, 252
Wood, Matt, 99, 101, 104
Wright, Peter, 207
Wright reforms, 201
Wright, Tony, 117

Zahawi, Nadhim, 151

EU representative:
Easy Access System Europe
Mustamäe tee 50, 10621 Tallinn, Estonia
Gpsr.requests@easproject.com